INHERITANCE OF LOSS

STUDIES OF THE WEATHERHEAD EAST ASIAN INSTITUTE, COLUMBIA UNIVERSITY

The Studies of the Weatherhead East Asian Institute of Columbia University were inaugurated in 1962 to bring to the wider public the results of significant new research on modern and contemporary East Asia.

INHERITANCE OF LOSS

China, Japan, and the Political Economy of Redemption after Empire

YUKIKO KOGA

THE UNIVERSITY OF CHICAGO PRESS
CHICAGO AND LONDON

The University of Chicago Press, Chicago 60637
The University of Chicago Press, Ltd., London

Printed in the United States of America

25 24 23 22 21 20 19 18 17 16   1 2 3 4 5

ISBN-13: 978-0-226-41194-1 (cloth)
ISBN-13: 978-0-226-41213-9 (paper)
ISBN-13: 978-0-226-41227-6 (e-book)
DOI: 10.7208/chicago/9780226412276.001.0001

This book was generously supported by the Association for Asian Studies First Book Subvention Program

Library of Congress Cataloging-in-Publication Data

Names: Koga, Yukiko, 1969– author.
Title: Inheritance of loss : China, Japan, and political economy of
redemption after empire / Yukiko Koga.
Other titles: Studies of the Weatherhead East Asian Institute,
Columbia University.
Description: Chicago : The University of Chicago Press, 2016. | Series: Studies
of the Weatherhead East Asian Institute, Columbia University
Identifiers: LCCN 2016019383 | ISBN 9780226411941 (cloth : alk. paper) |
ISBN 9780226412139 (pbk. : alk. paper) | ISBN 9780226412276 (e-book)
Subjects: LCSH: Manchuria (China)—Relations—Japan. | Japan—Relations—
China—Manchuria. | Postcolonialism—Economic aspects—China—Manchuria.
Classification: LCC DS740.5.J3 K615 2016 | DDC 303.48/2518052—dc23
LC record available at https://lccn.loc.gov/2016019383

♾ This paper meets the requirements of ANSI/NISO Z39.48-1992
(Permanence of Paper).

In memory of my grandmother, *Obāchama*, who opened the door for me to see the landscape of after empire

CONTENTS

ILLUSTRATIONS

MAPS

FIGURES

PROLOGUE AND ACKNOWLEDGMENTS

In the black-and-white photograph, a Chinese man kneels in front of a trench, into which his severed head will fall a moment later. A Japanese soldier behind him prepares to swing a long sword down through his neck. When I first encountered this photograph in the Fake Manchukuo Museum in Changchun, the capital of Jilin Province in Northeast China, I felt not the terror and shock many Japanese tourists told me they had experienced in facing this image, which captured the brutality of Japan's invasion of China. Rather, I felt a strange sense of familiarity in seeing a scene I had imagined for so many years. My maternal grandparents had shared their experiences in Manchuria with me ever since I was little, and this story was the one they most often recounted.

My grandmother, the more talkative one, used to portray her life with my grandfather in their adopted homeland in great detail, capturing both the mundane and the eventful. As a new college graduate in 1937, my grandfather had taken a job at the headquarters of the South Manchuria Railway Company in Dalian, a port city in Japanese-ruled Northeast China, and my grandmother later joined him as a newlywed. Altogether, they spent nearly a decade in Northeast China until they were repatriated one year after the Japanese defeat in 1945. Over the years, my grandmother recounted again and again the stories that left the deepest marks on her memory: the ornate and festive wedding ceremony of their Chinese neighbor's charming daughter; how one of my grandfather's favorite Chinese subordinates, Mr. Li, once knocked on their door in the middle of night to ask for stomach medicine available only to Japanese, and how later in thanks he had brought a large jar of pickled plums—an increasingly scarce Japanese staple that he knew my grandmother longed for; how my grandmother later heard about the brutal killing of Mr. Li, beheaded by a Japanese soldier in front of a trench into which "his head fell like a ball" (*kubi ga koron to korogattatoyo*); how after the Japanese defeat, their downstairs Chinese neighbors, who owned a tofu store, often gave my grandparents tofu to help my grandmother in nursing my mother; how they hid my grandmother and my mother in their house when the Russians came to look for Japanese, especially young women; how, just before my grandparents' repatriation to Japan in 1946, a group of Chinese, my grandfather's former subordinates at the South Manchuria Railway Company, scraped together an elaborate going-away banquet for him and, worrying about his returning to a defeated nation, prepared a large basket filled with grilled sparrows and rice balls for the long trip back to Japan; how my mother contracted dysentery as they waited in a camp for the repatriation ship; how the doctor strongly suggested that my grandparents leave their baby daughter with a Chinese couple rather than have to cast her corpse into the sea en route; and how their daughter miraculously survived the brutal voyage home.

Tears welled in my grandmother's eyes and her face twisted with pain every time she told me of Mr. Li's beheading in her gentle and musical Nagasaki dialect, "*kubi ga koron to korogattatoyo*." For her, his death symbolized everything that went wrong with the Japanese puppet state Manchukuo, which existed from 1932 to the defeat in 1945. My grandparents often spoke of their moral debt to the Chinese people—they felt indebted because of the brutal violence and injustice the Japanese had visited upon the Chinese and because of the incredible generosity their Chinese acquaintances had shown them after the defeat. When I visited my grandparents, the dinner-table conversation almost always turned to Manchuria. They were troubled by not knowing to whom and how to address this long overdue debt, unsure even if their former Chinese acquaintances, who were associated with the Nationalists, had survived the civil war between the Guomindang and the Chinese Communist Party, a conflict that reignited after the Japanese defeat.

Rooted in this sense of moral debt inherited from my grandparents, this study is fueled by a strong desire to understand what it means to come to terms with violence that took place more than two generations ago. Coming to terms with the past has long been an inflammable issue between China and Japan, yielding repeated controversies, including ones involving Japanese government censorship of history textbooks; Japanese prime ministers' visits to Yasukuni Shrine, which honors not only fallen soldiers but also convicted class-A war criminals; the Japanese legal system's repeated rejections of claims by Chinese war victims suing the Japanese government and corporations, seeking official apologies and compensation for wartime slave labor, massacres, or human experiments; and Japanese politicians' general refusal to recognize Japanese wartime atrocities and the questionable sincerity of those apologies that have been made. These public controversies surrounding the so-called history problem primarily revolve around the recognition of responsibility and the expression of remorse.

Since my first visit to China in February 1990, I have returned numerous times, amazed at how a socialist society has transformed itself into one of the most vibrant market-oriented economies in the world. I have wondered about the role of the difficult and unaccounted-for past in the renewed and deepening, though still largely economic, relations between China and Japan, especially in Northeast China, the former site of Manchukuo.

My study took concrete shape during my first visit to this region in the summer of 1999. After my grandfather passed away that spring, I boarded a night bus from Beijing, where I was studying Chinese, with my curious husband in tow to visit the cities where my grandparents had spent nearly ten years of their young married life. I was struck not only by how much of the colonial architecture, built mostly by Japanese and Russians, remained intact but by how it dominated the cityscapes. The municipal governments had recognized long-neglected colonial remnants as their "inheritance" (*yichan*) in their efforts to compete in the contemporary global economy, and they restored many of these buildings to attract tourism and foreign direct investment. There was also a notable Japanese presence in the region. Japanese tourists flocked to the "former Manchurian" (*kyū Manshū*) cities such as Harbin, Changchun, and Dalian. Japanese foreign direct investment had increased rapidly during China's transition to a market-oriented economy since the 1980s. Japanese foreign direct investment in Dalian, for example, resulted in a cityscape filled with things Japanese, from Japanese products and entertainment venues catering to Japanese businessmen to branches of several major Japanese corporations, which provided coveted career paths for elite Chinese college graduates. I wondered how the past appeared in the present and how the physical remnants of the contested history might affect the renewed relations between the two countries. The frantic economic activities in Northeast China seemed to have opened up a new terrain for the current generations to reckon with a distant, yet still alive, past.

Memory and trauma were the key conceptual frameworks that I carried with me when I set out to do my fieldwork in Northeast China and Japan. But I soon realized that they were insufficient in capturing what was unfolding in the cities in Northeast China. There I observed the aggressive use of remnants from each city's colonial past in the service of an expanding economy. China's transition to a market-oriented economy was accompanied by small- and large-scale processes of recasting long-neglected and decayed colonial remnants as newly minted capital through the rhetoric of inheritance. This does not mean that memory and trauma of losses sustained through Japanese imperialism were not present. They were, and my presence as a Japanese national stirred them up amid the otherwise future-oriented rhythm of daily life, sometimes creating uncomfortable moments for local Chinese when they discovered that I was Japanese and linked to *that* history.

But there were noticeable traces of the past that could not be fully captured by the framework of memory or trauma. I attempt to capture these traces by exploring the inheritances of losses that continue to drive the desire for recovery, redemption, and repayment for debts, which I observed in ordinary Chinese and Japanese encounters with what remains in rhythms of everyday life in Northeast China. It is these traces, their effects, and their relation to memory and trauma that I seek to articulate through my ethnographies of Harbin, Changchun, and Dalian.

My need to understand what it means for the current generations to reckon with the past gained an added urgency when a tragic incident took place while I was in the midst of my dissertation fieldwork. On August 4, 2003, in the city of Qiqihar, a three-hour train ride north of Harbin, a group of men were hard at work on the construction site of an underground garage in the center of a housing development for Qiqihar's new middle class. While excavating the site, they discovered five corroded steel drums filled with liquid. The steel drums were sold to a scrap-metal collector, some of the contaminated soil was taken home by workers for their backyards, and the remaining earth was piled up into a hill, which instantly became a playground for school children. By dinnertime, people had begun to experience burning skin, vomiting, loss of vision, and high fever. Not until the following morning did anyone suspect poisoning. The workers who uncovered the drums had no idea that they contained mustard gas, probably left over from biochemical experiments by Imperial Japanese Army Unit 516, which had been based in Qiqihar. Li Guizhen, the scrap-metal collector who thought he had landed a windfall, died after excruciating suffering, his body burnt and corroded beyond recognition. Forty-three people, including three young children, were injured and burdened with lifelong effects from their exposure to the toxin.

This instance of what can be termed *delayed violence* affecting the current generation is one of the most visible consequences of long-deferred attempts to adequately account for Japanese imperialism. Meeting the victims in the subsequent months and becoming involved in their eventual lawsuit against the Japanese government brought a new immediacy to my core questions about the generational transfer of unaccounted-for pasts. While deaths and injuries from buried weapons grab the headlines in a way that everyday encounters in urban spaces or debates about colonial architecture do not, both ways of inheriting are deeply intertwined. This book is about the shared mechanism of inheritance that connects them, what I call the *political economy of redemption*, and how it emerges from Japanese and Chinese encounters with colonial inheritance across the cities of Northeast China.

This book is based on my two-and-a-half-year fieldwork in China and Japan in 2002–4 and yearlong fieldwork in 2012–13, as well as follow-up research in the summers between these extensive fieldworks. Over the course of my fieldwork, conversations tended to be long and iterative, often starting in the morning, moving on to lunch, passing into the afternoon, and then continuing over dinner with family members. Establishing trust required me to say a lot about myself. My fieldwork itself was an integral part of the redemptive economy that I explore in this book. I carried with me both my Japanese name, which bears a particular historical burden within the East Asian context, and my family history, which ended up opening more doors than closing them. I was grateful that most people I encountered in China considered my eagerness to learn their language and culture as a sign of reconciliation. And for me, the return to the beginning—to the brutal yet familiar image of Japanese atrocity and the sound of Chinese words that my grandparents used in recounting their life there—led me to start conversations my grandparents had wished to have but did not know how to begin. China was never a completely foreign country to me, but rather, as my grandparents put it, "a country that could have been your homeland." My grandparents' stories again and again reminded me how "elusive the nation-state can be," as my grandmother often put it.

My fieldwork became a constant process of crossing, blurring, and unsettling boundaries. On many occasions, my relation to markers of belonging was defined through how others saw me. I was simultaneously both inside and outside, both Chinese and Japanese and, at the same time, "neither Chinese nor Japanese." My "both and neither" presence became particularly pronounced when I worked as an official guide at the Palace Museum of the Puppet Emperor Puyi in Changchun, explaining Japanese atrocities to groups of Japanese tourists in front of panel after panel of black-and-white photographs of gruesome violence committed by the Imperial Japanese Army. Many confided how glad they were to have a Japanese guide with whom to face this deeply uncomfortable past, while *Manshū hikiagesha*—Japanese repatriates from Manchuria—considered me "one of them," someone who could understand the "neither-nor" identity.

After my three-hour tours at the museum, I would often discuss the reactions of Japanese tourists with my Chinese colleagues, or simply gossip and chat over tea and sweets. As the only Japanese working for this state-run work unit, a holdover from prereform China, I shared daily meals in the canteen with my colleagues, carrying my iron bowl with several dishes piled up over heaping rice. I was an object of great curiosity for everyone in the museum—from kitchen staff to vendors to archivists to administrators, and especially for my young coworkers in the propaganda department (to which we tour guides belonged), for whom I was often the first living Japanese with whom they had spoken. They were eager for details of how "modern" Japanese society must be, and they wanted to know what I thought about the "progress" that Chinese society was making. They wanted to learn about everything—from the latest Japanese television dramas and popular culture to politics and lifestyles. There were moments when they treated me as non-Japanese, as when they would whisper into my ear comments about Japanese tourists or Japanese society in general, with the caveat "Don't tell this to Japanese, but . . ." I was, on many occasions, neither Japanese nor Chinese in their eyes. My ambiguous positioning was a particularly effective icebreaker when I met Chinese working for Japanese corporations in the Dalian special economic zone. They projected their own border-crossing experiences onto my experience of living in the United States. And my US background gave them more room to talk comfortably about Japan with me, since, as one of them put it, I wasn't "really Japanese after all."

Back in my hometown, Tokyo, I was also an insider and outsider. I spent much of my time there with Chinese war victims who had filed lawsuits against the Japanese government and corporations; with Japanese repatriates from Manchuria, many of whom were active participants in repatriate groups such as the Dalian Association, Changchun Association, or South Manchuria Railway Association; and with the so-called *Chūgoku zanryū koji* (Japanese orphans left behind in China at war's end who were adopted and raised by Chinese parents) who had decided to "return" to Japan. These were all people caught in the tide of history who projected different identities onto me—Japanese, Chinese, American, and, most of all, that of living on borders. Chinese war victims saw me as a bridge between themselves and the Japanese lawyers representing them, and sometimes as a bridge between themselves and Japanese society at large. It broke my heart when one of the plaintiffs in the "comfort women" lawsuit asked me in a whisper how to read some characters in her Chinese-language testimony because she was too embarrassed to let the Japanese lawyers know she was illiterate. In the center of Tokyo, at the district court, I listened to *zanryū koji* in their collective lawsuits against the Japanese government appealing to the judge in Chinese (their only language) to explain how as Japanese citizens they deserved more humane living conditions. My nights out at a karaoke club with elderly repatriates from Manchuria in their seventies and eighties often ended with Chinese songs.

This book is woven through these encounters, which opened up a space for us to reflect upon encounters that had taken place decades earlier. Many of my Chinese acquaintances expressed a very similar sentiment, that "it's *yuanfen* (karma, entanglement) that you are here to do research on this issue between China and Japan." *Yuanfen* was one of the most beautiful words I encountered during my years of field research in China. In encapsulating the difficult history between China and Japan in such a generous expression, the word also captured the generosity with which people greeted my intrusion into their lives.

My long journey to seek ways of repaying the moral debt that I inherited from my grandparents has incurred even more debts. Many of those whom I am deeply indebted to must remain anonymous in this book, and I cannot acknowledge their names here to thank them. I can only express my gratitude to them through a new set of questions, discussions, and dialogues that I hope this book will invite.

Living in a foreign country is a humbling experience. Living in China as a Japanese was even more so. Without the generosity of so many who opened up their doors and hearts to me, I would not have gained the kind of insight that I am about to present to you in this book.

In Harbin, local historians introduced me to the rich history of Harbin and the dramatic and engaging world of Harbin historians. Their guidance and friendship were indispensable for my introduction to life in Harbin and my exploration of the traces of the city's earlier history. My sincere respect and gratitude go to Bu Ping, whose intellectual rigor, open-mindedness, and generosity to his colleagues and students inspire great admiration. His family made me so much at home by often inviting me to their family meals after my hours of discussion with him. Duan Guangda went to extraordinary lengths to provide me with every possible support, intellectual stimuli, and a warm home away from home with his delightful family. Ji Fenghui provided wonderful friendship and gave me insights into intricate complexities within Chinese society. Li Shuxiao's vast knowledge of Russian and Jewish life in early twentieth-century Harbin was crucial for my understanding of the city's history. Gao Xiaoyan, along with Bu Ping, guided me in my efforts to trace and understand the contemporary devastation wrought by chemical weapons left by the Imperial Japanese Army at the war's end. Meng Lie is living history, a formidable intellectual, and a wonderful storyteller. Hou Youbin offered his expert knowledge on Harbin architecture and the politics behind the historical preservation policy, and so did his student Liu Yang, whose friendship I cherish. Zeng Yizhi is a truly wonderful friend, whose keen sense of justice is a source of my admiration. She took me along with her on journalistic expeditions to seek traces of Old Harbin from the early twentieth century, which introduced me to fascinating people and their life stories, rituals, and the incredibly complex dynamics that played out in both past and present Harbin. James Carter, Patrick Shan, and Mark Gamsa, historians of Harbin, gave me wonderful company going through archival materials and exploring physical traces of colonial Harbin in the rapidly changing cityscape. I am grateful to the late Han Xiao, the founding director of the Unit 731 Museum, for his support and for sharing the afterlife of this Japanese human experimentation site before it was turned into a historical museum. My gratitude and respect go to Su Xiangxiang and Luo Lijuan, dedicated Harbin lawyers who cooperated with Japanese lawyers representing Chinese victims of toxic exposures caused by abandoned chemical weapons left by the Japanese Army. They were tireless warriors during our investigative trips in Northeast China and our meetings in and outside of court hearings in Tokyo. Wan Jiyao generously gave me permission to include his striking black-and-white photographs from the Cultural Revolution era, long hidden in his closet, in this book. Yan Yansong at the Urban Planning Bureau in the Harbin municipal government introduced me to not only the world of Harbin urban planners but also many aspects of urban life in the city.

In Changchun, my heartfelt thanks go to Li Yiping and her family and Cheng Nina, who provided me with a home away from home and wonderful friendship. To my colleagues at the Palace Museum of the Puppet Emperor Puyi, where I worked every day as an official museum tour guide, I owe more than I can list: from training me as a tour guide, incorporating me into the daily rhythm of the life in their *danwei* (work unit), giving me full access to their archival materials, and sharing life's small pleasures as well as more difficult issues that lie between China and Japan. My special thanks go to Zhao Jimin, Zhang Wei, and Shen Yan. The Jilin Academy of Social Sciences generously gave me full access to their South Manchuria Railway Library and made every possible arrangement to make my research go smoothly, both in Changchun and elsewhere. Yuan Chengjun deserves special thanks for helping navigate the bureaucracy and providing support and friendship. Xie Xueshi, Sun Jiwu, and Li Maojie guided me with their expert knowledge on the history of Manchukuo. Liu Qinshi, Wu Yanzhi, and Wen Zhuming at the Changchun municipal government gave me access to their archival materials. Without the friendship of Dou Ping, Wang Ping, Wang Dapeng, Zhang Bin, and Wang Lili, life in Changchun would not have been so full of laughter, silliness, and joy. Sakabe Shōko provided wonderful friendship, support, and intellectual inspiration.

In Dalian, Jin Shoufeng played a pivotal role in bridging Dalian's past to the present by sharing with me his layered past and introducing me to the generation of people who experienced Dalian under the Japanese rule. Du Xingzhi, Tian Jinchuan, Du Fenggang, and Li Weiwei likewise helped me deepen my understanding of Dalian's past and present from both academic and personal perspectives. Sun Jian supported and helped my research with her journalist's keenness and provided warm friendship. Yu Tao and Shan Wenjun at the Dalian municipal government gave me indispensable support. Wang Xuan welcomed me with open arms to her trip to Dalian to investigate Japanese wartime human experiments. Wang Hui, Pan Fusheng, Wang Lan, Liu Zhipu, and Liu Wenge provided invaluable friendship and introduced me to the life of China's new middle class. Japanese CEOs in Dalian not only made every possible arrangement to make my research in their corporations possible but also provided me with wonderful friendship. This included facilitating my access to Japanese karaoke clubs, off-limits to a female researcher by herself. I am grateful to the young Chinese women I came to know there for sharing their complex emotions associated with working in these establishments to entertain Japanese businessmen.

In Tokyo, too, my research was only possible through the generosity of so many people. Yoshimi Shunya is a truly inspiring scholar and mentor, and I was lucky to have his guidance during my field research there. The University of Tokyo gave me not only every possible support and the freedom I needed to conduct my research but also opportunities to meet wonderful colleagues. Nishizawa Yasuhiko at Nagoya University, an expert on colonial architecture in Manchuria, gave me support and guidance. Gao Yuan and Umemori Naoyuki provided stimulating conversation and friendship, and Naoyuki also arranged library access for me at Waseda University. My heartfelt thanks and respect go to the Japanese lawyers representing Chinese war victims pro bono in their lawsuit against Japanese government and corporations. Their tireless passion and strong sense of justice forced me to drag my exhausted body every day to morning-to-midnight meetings, from early court hearings to meetings with Chinese plaintiffs and NGO members, to street demonstrations and even to investigative trips with the lawyers back to cities and remote villages in Heilongjiang Province in Northeast China.

And my deep feelings remain with the victims of Japanese imperial violence who shared with me their raw and intimate emotions during their court appearances in Tokyo and during my visits to their hometowns in China. For their friendship, despite all that they have gone through, I am at a loss for words. The *Manshū hikiagesha* welcomed me with open arms, as if I were part of the family, and shared with me their deep longings, disillusionment, and a strong sense of displacement. My thanks also go to the members of the Japanese Society for History Textbook Reform (*Atarashii kyōkasho o tsukuru kai*), who also welcomed me to their regular study-group meetings despite our conflicting political views.

Not all these people's voices can be directly heard in my ethnography, but their spirits are undeniably present in the following pages and reflected in my analysis, as they helped and challenged me in shaping and reshaping my thinking.

This book would not have come to being without my tremendous luck in meeting exceptional teachers at every stage of my academic training. Growing up in a traditional Japanese family in which learning was discouraged for women, I would never have dreamed of pursuing a higher education without the unconditional trust and encouragement of the late Seki Hiroharu. He took me under his wing and introduced me to the world of academia. His ceaseless passion for building peace, teaching, and research gave me the courage to take a big step away from the life trajectory expected of me, that of becoming a housewife and a mother, and eventually a step away from Japan. My senior year abroad at Dartmouth College opened up a vast, exciting, and completely new world. The late Gene Lyons guided me through my adventurous and often clumsy first year in the United States. Yakushiji Taizō at Keio University in Tokyo encouraged and supported at a distance my graduate study in the United States, which ended up encompassing many years in two disciplines at three institutions. At the Department of Political Science at Syracuse University, many teachers patiently guided me in my often awkward efforts to learn how to learn in English, while opening up an exciting world of theoretical thinking. Naeem Inayatullah, Lily H. M. Ling, Gavan Duffy, and Jim Bennett deserve special thanks. In the School of International Relations at the University of Southern California, the late Hayward Alker Jr. invigorated my thinking with his wildly imaginative and cross-disciplinary mind and unlimited intellectual curiosity. Richard Falk at Princeton University and David Sabean at UCLA played a decisive role in my decision to go beyond the world of political science. As a wonderful mentor and a friend, Richard inspired and supported my graduate study from the early years and suggested that I consider anthropology. David Sabean introduced me to the world of history and narratives, and even after so many years, I still vividly recall his exceptionally stimulating seminars at UCLA.

The Department of Anthropology at Columbia University was full of eclectic energy that embraced unbounded creativity, and my dissertation committee went above and beyond the call of duty to tirelessly shepherd me in extending and cultivating my imagination. I do not know how to thank Marilyn Ivy, a truly extraordinary advisor and a friend. Her ability to encase keen and rigorous yet free-spirited intellectual observation and imagination full of nuance and sensitivity in acutely sophisticated language continues to give me a sense of awe and inspiration. Without her support, encouragement, and guidance, this project would have either been left uncompleted or else taken a completely different shape. Above everything else, I have learned from her how to see and listen in a way I had never imagined before. My admiration and deep gratitude also go to Rosalind Morris, whose intellectual rigor pushed my thinking like nobody else's did. It took me many years after I left Columbia to grasp the meaning of her intellectual intervention into my thinking and writing, and I expect more revelation to come in the years ahead. And her sincere and conscientious attitude toward teaching and research is something I aspire to learn. Carol Gluck deserves a special place, and she is another teacher to whom I have difficulty articulating my gratitude. I can only hope to emulate her intellectual passion and intensity, boundless generosity to her students, keen sense of language, and earnest and playful outlook on life. Nicholas Dirks supported and encouraged me from the very beginning of my graduate experience at Columbia, and he initiated me into the intersecting world of anthropology and history. Harry Harootunian remains a source of great awe, with his intellectual rigors that are deeply grounded in his political and ethical concerns.

Other members of the department and beyond deserve my special gratitude for their intellectual guidance, stimulating conversation, and friendship: E. Valentine Daniel, John Pemberton, Michael Taussig, and Guobin Yang. I also benefited greatly from comments on earlier drafts of dissertation chapters from Tani Barlow, Peter Berton, David Buck, Myron Cohen, Anne Cronin, Kevin Hetherington, Neal Leach, Elizabeth Povinelli, Jordan Sand, Stig Thøgersen, and Madeleine H. Zelin.

My life at Columbia was blessed with friendship that I treasure. Ruchi Chaturvedi, Sofian Merabet, and Sonali Pahwa were with me to share all the joys and tears and everything in between. So were Tak Watanabe and Akari Maruyama, not only in New York, but also in Tokyo. The members of my dissertation-writing group, Ruchi Chaturvedi, Karin Jane Zitzewitz, and Tak Watanabe, tirelessly read numerous and messy earlier drafts of the chapters. Krista Hegburg spent hours copy editing my dissertation chapters past midnight to meet the deadlines in her usual manner of generosity and conscientiousness. I would like to thank Juan Obarrio, Nauman Naqvi, Kaming Wu, Lisa Mitchell, Roxanne Varzi, Emilio Spadola, Antina von Schnitzler, Michael Fisch, Jun Mizukawa, and Lori Watt for camaraderie in New York and beyond. In New York, so many friends have shaped this book directly and indirectly. There are too many to list, but I would like to thank especially Ashok Gurung, Aiko Sakurai, David and Monique Stark, Hugh Raffles, and Sharon Simpson.

It was my undeserving luck to start my teaching career at Brown University as a postdoctoral fellow. My students in my seminars, "After Empire: History, Memory, and Mourning," "Anthropology of Urban China," and "Accounting for Silence: Anthropology of Narrativity and Law," pushed my thinking in ways that none of my extraordinary teachers had. Michael Steinberg at the Cogut Center for the Humanities and Kerry Smith in the East Asian Studies Department provided me with support, encouragement, and a nurturing environment that were indispensable for my transition to a postdissertation stage. My special gratitude goes to Rey Chow for her belief in my work and engaging conversations that resonate with me so deeply that they came back to me again and again as I went through multiple revisions of this manuscript. The Nanjing-Brown Joint Program in Gender Studies and the Humanities was another exciting intellectual home that I was invited to take part in at its inception, and I would like to thank Lingzhen Wang and Elizabeth Weed for this unique opportunity and, above all, their wonderful friendship. The trip to Nanjing pushed me to set aside this project and start working on my next project in full swing, a detour that later became pivotal for reframing this book.

I am grateful for my colleagues at Brown for generous feedback on my earlier chapters, engaging conversation, support, and friendship. I would like to thank especially Bianca Dahl, Cathy Lutz, Catherine (Rina) Bliss, Ipek Tureli, Ipek Celik, Rebecca (Rivi) Handler-Spitz, Daniel J. Smith, Mark Swislocki, Ethan Pollock, Ian Straughn, Jessaca Leinaweaver, Kay Warren, Keith Brown, Lynne Joyrich, Matt Gutmann, Naoko Shibusawa, Paja Faudree, Samuel Perry, Sherine Hamdy, and Suzanne Stewart-Steinberg.

It was during my fellowship leave at the Harvard Academy for International and Area Studies at Harvard University that my manuscript went through a significant transformation. The intellectual environment that Jorge I. Domínguez has created was so uniquely nurturing and stimulating, and Jorge is such a truly extraordinary mentor, intellectual, and human being, that I do not know how to thank him. Larry Winnie, Kathleen Hoover, and Bruce Jackan ran the place with so much care and devotion that made our little gray house an unusual sanctuary that is both rigorously stimulating and forgiving. And my cohorts in this luxurious writing camp made all the difference. I would like to thank especially Naor Ben-Yehoyada, Yael Berda, Anne Clement, Arunabh Ghosh, Jeffrey Kahn, Elizabeth McGuire, Pascal Menoret, Ameet Morjaria, Raul Sanchez de la Sierra, and Elina Treyger for genuine camaraderie that was simply so special. I would also like to thank Marié Abe, Celeste Arrington, Ted Bestor, Mark C. Elliott, Vanessa Fong, Andrew Gordon, Nick Harkness, Henrietta Harrison, Michael Herzfeld, Arthur Kleinman, Doreen Lee, Elisabeth Köll, Franziska Seraphim, Susan J. Pharr, and Tomiko Yoda for mentorship, feedback on my chapters, and friendship that made my experience in Cambridge special.

Tani Barlow, Ian J. Miller, Jie Li, Lisa Rofel, and Ajantha Subramanian read the entire book manuscript at a critical stage and gave me invaluable comments and suggestions. Tani and Lisa in particular made long trips to Cambridge for my book workshop and offered the kind of intervention that any writer would only dream of. Likewise, the extensive comments from the anonymous reviewers for the Studies of the Weatherhead East Asian Institute series and the University of Chicago Press played a pivotal role in reframing and tightening my arguments. I am especially grateful for the reviewer for the Weatherhead series for pushing me to articulate the political and ethical stakes that had remained latent in my earlier draft.

My colleagues at Hunter College made me so much at home even during my job interview that I decided to call it my home institution even before they offered me the job. Their quintessentially New Yorker attitudes toward life and work, and their deep concern for social justice that comes through even in our faculty meetings, have provided me with the kind of environment that has reinforced my commitment to the issues I strive to address through my writing and teaching. I would like to thank especially Jacqueline Nassy Brown, Ignasi Clemente, Leo Coleman, Marc Edelman, Judith Friedlander and Ida Susser for mentorship, support, and good cheer. And my experience at Hunter would not be the same without Nala Fernando, who holds down the fort.

Aleksandra Jaeschke produced the beautiful maps that will guide you through the following chapters. Elizabeth Lee and Daniel Geist improved my writing considerably. Daniel Rivero and Ross Yelsey from the Studies of the Weatherhead East Asian Institute series and Priya Nelson, Ellen Kladky, and Trevor Perri at the University of Chicago Press have patiently shepherded me through the winding road of academic publishing.

This project would not have taken place without my maternal grandparents, who introduced me to the world of Manchuria and Japan's imperial aggression since my early childhood. This is a personal project as much as an intellectual one. My grandfather remained silent about his family members who perished in the atomic-bomb explosion in Nagasaki. It was only after his death that I learned of their existence and how his family had discovered bodily remains of their loved ones when they excavated their property to rebuild their house in the 1970s. To this day, my grandmother never fails to offer the first cup of green tea and the first scoop of freshly cooked rice to the home shrine of my grandfather's younger brother, who died of hunger during the war in New Guinea while waiting to be deployed in a human-torpedo suicide mission. Japanese imperialism and the subsequent war were never left in the past tense with my grandparents, in the form of both seen and unseen, present and absent. They showed me the land of in-betweenness, the ambiguous and ambivalent space that contains rich meanings and true tension. If people found me a good listener with whom they felt comfortable sharing their intimate feelings and difficult memories, sometimes things that they had never shared even with their family members, I owe it to my grandparents, who showed me the nuanced textures and complexities of our relations to the past, which often express themselves in silence.

My family history is silent about the life of my paternal grandparents when they spent their early marital years at the border of China and current North Korea in the 1930s under Japanese colonial rule. Subjected to abject poverty in Japan, my grandfather took a job as a border guard there. Since neither of my grandparents finished elementary school and both were illiterate and remained in dismal poverty in the postwar years, there is no written record, nor did they talk about these years. My grandfather died young without ever having access to written words, and my grandmother decided to learn how to read and write at the age of sixty. She sent me numerous letters with her beautiful handwriting with a traditional brush and ink, every single stroke filled with the joy of writing. It was only when one of the so-called comfort women, who was illiterate, asked me sheepishly in a whisper just before giving a testimony in court how to read some characters in her Chinese language testimony that

I belatedly understood the deep humiliation that my own grandmother must have harbored for decades before acquiring access to written language. The experience deeply humbled me to realize the vast unknowability of human experiences.

As much as both sets of my grandparents were deeply affected by and involved in the Japanese war efforts and colonial project, my parents are also deeply influenced by the war and its aftermath. With stability, social conformity, and pursuit of modest happiness as the valued goal in their life, it was an understandable disappointment and a source of great anxiety for my parents to see their daughter leave the expected life path as a homebound woman in a finally stable and prosperous Japanese society. Despite all the difficult years between us, my parents, Koga Tetsuhiko and Hiroko, have never given up on me, and I am indebted to them for their love and perseverance. During my father's desperate and last struggle to gasp for air with his cancer-filled lungs, he heard me deliver the news that the press had decided to pursue my manuscript, news that I hoped that he would take with him for his journey to the afterlife to assuage his anxiety about my future. Through his impossible breathing, his face brightened up with a wide smile one last time before his departure, and he squeezed out his last words, "I'll take it as a souvenir for my journey (*omiyageni motte ikuyo*)," and this image of his smile has sustained me through the arduous processes of revising this manuscript.

My maternal grandmother, Nōtomi Nobuko, has been a source of inspiration throughout this process in the truest possible sense. I am very grateful for my brother, Koga Daisuke, and his wife, Sachie, for their love and support during both good and challenging times and for creating such a loving and welcoming family with Daichi and Taiga, my sweet nephews. In the United States, I have found a new home and family, without which I would not be where I am. My in-laws, Suzanne and Robert Bach, have given me unconditional love, encouragement, and faith in me. They are a great source of joy, and they know my book intimately, from cover to cover. Bob left us in January 2015 after ninety-four years of full life, but he would have been most proud to hold my book in his hands. And the open-minded, funny, and *sympathique* Bach clan provided warmth, laughter, chocolate, and much more throughout the process. My deep gratitude extends to the Jiji clan, especially Latif and Vera Jiji, for their love and boundless generosity.

My greatest gratitude goes to my husband, Jonathan Bach, for more than I can even begin to name. He shared every moment, emotion, and word of my book and beyond. The following pages reflect our trips to Asia, countless discussions, and his patient editing of my endless versions of drafts. As much as I am the author of this book, this is a product of our life together over twenty years. This book is for him.

The field research and writing for this book have been generously funded by several institutions. My preliminary research was supported by the Ford Foundation Summer Research Grant for Research and Research Methods in the Developing World, the Scheps Summer Research Grant from the Department of Anthropology at Columbia University, and the Weatherhead Summer Training Grant from the East Asian Institute at Columbia University. The dissertation field research in China and Japan became possible with the support from the Social Science Research Council's International Dissertation Research Fellowship, the Wenner-Gren Foundation for Anthropological Research's Individual Research Grant, and the US Department of Education's Fulbright-Hays Doctoral Research Abroad Fellowship. The writing of the dissertation was supported by the Junior Fellowship in Japan Studies from the Weatherhead East Asian Institute at Columbia University.

A postdoctoral fellowship at the Cogut Center for the Humanities and East Asian Studies Department at Brown University as well as a Harvard Academy Scholar Fellowship at the Harvard Academy for International and Area Studies at Harvard University gave me the invaluable time and stimulating intellectual environment to develop my dissertation into a book.

A yearlong field-research grant from the National Endowment for the Humanities for Advanced Social Science Research on Japan for my next book project offered me a critical opportunity to reflect on and reframe my decade-long research for this book. Chapter 6 is a product of this fieldwork, which also compelled me to overhaul chapter 1. Any views, findings, conclusions, or recommendations expressed in this article do not necessarily reflect those of the National Endowment for the Humanities, the Japan-US Friendship Commission, or the other institutions that funded my research.

I am grateful for the First Book Subvention Award from the Association for Asian Studies to support the publication of this book. I acknowledge with gratitude permission to include texts previously published elsewhere. Sections of this prologue, chapter 1, and chapter 6 first appeared in "Accounting for Silence: Inheritance, Debt, and the Moral Economy of Legal Redress in China and Japan," *American Ethnologist* 40, no. 3 (August 2013): 494–507. An earlier version of chapter 2 was first published as "'Atmosphere of a Foreign Country': Harbin's Architectural Inheritance," in *Consuming the Entrepreneurial City: Image, Memory, Spectacle*, edited by Anne M. Cronin and Kevin Hetherington with a forward by Sharon Zukin, 221–53 (New York: Routledge, 2008), and it is reproduced with the permission of Taylor and Francis Group LLC.

I would like to thank Heilongjiang University in Harbin, Jilin Province Academy of Social Sciences in Changchun, the Institute of Socio-Information and Communication at the University of Tokyo, the Interfaculty Initiative in Information Studies at the University Tokyo, and the People's Law Office in Tokyo for offering me an institutional home, wonderful colleagues, and much more during my fieldwork in China and Japan. As a junior faculty at Hunter College of the City University of New York, I have been spoiled to the envy of my friends. It is my relief to be able to finally present this book.

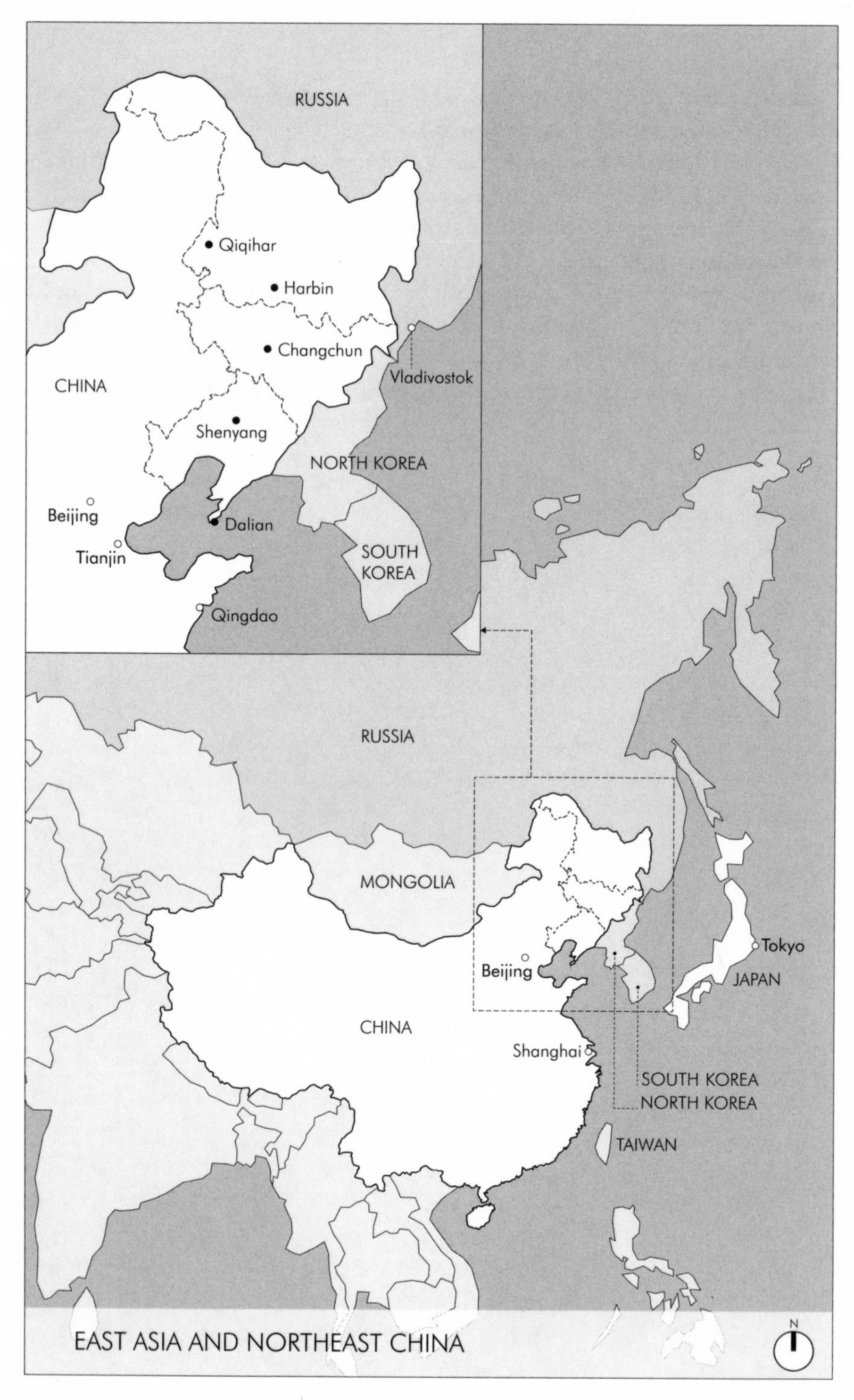

Map 1 Northeast Asia and Northeast China

CHAPTER ONE

Introduction: Colonial Inheritance and the Topography of After Empire

Just beyond the shoppers and strolling couples on Harbin's Central Avenue, an upscale pedestrian shopping street that ends at Stalin Park, scrap-metal hunters often comb the nearby riverbank for old weapons abandoned by the retreating Japanese Army in 1945. In this last major city in Northeast China before the Russian border, rusted missile heads, some containing deadly poisons like mustard gas, lie casually in the shadow of luxury high-rises and meticulously restored Russian and Japanese colonial buildings. Children occasionally play with the ordnance, and accidents—some fatal—are not uncommon. This unnerving juxtaposition echoes the stark contrast between Harbin's efforts to boost tourism through the restoration of its ornate, European-style colonial architecture and its ambivalent attitude toward the colonial violence that the city endured and its legacy, including the many victims of mustard-gas exposure who live in abject poverty, often stigmatized for their physical disfiguration and by an unfounded fear of contagion.

The neglected legacy of abandoned chemical weapons in Northeast China and the accentuation of colonial architecture after decades of neglect are intertwined inheritances from the "era of colonialism" (*zhimin zhuyi shiqi*), which is how the period from the mid-nineteenth century to the demise of the Japanese Empire in 1945 is referred to in China. This book is about how ordinary Chinese and Japanese, two to three generations removed from the direct experience of Japanese imperialism, now encounter each other and experience and navigate these inheritances. The settings for these encounters are three major cities in Northeast China, whose colonial legacies are etched on their cityscapes: Harbin, Changchun, and Dalian. All three have sought to benefit from newfound access to the global economy, refashioning their cityscapes to make them more attractive to tourists and foreign capital, and in the process generating new and often unplanned encounters with the past. The question of confronting the past is often relegated to the realm of politics, yet it is also through quotidian encounters in the workplace, on the streets, and in residential complexes that contemporary Chinese and Japanese are working out what it means to come to terms with the past.

Situated at the height of China's socioeconomic transformation in the 1990s and 2000s, this ethnography shows how the economic realm has become a key site for the generational transfer of difficult pasts. New economic relations generate wealth and a sense of redemption for both Chinese and Japanese, but they also summon the past, whether in heated debates over preserving colonial-era architecture—debates of unusual intensity in the contemporary Chinese context—or when construction for China's new middle-class apartments unearths chemical weapons buried by the retreating Imperial Japanese Army at the end of the war, as happened in 2003 in the city of Qiqihar, about 170 miles northwest of Harbin. As we shall see, the past also lingers surreptitiously in the offices and factories of the fast-moving, market-oriented Chinese economy.

In exploring how the second and third generations are coming to terms with the distant, yet still alive, past stemming from the era of colonialism, this book engages with the following questions: How do losses incurred through colonial modernity's violence travel across generations? How are a sense of historical responsibility and moral debt passed down to the second and third generations? How and where do unaccounted-for pasts manifest themselves, and with what effects? What happens to what remains, and who is responsible? How do these contemporary generations of Chinese and Japanese build new relationships *despite* the knowledge of not only past catastrophe but also deferred reckoning long after the end of the Japanese Empire? Last but not least, how has China's transition to a market-oriented society changed the dynamics of generational transmission, and what is the role of economy in the longstanding question of coming to terms with the past, which is generally consigned to the politics of memory?

To explore the workings of inherited losses and debts within the new Chinese economy, this book examines sites where long-neglected remnants from the era of colonialism are transformed into newly minted capital through the rhetoric of "inheritance" (*yichan*): losses are turned into capital to generate new value. My ethnography explores this *capitalization of colonial inheritance* as it is orchestrated by the municipal governments of Harbin, Changchun, and Dalian in their efforts to position their respective cities within the global economy. Such economic deployment of colonial inheritance as capital came to play a key role in the transition to a market economy in northeastern Chinese cities from the 1990s through the 2000s, for example, through the historical preservation of colonial-era architecture and the reincorporation of former colonial industries into special economic zones to lure tourists and foreign investors.[1]

Inheritance of Loss explores the face-to-face encounters between Chinese and Japanese set into motion at these sites of inheritance.[2] What I call *colonial capital* captures these processes of capitalizing on colonial remnants, and as my ethnography illustrates, colonial capital remains, reminds, and redeems. Through encounters in the realm of tourism and foreign direct investment, I identify a mode of generational transmission that I call the *political economy of redemption*. Here, the moral economy of seeking redemption for the unaccounted-for past is inexorably linked to the formal economy of exports, consumption, and the citywide pursuit of middle-class dreams. For both Chinese and Japanese, China's growing economy is channeling contradictory impulses toward erasing, confronting, or capitalizing on the past into new forms of production, consumption, and accumulation while at the same time exposing and amplifying new forms of anxiety arising from inherited legacies of colonial modernity.

The "loss" in the book's title refers to losses incurred during the era of colonialism, and it includes many kinds of loss: the loss of lives, physical and psychological injuries, material loss and damage, and forced displacement and mobilization, all of which have had lasting effects not only on those who were present at the time but on subsequent generations as well. The term also refers to failed empires, to a sense of failure to become modern, to a sense of humiliation and disgrace, and to a loss of faith in modernity's promise. My ethnography shows how these losses and their recovery—through redeeming the past and the scarred nationality of "Chinese" and "Japanese"—have become an integral part of the pursuit of "modern life" (*xiandai shenghuo*, a buzzword in today's China) in these cities in Northeast China.

Attempts to make up for the losses stemming from the era of colonialism are in fact everyday, ubiquitous, and publicly visible activities. At one end of the spectrum, we have anti-Japanese sentiments and increasing demands for official apology expressed on the street, in cyberspace, and through official government channels. At the other end of the spectrum, there is the eager capitalization of colonial remnants, explicitly named "inheritance," such as colonial-era architecture, factories, and human resources (as in the case of Dalian, for instance, which boasts a long tradition of linguistic and cultural fluency in Japanese). Focusing on the economic realm, this book uses the concept of *colonial inheritance* to make visible contemporary generational responses to the losses incurred through colonial modernity, as set in motion through China's transition to a market-oriented society.

CAPITALIZATION OF COLONIAL INHERITANCE

The physical marks on the urban landscapes of these cities in Northeast China reflect a history of competing ambitions of modern nation-state building in East Asia.[3] In the mid-nineteenth century, when China faced the threat of Western imperialist expansion, Russia played a significant role in ending the Second Opium War (1858–60) by mediating between Qing China and Britain and France. In return, the Qing dynasty awarded Russia the coastal Northeast region. Construction of the Siberian Railroad between this newly acquired region and the Russian heartland began in 1891. Its terminal, Vladivostok, was not a warm-water port, and Russia thus sought access to such a port on the Liaodong Peninsula, on the southeastern tip of Manchuria. The Japanese victory in the Sino-Japanese War (1894–95) resulted in the Japanese acquisition of Liaodong, along with Taiwan and a large monetary indemnity. Russia, France, and Germany, each with its own ambitions for imperial expansion in China, protested this annexation in the so-called Triple Intervention of 1895, and Japan agreed to withdraw from the Liaodong Peninsula in exchange for an additional indemnity from the Qing government. In 1898, Russia negotiated an agreement with the Qing authorities to lease the southern part of Liaodong Peninsula, including the warm-water port of what came to be Dalian, and began to build the Chinese Eastern Railway. The Russians showcased their modernity through flamboyant architecture and concerted urban planning in the cities of Dalian and Harbin.

Just a few years later, however, Japan's victory in the Russo-Japanese War (1904–5) led to the Japanese takeover of the Russian-leased territory. Like the Russians, the Japanese continued to expand the cities along the region's railroads, filling them with ornate European-style architecture to signal their own modernity. Established in 1906 as a semigovernmental, semiprivate corporation, Japan's South Manchuria Railway Company moved its headquarters to Dalian the following year with a mandate that went beyond building and maintaining the railroad. Despite its appearance as a corporation, it was an integral part of the Japanese government and became the central organization for developing and governing the region. This imperialist enterprise, pursued through railway and settler colonialism, took place against the background of competing Chinese nationalist movements.

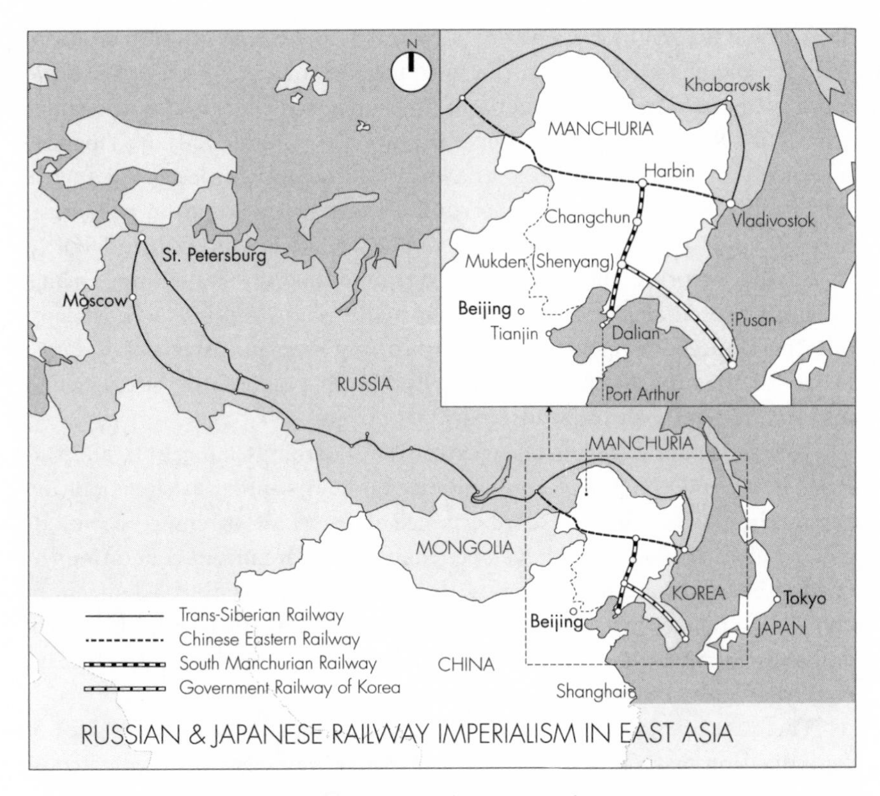

Map 2 Russian and Japanese railway imperialism in East Asia

When Manchukuo was created in 1932, approximately three hundred thousand Japanese were already living in the region known to the Japanese as Manchuria (*Manshū*), referring to the ethnic home of the Manchu, and to the Chinese as the Three Eastern Provinces (*Dong san sheng*). As part of the sphere of Japanese imperial ambitions—which by the end of the First World War encompassed Taiwan, Korea, the southern half of Sakhalin, and Pacific island chains—Manchuria attracted Japanese of different backgrounds, social strata, and political affiliations. The establishment of Manchukuo propelled Japanese colonial expansion in China to a new level. Puyi, the last emperor of the Qing dynasty, was made the emperor of Manchukuo, which Japan tried to present as an independent state. The Chinese, however, often referred to it as *Weiman* (Fake Manchukuo) to emphasize that it was a Japanese state with a puppet Manchu emperor.

In the beginning, the Japanese Kwantung Army controlled the area's defense and the South Manchuria Railway Company ran its administration. With the establishment of Manchukuo, Japanese colonial operations became more systematic in mobilizing natural resources and controlling the population. In addition to improvements in infrastructure to facilitate Japanese migration to Manchurian cities, the Japanese government launched a mass migration of Japanese farmers to rural areas. The exploitation of natural resources was accelerated by the use of cheap Chinese and Korean labor in mines and factories, and Manchuria became deeply integrated into Japan's expanding colonial economy. Changchun, renamed Shinkyō, or "new capital" in Japanese, developed into a city of imposing ministerial buildings. Dalian and Harbin, with their ornate European-style architecture, became major commercial cities for international business.

Today, each of my sites of investigation—Harbin, Changchun, and Dalian—has turned long-neglected colonial remnants into wealth-generating capital through the rhetoric of inheritance. In each case, attempts to capitalize on colonial inheritance have opened up space for current generations to encounter, confront, and reckon with complex pasts. Harbin, Changchun, and Dalian represent different modes of appropriating the past in the newly embraced market-oriented economy, and together they highlight the layered complexity of coming to terms with history.

The quotidian dynamics captured in my ethnography in these sites of capitalization make fewer headlines than such issues as the so-called comfort women (victims of wartime sexual slavery), the Nanjing Massacre, or the biochemical experiments conducted on human subjects by the Imperial Japanese Army.[4] These sites of Japanese wartime violence have provided symbolic images for public discussion on the "history problem," as the Japanese inability to reckon with its imperial aggression is referred to in East Asia.[5]

Yet the dynamics of the mundane rhythms of everyday life that my ethnography elucidates are not only reshaping contemporary Chinese and Japanese relations but also casting light on the mechanism of, and stakes in, inheriting losses. While much attention in recent years has been paid to making trauma socially visible by making victims' voices heard, my primary concern in this book is to explore the workings of losses as they seep into the "folds" of daily rhythms of newly emerging relations, which Veena Das calls the "descent into the ordinary."[6] It is within this realm of the everyday where effects of losses linger even after these losses are displaced, misrecognized, or given other names. It is in this everyday realm where current generations of Chinese and Japanese with no direct experiences of Japanese imperial aggression encounter latent losses, often unexpectedly, beyond the visible traces of wartime violence.

This quiet drama draws our attention to the larger context of what Tani E. Barlow calls "the project of colonial modernity."[7] This project is the pursuit of modernity, intricately linked to the development of colonialism, which shaped East Asia since the mid-nineteenth century and culminated in one of the most brutal wars the region experienced in its modern history. The era of colonial modernity was a period when the pursuit of modernity was deeply entwined with the development of capitalism, imperialism, and colonialism.

It is the material remnants of this colonial modernity that the municipal governments in Northeast China have been appropriating, re-presenting, and consuming en masse in recent years while using the rhetoric of inheritance. Plaques on landmarked buildings highlight the restoration and preservation of distinctive architectural styles that embody the region's history—early twentieth-century European-style architecture in Harbin and Dalian and a colonial hybrid called *teikan* style (emperor's crown style) in Changchun, which combines neoclassical facades with Asian-style roofs. The Japanese used Changchun, the colonial capital of Manchukuo, as an urban canvas to showcase this unique architectural style, which was considered as an expression of imperialism with an Asian twist.[8] Originally developed in Japan in the 1920s as an architectural style expressing Japanese modernity—an architectural echo of the Showa Emperor in Western clothing—the emperor's crown style was deployed throughout Changchun to express "the spirit of Manchuria," as Sano Riki, chief advisor for the National Capital Construction Plan, put it.[9] To reflect the idea of *gozoku kyōwa* (peaceful coprosperity of five ethnic groups), the stated political ideology of Manchukuo, the ministerial buildings in Changchun adopted the style with slight modifications, such as roofs with a "pan-Asian" mix of Japanese and Chinese features.[10]

While all three municipalities use landmark protection to capitalize on colonial edifices, the cities draw on their architectural inheritance for different ends and according to different criteria. In Harbin, the historical preservation policy revolves around the discourse of *wenming* (civilization). The architectural remnants here are meant to symbolize not colonial violence but cosmopolitan aesthetics and culture. The criterion for granting landmark status is aesthetic value rather than historical significance, which reflects the stated goal of redesigning and redefining Harbin as a modern city in a global economy. Dalian's municipal government goes further, mandating that new buildings be designed in the style of colonial-era architecture, reviving factories from the colonial era, and aggressively courting Japanese investment in the city's special economic zone. In Changchun, the historical preservation policy aims to preserve material witnesses to its colonial past. Many of the plaques on landmarked buildings in the city bluntly proclaim their purpose: "This building is granted landmark status in order to remind us of our national humiliation (*guochi*)."

Regardless of their stated rationale for putting these edifices under protection, the municipal governments of all three cities now acknowledge the remnants of colonial modernity—left to decay not so long ago—as vital capital for repositioning themselves within China's new economy. The citywide historical preservation of colonial-era architecture in Harbin underscores its cosmopolitan past: local guidebooks boast how the city offers the "atmosphere of a foreign country," and the preservation here has boosted both domestic and foreign tourism. Taking a train several hours south to Changchun, one finds that the former capital of Manchukuo has turned its cityscape of Japanese-built emperor's-crown-style architecture into a literal city museum of the former puppet state. Although the *Lonely Planet* guide describes Changchun as unworthy of a stop, *Chikyū no arukikata* (Walking around the globe), the Japanese equivalent, devotes fifteen full-color pages to Changchun. This travel guidebook, hugely popular among younger Japanese, presents the city as the former capital of Manchukuo and guides the reader through detailed accounts of the city's architectural inheritance from the era. Every day several hundred Japanese tourists seek "authentic" history in the Imperial Palace Museum of the Puppet State Manchukuo, the Fake Manchukuo Museum in the former State Council building, and the row of former ministerial buildings in the emperor's crown style, among numerous other structures built by the Japanese. The revenue from tourism provides significant income to this city in China's rustbelt.

Departing Changchun toward the south, one's train passes through Shenyang—the site of the 1931 Manchurian Incident and now the struggling postindustrial capital of Liaoning Province[11]—and within a few hours arrives at the terminal station of Dalian, a bustling port city that proclaims itself the "Hong Kong of the north." Like Harbin, Dalian boasts beautifully restored turn-of-the-century European-style architecture, built mostly by the Russians and Japanese. A significant number of more recent structures cater to the large Japanese business community, the predominant foreign investors here, from sleek office buildings and hotels to Japanese restaurants and karaoke clubs. New housing developments for the growing local middle class echo the architectural style of the colonial era. In a nod to the city's longstanding ties to Japan, one high-end residential development has a public installation of life-size statues of smiling Japanese women in traditional kimonos. With more than 60 percent of the city's foreign direct investment coming from Japan at the turn of the twenty-first century, the Dalian Economic and Technological Zone on the outskirts of the city feels like a modern-day foreign concession. Brand-name Japanese corporate campuses are arrayed one after the other in one section, while Korean, European, and American corporations occupy their own areas of the Zone. Dalian's urban renewal encompasses not only the historical preservation of colonial-era architecture but also the adaptation of the colonial aesthetic to new structures catering to Chinese middle-class tastes and the reincorporation of colonial-era industry in the special economic zone.

These developments in the economic sphere have taken place against the eruption of crises over history between China and Japan. Chinese protests against Japanese prime ministers' visits to Yasukuni Shrine, which enshrines class-A war criminals among other war dead, and demands for official apologies for Japanese atrocities in China are public expressions of the sense that Japan has not adequately accounted for its wartime violence.

While much of the public discussion on the question of coming to terms with this contested past has been consigned to the realm of politics, my ethnography demonstrates that the economic sphere is equally crucial to this longstanding question of delayed reckoning. Similarly, while much attention has been paid to the question of apology and historical responsibility for Japan's wartime violence,[12] my ethnography points to the importance of framing this history problem through the lens of colonial modernity, which encompasses larger structural relations—Japanese imperialism and colonialism—that culminated in wartime violence.

In this analytical shift from *postwar* historical responsibility to what can be called the question of *after empire*, I locate the activation of colonial inheritance in recent years. By highlighting the afterlife of colonial modernity, the framework of after empire situates the history problem within intertwined processes of postimperial, postcolonial, and postwar dynamics. I identify these dynamics within the daily rhythm of urban life in Northeast Chinese cities that are buzzing with frenzied economic activities, and I shift our attention from high politics to the realm of the everyday for ordinary Chinese and Japanese. In doing so, *Inheritance of Loss* elucidates the mechanisms and effects of the generational transfer of the remainders of colonial modernity. This book thus explores the recent capitalization of colonial inheritance in Northeast China as a pivotal and underexplored site for the generational transmission of unaccounted-for pasts.

FROM WAR MEMORY TO COLONIAL INHERITANCE

The turn of the twenty-first century marked a major turning point in Sino-Japanese relations. Rapidly deepening economic relations created new dynamics between market and history, which simultaneously highlight *and* disguise shared yet contested pasts. With intense media focus on demands for an apology for Japanese wartime violence and protests concerning Yasukuni Shrine, it is easy to forget that these issues were dormant for many decades after 1945. The public proclamation of China's victimhood was not at all a historical given. The "history problem" between China and Japan has gone through several different manifestations, including the Chinese state's decades of refusal to recognize its own citizens' victimhood. The distinctive character of the current manifestation becomes apparent only when viewed in this longer historical context.

As the following section details, for nearly three decades after Japan's defeat, Sino-Japanese relations developed through a delicate dance in the absence of formal diplomatic ties. In a dynamic of what can be called *inverted victimhood*, Chinese victimhood became invisible within the Communist hero narratives, while Japanese victimhood was highlighted. In the second phase, a clumsy courtship followed in the wake of the signing of the Joint Communiqué in 1972, which reestablished diplomatic relations, and the Peace and Friendship Treaty in 1978.

Together these paved the way for economic cooperation within a diplomatic framework that I call *(for)given time*, in which the Chinese government, still in the midst of the Cultural Revolution, renounced reparation claims in exchange for economic assistance and cooperation from Japan. In subsequent decades, economic relations between the two countries developed rapidly. In the third phase, beginning in the 1980s, Chinese society reemerged from the turmoil of the Cultural Revolution while Japan emerged as a new world economic power willing to invest in a then-uncertain Chinese market.

The growing economic friction between the two countries, in addition to the legitimacy crisis within the Chinese state and the resurgent right-leaning rhetoric among Japanese politicians, led to the Chinese government's *political deployment of war memory*, most prominently through the establishment of historical museums displaying Japanese wartime atrocities. In the fourth phase of relations, beginning in the mid-1990s and continuing through the 2000s, which is the scope of my ethnographic study, China rapidly prospered in the global economy while Japan sank deep into a decades-long recession. Here we find a significant shift from the previous decade's political deployment of war memory to the *economic deployment of colonial inheritance*.

Inverted Victimhood

In the years immediately following Japan's defeat in the Second World War, despite the many physical reminders of Japanese imperialism in Northeast China, a curious thing happened. Chinese victims disappeared from the post-Liberation discourse of the "New China," while the postwar Japanese discourse of "newborn Japan" stressed Japanese victimhood through a narrative emphasis on the atomic bombs and the US occupation.[13] The inversion in Japan—where, collectively speaking, perpetrators became victims—was inadvertently reinforced by the discursive shift in China, where the narrative of victimhood was overshadowed by a focus on heroism, liberation, and declarations that ordinary Japanese were also victims.

This *inverted victimhood* characterized the first three decades of post-1945 Sino-Japanese relations: Chinese victims became invisible in the hero narrative put forth by the Chinese Communist Party (CCP), while the Japanese highlighted their own victimhood. The Japanese public discourse reduced the country's imperialist aggression to the Asia-Pacific War experience, or even more narrowly to the Pacific War against the United States (*taiheiyō sensō*, as this war is often referred to in Japan), highlighting Japan's *postwar* while erasing post-1945 Japan as *postimperial* Japan. The sudden and formal disappearance of the Japanese Empire was accompanied by the public erasure of imperial consciousness and the wars Japan had launched against other Asian countries.[14] Most telling of Japan's imperial amnesia is how "postwar" became a measure of time relative to 1945, such as "postwar year seventy." The endorsement of this Japanese narrative of victimhood by the CCP reflected Mao Zedong's idea that ordinary Japanese had been victims of the Japanese militarists.[15] The founding narrative of the new Communist Chinese nation primarily revolved around its courageous revolutionary victory over the Guomindang, and both the war against Japan and Chinese victimization in that war played only marginal roles.[16] Cold War politics in Asia, which led to hot wars in Korea and Vietnam, intensified US willingness to overlook Japan's historical responsibility in favor of rebuilding the country as a geopolitical and economic ally.

In both China and Japan, inverted victimhood was thus a centerpiece of national narratives after empire, which for more than three decades excluded postcolonialism and postimperialism as discursive genres and terms of analysis.[17] By detaching "modernity" from "colonialism," these narratives were part of an attempt to undo the project of colonial modernity that had shaped East Asia. Yet the afterlife of colonial modernity has proved surprisingly resistant to this severing.

(For)given Time: The Zero Hour of Postwar Sino-Japanese Diplomatic Relations

The signing of the 1972 Joint Communiqué, followed six years later by the Peace and Friendship Treaty, marked the zero hour of postwar Sino-Japanese relations in which the two countries officially put the issue of Japan's war responsibility on the table but then set it aside in favor of formal economic relations and the pursuit of economic cooperation.[18] These state-to-state agreements located the moral economy of accounting for Japanese imperial violence in an ambiguous relationship with the formal economy. By renouncing reparation claims in the Joint Communiqué, which the Japanese side feared the Chinese would demand, the Chinese government in effect gave a "gift" to Japan. Instead of war reparations, the new Sino-Japanese relations centered around Japan's Official Development Assistance (ODA) to China, at a time when other countries were reluctant to invest in the country, which was just beginning to recover from the turbulence of the Cultural Revolution. But the Japanese ODA was never declared a substitute for war reparations, and the "gift" from China came with the expectation that Japan would not revert to the imperialism of its past.[19] A gift demands reciprocity and thereby becomes a debt to be repaid.[20] In 1972, the Japanese received a gift—China's renunciation of war-reparation claims—and in turn incurred a debt that they would find difficult to repay, since it was measured in their attitude toward the past rather than in currency or concrete demands.[21] The 1972 agreement gave the Japanese not forgiveness but the gift of time to repay this moral debt.[22]

It is this *(for)given time* that set the stage for the new phase in Sino-Japanese relations: the robust development of formal economic ties, initially through the ODA, which started in 1979, and then increasingly through direct Japanese investment in China.[23] This new and official postwar Sino-Japanese relationship, which had been delayed by twenty-seven Cold War years, privileged formal economy over moral economy in accounting for Japanese imperial violence. *(For)given time* became a diplomatic framework produced through the Japanese and Chinese governments' shared project of deferring redress in favor of wealth accumulation. Structurally, it became a silencing mechanism that forced many Chinese victims to maintain their long years of silence and become socially invisible in both countries.

The Political Deployment of War Memory in the 1980s

In the mid-1980s, the issue of unpaid moral debt found political expression in the new socioeconomic context of East Asia: Japan's rise as an economic power and the rise of neonationalism, increasing trade friction with China, and the CCP's legitimacy crisis stemming from the post-Cultural Revolution democracy movement and the "reform and opening" policy under Deng Xiaoping. It was during this period that the physical remainders of the brutality of Japanese militarism first became official sites for the commemoration of Chinese suffering, and only since then has the discourse of antifascist, anti-Japanese struggle moved to the center of the Chinese national narrative.[24] A series of events that signaled the resurgence of nationalism in Japanese society—history textbook revisions by the Ministry of Education in 1982 and Prime Minister Nakasone's official visit to the Yasukuni Shrine in 1985, the first by a sitting prime minister—as well as increasing trade deficits with Japan, which some Chinese described as the consequence of an "economic invasion" (*jingji qinlüe*), generated widespread anti-Japanese sentiment and student protests.[25]

The war against Imperial Japan came to play a pivotal role in the redefined narration of the Chinese nation and its history. This new emphasis on remembering the war culminated in a political campaign in 1994 that resulted in the marking of sites of Chinese victimhood—including the Nanjing Massacre, the Manchurian Incident in Shenyang, and the Unit 731 human experimentation laboratory on the outskirts of Harbin—as "bases for patriotic education."

Most of the long-abandoned Unit 731 facility, the biological and chemical warfare research and development headquarters of the Imperial Japanese Army,[26] had been demolished by the late 1960s. A political initiative to establish a museum began only in 1982 when the Japanese writer Morimura Seiichi visited the site to complete his *Akuma no hōshoku* (Devil's Gluttony), a graphic exposé of the wartime biological experiments that took place there.[27] Han Xiao, the founding director of the Unit 731 Museum, told me in 2002 that the site, including abandoned germ-incubation boxes, was still largely untouched when he took a job in 1956 at the airplane-parts factory next door. Many of the buildings were demolished in 1958 to salvage steel during the Great Leap Forward. In the spring of 1969, amid the Cultural Revolution, around three thousand people participated in destroying most of what remained. Han Xiao began his own research on Unit 731 around this time, but it was not until after Morimura's visit that he succeeded in opening the museum in 1984.

Through the transformation of sites of Japanese military aggression into museums across Chinese cities after the mid-1980s, the era of colonialism in China was assigned to demarcated spaces.[28] The past became confined to the museum so that the present outside the museum's walls could forget it, similar to Andreas Huyssen's description of the museum as a "burial chamber of the past."[29] Here, the political use of war memory in the 1980s resulted in a form of betrayal: displaying the past in a museum context meant hiding it in plain view while leaving those physical remains of imperialism unsuited to that context—such as colonial-era buildings and factories—to decay, what Ann Stoler calls "imperial debris."[30] The political deployment of war memories in the 1980s, which went hand in hand with the party-state's tight control over the interpretation of the era,[31] involved a spatial demarcation of *postwar* from *after empire*.

The Economic Deployment of Colonial Inheritance since the 1990s

The decade between the mid-1990s and the mid-2000s proved another major turning point in Sino-Japanese relations as new debates and negotiations emerged over China and Japan's shared history. While the political deployment of war memory in the 1980s harnessed the wartime past in the demarcated space of museums, the economic deployment of colonial inheritance that began in the mid-1990s made physical remnants of imperialist aggression publicly visible by naming them "inheritance" and recognizing them as value-generating "capital." Responding to municipal governments' eager invitations, Japanese flocked to Northeast China not as colonizers but as business partners reinvesting in former colonial factories or as tourists admiring restored colonial architecture.

This shift from the political to the economic was particularly notable in Harbin. In the early 2000s, the municipal government poured money into a colonial-architecture-restoration project in the city's downtown area, while the long overdue renovation of the Unit 731 Museum was put on hold until the downtown project's completion. Even when the museum renovation finally did proceed, there were not adequate funds to restore historically significant parts of the facility where human experiments had been conducted. Meanwhile, the former Japanese consulate building was included in the downtown preservation project, yet the building's commemorative plaque fails to mention that the site served as the hub for transporting human subjects to Unit 731.

Harnessing the past became a pressing issue in the 1990s for the Chinese government, which was navigating uncharted terrain in steering the country to a market-oriented system. The historical coincidence of multiple "ends"—the end of the Shōwa era in Japan with the death of Emperor Hirohito in 1989 after a reign of more than six decades, the end of the Cold War in Europe that same year, and the end of China's state-owned, centrally planned economy—generated a sense of layered "posts" in the last decade of the twentieth century: post-postwar, post–Cold War, and postsocialism.[32] Facing so many dramatic "ends," the era conjured up the long absent and the invisible through the global phenomena of memory work.[33] Formerly "invisible" Asian war victims became featured in the media, the most widely known being the "comfort women." Their public appearance strengthened the sense that there was much still to be accounted for and triggered victims' movements across China.[34] While these movements were soon suppressed by the CCP, this development in China sparked a series of public debates in Japan over what it meant to come to terms with the nation's imperialist past. A surge of lawsuits filed in Japan against the Japanese government and corporations by Chinese war victims, inspired by similar lawsuits in Europe concerning the Holocaust, was one product of this historical moment.[35] In the face of an aging populace who had lived through the war, both the Chinese and the Japanese publics expressed a new urgency in making overdue attempts to come to terms with the past. These efforts unsettled narrations of the past as contained and tamed within historical museums and inaugurated a new chapter between the two countries.

Capitalization of colonial inheritance was, in this sense, no less political than economic, even though it revolved around the rhetoric of economic rationality with an explicit rejection of historicity. During my years of fieldwork, many younger Chinese often said to me, "history is history" or "it's all about making money," to underscore their indifference to the historical burden stemming from the era of colonialism. Through this rhetoric, they liberate the formal economy that they engage in from the past and the debts incurred there. I take this stated economic rationality seriously and examine the dynamics contained within it. As my ethnography shows, their claimed absence of historicity inadvertently implies its very presence: their felt need to wipe the slate clean, on which the current economic relations operate, ironically reveals the acknowledged debts attached to the perceived "rational" economy. The rhetorical erasure of historical burden thus actually reveals the publicly acknowledged debts and losses embedded in this economy. A supposedly rational formal economy has become a constant reminder of the underlying moral economy and its unpaid debts.

By shifting our focus from the realm of politics to that of economy through the concept of colonial inheritance, this book makes visible how the persistent question of coming to terms with the past is present in and through the rationalized rhetoric of modern life and economic prosperity as these play out in everyday spaces from factories to offices and from public places to private homes. At these sites, the inheritances of the second- and third-generation Chinese and Japanese converge amid China's frenzied transition to a market-oriented economy, illuminating the disappearance and reappearance of layered pasts. While at first glance, the economic deployment of colonial inheritance—appropriations of colonial remnants for economic gain—may seem to trivialize historical losses, if not erase them altogether,[36] the following chapters show how losses and their recovery—through redeeming the past and the "Chinese"—have become a motor behind China's new economy and an integral part of the pursuit of "modern life" in three major cities in Northeast China.

GENERATIONAL TRANSMISSION OF LOSS

How do we account for these forms of political, economic, and emotional engagement with the era of colonialism set within the sweeping transformation of contemporary Chinese society? How have different understandings of the past projects of modernity—colonial modernity and socialist modernity—informed and shaped the way in which the new market-oriented modernity is imagined, experienced, and perceived?

The Afterlife of Colonial Modernity in Contemporary China

While similar questions have been approached through postcolonial lenses in many parts of the world that experienced the brutal consequences of colonial modernity, there is a general reluctance or resistance within China studies to incorporate this analytical framework.[37] Anthropological studies of China's spectacular transition to a market-oriented society have devoted much effort to untangling the relationship between China's two forms of modernity—socialist and postsocialist. What is much less explored is contemporary Chinese society's relationship to colonial modernity, which is often consigned to the historical past of the pre–People's Republic of China (PRC) in footnotes, if at all.

Historians, meanwhile, debate the difficulty of generalizing postcolonial conditions in the case of China, since some regions experienced the forces of imperialism more intensely than others. Northeast China was one of the regions most directly influenced by imperialism in the first half of the twentieth century, first through railway and settler colonialism by the Russians and Japanese and then through the installation of Japan's puppet state Manchukuo. While some argue against the usefulness of the postcolonial lens in analyzing contemporary Chinese society due to the country's semi-colonial status,[38] Tani Barlow invites us to shift our focus away from the formalities of colonialism, which she argues obscure power dynamics rather than elucidate them. Instead, she suggests considering societal responses to the project of colonial modernity, which resulted in entwined networks of power relations that defy the simple binary categories of colonizer and colonized.[39] Barlow further shows how Cold War politics influenced an ongoing erasure of postcolonial analysis within China studies in the United States.[40]

In fact, as we shall see in the following chapters, the reluctance to analyze contemporary China in relation to colonial modernity is not limited to American academia. My ethnography makes visible how this reluctance also exists within contemporary China by illustrating how Chinese society's uneasy relationship to colonial modernity plays out in the everyday through recognition, misrecognition, omission, and displacement of losses. These range from municipal governments' attempts to obscure colonial modernity's extended reach despite their political deployment of anti-imperialist rhetoric, to the middle-class rhetoric of economic rationality that discounts the role of history ("history is history"; "it's all about making money"), to the appropriation of China's long-erased postcoloniality by municipal governments and individuals alike as they maneuver China's newly globalized economy. The concept of *colonial inheritance* brings to the fore the erasure of losses sustained through colonial modernity or the displacement of them by another name, and it approaches such absence itself as a site of exploration.

Instead of focusing on the degree or length of the formal history of colonialism, this book suggests that it is the relationship to what the Chinese call the era of colonialism—when competing, collaborating, or disparate social forces were entangled in and transformed through colonial modernity—that calls for the analysis of its prolonged hold in the present. The framework of *after empire* works as a prism for Chinese society's complex relations to the project of colonial modernity, revolving around both desire and disavowal (thus defying a simple dichotomy between colonized and colonizer and involving relationships even more intricate than collaboration between these categories).[41]

Through this lens, this book identifies the development of modern China as after empire in multiple senses.[42] As a result of the aggression of Western imperial powers and the co-optation and fall of the Qing dynasty, ending millennia of dynastic rule, China took the full blow of the brutal consequences of colonial modernity in the course of its transformation into a modern state. The Chinese term *guochi* (national humiliation) is often used to describe imperial aggression in China, and it is also often used specifically to describe the Japanese aggression.[43] The framework of after empire captures this deeply engrained sense of humiliation in China, combined with a strong desire for redemption for that loss and a persistent yearning to achieve modernity's promise, which defies attempts to reduce these senses of loss and redemptive desires to loss and injury incurred from wartime violence. The redemptive desires of after empire, then—first through socialism and more recently through its transition to a market-oriented society—are also about chasing after a new Chinese empire as a global power.[44]

By bringing colonial modernity and its afterlife into analysis, this book thus addresses the growing gap between the discursive silence about China's postcoloniality and the current lived experiences in which traces of colonial modernity not only are being made publicly visible again but also have become primary forms of capital under the rubric of "inheritance." Through the lens of colonial inheritance, this book brings to the fore this underexplored link between China's postsocialist modernity and colonial modernity, which has come to play a key role in redefining and articulating the relationship between socialist and postsocialist modernity. *Inheritance of Loss* locates China's relationship to colonial modernity—and the attendant sense of loss—at the center of my ethnographic exploration of China's transition to a market-oriented economy.[45] Looking into the capitalization of colonial remnants is thus an exploration of how *inheritance of loss is turned into capital* and with what consequences.

Inheritance of Loss

Colonial inheritance is an enigmatic manifestation of colonial modernity's remnants. As traces of Western imperialism, colonial remnants pose as *the other's* inheritance. Yet, as an integral part of the lived environment, they are also *one's own*. Is colonial inheritance part of one's tradition, or is it problematic to name it as such? Where does it belong, who has a claim to it, and with what consequences? What is the underlying mechanism of inheritance and of inheriting? And what does it mean to inherit a loss? Is it akin to inheriting debt, or maybe credit that anticipates future payment? Is it a loss or a gain?

The Chinese and Japanese characters for "inheritance" (the same characters but pronounced *yichan* and *isan*, respectively) capture the paradoxical qualities contained within this concept. The first character refers to the act of losing, leaving out, leaving behind, and forgetting, but also of involuntarily emitting and of presenting a gift. The second character refers to a property but also an act of producing, making, or giving birth. Together these characters capture how at the core of the concept of inheritance lies the dynamics of turning loss into gain/property through presenting and giving.

"Inheritance of loss" captures this inherent meaning of loss and discontinuity contained within the Chinese characters for "inheritance," which does not come through in English. In English, the term highlights continuity and possession and implies the unchanging quality of that which is handed down. In contrast, *yichan* and *isan* embody a sense of loss and recovery that is articulated in a gift economy. The etymology of *yichan/isan* further suggests that what is being presented is transformed through this process. In this sense, it is less "recovery" than "reincorporation" that takes place through the act of inheriting. My exploration of colonial inheritance in Northeast China is an exploration of this economy—how losses sustained through colonial modernity are incorporated into the new economic relations today to produce new value.

This lens allows me to examine how Chinese society, at the height of its transition to a market-oriented economy, has (re)discovered and negotiated those traces of losses sustained during imperial aggression that were once consigned to the margins. And importantly, colonial inheritance is an issue not only for the Chinese; it is problematic for the Japanese as well. The counterpart to China's market opening has been the Japanese (re)discovery of China in recent years as investors, business partners, and tourists. Here the Japanese also attempt to redeem colonial modernity's losses, bluntly inscribed onto the cityscape of Northeast China in the absent presence of Manchukuo.

I approach the losses inflicted by Japanese imperialism in China as both Chinese *and* Japanese inheritances—as a problematic doubled "tradition" for both. Because colonial remnants bear scars of colonial violence, they cannot be easily named as an integral part of China's "tradition," an issue that led to, for example, heated public debates in Harbin and a contested discussion behind closed doors in the Dalian municipal government. Yet "inheritance" allows Chinese municipal governments and locals alike to recognize, activate, and reincorporate these neglected and enigmatic remnants within *Chinese* history through the language of capital and market. Rather than effectively neutralizing its colonial origin, however, this recognition of inheritance as such in the economic sphere has produced excess that betrays secrets contained within what is being handed down. As the first Chinese character for "inheritance" suggests, acts of inheriting are accompanied by unexpected disclosure/exposure. The following chapters illustrate how multiple layers and forms of betrayal structure the process of inheriting. Through these dynamics of *inheritance and betrayal*, my ethnography seeks to reveal what is produced within this process of transmission, and with what effects.[46]

The Political Economy of Redemption

The question of loss and its prolonged hold on the present has been analyzed widely through the concept of memory. By turning to the economic sphere as an underexplored site for the transmission of losses across generations, *Inheritance of Loss* departs from existing memory studies in its exploration of how those who did not directly experience a catastrophe inherit losses through newly available sites of encounters, and it considers the role of economy in this transfer. The Chinese and Japanese encounters with their past, each other's pasts, and each other in the present shows how multigenerational transmission is not always linear, nor is the mnemonic community self-evident, contrary to assumptions often shared in memory studies, for example, in Marianne Hirsch's powerful concept of "postmemory," which captures how the generation born after a catastrophe comes to relate to personal and collective traumas of the previous generation through representative forms such as photography, literature, and testimony.[47] While Hirsch's postmemory effectively captures certain forms of mediated relationships to the traumatic past by second-generation Holocaust survivors—what Eva Hoffman refers to as "postgenerations"[48]—my ethnography points to different dynamics that emerge through Chinese and Japanese postgenerations' relationships to what remains.

As my ethnography in chapter 3 demonstrates in detail, the optic of colonial inheritance elucidates dynamics that escape that of postmemory. Attempts by Chinese and Japanese postgenerations to come to terms with Japanese aggression in China simultaneously reaffirm and defy assumptions about mnemonic communities and certainties about which past is being transmitted. What is recognized as loss is not so much self-evident as assumed. What the lens of colonial inheritance makes visible is akin to what Michael Rothberg calls "multidirectional memory."[49] Instead of presenting memory as a representation or trace of the past event in one-on-one correspondence, Rothberg illustrates memory's emergence at the crossroads of multilayered and multidirectional recollections of past events among different actors.[50] Memory, as he sees it, is a product of multidirectional "negotiation, cross-referencing, and borrowing,"[51] and he argues that "memory is thus structurally multidirectional, but each articulation of the past processes that multidirectionality differently."[52]

The rhetorical shift in the public discourse in Northeast China to name colonial remnants as "inheritance" supports Rothberg's insight that memory cannot be reduced to a single origin (the original moment when the event took place) that can be captured as either representation, trace, or aftereffect, akin to trauma's relationship to the original injury. As the following chapters show, inheritance sometimes contains multiple origins, since the passage of time can add additional layers of losses and accompanying historical responsibilities. While Rothberg uses the term *memory* as a shorthand for "our relationship to the past,"[53] my ethnography of multigenerations—and a significant passage of time between them—suggests that *memory* as a general umbrella term may obscure certain dynamics that shape our engagement with difficult and now distant pasts.

For example, Harbin's colonial inheritance, discussed in chapter 2, contains at least three moments of "original" loss: colonial, socialist, and postsocialist. To call such relationships to layers of the past "memory" seems the wrong category here. More importantly, doing so could obscure layers of losses and attendant historical responsibilities. In Changchun, young Japanese tourists visiting the former faux capital of Manchukuo in search of postmemory encountered *that* history that they felt missing in Japan: the cityscape full of Manchukuo architecture in the emperor's crown style, the Fake Emperor's Palace Museum, and the former palace of Manchukuo emperor Puyi. But the nature of their encounter did not let them consign this history to the past. These Japanese tourists became aware of the local Chinese gaze, which turned the spectators into spectacles, as part of the Manchukuo artifacts in the present. This gaze of the Chinese, as imagined as it may have been, made the Japanese tourists keenly aware of their position as inheritors of this past without choice, which many described as "the negative inheritance" (*fu no isan*). The character for "negative" (*fu*) means a burden, to bear, to carry on one's back, responsibility, debt, to betray, or to lose in a war or game. Young Japanese visitors to Changchun often used this term to acknowledge having inherited not only legacies of Imperial Japan but also a sense of debt deriving from the lack of accountability during the postwar years, as seen (so they imagine, accurately or not) through the eyes of local Chinese.

Rothberg's insightful intervention into memory studies does not explicate what, when, and how structural forces generate particular instances of multidirectionality. My turn to the economic sphere elucidates these forces behind a multidirectional form of transmission that I call the *political economy of redemption*, which brings to light latent loss, debt, and moral economy.[54] I use *political economy of redemption* to show how at the core of the moral economy lies a sense of debt and unfulfilled promise inseparable from the formal economy of wealth accumulation.[55] Originally primed to see examples of the further separation between the formal and moral economies through the capitalization of colonial inheritance, I discovered instead how the moral economy shaped, redefined, and fueled Sino-Japanese formal economic relations beneath seemingly apolitical and ahistorical uses of colonial remainders under the rubric of economic rationality.[56]

Colonial inheritance is a hinge between the otherwise seemingly separate accumulation of moral debts and the accumulation of wealth. While recent anthropological use of the term *moral economy* refers to a moral regime that emerged around the concept of trauma, as in the work of Didier Fassin and Richard Rechtman, who employ "economy" metaphorically,[57] this book points to a literal economy (formal economy) as central to the workings of moral economy.[58]

The political economy of redemption in turn enriches our understanding of "economy" by making visible the workings of moral economy as it drives, shapes, and gives meaning to formal economy. By casting light on the past, the political economy of redemption further allows us to see underexplored dimensions of China's new economy. Whereas speculative economy, which has become the driving force behind the new Chinese economy, is usually associated with the future, this book shows how the Chinese economy also speculates on its past. The etymology of *speculative* shows how the term developed from its original usage, referring to vision or reasoning based on incomplete knowledge without positive evidence, to a later usage referring to investment through risk-taking. As these usages indicate, at the core of speculation lie secrets invisible in the present. While the unknown in speculative economy is often associated with the future within the world of finance, my ethnography foregrounds the dynamics in which past secrets cast risks and opportunities in the future. It tells a story of how China's new economy activates dormant imperial debris and with what effects.

Seen through the lens of colonial inheritance, then, what is usually described as China's "transition" to a market-oriented economy (or else subsumed under the rubrics of globalization or neoliberalism) is revealed as an integral part of a larger economy of inheriting—inheriting socialist modernity, inheriting colonial modernity, and the dynamics between the two in navigating what is to come. *Inheritance of Loss* tells a story of this economy, which has taken a particular shape in Northeast China through the orchestrated capitalization of colonial inheritance that has opened up new sites of encounters. These encounters have resulted in what I call a *refractive structure of transmission.*

Awase kagami: The Refractive Structure of Transmission

The capitalization of colonial inheritance set in motion face-to-face encounters between Chinese and Japanese through tourism and foreign direct investment, and these encounters have generated a new mode of generational transmission. In this mode, the role of the other becomes key to one's acknowledgment of inheritance within this newly available theater of after empire.[59] The idea of theater is not just a metaphor here, and role-playing is key. Within this landscape of after empire full of reincorporated remnants of colonial modernity, the adjectives "Chinese" and "Japanese" are not innocent, and participants are assigned roles as inheritors in the name of the nation. It is a complex play: participants are simultaneously actors and spectators.

This theater produces effects akin to the Japanese concept of *awase kagami* (two mirrors arranged at such an angle that you can see your own back). You find your otherwise invisible back through the reflection in the mirror held by someone else behind you, which is reflected in your own mirror (just as in a hair salon). The mirror in front of you captures more than the doubled image of yourself: you see your face as a reflection, and you see your back through a reflection of a reflection. The mirror in front of you also captures the image of the other who holds another mirror behind you. What you see in the mirror facing you is a *refractive* image, a product of multiple doubling reflections. Through this refraction, you see what naked optics fail to capture. The mirrored refraction thus not only doubles the original but also reveals more than the original. According to legend, through this refractive power, *awase kagami* conjures up ghostly images invisible to the naked eye. This legend captures well Chinese and Japanese encounters with colonial inheritance set in motion through the capitalization of colonial remnants.

In Changchun, where Manchukuo remnants are the architectural vernacular, young Japanese visitors come to acknowledge their own postimperial positioning as if seeing their backs in a mirrored refraction. They see themselves in the twice-reflected image in the mirror held by the local Chinese, whom the Japanese imagine are watching them as part of the Manchukuo spectacle. Through refraction, the structural position of the Japanese within the landscape of *(for)given time* and the underlying debts they have inherited become visible to them. They discover the "negative inheritance" of

Japanese. The mirror reflects their otherwise invisible backs that bear a historical burden, but it also reflects the ones holding the second mirror, the Chinese. In this mirrored refraction, the Japanese discover the Chinese inheritance as well. The refractive structure of transmission has resulted in acknowledgment of not only one's own inheritance but also the other's. At the same time, acknowledged inheritance is a product of the gaze of the other in the mirrored refraction, however one imagines the intent of that gaze.

My ethnography demonstrates this refractive doubling quality at the core of the generational transmission of unaccounted-for pasts. The layered doubles illustrated in this book are the sign of oft-unarticulated "entanglements," to borrow Rey Chow's term, which simultaneously amplify and unsettle hierarchical distinctions.[60] These entanglements include the afterlife of asymmetries and the interrelations inherent in colonial modernity on the one hand, and Chinese and Japanese attempts to redeem inherited doubles and duplicity on the other. Rather than focusing on where the afterlife of "imperial formations" cuts through boundaries of modern nation-states, as suggested by Ann Laura Stoler, my use of *double inheritance* instead seeks to explicate the core contradictions *and* refractive structure of colonial modernity and its afterlife, including the propensity of doubles to produce even more doubles around the figure of a "national thing," which bears the scars of history.[61] My ethnography suggests that the crux of the long-standing question of coming to terms with Japanese imperialism in China lies in this doubled structure of inheriting.

Accountability after Empire

The landscapes of responsibility that emerge out of this refractive transmission complicate not only the expected narratives of victimhood and perpetration but also how loss is recognized and articulated as loss. More than a temporal framework at the intersection of postimperial, postcolonial, and postwar, after empire is a lived reality among remainders—where formerly and formally defined categories such as colonizer/colonized and perpetrators/victims become fluid, contested, and conflated with the passage of time while, at the same time, exposing the mutually implicated and deeply intertwined nature of these historical relations.[62] *Inverted victimhood* is one such example of these entangled categories. The inversion of victimhood and perpetration in former colonial and imperial societies is not limited to East Asia,[63] and it compels us to consider elisions, displacement, and duplicity incurred through the process of inheriting empire's remnants, which have made certain populations socially invisible and outside the purview of accountability.[64]

Inheriting itself is accompanied by losses and debts, and this book explores how gaps, folds, and voids created by postcolonial, postimperial, and postwar entanglements have propelled capitalization and abandonment, twin processes of inheriting. The topography of after empire exposes historical responsibility for losses incurred *after* the end of empire through these processes—for example, the *delayed violence* inflicted by abandoned and long-neglected chemical weapons, as we shall see in chapter 6.[65] As an articulation of the long reach of colonial modernity, the *double inheritance* presents itself not as a trace of the past, such as a legacy or memory, but as a reckoning with the present that comes with compounded losses and accrued interests on debt over time.[66] It directs us to see structures of violence and injustice *after empire* as an integral part of the colonial inheritance that the postgenerations have no choice but to inherit.

THE TOPOGRAPHY OF AFTER EMPIRE

During the period from the 1990s to the 2000s, Japanese direct investment in China increased steeply, soon surpassing the ODA. Trade flourished along with investment. Even with the downturn caused by the Asian financial crisis of 1997–98, China remained Japan's major trading partner along a classic export model: parts and raw materials were exported to China for assembly, and finished products were exported back to Japan. In 2002, Japanese imports from China exceeded those from the United States for the first time, and Japan was China's largest trading partner until 2004, when it was surpassed by the United States and the European Union.[67] In 2007, leapfrogging the United States, China became Japan's biggest trading partner. Facing China as an emerging economic superpower, some Japanese described Japan's dependence on the Chinese economy by saying that "when China sneezes, Japan catches cold," a twist on the familiar expression from an earlier era when the United States was doing the sneezing.[68]

Despite apprehensions about the rise of China as an economic superpower, this robust economic relationship led many Japanese to rediscover in China the benefits and excitement of pursuing modernity. The challenge proved especially attractive to many who had lost confidence in the promise of modernity during Japan's long recession beginning in the 1990s.[69] In Japan, countless books on doing business in contemporary China filled the bookstores. Chinese became the foreign language of choice; Chinese-run schools that once catered only to Chinese living in Japan were now flooded with Japanese students whose parents wanted their children to learn the language of the future. Japanese flocked to China as tourists and business people, encountering a China not captured in the standard media representations. For many Chinese, whose opportunities to go abroad were still limited, Japanese visiting or living in China often provided their first postwar encounters with people from Japan. Such face-to-face encounters challenged the polarized portrayals in the Chinese media that tacked between Japan as an object of disdain, as portrayed in anti-Japanese war movies as well as news reports about Japanese denials of war responsibility, and Japan as an object of emulation as a modern society, represented by Japanese products and popular Japanese television dramas. This shift from virtual to real encounters—Japanese reencounters with "former Manchuria" in Northeast China and Chinese reencounters with "real" Japanese—set the stage for the developments explored in this book.

Chapter 2, "Inheritance and Betrayal: Historical Preservation and Colonial Nostalgia in Harbin," shows the dynamics of *inheritance and betrayal* as they play out in the politics surrounding the city's historical preservation of colonial-era architecture, built mostly by Russians and Japanese in the beginning of the twentieth century, and the ensuing nostalgia industry related to "Old Harbin," as locals affectionately refer to Harbin during the era of colonialism. The chapter explores the heated and public "historians' debate" on Harbin's colonial origin in preparation for the city's ill-fated centenary celebration in 1998; a concomitant photography exhibition on the history of Old Harbin in the beautifully restored cathedral in the center of the city; and the virtual resurrection of Russian-built St. Nicholas Church, destroyed during the Cultural Revolution. We see how the Harbin municipal government's capitalization on colonial inheritance through preservation unintentionally questioned the legitimacy of the party-state and called forth an unexpected ghost of a different sort—the Cultural Revolution. Through the dynamics of inheritance and betrayal, the case of Harbin illustrates how multilayered losses from different historical sediments—losses from colonialism, socialism, and postsocialism—unexpectedly emerge through the capitalization of colonial inheritance.

Chapter 3, "Memory, Postmemory, Inheritance: Postimperial Topography of Guilt in Changchun," examines Japanese tourists' encounters with Manchukuo remnants in Changchun, the faux-imperial former capital of Manchukuo, which has become a location for the displacement of guilt and "real history" in the Japanese popular imaginary of recent years. Through my participant observation as an official tour guide at the Palace Museum of the Puppet Emperor of Manchukuo, I follow Japanese visitors—repatriates (*hikiagesha*), schoolchildren, backpackers, businessmen, and farmers—to examine their encounters with the museum's atrocity exhibition as well as local Chinese perceptions of the Japanese visitors flocking to their city, which many locals think offers "nothing else but Manchukuo remains."

I demonstrate how, through the *refractive structure of transmission* in the manner of the Japanese concept of *awase kagami*, Japanese postgenerations' encounters with Manchukuo remnants, which they hoped would allow them to attain postmemory—the "real history" that they feel missing in Japan plagued with imperial amnesia—actually reveal something else: the *double inheritance* of their own *and* of the Chinese, as well as moral debts not only from Japanese colonial violence but also from the lack of accountability after the empire's demise. We shall see how Japanese postgenerations' encounters with traces of the unaccounted-for past simultaneously reaffirm and defy the assumed mnemonic communities of former colonizer and colonized and further unsettle certainties about which loss is being transmitted. The case of Changchun suggests how Japanese and Chinese attempts to come to terms with the past are intricately connected, implicated, and affected by each other.

If in Changchun the generational transmission of their inheritances seemed to result in parallel monologues, in Dalian the robust economic cooperation turns this otherwise problematic transmission into wealth production. Chapter 4, "The Political Economy of Redemption: Middle-Class Dreams in the Dalian Special Economic Zone," looks into the *political economy of redemption*, a mode of generational transmission where the moral economy of seeking redemption for the unaccounted-for past is inexorably linked to the formal economy of exports, consumption, and the citywide pursuit of middle-class dreams. Against the backdrop of a national mythology premised on anti-Japanese struggles, the municipal government literally invited the Japanese back in and turned the city into a nonstop performance to lure Japanese capital, businessmen, and tourists to its factories, office blocks, and beautifully restored colonial architecture. Increasingly common because of the considerable Japanese corporate presence, face-to-face interactions between Chinese and Japanese changed colonial inheritance into a productive force within the rhythm of everyday life. An analysis of "modern life" (*xiandai shenghuo*), especially in the Dalian Economic and Technological Zone, reveals how the everyday pursuit of middle-class modern life, from factory floors to karaoke clubs, has become a primary site for incorporating and coming to terms with the city's colonial history. We shall see how at sites of encounters between Chinese and Japanese, the supposedly rational formal economy has become a constant reminder of the underlying moral economy and accompanying unpaid debts, propelling desires from both sides to reckon with what remains unaccounted for through day-to-day economic activities. Dalian's new economy channels desires to redeem the past into new forms of production, consumption, and accumulation.

While the political economy of redemption channels debt into productive relations, it also produces excess in the form of latent anxiety about modernity among Dalian's postgenerations. Chapter 5, "Industrious Anxiety: Labor and Landscapes of Modernity in Dalian," looks into this excess through the Chinese concept of *renzhen* (conscientiousness/conscience). This term is often used to describe the Japanese character as having both an excessively conscientious work ethic and a lack of conscience when it comes to apologizing for past violence. This double usage captures the tension between Japan as a model to emulate and Japan as an object of hostility, and this chapter examines this double usage in young middle-class Dalianites' encounters with colonial inheritance at two major industrial sites in Dalian: the Onoda Cement plant located on the outskirts of the Zone, which is one of the first former colonial Japanese corporations to "return" to the city, and the former grounds of the Fukushō Chinese Labor Company, which was one of the outfits in charge of the Japanese use of wartime forced labor. I look at how the ghostly echoes of forced labor at the prewar precursor of the cement factory took concrete form during a visit to Dalian by national heroine and social activist Wang Xuan as part of her investigation of the Imperial Japanese Army's wartime biological human experiments at Fukushō.

The double usage of *renzhen*, elicited through these encounters, allows us to see what lies behind the rhetoric of "not enough apology" and repeated surges of anti-Japanese sentiment. The double usage points to how a conscientious work ethic does not always translate into good conscience at the collective level but rather can potentially contribute to state violence. The chapter suggests that even with "enough apology" in good conscience from the Japanese, that apology could never satisfy the unarticulated anxiety about how modernity evades individual accountability and good conscience while celebrating the diligence and conscientiousness of modern workers, the perverse combination that once led Japan to its violent colonial aggression in the name of the state. The ethnography in this chapter directs attention to how the perceived lack of acknowledgment of historical truth and accompanying apology by the Japanese may be misplaced as the crux of failed reckoning. Rather, anxiety projected onto the figure of Japanese workers suggests that, for the current generation, the crux of the issue is less the question of seeking historical truth and apology than the question of accountability within the topography of after empire.

Since I first conducted the fieldwork, the doubled structure of transmission has become more visible in the political sphere. Chapter 6, "Epilogue: Deferred Reckoning and the Double Inheritance," takes us to the second decade of the twentieth-first century, pervaded by heightened political tension over Japan's "history problem" within East Asia's new geopolitical context. We will find the victims of the mustard gas exposure in Qiqihar in the Tokyo High Court, awaiting the ruling in their lawsuit against the Japanese government. Through this High Court ruling, I show how the issue of accountability, which remains latent in the economic sphere, becomes publicly recognized as an issue of political accountability articulated in the form of *double inheritance*, bringing with it new challenges and possibilities for reckoning with the past.

Inheritance of Loss makes visible the entangled processes of after empire, which unfolds under the guise of persistent aspirations *and* anxiety for modernity's potential. Through experiences in the semiperiphery, this book explores how persistent redemptive desires—often articulated through a refraction of Western modernity—have channeled such aspirations and anxiety into new economic relations, including desires for going after empire.[70] The topography of after empire that I map out in this book thus brings to the fore the entwined and often ambivalent relationship between market and history as it entered a new phase with China's ever-tighter embrace of the market-oriented economy at the turn of the twenty-first century. The intricacies of such a relationship, its mechanisms of desire and disavowal, of inheritance and betrayal, and of possibility and peril, are what the following chapters seek to elucidate.

Map 3 Harbin, Heilongjiang Province

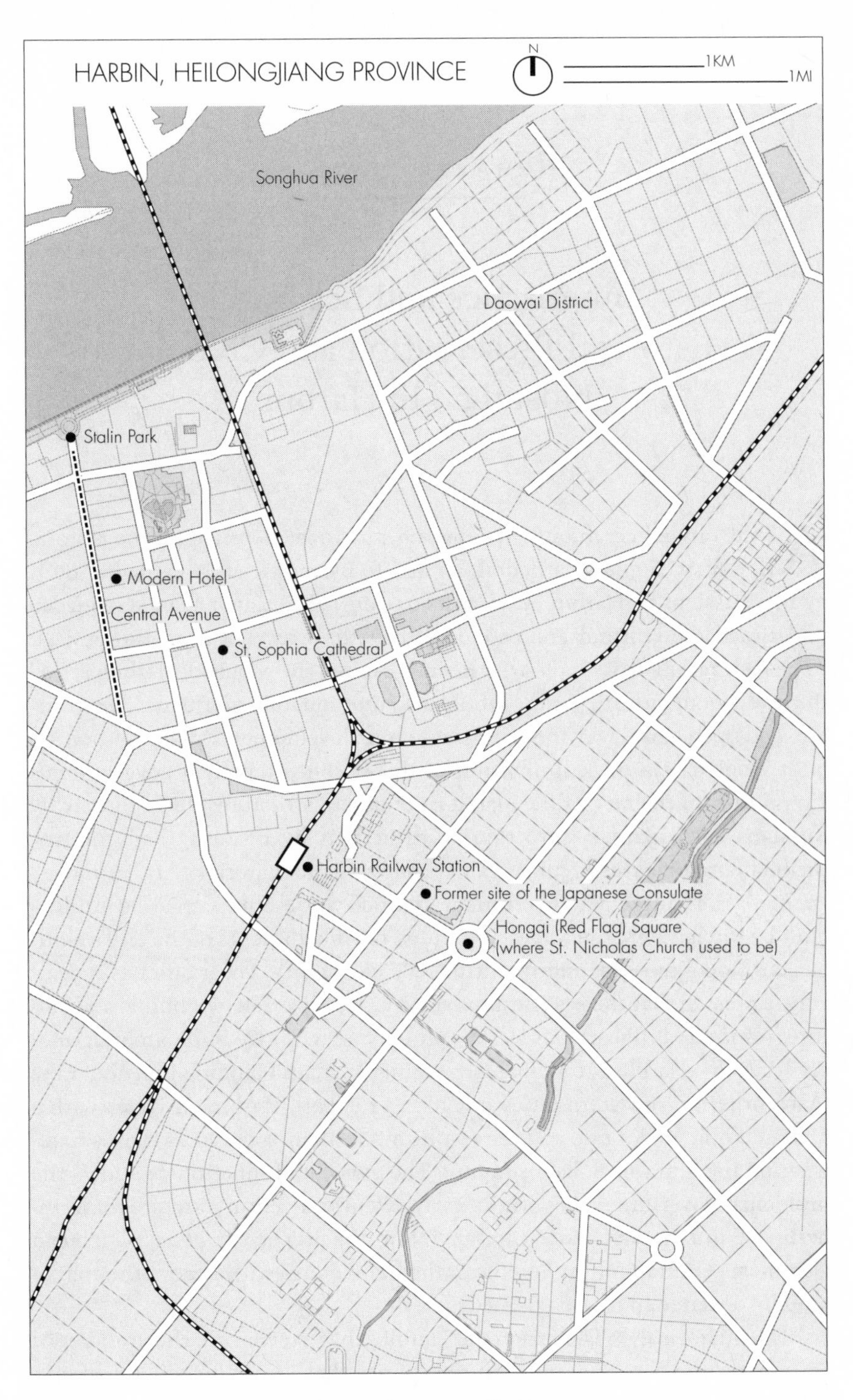

Map 4 downtown Harbin

CHAPTER TWO

Inheritance and Betrayal: Historical Preservation and Colonial Nostalgia in Harbin

At the official ceremony on September 2, 1997, to celebrate the restoration of St. Sophia Cathedral, an ornate Byzantine-style cathedral built by the Russians in Harbin between 1907 and 1932, Mayor Wang Guangdao underlined the cultural and economic benefits expected from the project: "The restoration of St. Sophia Cathedral inspired the people of Harbin, raised the level of our culture, let the whole of China and foreign friends know Harbin, and opened the way for faster economic development." The restoration of St. Sophia was the culmination of the Harbin municipal government's efforts to turn the city's dilapidated colonial-era structures, built mostly by Russians and Japanese, into tourist attractions by restoring and granting them landmark status (figure 2.1). By deploying the rhetoric of "inheritance" (*yichan*), the municipal government claimed these European-style edifices built by foreign imperial forces as their own, embodiments of the city's glorious cosmopolitan past and its future as a global city. Local officials repeatedly expressed that these structures signified civilization (*wenming*) and culture (*wenhua*). Billboards in Harbin proudly stated, "We build architectural civilization—Harbin Municipal Government Urban Planning Bureau." Like many other northeastern cities in China's rustbelt, Harbin struggles with a high unemployment rate and the resulting social unrest even as it tries to reposition itself in the global economy. The concept of inheritance allows the municipal government to turn its early twentieth-century architectural inheritance into much-needed capital. "Now, the property (*zichan*, which can also mean 'capital') of St. Sophia Cathedral belongs to Harbin," the mayor proudly declared in his 1997 speech.[1]

The historical preservation in Harbin that started in the mid-1990s epitomizes the core dynamics of inheritance that I introduced in chapter 1 through the etymology of the Chinese and Japanese terms *yichan* and *isan*:

2.1 St. Sophia Cathedral in downtown Harbin: Long neglected and effectively invisible during the Mao era, St. Sophia Cathedral (built by Russians, 1907–32) was completely restored in 1997 and is now the face of the city. It houses the popular Harbin Architecture Art Center. Photo by author, 2002.

to turn losses into gains/property through presenting. The mayor's speech encapsulates how colonial remains are incorporated into today's economic relations to produce new value. The citywide historical preservation efforts and the celebration of colonial-era architecture as the face of Harbin further illustrate a dramatic shift from the *political deployment of war memory* to the *economic deployment of colonial inheritance* through the erasure of colonial modernity's violence. It was only a decade earlier that the government had marked a site of Japanese wartime violence by establishing a historical museum in 1984 on the city's outskirts at the former base of Japanese Army Unit 731, infamous for conducting human experiments for developing chemical and biological weapons, and turning it into a prime destination for the newly instituted patriotic education (figures 2.2 and 2.3).

In contrast, Harbin's historical preservation is characterized by a deliberate absence of such markings of losses sustained through colonial modernity, highlighting instead the colonial structures' aesthetic and cultural value under the rubric of *wenming* as well as their economic value as capital.[2] The

2.2 The former site of Imperial Japanese Army Unit 731 in Harbin: On the outskirts of Harbin, the remaining structures of Unit 731, the headquarters for developing biochemical weapons through human experiments, had been left to decay for decades. The site is now a museum. Photo by author, 2013.

2.3 Gas masks displayed in the Unit 731 Museum: In one exhibition hall at the Unit 731 Museum, the Imperial Japanese Army's biochemical weapon development is evidenced through gas masks on display. Photo by author, 2013.

plaque on the beautifully restored and landmarked former Japanese consulate building in the center of Harbin does not mention that its basement was used as a hub for the transport of human subjects to Unit 731. And the erasure of colonial modernity's violence goes beyond the effacement of wartime violence. It extends to obliteration of losses sustained through railway imperialism and settler colonialism by the Russians and Japanese—two manifestations of colonial modernity that played key roles in the formation of Harbin as a modern city—which later culminated in a formal colonial enterprise with the establishment of the Japanese puppet state Manchukuo, followed by a full-fledged Japanese military invasion of China. There is no acknowledgement of the losses incurred through the foreign exercise of administrative rights along the Russian-founded Chinese Eastern Railway (CER), which put significant portion of Harbin under extraterritorial jurisdiction with large military presence. Settlers in this jurisdiction enjoyed special privileges, even during a brief period in the 1920s when the Chinese seized some administrative rights and established the Special District of the Three Eastern Provinces (*dongsansheng tebie qu*).[3]

While historical preservation has opened up new sites of encounter with the past by presenting the landscape of after empire to the public with a flair of cosmopolitanism, these encounters have resulted in recognition, misrecognition, and displacement of losses incurred through colonial modernity. These elisions and excesses produced through the capitalization of colonial inheritance provide a window through which to explore what is at stake for postgenerations in inheriting colonial remnants today. Through the prism of historical preservation that has turned long-neglected colonial edifices—what Ann Laura Stoler calls "imperial debris"[4]—into colonial capital, this chapter illustrates this economy of inheriting, which simultaneously displays, discloses, and displaces losses that one inherits.

Inheritance, then, is more than a simple transfer of property from one generation to another. Inheritance also betrays secrets contained within what one inherits. As my ethnography illustrates, displaying long-neglected colonial remnants through historical preservation discloses layers of historical sediments, including losses incurred during the Mao era. Elision of colonial violence through the capitalization of colonial inheritance inadvertently makes visible, for instance, the long-hushed-up violent destruction of the beloved St. Nicholas Church by the Red Guard during the Cultural Revolution. The loss of St. Nicholas, whose absence became highlighted through the restoration of other remaining colonial edifices, symbolizes losses incurred during the Mao era that are more immediate to the current generation than colonial violence. Historical preservation thus generates excess that betrays the party-state.

While the deployment of the *wenming* discourse by various officials in Harbin conveys how the burst of productive energy during the reform era remains under the control of the party-state rather than set loose as a self-regulating market force,[5] the economy of inheriting points to surplus beyond the intended control of the past. Harbin's preservation policy set in motion a complicated play between official attempts to control the city's colonial remnants and the inability to stem the betrayal of secrets contained in its architectural inheritance. This chapter brings to the fore this dynamic of *inheritance and betrayal* at the core of the economy of inheritance.

The common usage of *betrayal* illuminates the logic of inheritance in the case of historical preservation in Harbin. Its most common usage signifies an act of treason and disloyalty. A second usage refers to the act of revealing, disclosing, showing, or exhibiting. And yet a third refers specifically to the disclosure or revelation of what should be kept secret. Since inheritance embodies the multiplicity of the past, displaying inheritance could reveal what is supposed to be unseen and therefore become a betrayal in all three senses. What the case of Harbin illustrates is the tension brought forth by the play of these three workings of betrayal contained within its architectural inheritance. By exposing through historical restoration what has long been invisible, the capitalization of colonial inheritance becomes burdened by an unexpected excess that disturbs long-held narratives of the past. The dynamics of inheritance and betrayal thus defy attempts to harness the past through the capitalization of colonial inheritance.

The historical preservation policy was one of the most visible manifestations of Harbin's transition to a market-oriented economy, and the resultant new encounters with the landscape of after empire generated two significant developments: the "historians' debate" over the origin of Harbin as a colonial city and the proliferation of "Old Harbin" (*lao Haerbin*) nostalgia. Through ethnographic analyses of these public engagements with Harbin's colonial inheritance, I demonstrate how Chinese society's reckoning with its socialist past is intricately entwined with its reckoning with its colonial past, as well as how the contemporary envisioning of Harbin's future and "modern life" is inseparable from the task of wrestling with these two past forms of modernity and their attendant losses. Through exploring this landscape of after empire, this chapter tells a story of contemporary China's resilient yet oft-unarticulated relationship to colonial modernity, which has resurfaced in new guises as a result of urban reconfigurations in the midst of China's mad rush to the market.

"THE ATMOSPHERE OF A FOREIGN COUNTRY": INHERITING THE OTHER

Following the 1997 opening ceremony and media coverage of St. Sophia Cathedral and the Harbin Architecture Art Centre housed within, the municipal government began planning for the city's centenary the following year, a gala celebration meant to involve numerous ceremonies, publications, and sales of commemorative gold plates. At the last moment, the government cancelled all the centenary events under pressure from a growing chorus of voices opposed to a "colonialist historical perspective" (*zhimin zhuyi lishiguan*).

This opposition had emerged from the debates of local intellectuals over the city's disputed origins, which revolved around the question of the role of colonial modernity in the development of Harbin as a modern city. A series of public debates that started in 1992 among local intellectuals in anticipation of the 1998 centenary celebration raised this sensitive question through arguments over the city's "birth year" and the nature of Harbin's existence before the arrival of the Russians in 1898. The initial debate was carried out in the local daily *Xinwanbao* (New Evening News), which published fourteen essays from April to June 1992 under the series title "City Origin Debate," written mostly by scholars at local universities and social-science academies. The core tension illuminated in the essays continues today.

Wang Yulang, one of the most vocal critics of the colonialist historical perspective, traces the origin of Harbin to the Jin dynasty (1115–234 AD).[6] He rejects Harbin's colonial origin by claiming the city predated the Russian arrival. Against this view, Wang Dexin cautiously differentiates between the archeological origin of the city (*chengshi qiyuan*) and the city's origin (*chengshi jiyuan*), and he claims the primacy of the latter, concluding that "there is no doubt that the construction of the [Russian-built] Chinese Eastern Railway is considered the historical incident that marks the origin of the city."[7] In a subsequent essay published three days later, however, he preempts certain criticism by stating, "Any one of the historical moments that embody invasion and colonialism, such as signing for the construction of the railroad, cannot be the origin of the city, since that is not what proud Chinese would be willing to accept."[8] To avoid any date that might have imperialist resonance, he diplomatically suggests January 1, 1900, as the date of Harbin's founding.

Despite the critiques of the colonialist historical perspective, the opponents reached a tentative consensus in December 1994 and agreed to set the origin of Harbin in 1898, when the Russians began the construction of the Chinese Eastern Railway.[9] Yet the sensitive question of colonial inheritance again resurfaced. Sociologist Shang Zhifa, for one, strongly objected to recognizing 1898 as the origin of the city by asking, "Should all the colonial cities in the world that were constructed after colonial invasions commemorate the moment of oppression?"[10] In private conversation, Tian Qiang, a prominent local intellectual pointed out to me how inappropriate it would be to date the origin of the Americas to Columbus's first landfall in the West Indies. He asked, "What would the Maya think of such a historical interpretation?" He continued, "It is not true that the arrival of the Russian ship started Harbin. The city was built by the Chinese, who laid bricks one by one. . . . To think that the city was born when the Russians arrived is a colonialist perspective, and that is why I cannot agree with this view."

According to some of the debate's participants, opponents of the consensus date of 1898 went to the local Security Bureau while the preparation for the citywide centenary celebration was under way. The bureau took the issue to the Foreign Affairs Ministry in Beijing, and a high-level directive came back to Harbin to cancel the celebration. The government decision to cancel the centenary commemoration resulted in immediate censorship. Local newspapers refused to publish articles advocating 1898 as the date of the city's origin, and some writers even faced the threat of arrest by the Security Bureau. The fall of 2003 witnessed another wave of heated discussion. In the midst of this renewed debate, one of the most vocal advocates of 1898 disappeared without a trace, and his main opponent was suddenly transferred to a university in another city. People were reluctant to talk about these mysterious incidents, and many indicated to me that I had better not stick my nose into the matter. Repeated eruptions of the historians' debate over the past decades signal the volatile nature of coming to terms with the city's colonial inheritance.

The ambiguous role of colonialism in Harbin's history is highlighted by a cityscape that maintains unambiguous foreign traces. Once called the "Paris of the East" in the first half of the twentieth century, Harbin still appears more European than Chinese with its elegant Art Nouveau architecture and variety of other European-style colonial structures in a bricolage of styles: Renaissance, Baroque, Classical Revival, Romanesque, Judaic, Byzantine, Russian, "Chinese Baroque,"[11] Eclectic, sober socialist-style buildings from the 1970s and 1980s, monoliths of mirrored glass and steel that embody the "modern" ideology of the Beijing government of the 1990s, and more recent so-called European-style (*oufeng*) buildings that echo colonial-era motifs (figures 2.4, 2.5, and 2.6). Many locals proudly and fondly describe the urban space of Harbin as exotic (*yiguo qingdiao*—the atmosphere of a foreign country). Likewise, many postcards and local guidebooks feature glossy photographs of colonial-era structures that dominate the visual composition of the city.

With the historical preservation policy that started in 1996, the Harbin municipal government has turned once purposefully neglected and dust-covered symbols of colonialism into a significant part of Harbin's inheritance rather than demolishing them.[12] The focus on tourism is not ancillary to the economy. This freezing rustbelt city suffers from high unemployment due to the privatization of state-run heavy industries, and cash revenue from tourism and related employment opportunities is a matter of survival.[13] Although media coverage of social unrest remains prohibited by the authorities, protests by unemployed workers are quotidian events (figure 2.7).[14] It is in this context that the preservation policy has been eagerly promoted by the government as a way of transforming its colonial inheritance into profit-generating capital.

The steady influx of visitors from Hong Kong, Taiwan, Japan, and Russia speaks to the success of this conversion of the colonial remnants into a tourist attraction. The famous January ice festival and European atmosphere beckon Chinese from the wealthy south, while Japanese tourists

2.4 The Modern Hotel on Central Avenue: The Modern Hotel, originally built in the 1910s by a French Jewish businessman, was restored to its former glory in the late 1990s. It is the centerpiece of Harbin's main shopping street, which is lined with colonial-era architecture in pastel colors. Photo by author, 2002.

purchase tour packages to this "former Manchurian" city and "discover" a modern city that is simultaneously a historical artifact. The once vibrant communities of White Russians and Russian Jews of the first half of the twentieth century have been replaced by poor Russians from Siberia, who hawk military binoculars and army watches in street markets to buy their daily meal, even as well-to-do Russian tourists come to admire the Russian-style architecture of the previous fin de siècle. Harbin officials acknowledge the tourists' gaze and seek to recreate cosmopolitanism through large projects and small gestures, such as bilingual (Chinese and English) plaques that describe the history of protected colonial architecture in positive terms.

The traces of the West so undeniably inscribed in Harbin's urban space were notably absent from official historical narratives of the city written during the Mao era.[15] In these narratives, the West suddenly disappeared after the Liberation in 1949 until the historical preservation policy in the 1990s unearthed what had long been invisible to the public.[16] This discursive disappearance of colonial traces was part of the government's longstanding attempt

2.5 Xinhua Bookstore on Central Avenue: Across the street from the Modern Hotel is Xinhua Bookstore, housed in a baroque building originally built by Japanese (and designed by a Russian architect) to accommodate a Japanese department store. Photo by author, 2002.

to construct a history of the Chinese vis-à-vis "foreigners," and it went hand in hand with the "disappearance" of ethnic groups.[17] Through this process of fixing Harbin within the master narrative of Maoist nation-state building, the municipal government avoided highlighting Harbin's "exotic atmosphere." The ideology that produced such invisibility is now being challenged by both internal and external pressures.

Historical preservation projects oriented toward tourism are often criticized for reproducing the colonial gaze. Writing on the visual consumption of history in Hong Kong, Ackbar Abbas argues that the preservation of colonial-era buildings reduces historical memories to kitsch "by aestheticizing them out of existence."[18] Historical sight, he warns, substitutes for the disappearance of historical site. This critique speaks to the situation in Harbin, where the preservation project celebrates the cosmopolitan element of imperialism and effaces losses sustained through colonial modernity. Yet,

2.6 Chinese Baroque architecture in the Daowai district: Most of the Chinese construction workers who built the European-style colonial-era architecture in downtown Harbin mass migrated to the city from Shandong Province. They used their acquired skills and aesthetics to build their own housing in the Daowai district adjacent to the downtown area in an eclectic architectural style often referred to as "Chinese Baroque" style. Photo by author, 2002.

2.7 Sit-in protest in front of the Heilongjiang Province Communist Party Headquarters: Against the background of the beautified cityscape, sit-in protests like this one in front of the Heilongjiang Province Communist Party Headquarters are not uncommon in this rustbelt city. Laid-off workers from state-run work units demand compensation and jobs while the police chase away onlookers. As I was taking this picture, a plain-clothes policeman demanded that I surrender the film. Photo by author, 2002.

however apposite this critique, spatial politics in Harbin present an even more complex dynamic beneath the façade of aestheticized colonial space.[19]

COSMOPOLITAN IMPERIALISM AND OLD HARBIN NOSTALGIA

One of the most heralded events in the recent history of the city was the resurrection of St. Sophia Cathedral. Although the cathedral's sturdy structure evaded its intended destruction during the Cultural Revolution, its empty hull became a warehouse for a nearby state-run department store. Its windows were bricked up, and saplings grew from the roof.[20] Prefabricated concrete high-rises boxed it in on all four sides, coming within yards of its walls, making the cathedral inaccessible and invisible from the street. For decades, it remained the invisible center of the city, surrounded by decoration-material stalls, an auto-body shop, a pen factory, and apartments for city-government employees, until the Beijing government designated the cathedral a national cultural heritage site in 1996 as part of a nationwide campaign to protect historical sites. This prompted a newspaper article about the "hidden" cathedral[21] that spurred donations from local corporations, small businesses, and workers at nearby department stores to restore the cathedral and renovate the square in front of it.[22] A total of twelve million yuan (approximately 1.5 million US dollars) was eventually raised,[23] and by 1997, the cathedral was once again visible. The change was dramatic: the surrounding buildings were torn down, and the new Harbin Architecture Square showcased the cathedral with a huge new fountain at its entrance. The opening celebrations were suitably spectacular.

With this municipal government decision, the European-looking space was given new meaning as an embodiment of culture and art and was represented to the public as the city's proud inheritance. As then-mayor Wang Guangdao repeatedly declared, "The purpose of the historical preservation of St. Sophia Cathedral is to restore the architecture unique to Harbin and turn it into a tourist destination."[24] Harbin guidebooks feature the cathedral on their covers, proclaiming the city's exotic atmosphere. The cathedral and the restored Central Avenue are now touted as the symbolic center of the city, bustling with locals and tourists alike and signifying "civilization, culture, and art."[25]

Inside the cathedral, brand-new reproductions of Orthodox icons look down at the visitor, in sharp contrast to the battered ceiling, faded frescos, and peeling paint, all bespeaking the days before restoration. A photography exhibit portrays early twentieth-century Harbin as a cosmopolitan city where "the fashion in Paris flies to Harbin in two weeks."[26] The exhibit, which remains popular years after its opening, traces the development of Harbin from the late nineteenth century, when the Russians built the first railroads in the region, to the early 1940s. More than three hundred photographs are arranged around scale models of St. Nicholas Church, the central Orthodox church in Harbin destroyed during the Cultural Revolution, and St. Sophia Cathedral itself (figure 2.8). The placement of St. Nicholas Church at the center of the exhibit, accompanied by a mournful textual commentary on its destruction, highlights the church's absence. The caption for the old photograph of St. Nicholas reads, "The scale of the church was magnificent, and its exquisite architectural details were world renowned. It was built in a Russian style, typical wooden well-casting structures with steeples. It was destroyed during the Cultural Revolution." One's eyes move to the enlarged photographs with descriptive captions covering the surrounding walls, twisting through small

2.8 Old Harbin photography exhibition in St. Sophia Cathedral: St. Sophia Cathedral houses the Harbin Architecture Art Center, with its popular Old Harbin photography exhibition that illustrates the history of the city since the late nineteenth century. The scale model features St. Sophia Cathedral and St. Nicholas Church, a beloved central Orthodox church that was dramatically destroyed during the Cultural Revolution. Photo by author, 2002.

alcoves as the history of Harbin unfolds. Many of these pictures come from postcards proudly produced by Russians and Japanese in multiple languages (commonly Russian, Japanese, and English) to show off *their* modern monuments, and they reveal the cosmopolitanism of Old Harbin and also the unusual nature of the exhibit in light of the official narrative of the colonial past.

The exhibition conveys nostalgia for the era affectionately referred to as "Old Harbin." The preface to the exhibition (in both Chinese and English) reads, "Old pictures are true records of what happened, and they provide accurate answers to unsettled issues in history. . . . Leaping over time and space, here we have reproduced her ethos and beauty" (my translation). After a long description of the cosmopolitan past, the text in a few brief sentences recalls the difficult years under the Russians and Japanese.[27] In closing, it encourages visitors to interpret and ponder the messages contained within the exhibition. In contrast, other historical museums in the city, such as the Heilongjiang Province Museum, the Northeast Martyr Memorial Museum, and the Japanese Army Unit 731 Museum, seek to educate the public in anti-imperial discourse and to call attention to past tragedies and atrocities.

The exhibition is organized into three sections: "The Early Days of the City: The End of the Nineteenth Century," "The Old View of the City: The Penetration of Western Culture," and "Quotidian Vignettes: The Early Twentieth Century." The first section attempts to capture the role of the Chinese community in constructing Harbin as a city. Many photos show one-story buildings in Fujiadian, the Chinese district populated predominately by migrant construction workers from Shandong Province. The second section demonstrates the influence of Western culture on the city's architecture, claiming that the variation and number of Harbin architectural styles are unique in the world. The captions, in Chinese only, state each building's original name, the year it was built, the name of the architect if known, and its current name, along with a brief description of its architectural style. Some captions mention that the buildings were destroyed during the Cultural Revolution. The last section depicts Western culture in the daily life of Harbin in the early twentieth century. The accompanying text points out how "the liberal thought that came along with the Western culture lashed out against the corrupted feudal social elements."[28] The exhibition closes with a celebration of the cosmopolitanism that existed in Old Harbin. To those used to historical museums in China, the tone of the exhibit is quite unusual, and it probably contributes to its sustained popularity compared with other historical museums in the city that are usually nearly empty of visitors.

The photography exhibition paints a picture of competing imperial forces liberating Harbin from feudalism and bringing cosmopolitanism, echoing the sentiments I heard expressed among local intellectuals. Old Harbin nostalgia is at once a reevaluation of losses incurred through colonial modernity *and* an articulation of losses incurred through the party-state, albeit in a displaced manner. By highlighting cosmopolitan imperialism, Old Harbin nostalgia challenges the one-dimensional portrayal of the colonial era in the party-sanctioned national rhetoric of anti-imperialism. At the same time, the rosy portrayal of cosmopolitan Harbin points to layers of losses sustained under Communist rule: those incurred through the city's transition to socialism after the Liberation in 1949 and then through the more recent transition to a market-oriented society.

Dinner-table conversations with local intellectuals often revolved around contrasting Old Harbin, which they praise for its openness, diversity, and culturally rich life, to Harbin today, which they feel constrains their intellectual pursuits and cultural life. Li Keqian, a Harbin native in his midforties who is known in local intellectual circles for being very careful about what he says in public, spoke eagerly about how cosmopolitan and multicultural Harbin once was: "Can you believe that in the 1920s there were more than one hundred foreign language newspapers in this city? Diverse cultures really flourished in Harbin at that time. Yet look at Harbin today. We are so closed, provincial, and backward. And the intellectual culture is dead. We cannot say what we want to say, you see." Nostalgia for Old Harbin is a displaced form of social criticism of contemporary Harbin. After listening to my conversation with his teenage daughter at the dinner table, he murmured, "With kids like her you really get what they are thinking about. We [adults] think twice or three times before speaking out loud about anything."

Wu Liang, another local intellectual, put it more bluntly, describing how nostalgia for Old Harbin reflects the deeply felt and widely shared resentment toward the Chinese Communist Party (CCP) among ordinary people in Harbin:

> Without the resentment towards the current government, there wouldn't be nostalgia (*huaijiu*) for Old Harbin. The sudden flourishing of the Old Harbin industry in recent years speaks of such bitterness among common people here. Those elderly people I chat with when I exercise in the park in the morning gnash their teeth in rage and are bitterly angry with the Communist Party (*yaoya qiechi tongtong hen Gongchandang*), mainly because of political corruption. Of course, Chinese society experienced serious problems at other times in the past, especially during the Cultural Revolution. But now people are very bitter because some are milking the open-market policy while many others are left behind, and

> the gap between the rich and the poor is widening. When everybody was poor, it was much easier to accept the authorities. But now that people see the wealth, which is distributed quite unevenly, they cannot but feel resentful at the party.

The published works of local intellectuals rarely include explicit critiques of the party, even though these intellectuals, over many meals, openly and eagerly shared their views with me, a researcher from abroad, whom they considered a safe audience for their frustrations. Among the few exceptions to this intellectual silence in the public realm are Zhao Yihong, a senior journalist at the local newspaper *Harbin ribao* (Harbin Daily), and Liu Jun, a local intellectual.[29] Zhao Yihong contributes weekly full-page feature articles to her paper. By investigating human dramas surrounding historical architecture, her strong nostalgia for Old Harbin is redirected into criticism of the current government for its injustice, political corruption, and what she sees as modernization without serious consideration for Harbin's rich historical inheritance. Her articles receive immediate and passionate responses from her readers. "The municipal government doesn't like me," she told me, breaking into a big laugh.

> Because they know I'm not afraid of criticizing what they are doing. These days when I try to call the government, they just hang up when they recognize my voice. But I receive a lot of phone calls and letters from my readers, who support and encourage me with great enthusiasm. . . . I want the people in Harbin to be aware of what they are losing in this rapid urban transformation. The historical preservation policy is limited to superficial preservation of certain areas without real understanding of the history of Harbin. Harbin was once an extremely culturally rich society. It was very diverse and tolerant of different nationalities and cultures, something we should emulate now to create a new Harbin. I want to bring out these stories buried beneath the rapid urban reconfiguration.

Many intellectuals in Harbin use almost identical language to describe this energetic woman in her midforties with an infectious smile: "She is a person with a very strong sense of justice, and she is not afraid of the authorities." She treasures remainders from Old Harbin and was eager to take me along on her journalistic excursions to trace and capture the disappearing past—from visiting neglected architectural jewels that have not received landmark status to celebrating Russian Orthodox Easter with the last living

Russians from the Old Harbin era. For Zhao, these remainders testify not only to the Harbin that once was but to the Harbin that might be.

The tenacious presence of xenophobia (*paiwai zhuyi*) within the municipal government, despite its stated goal to make Harbin into a "major international economic city of Northeast China," frustrates many historians of Old Harbin and leads them to view Old Harbin in a rosier light than they might otherwise. Local historian Liu Jun, also in his midforties, is a vocal critic of local authorities' xenophobia through his nostalgic accounts of Old Harbin. Writing on the encounter between Harbin and the West, Liu highlights positive Western influences on Old Harbin. He claims that Western civilization destroyed feudalism in China while "normalizing" Chinese perspectives by introducing such concepts as democracy, humanity, freedom, and the rule of law. As a result, Liu argues, Harbin developed a "uniquely tolerant and peaceful attitude." He claims that "in the face of rising nationalism around the world, citizens of Harbin did not have strong exclusionist sentiments or mass protests against foreigners." His embrace of Old Harbin as an open-minded, cosmopolitan city is in turn used to criticize the post-Liberation Communist discourse of anti-imperialism and anticapitalism. He writes, "Since the Liberation, historians of Harbin have produced a considerable amount of work exposing the imperialists' invasion and praising people's anti-imperialist struggles. This is entirely accurate and necessary; however, it only captures one aspect of Chinese and foreign relations in Harbin. The fact that the Chinese and Western people built friendships and together constructed and developed Harbin is also an important aspect." He argues that the post-Liberation discourse, which he sees mired in political struggles, reduces capitalism to imperialist invasion: "In the academy in Harbin, studies of Harbin from the perspectives of modern social development and political struggles are plentiful. Yet perspectives considering cultural development remain underdeveloped. As a result, the study of Harbin's historical development tends to be subsumed by the theoretical restraints set by political struggles. In this process, they emphasize the brutal invasion by capitalism while omitting another aspect of capitalism, which is pervasive. And this aspect influenced Harbin greatly."

Belonging to the same generation as Zhao Yihong and other influential intellectuals of Harbin who were part of the first college graduating class after the Cultural Revolution, Liu experienced the underground democracy movement in 1981. "Many people got arrested, but I escaped from being busted because I wasn't one of the big guys in the movement," he recalled. "I'm not interested in radical change any longer. Rather, I'd like to gradually change the ways in which people think about history through my writings."

He wants to "slowly and quietly brainwash his readers" so that "they can see alternative narratives of history to the official one." This is what he calls "*dixia faxin*"—underground activity in broad daylight—which he pursues while securing political protection by cultivating networks of personal connections (*guanxi*).[30] I wondered why his book appears to be a volume edited by several people. Liu explained that the other editors are a protective umbrella (*baohusan*) in case the book upsets the authorities: "I paid 1,000 yuan [approximately 120 US dollars, about half of his monthly salary and more than the monthly average for workers in Harbin] to ask a politically influential person to provide calligraphy for the title of the book and to sign the preface. It works this way in China. I almost got arrested by the Security Bureau with my first book because I didn't do this." Then he proudly flipped through some pages to show how he had slipped in a bold critique of the party among his otherwise nostalgic, anecdotal accounts of Old Harbin.

As Liu indicated, public criticism of the authorities, especially by prominent intellectuals, remains dangerous terrain. When I spoke with the director of the Japanese Unit 731 Museum, I mentioned that nostalgia for Old Harbin could be interpreted as displaced social criticism. The director, who previously had held a high government position, reacted in alarm: "Who gave you that idea? Tell me the name of the person who told you this!" My reply that it was something *I* thought possible calmed him down immediately, but he pressed the point that this was not at all the case in Harbin. I asked him at the end of our meeting if I could have a copy of the notes his secretary had taken during our meeting for an accurate recounting of our discussion. After lengthy deliberation, he rejected my request.

This encounter illustrates the stakes involved for the intellectuals who curated the Old Harbin photography exhibit. Making the colonial inheritance publicly visible in the cityscape brought turmoil within the Harbin municipal government. After previewing the photography exhibit, one high-ranking official complained that it included too many pictures of Western structures, echoing concerns about the "colonialist historical view" expressed in the historians' debate and anticipating the embarrassing cancellation of the centenary celebration in 1998.[31]

Since 2001, St. Sophia has also hosted a separate, underground exhibit concerning the present and future of Harbin, installed along with an exhibit of religious artifacts recently unearthed in the crypt. Almost hidden down a dark staircase in a dimly lit basement smelling of cool concrete, visitors come upon an illuminated scale model of the Harbin of tomorrow: a city of skyscrapers, sprawling apartment blocks, and multilane highways. The exhibit consists of three parts. The first, "Historical Cultural City," displays large-scale photographs of colonial structures, both present and absent, the former in color, the latter in black and white. The last two parts form the substantive core of the exhibit and illustrate the urban renewal and historical preservation since the 1990s. The preface to this Chinese-language exhibit is reminiscent of the political turmoil over Harbin's origin: "Historically, Harbin was once part of the Jin dynasty, the birthplace of the Qing dynasty. With the construction of the Russian Chinese Eastern Railway and the influence of the two world wars, Harbin became a crossroads of foreign trade in the early twentieth century. Tens of thousands of foreigners settled in this well-known international trading city and constructed a large number of Western-style buildings, which defined the characteristics of the city." As a gesture toward the criticism of the colonialist historical perspective, the origin of Harbin is here set in the Jin dynasty and is otherwise left intentionally vague. Yet later text, accompanying the section of the exhibit called "The Development Process," explicitly states that the advent of the Russians in 1898 marked the birth of Harbin as a modern metropolis: "The construction of the Russian Chinese Eastern Railway in 1898 transformed a small fishing village into a modern city."

Instead of following the development of the city in a continuous fashion after 1949, visitors walk past panel after panel of enlarged photographs of factories, bridges, highways, skyscrapers, and apartments built in the late 1990s, all demonstrating the modernity of Harbin. The scale model in the center of the Harbin of tomorrow shimmers like Shanghai, the architectural icon of new capitalist China. The missing "development process" of the city between 1949 and the mid-1990s corresponds to the sudden disappearance of the "West" in historical writings of this period. The absence of photographic representations from this period—except for the ghostly apparition of memories of the Cultural Revolution in the old photography exhibit upstairs and the few black-and-white photographs of destroyed colonial-era structures in the section on the "Historical Cultural City"—corresponds to the official silence concerning the history of this period. No photography, no history. The historical narrative of the city bypasses socialist China, connecting cosmopolitan Old Harbin directly to the present-day Harbin of economic spectacles.

Referring to the photography exhibit while celebrating the renovated cathedral, the mayor drew a striking link between Old Harbin, which he described as an "open city" (*kaifang de chengshi*), and contemporary Harbin under the open economic policy.[32] Terms such as "openness," "level of culture," and "economic development" all contribute to the idea that Harbin's architectural culture will achieve a "synthesis of cityscape and the open economic policy."[33] The Communist government repeatedly deploys the discourse of *wenming* to control the meaning of the "West" set loose by historical preservation policies. Colonial structures are renewed as an aesthetic category embodying culture and civilization. Since the discourse of *wenming* embraces the aesthetic element of the architectural inheritance from the colonial era, it simultaneously reveals a past whose history was repressed during the Mao era while itself repressing the new politics of inheritance and the socialist history of the city after empire.

Layers of repressive politics were evident not only in the narrative spun by the mayor but also in speeches by other officials at the ceremony. While the mayor briefly mentioned colonial violence,[34] other officials displaced the sensitive issue of colonialism with the supposedly less controversial issue of religion in arguing about the appropriateness of including religious architecture in historical preservation.[35] The anti-imperialist discourse, omnipresent under Mao when authorities repressed the presence of the West, is now reduced to a matter of religion, providing cover for the elevation of such a material witness to imperialism as St. Sophia to its current position as the city's most prominent symbol of culture and civilization.

The discourse of *wenming* is also manifest in how Harbin residents outside of government and intellectual circles, when asked about their unique heritage, talk about colonial structures in the language of aesthetics. "Culture is culture" and "Art is art" are frequent responses to the question of whether certain objects represent the imperial domination of Harbin. Most of all, people are proud of the newly restored beauty of these structures. As soon as locals found out that I was not from Harbin, they would eagerly ask, "Have you seen St. Sophia yet?" and "What do you think?" They were very satisfied to hear my praise. A Japanese tourist to the city told me that her taxi driver, upon finding out where she was visiting from, insisted on driving her around St. Sophia, circling around the cathedral as if to show off his baby, before driving her to a hotel.

Yet Harbin's historical preservation policy has a double face: if one face preserves colonial structures, the other relentlessly demolishes old structures and neighborhoods that do not fall within the preservation policy. In the rush to urban renewal, historic buildings disappear overnight, while those selected for preservation receive princely revitalization through structural and cosmetic renovation. High-rises replace old structures, drastically shifting Harbin's skyline from early twentieth-century cupolas to modern boxy fortresses. Recently constructed luxury buildings echo colonial-era motifs in what is called "European-style" architecture. Harbin's nouveau riche purchase luxury condominiums in these full-service buildings with modern amenities. Meanwhile, the majority of the population is stuck in housing that lies between the poles of historical preservation and the newly available "modern life" (*xiandai shenghuo*).

Most people in Harbin live in gray, rusty, multistory Communist-style walk-up buildings built in the 1970s and 1980s. Concrete walls are cracked and stained, dim hallway lights flicker if they work at all, and many apartments do not have baths. The supply of water and electricity is never reliable, and the fundamental shortage of these resources makes their allocation a political matter, subject to political corruption.[36] In the impoverished district of Daowai—known in Old Harbin as Fujiadian—a shantytown spreads along the river. Shacks are built with cinder blocks, pieces of wood, cardboard, or whatever is available to shield residents from the elements. Flimsy cardboard ceilings barely protect inhabitants from the harsh winters, during which temperatures regularly drop to thirty degrees below zero Fahrenheit. Unemployed middle-aged men and women with expressionless faces and sunken eyes stand on dusty, unpaved street corners with hand-written cardboard signs hanging from their necks, which read "plumbing," "welding," or "mechanic," hoping for a day's labor. In downtown Harbin, many men and women in ragged and faded clothing line up on sidewalks to sell roasted sunflower seeds and pine nuts from dusty baskets. They are the unemployed, most likely laid off by state-run companies that were privatized, who receive a monthly subsidy of two hundred yuan (approximately twenty-five US dollars and about a quarter of what average workers make in Harbin) from the city in return for selling these goods on the streets.

China's transition to a market-oriented society has generated a considerable sense of loss among many for whom the widening socioeconomic disparity defies the promise of "modern life."[37] In this socioeconomic context, the historical preservation opens up space for publicly expressing the latent sense of loss that the *wenming* discourse gives cover for, and it generates effects that exceed the disciplinary power of the party-state and its civilizing practices. In Harbin, the *wenming* discourse, which is a discourse of both lack (of modernity, of civilization) and transformation (modernization, Westernization), slips into yet another discourse of lack: nostalgia for cosmopolitan Old Harbin. The sense of loss that fuels this nostalgia does not emerge from firsthand experience, since most of the city's population never experienced Old Harbin. Their sense of loss is of something already lost before their time.[38] Despite its imaginary nature, this sense of loss is exacerbated by the disappearing physical landscape of Old Harbin under urban renewal. The urban space turns an imaginary loss into a real one, bridging the past and the present. The simultaneous reappearance of Old Harbin through the historical preservation policy and its disappearance as a consequence of urban renewal give substance to the nostalgia.[39] While government efforts to turn Harbin's architectural inheritance into capital has increased tourism revenue and invigorated the real estate market, the proliferation of Old Harbin nostalgia as a result of the preservation policy has opened up a public space for articulating losses in the present, and the image of cosmopolitan Old Harbin has become a displaced forum for criticizing the party-state.

INHERITANCE AND BETRAYAL: THE RESURRECTION OF ST. NICHOLAS CHURCH

The simultaneous workings of the *wenming* discourse—legitimizing the pedagogical party-state in the reform era as well as generating nostalgia for cosmopolitan Old Harbin as a displaced form of social criticism—bracket the Mao era. It is as if embracing the city's architectural inheritance effaces the lived experience of this period. Yet the logic of inheritance has not let the city capitalize on its inheritance without paying interest on its debt. In the process of excising the Mao era, the preservation policy and Old Harbin nostalgia have unexpectedly uncloaked the violence of the Cultural Revolution, epitomized by the spectacular destruction of St. Nicholas Church, a beloved architectural icon in the center of the city. The same policy that exalts some colonial structures highlights the absence of others, which evokes losses inflicted under the CCP's own watch. This publicly acknowledged loss is supplemented by various forms of reproductions, such as the scale model of St. Nicholas Church within St. Sophia and enlarged photographs of other structures destroyed during the Cultural Revolution with captions plainly stating the historical fact.

One of the byproducts of the sudden public interest in Old Harbin in the 1990s was the first public appearance of a set of photographs that capture the destruction of St. Nicholas Church by the Red Guard in 1966. In 2000, *Xinwanbao* (New Evening News) published a special issue devoted to the preceding century of Harbin history with more than one hundred photographs, which sold out immediately after the copies hit newsstands. Although primarily focused on Old Harbin—the city before the Liberation—the special issue also covers the era after 1949, unlike the cathedral photography exhibit. Like that exhibit, the *Xinwanbao* edition documents the early development of Harbin with numerous images of colonial structures, but then four striking black-and-white photographs of St. Nicholas Church and its ruins in 1966 follow. In the first picture, St. Nicholas stands draped with banners and slogans held by men occupying the structure while onlookers surround the church (figure 2.9a). The white banners dangling from railings

of the church are reminiscent of a traditional funeral scene, which, in a sense, was to follow moments later. The second picture is a close-up of two young men climbing down from the cupola top, where they have placed a national flag and a Red Guard flag beneath it (figure 2.9b). In the next picture, the cupola lies on the ground as if dead, amid the flushed faces of young Red Guard members (figure 2.9c). The last shot captures a triumphant funeral procession, with the cupola in the back of a shiny black truck guarded by students (figure 2.9d).

These pictures, taken by photojournalist Wan Jiyao for *Heilongjiang Daily*, had been hidden deep in his closet for more than thirty years. They are among the few remaining photographic traces of the 1966 incident, except for those possibly locked away in the city archive.[40] Wan managed to hide his film while the authorities destroyed the pictures that a colleague of his had taken from the same vantage point. The violence that these pictures evoke in this otherwise nostalgic and celebratory special issue is almost anachronistic. In his discussion of Japan's war responsibility, philosopher Takahashi Tetsuya points out that chronology (*chronos* + *logos*: logic of time)

2.9a–d The destruction of St. Nicholas Church in 1966 during the Cultural Revolution: The destruction was captured by a local photo journalist, Wan Jiyao, who happened to be in a hotel facing the square at the time. The authorities confiscated the film from his colleague as they were leaving the hotel, but Wan managed to conceal his film and keep it hidden for decades. Photos courtesy of Wan Jiyao, 1966.

is a force behind turning forgetting into normality, while anachronism (*ana* + *chronos*: movement against time's order) works against the logic of forgetting.[41] Anachronism is what comes back when the logic of forgetting starts to dominate, and it demands that the work of mourning be finished. One wonders if these photographs signal the return of the repressed after more than three decades of collectively suppressing public discussions of the Cultural Revolution.

Nostalgia for the Cultural Revolution emerged in 1990s China, with the proliferation of Cultural Revolution–themed restaurants (serving slightly upgraded versions of peasant food amid a décor of slogans and reproduced posters from the era), the publication of memoirs and photography books, and online chat groups, to name a few examples.[42] A closer look at these nostalgic phenomena shows how the proliferation of certain forms of Cultural Revolution memories predominantly functions to mourn the present. What is mourned is not the Cultural Revolution per se but the social relationships under strain as a result of China's rapid transformation in the last decades. Even in its nostalgic appearance, the Cultural Revolution is constantly displaced without being actually signified; therefore, it hardly can be the object of mourning.[43]

The displacement of losses is particularly visible in the Cultural Revolution nostalgia expressed in photographic forms. *Zhiqing lao zhaopin* (Old Zhiqing Photos), a widely popular publication among the Cultural Revolution generation, chronicles the daily lives of the *zhiqing*, the educated urban youth who were "sent down" to the countryside. The photographs show groups of *zhiqing* youth among themselves, sometimes with local peasants, most against the backdrop of a raw and harsh natural environment.[44] The young faces captured almost uniformly beam with hope, fulfillment, and direction. In his analysis of the production and consumption of this publication, David J. Davies shows how these nostalgic photos evoke the struggles of the former *zhiqing* generation in the reform era.[45] He points out that the *zhiqing* photos are "future-oriented photography," for they "were not taken for memorial value, but attempted to capture . . . images of the desired future."[46] As Davies sums up, in "future-oriented photography," individuals became abstract props, symbolic workers and peasants in an idealized social order.[47]

In contrast, the four pictures of the destruction of St. Nicholas Church were taken with a journalist's instinct to seize the moment. Wan Jiyao was attending a conference at the International Hotel across the street from St. Nicholas when the Red Guard started to surround the church. He had the perfect vantage point from which to observe the unfolding of this historical event, and he and his colleague instinctively started taking pictures from their window. Unlike "future-oriented photography," these four pictures mercilessly lift the veil of socialist utopian imagery. The anachronism and anxiety they evoke derive from the individuality they betray. The individuals photographed are not props but distinct persons participating, wittingly or unwittingly, in an event. At the same time, in exposing individuality, the photos also convey a sense of collective loss. Whether you were a Red Guard member on the cupola or one of the onlookers encircling the church, the indisputable loss of a physical constituent of the city's symbolic landscape is something all residents of Harbin can safely share in mourning.

In Harbin, the proliferation of Old Harbin nostalgia has vastly overshadowed the Cultural Revolution nostalgia. I sensed a widespread and persistent desire to remain silent about the Cultural Revolution. Many intellectuals I encountered had been "sent down" to the surrounding region, and after the Cultural Revolution, they settled in the city. Most of them talk only reluctantly and tersely about their experiences, without giving specifics. Their narratives omit proper names except for categorical nouns. One professor, when recounting vivid accounts of the war against Japan and its aftermath, paused with clear hesitation on his face when I asked him about the local situation during the Cultural Revolution. After a deep silence, he finally opened his mouth: "Talking about that era is really difficult and tricky, because people from all sides now have to work together as colleagues. Not to talk about it is a way to conduct our daily life without bringing up unnecessary memories of who did what." Only in complete silence about the past can they work and live together.

For the Cultural Revolution generation, now in charge of every aspect of sociopolitical life in Harbin, wounds from the "ten years of turmoil," as it is often referred to, are more tangible than those from the fourteen-year Japanese occupation, whose effects they experienced indirectly. Yet despite official acknowledgement that the Cultural Revolution was a mistake, criticism of it is strictly limited by both the government and individuals themselves, who are afraid of conjuring up unwanted ghosts. As a result, memories of the horror remain fragmented and knowledge of its scale unavailable to most individuals, who have effective access solely to their own experiences.

The absent colonial structures thus potentially become a site for collective mourning for a past that cannot be shared. Standing out from the highly stylized photographic memories of the city during the Cultural Revolution—mostly in the form of Mao portraits, shots of Red Guards marching in uniform, or portraits of youths posing in idealized socialist tableaus—the re-presentation of the death of St. Nicholas Church provides a site for mourning. Despite the general unwillingness to talk about the Cultural Revolution, many people openly expressed their regrets at the loss of St. Nicholas. Xu Jianguo, a native Harbinite in his late sixties, spoke to me while showing me his collection of old pictures of Harbin, which included a black-and-white photograph of St. Nicholas:

> After the Cultural Revolution, sometime in the early 1980s, when Wang Huacheng was the mayor of Harbin, many people in the United States told him that they would be willing to donate money to rebuild St. Nicholas Church. . . . Even nowadays, people ask me to lend them this old picture of St. Nicholas, mostly for planning to rebuild the church. For instance, one architecture professor called me to send him a clear picture of the church in its early days. . . . Poster-size blow-up photographs of St. Nicholas became available in the market in the 1950s, which many people bought, including myself. . . . Now I feel that the church shouldn't be rebuilt, since such a resurrection would make us regret the loss of St. Nicholas even more. Our generation grew up with the sound of the bell from the church.

This deeply held anxious desire to rebuild St. Nicholas has found ironic expression in Harbin's famous ice festival. Every year, a life-size St. Nicholas Church is meticulously recreated with bricks of ice and lit up in dreamy pastel colors as one of the festival's centerpieces (figure 2.10). In its resurrection with electric cosmetics, St. Nicholas Church stands not as the victim of the Cultural Revolution but as the embodiment of the glorious Old Harbin and Harbin's future. Its ephemeral yet grand presence in this winter festival epitomizes the longing for Harbin's origin unencumbered by the official discourse. Hence St. Nicholas church has become what Marilyn Ivy calls "a *memorial* marker, a monument to an absence, to a loss that must be perpetually recovered."[48] Yet the loss itself is constantly displaced by the recovery of something else. The loss of St. Nicholas conjures up the Cultural Revolution, while its resurrection signifies Harbin's lost glory.

As if to console the ghost, one of the students photographed on the cupola, now a man of fortune in Hong Kong, made an unofficial offer to rebuild St. Nicholas, which the city government declined. The graveyard of St. Nicholas, now called Red Flag Square, is blemished by what many describe as one of the ugliest structures in the city. In the center of a huge rotary bustling with pedestrians, bicyclists, buses, and cars crossing and circling in a mad rush, galvanized iron sheets form the ceiling and air ducts for a three-story underground shopping mall on the site of the church (figure 2.11).[49] Covered with dust and exhaust, the mall's lack of any design gesture to aesthetic

2.10 Resurrected St. Nicholas Church at Harbin's annual ice festival: As local Harbinites continue to debate year after year whether or not to reconstruct St. Nicholas Church, the church is resurrected annually in the city's famous ice festival in this ephemeral form. Photo by author, 2003.

2.11 Red Flag Square where St. Nicholas Church once stood: To fill the absence left by the destroyed St. Nicholas Church in Red Flag Square, this geographical center of Harbin has featured various structures over time. Today, an air duct and a skylight for a three-story underground shopping mall occupy the beloved church's former site. Photo by author, 2002.

pleasure is more noticeable than ever due to the virtual resurrections of St. Nicholas taking place all across the city.

The rehabilitation of St. Nicholas Church as the embodiment of both glorious Old Harbin and the embarrassment of the Cultural Revolution hints at the "return" of the absent Mao era.[50] What is foreign, what is frightening, and what is full of secrets is the Mao era, China's supposed national origin, while the supposedly foreign Old Harbin, with its "atmosphere of a foreign country," is domestic and familiar and accorded the status of authentic origin.[51]

The capitalization of colonial inheritance through historical preservation thus has revealed layers of pasts beyond the originally intended public display of colonial-era architecture as the symbol of *wenming* and the future of Harbin as a global city. The dynamics we have seen suggest that inheritance involves something more than the classical economic conception of the circulation of property, although they are intricately entwined. The effectiveness of inheritance goes beyond the simple transfer of remainders of the past from one generation to another. Inheritance contains secrets, which open a possibility of betrayal—what one inherits is opaque, yet one has no choice but to inherit.[52] It is through this generational transmittal that unexpected losses emerge, and the dynamics of inheritance and betrayal thus defy attempts to harness the past through the capitalization of colonial inheritance.

ENCOUNTERING LOSS THROUGH INHERITING

Despite the municipal government's attempt to assert *Chinese* Harbin in a multivolume city history published to accompany the (ultimately aborted) centenary celebrations in 1998,[53] the historical preservation policy has highlighted Harbin's unique postcoloniality in the landscape of after empire, as seen in how the historiographical practices of local intellectuals have contributed centrally to the proliferation of Old Harbin nostalgia. Analyzing the historiography in late-1980s Harbin, Søren Clausen and Stig Thøgersen observed that history writing has become rewriting history for the purpose of asserting Chineseness in a city full of memories of imperialism: "Contemporary historiography in Harbin is by necessity a *rewriting* with the purpose of writing China and the Chinese back into the history and establishing a proper and dignified role for them in this City of Many Masters."[54]

More than a decade has passed since Clausen and Thøgersen observed this renewed interest in local history and described how historiographical practices among local historians were shifting toward a more forceful assertion of Chineseness. Government-sponsored historical narratives continue to revolve around anti-imperialist discourse, as the centenary history demonstrates.[55] But other forms of historical writing, many of which fall into the category of coffee-table books produced by professional historians, deploy a nostalgic tone that indicates the emergence of a different type of writing practice.[56] In their efforts to highlight multicultural Old Harbin, references to colonial violence and exploitation have receded in scholars' narratives. Their nostalgic accounts primarily revolve around Harbin's rich social history, featuring a colonial-yet-cosmopolitan version of the city.[57] The imperialism portrayed in these historical narratives is quite different from that in the anti-imperial discourse. Recent scholarly writings on "colonial" Harbin work to undo the image of "Chinese" Harbin. These writings also reveal a certain absence of colonial violence in the description of Old Harbin. For instance, in the introduction to *Dongfang xiao Bali* (Paris of the East), a glossy coffee-table book with artistic shots of colonial architecture published in 2001, the author/photographer only briefly hints at colonial violence and moves quickly to describe how cosmopolitan the city once was: "After Tsarist Russia robbed China of the right to develop the railway, Harbin developed around the Chinese Eastern Railway. In the early twentieth century, Russia, England, Japan, Czechoslovakia, etc. opened up general consulates in Harbin, and Germany, France, Italy, etc. opened up consulates, and within fifty years Harbin developed rapidly into a unique international metropolis."[58] These new historiographical practices thus mark a significant shift from the postcoloniality of asserting Chineseness that Clausen and Thøgersen observed in the late 1980s.

Within the new discourse of cosmopolitan Harbin, the inherited past is no longer contained within the demarcated space of prehistory—history before Mao. As the reborn St. Sophia symbolizes, Old Harbin provides the inheritance and the promise of Harbin's future success in the global economy. The belatedly acknowledged postcolonial consciousness poses a potential threat to the founding myth of the CCP. As the virtual resurrections of St. Nicholas epitomize, the new manifestations of postcoloniality lead many locals to acknowledge the uncanniness of the Mao era and raise uncomfortable questions about the party-state.[59]

In her analysis of nostalgia for historic St. Petersburg in 1990s Russia, which curiously resembles Old Harbin nostalgia, Svetlana Boym observes the inside-out sensations evoked through this nostalgia: "For many local residents, the historic St. Petersburg facades have become the private architecture of their dreams; exteriors were internalized and appear more intimate than their actual impoverished interiors."[60] Façades of colonial Harbin architecture similarly hide dilapidated interiors, material traces of the city's Communist past with their grey, cracked walls, divided rooms, and multiple households living in what were intended to be single-family units. The foreign-looking exterior has become intimate and familiar to locals, while the interior—embodying the lived experience of the Mao era—is seen with great suspicion. The restoration of European-style structures has resulted in effacing the Mao era, reversing that very era's effacement of the West. With Old Harbin nostalgia, people's desire for attaining "modern life" (*xiandai shenghuo*) often acquires what seems like a pro-Western outlook by locating authenticity in the city's colonial-era architecture. The anti-imperialist discourse is not just government propaganda; for most locals, Japanese colonial violence, whether directly or indirectly experienced, persists as transgenerational pain. Yet most locals find no contradiction in harboring Old Harbin nostalgia, which clearly undermines colonial violence, since, after all, Old Harbin is their own.

The politics of inheritance in Harbin demonstrates how a deep, unarticulated postcolonial consciousness remains in this city, dominated by visible traces of its colonial past. Much deeper, more textured, and more complex than the official discourse of anti-imperialism or the passionate and deep-rooted hatred for the Japanese, postcoloniality is now resurfacing from Chinese society's unconsciousness, taking the form of something intimate and seductive, yet dangerous. The government and citizens alike in Harbin are facing this delicate coupling of desire and disavowal faced by many postcolonial societies and that most in China had been shielded from until recently. This intersection of postsocialism and postcolonialism signals the opening of a new chapter of Harbin's history.

The story of inheritance of loss and its redemption in Harbin suggests an elusive location of loss that is redeemed through the capitalization of colonial remnants. Despite the seemingly obvious inscription of loss onto Harbin's urban landscape—colonial modernity's violence reified in the form of edifices built by imperial powers—we have seen how unexpected losses emerged in this generational transmission while the losses sustained through colonial modernity were given another name. The rhetoric of inheritance, through which colonial remnants were reincorporated into the cityscape, brings to light the double face of modernity—its promise and destructive potential. Historical preservation plays out this doubled nature contained within colonial inheritance and highlights colonial modernity's promise through the language of *wenming* while undermining its violence. Yet through the dynamics of *inheritance and betrayal*, the effort to capitalize on colonial inheritance through historical preservation has resurrected an uncanny inheritance from the Cultural Revolution era, a past that exceeded its narrative the moment it seemed to be under control.

As I discussed in chapter 1, the Chinese and Japanese etymology of "inheritance" not only embodies a sense of loss and recovery but also suggests what is being transmitted is transformed through this process. Inheritance and betrayal capture these transgenerational dynamics: acts of inheriting reveal and articulate "loss" (the thing that one inherits) through the very processes of inheriting (recovery/redemption/reincorporation of what is being lost). Only through the process of inheriting does one discover what she inherits. In this process, the original loss, sustained through colonial modernity, is assigned new meanings, while losses from a different time period—the Cultural Revolution era, in the case of Harbin—emerge as an integral part of what one inherits. What is being transmitted, it turns out, are not only the original loss from the colonial era but also losses from the Mao era, which are compounded by a keen sense of loss felt by many as a consequence of

China's ongoing transition to a market-oriented society. The dynamics of inheritance and betrayal, then, extend the temporal scope of one's inherited loss. The next chapter explores how this mechanism of generational transmission complicates not only the temporal scope of loss (the question of which past is inherited) but also its geographical scope (the question of *whose* loss one inherits).

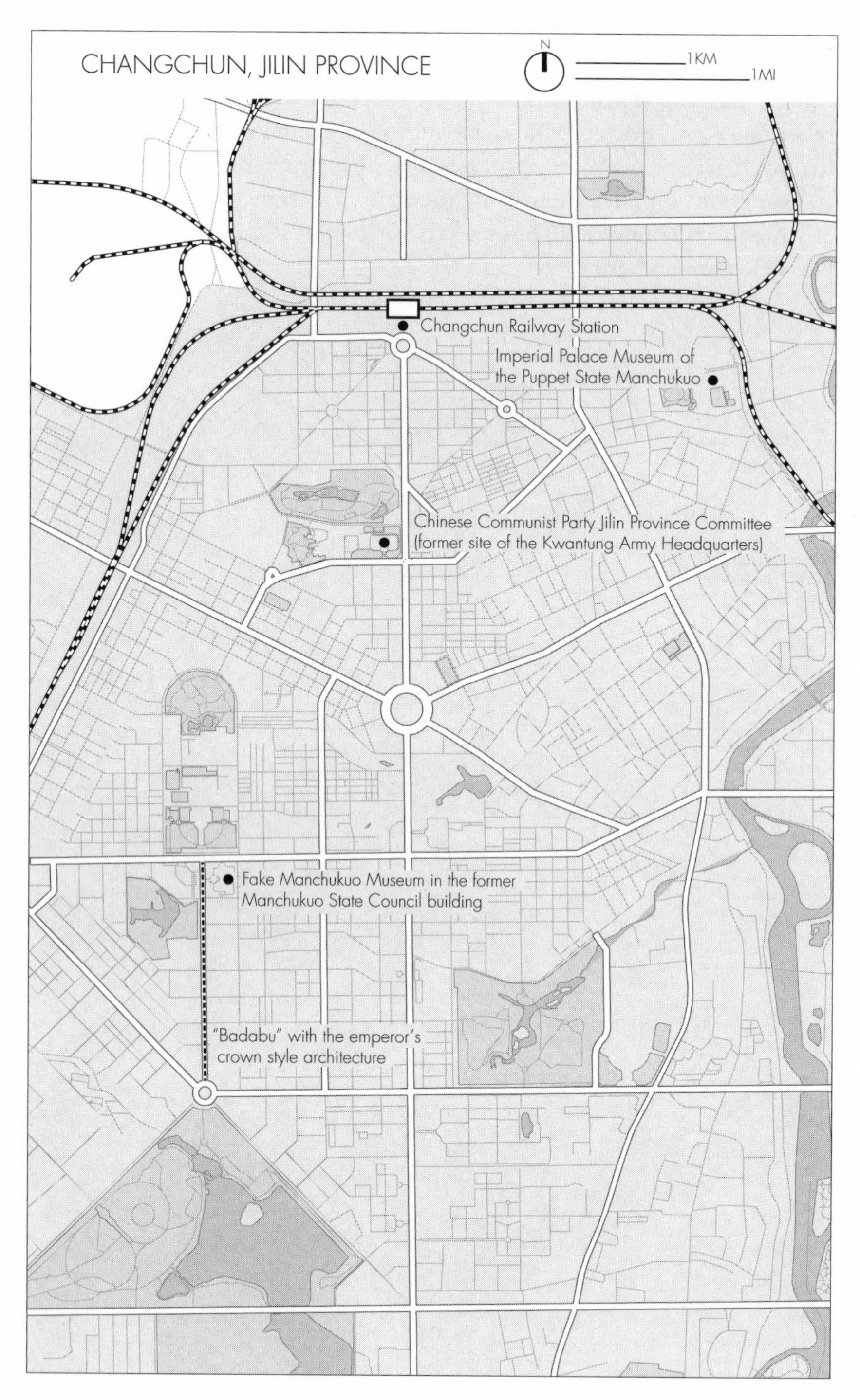

Map 5 Changchun, Jilin Province

CHAPTER THREE

Memory, Postmemory, Inheritance: Postimperial Topography of Guilt in Changchun

In August 2001, the Osaka branch of the Japan Travel Bureau (JTB) opened the Consultation Center for Nostalgia Tours to Former Manchuria (*Chūgoku natsukashi no chi hōmon sōdan sentā*) to assist Japanese repatriates from Manchuria (*Manshū hikiagesha*, or *hikiagesha* for short) in visiting their former hometowns, nearly a hundred years after the opening of the Dalian branch of the JTB in Northeast China in 1914 to promote tourism to what later became Manchukuo.[1] Elderly *hikiagesha* have sought to visit the home that they have silently remembered even as Manchuria became "former Manchuria" in postwar Japan, their adopted homeland. Along with "*nōkyō* tours" (groups organized by agricultural co-operatives), businessmen, and a sizable number of students, these tour groups account for a substantial portion of the Japanese tourists in Changchun. Their tour buses arrive one after another before the imposing cast-iron gate of the Imperial Palace Museum of the Puppet State Manchukuo, which is housed in the former palace of the Manchukuo Emperor Puyi, the city's major tourist attraction. They take group pictures in front of a large stone monument with the inscription "Never Forget 9.18 [Manchurian Incident]" located in the center of the museum's front courtyard (figure 3.1). The young Chinese tour guides of the Palace Museum roll their eyes at the sight and wonder why so many Japanese flood this city, which *Lonely Planet* deems unworthy of a stop.

Every day during the tourist season between May and November, two hundred to three hundred Japanese, more than 10 percent of all visitors to Changchun, tour the city.[2] Developed as an ideal modern city by the Japanese government in the 1930s, Changchun is characterized by *teikan* architecture (*teikan yōshiki*, or emperor's crown style), often described as fascist architecture with Asian-style roofs, an attempt to express modernity with a Japanese

3.1 Japanese tourists taking a group picture in the Imperial Palace Museum of the Puppet State Manchukuo in Changchun: The museum, which is housed in the former palace of the Japanese puppet emperor Puyi, is one of the main tourist attractions in the city and attracts busloads of Japanese tourists of various backgrounds and generations. They take pictures in front of the stone monument with an epitaph that reads, "Never forget 9.18 [Manchurian Incident]." Photo by author, 2002.

face.[3] Built in the emperor's crown style with a few Chinese elements, the former ministry buildings of Manchukuo line both sides of Xinmin Boulevard (figures 3.2 and 3.3), stretching for miles from the planned palace for Puyi, the last emperor of the Qing dynasty and the first and last emperor of Manchukuo. Once symbols of colonial power, these buildings now house Communist Party ministries and universities. To many locals, these buildings have lost their colonial reference, especially now that new buildings in the area imitate the style, which is even thought to represent authentic "Manchu-style" architecture. In contrast, Japanese visitors project Japan's imperial past onto these colonial structures. For those in Japan who are referred to as the "postwar generations" (those born after the defeat in 1945) in particular, Japan's imperial past is not visible in the urban landscape of Tokyo.[4] That history is to be found in "former Manchuria." The distant city allows Japanese to seek "real" or "authentic history" (*hontō no rekishi*), which appears to exist only in fragments in Japan, where the inability to come to terms with its imperialist past has been acknowledged as a national syndrome.

Since the 1990s, Changchun has become a popular tourist destination for Japanese, and to accommodate this demographic, tourist attractions have begun to hire Japanese-speaking tour guides. Based on my participant-observation as an official tour guide at the Palace Museum, this chapter follows Japanese visitors of various generations—repatriates (*hikiagesha*), schoolchildren, college students, businessmen, and farmers—and tracks local Chinese perceptions of these Japanese visitors flocking to their city, which offers "nothing other than Manchukuo remains," as many locals put it. By ethnographically examining the engagement of prewar and postwar generations of Japanese with the atrocity exhibition at the museum and the haunting urban landscape full of Manchukuo remnants, this chapter explores the generational transmission of unaccounted-for pasts through tourism. As we

3.2 The former Manchukuo Ministry of Military in the emperor's crown style architecture (currently Jilin University Medical School): The former Ministry of Military was built in the emperor's crown style, an architectural expression of Japanese imperialism with a pan-Asian flavor, which was the chosen style for the capital of Japan's puppet state Manchukuo. The boulevard that stretches to the south is lined with buildings in this style of architecture. Photo by author, 2002.

3.3 The former Kwantung Army Headquarters (currently Jilin Province Committee of the Chinese Communist Party): The former Kwantung Army Headquarters was built in the style of traditional Japanese castles. Photo by author, 2002.

shall see, the concept of memory alone cannot capture the experiences of these tourists in Changchun.

In searching for the lost memories of Japan's Manchukuo in the Changchun cityscape, the Japanese encounter instead what can be called the *postimperial topography of guilt*. It is within this moral landscape of after empire that postwar Japanese visitors to the city come to recognize not so much the missing memory of Japanese colonial violence, as they expect, but rather a form of *colonial inheritance* from the previous generation that they have no choice but to accept.

My exploration of these visitors' experiences through the lens of colonial inheritance adds new dimensions to recent attempts within memory studies to address generational aspects in our relationship to difficult pasts. Recognizing the fundamental difference in the memory of the Holocaust between survivors and the second generation, Marianne Hirsch introduces the term "postmemory."[5] Postmemory captures the mediated relationship to the traumatic past among what Eva Hoffman refers to as "postgenerations."[6] Produced by the generation that follows catastrophic events, Hirsch shows how this memory is mediated through representational forms such as photography and literature. While Hirsch's study revolves around second-generation Holocaust survivors, she suggests that the structure of transmission also applies to second-generation perpetrators.

The case of Changchun sheds light on a different structure of generational transmission—that among the postgenerations of Japanese who visit Northeast China as tourists. My ethnography complicates Hirsch's assumed boundaries of mnemonic community and certainties about which past is being transmitted. Situated at the intersection of market and history in Manchukuo tourism, we will see in Changchun the dynamics that thwart the attempts of second and third generations of Japanese to seek postmemory in this city filled with remnants of Japan's failed empire.

REMNANTS OF MANCHUKUO IN CHANGCHUN

With its architectural remainders and recognizable urban planning from the Manchukuo era, Changchun cannot hide its colonial history. Shinkyō (New Capital), as Changchun was once called in Japanese, vanished with the disappearance of Manchukuo in 1945, only to return with the thawing of the Cold War. To Japanese eyes, this faux-imperial capital of Manchukuo is like both a well-preserved archaeological find of the lost empire and, given the current use of some buildings by the Chinese Communist Party (CCP) and the museumization of others, a theme park.

The "real" and "authentic" (*hontō, honmono*) that the Japanese tourists to Changchun encounter now is the product of the Japanese imaginary in the 1930s. When the Japanese occupied Changchun in 1932, it was not much bigger than a town.[7] Meticulously planned and expanded as Shinkyō, the capital of Manchuria was to be a futuristic, modern city. Changchun showcased Japanese modernity through architecture and urban planning in a way impossible in the overbuilt metropole of Tokyo.[8] In Changchun, Japanese architects and urban planners could experiment and implement their fantasies of modernity. Its urban planning copied nineteenth-century Paris: wide tree-lined boulevards fed into large rotaries, all adorned with early twentieth-century Western-style structures. Residential houses had flush toilets and central heating systems, rarities in Tokyo at the time. The urban space of Shinkyō was far more modern than anything in Japan.

Minimally damaged during the war,[9] Changchun went through a turbulent transition period after the Japanese defeat on August 15, 1945.[10] The Manchukuo Emperor Puyi abdicated on August 17, and the Soviet Red Army took control of the city on August 19, followed by the establishment of the Changchun municipal government by the Guomindang on November 8. On April 14, 1946, the Soviet Army withdrew from the city at the Guomindang's request. In the wake of the Soviet withdrawal, the conflict between the Guomindang and the CCP intensified into a vicious civil war; the Guomindang established control over Changchun on May 23, 1946 and changed Japanese street names to Chinese ones in July. The critical issue of redistribution of properties formerly owned by the Japanese led to serious clashes within the Guomindang as well as with the CCP. Shut out of Changchun, the Communists laid siege to the city for months, during which tens of thousands of people starved to death.[11]

When the Communists took control of the city on October 19, 1948, Changchun had become "a ruin, with no running water or electricity, its transportation system paralyzed, factories and stores closed, parks turned into wastelands, and the city's basic infrastructure destroyed," as chronicled in *Changchun erbai nian* (Two-Hundred-Year History of Changchun), compiled in commemoration of the city's second centennial.[12] The new Changchun municipal government's first task was to save the starving citizens and to bury the nearly sixty thousand corpses that lay abandoned on the city's streets. Even after those turbulent transitional years with its succession of rulers, the cityscape remained more or less the same, except that approximately 30 percent of the buildings in the city had been destroyed.[13] Structures in a neoclassical "Chinese ethnic" style resembling the Japanese emperor's crown style were erected on the sites of destruction. Communist Party ministries took over the Japanese-built ministerial buildings. Many locals moved into residential buildings with Japanese-style *tatami* mats on the floor, a Japanese practice that they had quickly adopted. The first major transformation of Changchun's cityscape occurred only after the Cultural Revolution, between 1985 and 1993, when multistory apartment buildings replaced Japanese-built residential houses in an effort to accommodate the city's growing population.[14]

During this major reconfiguration of the cityscape, the Changchun municipal government decided to put structures from the Manchukuo era under protection. Major edifices of *Weiman* (Fake Manchukuo, a Chinese term used to refer to the Japanese puppet state) received landmark status, with plaques affixed explaining their history. This government decision was in stark contrast to the South Korean government's decision in the mid-1990s, after long and heated debates, to demolish the former Imperial Japanese headquarters building in Seoul. A local Chinese man in his eighties expressed to me a sentiment shared by many Changchunites, especially those who remember the Manchukuo era:

> It is meaningless just to erase physical remainders if the ideology bestowed onto them does not change. What's important is not whether or not these remainders exist but how you acknowledge them. Furthermore, these buildings are, after all, eyewitnesses to the Japanese invasion. I believe that it's better to educate our future generation by using these physical remainders of the past. If we just demolish them, it is equivalent to abandoning history. If we demolish traces of history, does it mean that history disappears? That's not how things work. Besides, the meanings of these structures are changing. For our generation, of course, these remainders remind us of the past, since these buildings once symbolized the Japanese colonial power. But for the younger generation of Chinese, it's a different story. I wouldn't say that these structures don't have any emotional effects on them at all, but I can safely say that many of them are indifferent to their presence.

In Changchun, the Bureau of Cultural Relics administers the preservation of Manchukuo architecture as a way of preserving material witnesses to its colonial past. Many of the plaques on landmark buildings clearly state this purpose: "This building is granted landmark status in order to remind us of the national humiliation (*guochi*)."[15] This is in sharp contrast to the situation in Harbin, where young planners and architects in the Urban Planning Bureau led the historical preservation of colonial architecture as an integral part of redesigning and redefining the identity of Harbin as a modern city in a global economy.

The Changchun cityscape stands out due to the emperor's-crown-style architecture, which often combines Western neoclassical style with a Japanese-style roof.[16] Originally developed in Japan in the 1920s to express Japanese modernity—an architectural echo of the portrait of the Showa Emperor in Western clothing—examples of this style are still found in Japan in the Kanagawa Prefecture Hall (planned in 1926 and completed in 1928), the Nagoya City Hall (1930–33), the Takashimaya Department Store (formerly the Japan Life Insurance Building, 1930–33) and the Kudan Building (formerly the Military Officers Building, 1930–34) in Tokyo, and the Aichi Prefecture Hall (1938). Sporadically employed within Japan, in Changchun it was deployed on a citywide scale in the 1930s. The chosen architectural style for the ministerial buildings was meant to express "the spirit of Manchuria," according to Sano Riki, the chief advisor for the National Capital Construction Plan, who as architect of the Kanagawa Prefecture Hall had been among the first to work in the emperor's crown style.[17] Behind "the spirit of Manchuria" is the idea of *gozoku kyōwa* (peaceful coprosperity of five ethnic groups), the stated political ideology of Manchukuo.[18] For this purpose, the ministerial buildings in Changchun adopted the emperor's crown style with slight modifications—in particular, roofs meant to look pan-Asian, mixing Japanese and Chinese elements—to express this ideology of ethnic coprosperity.

That the emperor's-crown-style architecture in Japan does not conjure up the ghosts of empire to local Japanese, while the same style in Changchun does to Japanese visitors, reflects the Japanese moral landscapes of after empire. As we shall see in the next section, what Japanese public intellectuals often refer to as "imperial amnesia" makes Japan's imperial remnants socially invisible to the public, which then generates desires to seek that missing history elsewhere. As many have observed, postdefeat national narratives foregrounded Japan's own victimhood, while its role as a perpetrator was effectively erased by a focus on the atomic explosions in Hiroshima and Nagasaki and the American occupation.[19]

These narratives thus highlighted Japan's *post-war* status while pushing aside its story of after *empire*, which in effect created a geographical division of moral topography: Japanese victimhood is projected onto Japan's physical territories, and Japanese perpetration is projected onto Changchun's cityscape, the former capital of Japan's puppet state Manchukuo.

AMNESIA AND OBSESSION

The Historians' Debate in Japan

The postwar narrative of Japanese victimhood has often been described as a manifestation of amnesia about the country's imperial past. While the imperial past is often actively denied, amnesia is a misnomer for this phenomenon. Amnesia implies both an involuntary forgetting and a total erasure of the memory in question. In the case of Japan's imperial past, the forgetting was neither involuntary nor complete.[20] Quite to the contrary, the enormous and persistent cultural production of books, films, comics, and commentaries on Japan's Manchuria and the war speak to an obsession. And herein lies the peculiar quality of "imperial amnesia" in Japan: the tangible lack of post-imperial consciousness in Japanese society, with its absences, taboos, and elisions of Japanese imperial violence, creates a desire for more discussion of it. Like the famous episode of the British television series *Fawlty Towers* in which the British innkeeper tries so hard *not* to talk about the war to his German guests that all he does is talk about it, the imperial past is ubiquitous in Japan while its absence from consciousness is acknowledged.[21]

The reaction to this interplay of amnesia and obsession takes two related forms within Japan: memory work and historical revisionism, each of which provokes the other. The resurgence of neonationalism in Japan since the mid-1990s is partly a reaction to the resurfacing of the long-deferred task of coming to terms with the past as a result of the end of the Cold War. It is also a reaction to the burst of the economic bubble and the subsequent economic recession that betrayed the dysfunctional state of "Japan, Inc.,"[22] the depository system of values such as order, family, and lifetime employment.[23] Revolts against memory work have appeared in many corners of society. For example, in 2004, the pressure to raise the national flag and sing the national anthem in public school ceremonies became so strong that nearly three hundred teachers and principals were punished by the Tokyo Board of Education for refusing to do so during graduation and entrance ceremonies. The dissenting teachers claimed that the national anthem, "*Kimigayo*" (His Majesty's Reign)—which, as the title suggests, praises the emperor—is not only inappropriate for a democratic society but also insensitive to other Asians who suffered under Japanese imperialism.

This obsession with the past and unaccounted-for Japanese guilt can be found in the sentiments of the political right. Many members of the Japanese Society for History Textbook Reform (*Atarashii rekishi kyōkasho o tsuku-kai*), which promotes neonationalist agendas through the revision of history textbooks and educational plans and is one of the most vocal groups advocating revisionist history, have expressed sentiments similar to what one member confided to me during their weekly study-group meeting: "For many years, until recently, we felt that our voices were marginalized and repressed within Japanese society, which chanted the mantra of peace and war responsibility." Beneath the alleged amnesia lie recurrent debates and movements to undo or reaffirm amnesic practices that swing like a pendulum.[24] The recurrent "historians' debates" (or "historical subjectivity debates") and social movements in Japan's postwar years attest to this dialectic of memories.[25] The publication in 1995 of "On Postdefeat" (*Haisengo ron*) by literary critic Katō Norihiro and its critique by philosopher Takahashi Tetsuya in "On the Memories of Disgrace" (*Ojoku no kioku o megutte*) triggered a major public debate that captured the public sentiment of the era.[26] This debate reflects the moral landscape of after empire and its attendant tensions that Japanese tourists take with them to Changchun.

Katō argues that in order for Japan to fulfill its responsibility for the war, it must establish the national subject, "we Japanese." To do so, he says, "we" have to be able to mourn "our own" losses—in particular, those of the three million "disgraceful invaders"—before mourning for the twenty million

Asian dead. In so doing, Katō rhetorically asks whether it is possible to think about justice outside the nation-state when the original violence was done in the name of the nation-state.

A cultural industry of "postdefeat" ensued with many prominent intellectuals responding to Katō.[27] Katō was intensely criticized, especially by left-wing intellectuals, who attacked him as a symbol of the resurgence of nationalism that many feared latent in Japan. Claiming that Katō's view of a "we Japanese" consciousness as the foundation of the "national subject" is built upon an essentialist understanding of the "Japanese people," Takahashi argues that Katō assumes the existence of "the Japanese" as a given unity, leaving no room for Others. Takahashi finds this manner of constructing a self-identity without the Other as referent both impossible and violent.[28] He warns of the possibility of repeating the violence of exclusion in the name of the "national thing" if one accepts Katō's approach, which locates the "national subject" as a presumed a priori unity.[29] Other critics share Takahashi's concern that Katō's argument constitutes a dangerous spark that could ignite the embers of violent nationalism. For instance, Karatani Kōjin argues that Katō abets a neoconservative trend by precluding the presence of non-Japanese readers.[30] Behind these criticisms is the concern expressed by Nishikawa Nagao that the postwar generation, including Katō, is resurrecting "a monster called the nation (*kokumin*)."[31]

Many critics see Katō's plea for the reestablishment of "we Japanese" as a response to the representational crisis in late modernity. As Yumiko Iida summarizes in her analysis of the emergent hegemony of the virtual and new nationalism, "The former anti-essentialist position is pregnant with the possibility of the latter, the eruption of suppressed reactionary sentiment that is the precursor to the rise of a sublime superego."[32] "We Japanese" (*wareware nihonjin*) is something to be disavowed yet yearned for, generating a question brought to the fore by Katō, "Can we mourn without enunciating 'we' the Japanese?" Katō's question echoes the question posed by Eric Santner in his analysis of the inability to mourn in postwar Germany, where the pronoun "we" bears the scars of history.[33]

The link between the question of mourning and the question of inheritance has become more and more prominent as the postwar generations have become the majority of those dealing with this issue. Katō's question—can we mourn apart from "we Japanese" when the original violence was committed in the name of "we Japanese"?—is not only a neonationalist question, as leftist intellectuals prefer to portray it. Rather, it is a question of an era when the work of mourning the Second World War has increasingly become the task of the postgenerations who inherit the burdens of unaccounted-for past violence in a time when essentialism is suspect as a means of constituting identity.

But it is not only the scarred nationality or the general suspicion toward essentialized identities that produces anxiety over the pronoun "we" among postgenerations. As the following ethnography demonstrates, it is also the very processes of inheriting unaccounted-for pasts that challenge assumptions about who constitutes the mnemonic community of inheritors and *whose* loss the Japanese postgenerations are inheriting in the name of the nation. What does it mean for the Japanese to inherit losses sustained through Japanese imperialism as postgenerations of *both* perpetrators *and* victims? Against this background of public sentiment in Japan, which continues to display a deep suspicion toward the enunciation of "we Japanese," Japanese tourists to Changchun encounter the remnants of Manchukuo.

The Palace Museum of the Puppet State

The major tourist attractions in Changchun are the Imperial Palace Museum of the Puppet State Manchukuo in the former palace of the Manchukuo Emperor Puyi, the Fake Manchukuo Museum in the former State Council building, the row of former ministerial buildings in the emperor's crown style (the so-called *Badabu*, the eight ministries), and the Changchun Film Studio, which succeeded the former Manchurian Film Studio.

The largest in scale and the most popular is the Imperial Palace Museum of the Puppet State Manchukuo (Fake Emperor's Palace, *Wei huanggong* for short), located on the northeastern edge of the city. Every day, large tour buses carrying tourists from all over China—as well as Japan, South Korea, and a small number of other countries—crowd its parking lot. Its walled grounds contain several buildings, some original and some restored to their original state. Part of Emperor Puyi's living quarters and the palace's administrative wings have carefully restored interiors populated by life-size wax figures, while other parts are used for permanent and temporary historical exhibitions of photographs and artifacts. The museum brochure handed out to visitors along with their admission tickets is worth quoting in its entirety:

> Jixi Building was the living quarters for Puyi and his wives. It was originally built as an office building for a state-owned salt company and was turned into a palace. Puyi spent fourteen years of his life here as a puppet emperor. Qinmin Building was Puyi's office, where he received Japanese and "Manchukuo" officials and foreign delegates. In the main reception

> hall, Puyi accepted the emperor's throne for the third time. Huaiyuan Building was built in 1934 to enshrine Puyi's ancestors. It also housed the main office of the palace. Tongde Building was designed in 1936 and completed in 1938. It combines Chinese and Japanese architectural styles, and as the name indicates, it attempted to express the unity of Japan and "Manchukuo." Tongde Building was originally designed as a palace that combines office, recreation, and living spaces for the emperor's family. Puyi, however, never lived here, because he suspected that the Japanese had built in eavesdropping devices. East Imperial Garden was designed by a Japanese landscape designer and completed in 1938. It is 11,100 square meters and the largest garden in the palace. Later the Japanese built the "National Foundation Shrine" and enshrined the Japanese Shinto deity. They also built two air-raid shelters: one for the emperor's family and the other for the Shinto deity. After the defeat of Japan, the garden was abandoned, but it was restored to its original state in 2002.
>
> These grounds, which used to be the palace of Puyi, the last emperor of the Qing dynasty and the emperor of the Puppet State "Manchukuo," have now become a museum. It contains the original buildings and some thematic exhibitions, portraying the old days of the palace. Through the use of historical artifacts and photographs, the museum illustrates the history of Puyi and the fourteen years of Japanese occupation. This museum serves as historical testimony to the Japanese imperialist invasion of Northeast China. Puyi was born in 1906 and became the tenth and the last emperor of the Qing dynasty at the age of three. Dethroned at the end of the Qing dynasty in 1911, Puyi was later officially enthroned as emperor of the puppet state of "Manchukuo" in 1934, two years after the puppet state's establishment by the Japanese. The palace, which comprises 137,000 square meters, became his office and living space for fourteen years. Since its opening in 1984, the museum has hosted exhibitions such as "The Manchurian Incident: Never Forget," "From Emperor to Citizen," and "The Historical Artifacts of the Imperial Palace of the Puppet State" to illustrate the crimes committed by Japanese imperialism and Puyi's complicity in them. (translation mine)

This brochure as well as the government plaque identifying the site as a "patriotic education base"[34] on the entrance gate indicate that the museum is designed to educate its visitors on the history of the fourteen years of Japanese rule in Northeast China through the life of Puyi.

When I approached museum officials in the spring of 2002 and suggested I work as a Japanese-speaking tour guide, they jumped at my proposal, keenly aware of the opportunities they had lost by not offering guided tours to the rapidly growing number of Japanese tourists. I was hired on the spot as the sole Japanese-speaking tour guide in the propaganda department of the museum, which had approximately fifteen Chinese-language tour guides, most in their early twenties. I shared an office and daily meals in the work-unit canteen with my Chinese colleagues, who taught me how to give a nearly three-hour-long tour of the museum based on a written script in Chinese. I followed their tours several times before starting to give my own in Japanese, in which I followed the narrative outline and the specific descriptions of the Chinese version. I gave a few tours daily to numerous Japanese tour groups of all ages and social backgrounds. When I was not giving a tour, I would chat with my colleagues over tea and sweets on topics ranging from family to history to the latest Japanese television dramas, hang out in the museum's archive department, or observe Chinese tourists' responses to my colleagues' tours. At lunch, we would grab our metal bowls and rush to the basement canteen, where everyone in the museum from the director to the cleaning crew ate breakfast and lunch. We would pile up several dishes on top of a heaping bowl of rice while balancing steaming soup in the deep lid. In one of the last holdouts of the "iron rice bowl system" in slow transition to a profitable tourist industry, I observed how Japanese tourists found themselves in the temporal nexus of the past and the present and the geographical nexuses of "former Manchuria" and Northeast China *and* of China and Japan.

THE POSTIMPERIAL TOPOGRAPHY OF GUILT

Inability to Mourn: Japanese Repatriates (*Hikiagesha*) and Nostalgia Tours

Into this setting one autumn afternoon in 2002, a group of twenty Japanese tourists, mostly in their sixties and seventies, walked through the Imperial Palace Museum, their excitement tangible though restrained. Following the exhibition portraying the turbulent life of Emperor Puyi through more than one hundred large photographs and artifacts, the group walked through restored rooms in a two-story gray brick building that Puyi and his family had inhabited. The family quarters, which many visitors find modest for an emperor's family, are furnished with traditional Qing dynasty furniture. Ornate, colorful silk fabrics provide warmth to the dark wood furniture and decorative curved wood panels on the walls and ceilings. A man in his early seventies walked through the exhibition with his wife, who carried a laminated sepia-colored family portrait, to which she showed every single room they walked through, while talking quietly to the photograph: "Father, this is the room where Emperor Puyi used to pray for his ancestors, and that was his office where he had daily meetings with Japanese officials."

Their procession through the artifacts of the emperor of the disappeared empire called forth a funereal scene of affectionate, tender, and resolved mourning. They mourned for deceased family members whose intimate yet distant memories had been sealed by the tides of history. Kawashima Hiroshi, the husband, was born and grew up in Shinkyō and repatriated to Japan at the age of fifteen. His father, who died three years before, had been a civil servant of the Manchukuo government with an office in the former State Council building, now another major tourist attraction. Before visiting the museum, Kawashima and his wife tried to visit his old school, but they discovered that it had been demolished only two weeks earlier. Yet he seemed content. "It's very calming to be here. My mind doesn't feel a kind of disturbance that I often feel when I visit new places. I'm overwhelmed with excitement," he said, his face radiant. His wife later whispered to me, "It's been fifty-six years since my husband left here. . . . Seeing my husband's hometown, about which I've heard so many times from my in-laws and my husband, is so important for me to understand him—to know where he is coming from and what he lost."

A story that three Japanese tourists to Changchun—eighty-five-year-old Sasaki Kimiko and her two children, Yoshiko and Takashi—told me illuminates not only the unsettling and layered identities many *hikiagesha* felt in "returning" to Japan after the demise of Manchukuo but also the meaning of "coming back" to former Manchuria.[35] Yoshiko was five and Takashi was four when they left Northeast China for Japan in 1946. Their father had gone to Changchun in 1937 to work for the South Manchuria Railway Company as a radio technician. He passed away at the age of sixty-one in 1972, the year Japan and China normalized relations, so it would have been unthinkable for him to revisit Northeast China in his lifetime. Yoshiko and Takashi had always wanted to visit the hometown that they vaguely remembered, while their mother had demurred, as she did not have good memories of her life in China. She had been "afraid to come back," she murmured while carefully examining the map of Changchun next to the reproduction of the old map of Shinkyō that they had purchased at the Fake Manchukuo Museum, located in the former State Council building. But after visiting the places where they used to live, she said she felt that her "life has finally come to completion." For her children, who grew up in postwar Japan without being able to speak about their experiences in Manchuria or even to tell others that they were born there, the trip offered a crucial opportunity for filling a blank space in their lives. Their childhood after repatriation had not been a smooth one. Parents of their classmates hesitated to let their children befriend Yoshiko and Takashi once they found out that they were repatriates from Manchuria. When they told their friends that they were born in Manchuria, many of them did not know where it was. So Yoshiko and Takashi learned to lie and tell people that they were born in Tochigi, where they settled down after repatriation. "Coming back here makes me feel complete and whole again, finally," commented Takashi.

Their homeland was doubly erased—through the sudden disappearance of Manchukuo at the war's end and the discursive suppression of people's roots there during the postwar years. Like Sasaki Kimiko and her children, many of these repatriates feared discrimination and hid their origins in the postwar years. Their brief visits to Northeast China provide them with a space where they can share their long-repressed memories of life in Manchuria. Tanabe Satoshi, another *hikiagesha*, who was also born in Changchun, explained to me that Japan never really became his home, a sentiment echoed by many others. The trip back to China, especially for those who were born and grew up in cities there, confirms their long-held sense that they are not quite "Japanese" but rather "Changchunite" (*Chōshunjin*) or "Dalianite" (*Dairenjin*), cosmopolitan urbanites who refuse to be confined within the nation-state.

Many of them told me that their trips back "home" bring a painful joy and the pleasure of being able to share such painful pleasures. "It's heavy," Maeda Hajime, in his late seventies, murmured as he stepped into another tourist attraction, the Changchun Film Studio, formerly the Manchurian Film Studio (*Man'ei*). "Visiting the Palace Museum yesterday was exhausting. Going through that history is really heavy for me, you know, I was part of that picture—I was waving flags as a teenager." Maeda continued, "I'm so happy to be back in my hometown, but my joy comes with painful bitterness for the wrongful history that I took part in."

For many who were born and spent their formative years in Manchuria, their trips to their hometowns often result in bittersweet acknowledgments of paradise lost.[36] Changchun's urban space betrays their nostalgia with its new buildings, Chinese-language signs, and unfamiliar population. Okada Masashi, who was born in Changchun, sheepishly confided after growing comfortable with me,

> Intellectually I understand that this is a Chinese city and that it's wrong for me to be nostalgic about my home in Manchuria. That was a wrong

> country built on a wrong idea. But I can't help missing my home. I can't help missing Changchun. To be very honest with you, I sometimes resent the fact that my hometown is now a Chinese city. I sometimes can't help feeling resentful that I have no claim to this city any longer. And then I feel guilty feeling that way. I feel guilty showing my nostalgia in front of the local Chinese.

Nostalgia expressed by Okada and many other *hikiagesha* like him is entangled with a deep sense of guilt.[37]

The influential Japanese literary and cultural critic Takeuchi Yoshimi wrote in the early 1960s that Japan never carried out the funeral of Manchukuo.[38] These tours to Changchun now seem like enactments of a funeral that is long overdue, which the participants need, as many of them put it, to come to "a sense of closure" by "filling in the missing pages" (*kūhaku o umeru*) in their personal histories. Their felt inability to mourn the sudden loss of their home, because the object of the loss is the negation of what the postwar present is about, has left an absence that persistently implicates the loss yet prohibits its mourning.

Their decades-long inability to mourn is closely linked to their inability to talk about their loss as a loss. Okada articulated a widely shared sentiment: "What we call our 'real home' was once the home of Chinese, which we Japanese forcefully took away from them. There is a sense of guilt associated with my calling it my home and with my mourning that loss." The Chinese loss is what enabled the Japanese to call Changchun home and what now prohibits them from mourning its loss. Okada's sense of closure only comes when the Other's loss is implicated in his own. It is through refraction of the Other's loss that one's own loss is simultaneously articulated *and* forbidden to be named as such.[39]

Overwhelmed by a flood of memories and emotions, *hikiagesha* reluctantly leave Changchun, many of them murmuring, "This is my homeland, not Japan"—an utterance long repressed in Japan and pronounced in a hesitant manner in Changchun. Many repatriates from Manchuria have lived between the fictional and the real, here and there, now and then. They are ambivalent about the nation-state; repatriates often exclaim that "the nation-state is, after all, elusive and ephemeral,"[40] while, at the same time, they attempt to redeem its broken promise by assigning new meanings to it. Some older repatriates, who spent their teenage years in Manchukuo, attempted in postwar years to reclaim their shattered ideals by acting in the spirit of *gozoku kyōwa* (coprosperity among the five ethnic groups), the failed ideological promise of early Manchukuo. Many are involved in various activities to promote China-Japan friendship and try to stay in practice with their fading if not broken Chinese, and they show a desperate desire to promote the idea of multiethnic society, in keeping with the unfilled promise of *gozoku kyōwa*, by looking after Chinese students in Japan and reconnecting with their Chinese classmates. Acting according to *gozoku kyōwa* is seen by some as a way to make amends for their "disgraced" upbringing, which they feel is, as one put it, "stained with the blood of Asian others." On many occasions when I participated in reunion dinners and parties with repatriates in Tokyo, held by various societies such as the Dalian Association (*Dairen-kai*) or Changchun Association (*Chōshun-kai*),[41] some insisted on talking to me in Chinese, as if the sound of Chinese was consoling, as if Chinese utterances were signs of their attempts to undo the colonial hierarchy. For others, the sound of Chinese is simply soothing, and our trips to karaoke clubs after these reunion dinners often ended with Chinese songs.

Referring to their former home as "former Manchuria" is itself contentious. I was invited to a dinner meeting of the Dalian Friendship Association (*Dairen tomo no kai*), a group of former CEOs of Dalian branches of Japanese corporations that started (re)investing in Dalian in the early 1990s. Some members were ex-repatriates from Dalian who had gone back to their hometown in the 1990s as businessmen. An elegantly dressed and soft-spoken man in his seventies seated next to me was one of these former Dalianites (*Dairenjin*), as they often call themselves ("We are not Japanese but *Dairenjin*," they claim proudly). After learning that he was born and raised in Dalian, I asked him when he had first gone back to former Manchuria. He replied with a slightly alarmed tone in his voice, "'Former Manchuria'—you mean *Dongbei* [Chinese for 'Northeast'], right?" I replied, "Yes, that's what I meant," thinking that it was unusual for a Japanese man of his age to be so explicitly "politically correct" by referring to the region as it is addressed in Chinese (*Dongbei*). He murmured, unable to hide his astonishment, "So nowadays young people like you call that region 'former Manchuria' instead of *Dongbei*?" At this point, I realized that he had mistaken me for Chinese and wanted to make sure that he would not insult my feelings by referring to this historically contested region with a name that bore the trace of the Japanese invasion. "Former Manchuria" (*kyū manshū*), as Northeast China is usually referred to in Japan when its historical connection to Manchukuo is highlighted, is carefully put into quotation marks, if not more proactively replaced by *Chūgoku tōhokubu* (Northeast China), linguistically reproaching the inerasable trace of history.

The Vanished Empire: "Former Manchuria" in the Postwar Japanese Imaginary

As my ethnography demonstrates later in this chapter, most postgeneration Japanese visit Northeast China with a clear sense of what they expect to see. The gap between these expectations and what they acknowledge they see, and the negotiation between the two, reveals the structure of transmission of unaccounted-for pasts. Most Japanese without the firsthand *hikiagesha* experience of Manchukuo draw their knowledge of Manchuria through various forms of representations in the robust "former Manchuria" cultural industry, from memoirs and fiction to news reports, films, and comic books. Decades without diplomatic relations between the two countries during the early Cold War led many Japanese to project not only the past onto "former Manchuria" but also their imagination of contemporary China under the Communist Party. Even after the establishment of diplomatic relations in 1972, before travel to the region became common two decades later, "former Manchuria" continued to exist for most Japanese only in abstract or media representations—a land of phantoms hovering between the imagined and the real, the past and the future.

It is, therefore, crucial to understand the images of "Manchuria" that many Japanese tourists take with them in order to understand what they expect to see, what they then project onto today's cityscape in Changchun, and what their encounters with this urban space produce. We will take an important detour here, away from Changchun, and shift our eyes to Japan to see how the changing representation of "Manchuria" in the Japanese cultural industry over the years has shaped the images that many Japanese tourists now carry with them to Northeast China as they seek remnants of Japan's Manchukuo.

In the Japanese imaginary, "Manchuria" has never existed only in the present: the popular imagination saw Manchuria as the future in prewar Japan and as the past in postwar Japan, reshaping, in both periods, Japan's self-recognition and self-presentation. Louise Young's observation that, just as Japan shaped Northeast China as its colonial space, "Manchuria" also reshaped Japan during the war remains valid even after Manchuria's disappearance.[42] Manchuria in the twentieth century provided a space where Japanese society worked out—through physical intervention or mythmaking—its pathologies and phobias. In the period between 1920 and 1940, Japan projected its desire to become a modern state onto Manchuria, a land of harsh weather, uncultivated nature, and opportunity, seemingly ripe for development.[43] The South Manchuria Railway Company's state-of-the-art railroad connected cities proudly represented in Japan as modern utopias in guidebooks, photo essays, and postcards. Not only representing the Japan of the future, Manchuria also served as a site for the working out of marginal and residual aspects of a rapidly modernizing Japanese society.[44] The process of empire-building was part of "social imperialism," which Young defines as "the projection overseas of the social discontents and dislocations engendered by industrialization at home."[45] With the abrupt and catastrophic disappearance of Japan's empire, Manchuria drastically changed course in the Japanese imaginary.

Following Japan's defeat in 1945, Manchuria as such ceased to exist. Yet this land of imagination made real persisted in the popular imaginary, functioning as a measure of the aspirations and achievements of postwar Japan. The postwar trajectory of "former Manchuria" shows how its image is conflated with Japanese understandings of contemporary China, which, until 1972, remained an almost entirely abstract, if not physically distant, country for most Japanese. Former Manchuria functioned largely as a site of refraction through which many Japanese perceived contemporary China for decades. The place where Japan once projected its future now became a rem(a)inder of the loss sustained in the creation of newborn Japan, with its embodiment of new ideologies of peace, democracy, and prosperity. No longer the projection of future fantasy, Manchuria rematerialized as a mixture of nostalgic past and backward present. It gave shape to Japan's unarticulated loss and provided a benchmark of pride in Japan's postwar status, at last, as a modern state. Former Manchuria in postwar Japan signified New China, even as it held the traces of what was once "Japan's Manchuria."

When the empire vanished in 1945, Manchuria disappeared from Japanese topography, both literally and metaphorically, followed by the unleashing of "postwar" (*sengo*) discourses in Japan. Yoshikuni Igarashi describes the construction of postwar discourses as a process of naturalizing forgetting.[46] The foundational narrative of the postwar portrays Japan as the colonial Other to the United States, a narrative that then led to the erasure of Japan as colonizer.[47] Igarashi's observation echoes Carol Gluck's claim that the postwar signifies the inversion of the prewar and that this process "turned victimizers into victims and atomic memory into imperial denial."[48] As a result of this inversion, the postwar functions to make the prewar disappear, while the war itself is frozen in time. If New China marked the establishment of the Communist state in 1949 as its zero hour, Japan marked 1945 as its zero hour, drawing a radical discontinuity between prewar and postwar Japan.

The advent of the Cold War reinforced this imperial denial, and Japan's postwar was constructed predominantly in relation to the United States within a version of the Cold War discourse that largely excluded Asian Others. What Gluck calls the "mythistorical" beginning—the creation of "the founding myth of 'Japan reborn'" in 1945—has led to Japan's "long postwar."[49] The term "postwar" (*sengo*) has functioned as a kind of *gengō*, a chronological system based on the emperor's reign, of this new era within Showa. Contemporary Japanese society, infamous for its historical amnesia, has ironically operated on a temporality marked by its moment of defeat, as attested by commonly used expressions such as "*sengo 70-nen*" (seventieth year of the postwar) or "*sengo sedai*" (postwar generation) even decades after the war's end.[50] Despite the official proclamation in a 1956 government white paper that the "postwar is over,"[51] *sengo* continues into the twenty-first century. In a policy statement on January 26, 2007, then–Japanese Prime Minister Abe Shinzō emphasized the importance of "departure from the postwar regime (*sengo rejīmu*)," indicating that the postwar is not over yet.

The multiple discourses of "postwar," be they the discourses of forgetting, inversion, or democracy, all contributed to generating the founding myth of newborn Japan. This myth requires a radical discontinuity with the past as a condition of embracing democracy, peace, and prosperity.[52] In so doing, the term "postwar" itself evades Japan's postimperial responsibility by de-emphasizing the fact that 1945 marked Japan's own period of after empire. This postwar myth of newborn Japan thus comes at the cost of institutionalizing an absence of postimperial consciousness, an absence that is felt more keenly since the "post-postwar" era dawned with the Showa Emperor's death in that international annus mirabilis of 1989.

Against this backdrop of the "long postwar" that dominated the Japanese discourse, "former Manchuria" primarily symbolized Japanese victimhood in the popular imaginary.[53] Only in recent years has that same region come to be recognized as the site of Japanese perpetration. As discussed in chapter 1, *inverted victimhood*, in which Japanese victimhood was highlighted against the background of invisible Chinese victimhood, characterized postwar Japan's "imperial amnesia."

Imperial Amnesia in the 1940s and 1950s

During the years immediately following the Japanese defeat, repatriates (*hikiagesha*) from the lost empire brought former Manchuria to war-torn Japan. The manner in which *hikiagesha* were reincorporated into the Japanese society epitomizes the workings of *inverted victimhood*. An array of popular cultural productions that depicted their ordeals after the Russian invasion of Northeast China, just before the Japanese surrender in 1945, served to highlight Japanese victimhood and Japan's postwar status, rather than Japanese perpetration and Japan's postimperiality after empire.

A popular autobiography, *Shooting Stars Are Alive* (*Nagareru hoshi wa ikite iru*) by Fujiwara Tei, captured their tearful ordeals of repatriation, which many did not survive.[54] In this national bestseller of 1949, which became a movie immediately after publication, Fujiwara illustrated her own desperate and fierce efforts to repatriate with her young children from Changchun to Japan via liberated Korea. Her moving account of their ordeal equated Manchuria with Japanese victimhood in the minds of many Japanese, who had encountered millions of *hikiagesha*. For most ordinary Japanese struggling to reconstruct their lives amid the Cold War, New China remained abstract, while former Manchuria evoked vivid memories of *their* own sufferings.[55] Representations of former Manchuria in popular culture captured the Japanese national imagination. Having gone through many reprintings, Fujiwara's book even now remains on recommended book lists at many schools. Such portrayals of Manchuria effectively turned it into a land of Japanese suffering and victimhood, rather than the site of Japanese railway imperialism and settler colonialism that culminated in a formal puppet state and a full-fledged war. It was a process not unlike how the use of the atomic bombs in Hiroshima and Nagasaki followed by the Allied occupation turned Japanese imperialism into a story of Japanese victimhood.[56]

Against this background of "amnesia of empire,"[57] Gomikawa Junpei's six-volume novel *The Human Condition* (*Ningen no jōken*) became a bestseller in the 1950s.[58] Published between 1956 and 1958, it was made into a highly acclaimed movie under the same title by director Kobayashi Masaki in 1958. Born and raised in Dalian under Japanese control, Gomikawa (1916–95) worked for Shōwa Steel Industry in Manchuria after graduating from college in Tokyo. He was drafted in 1943, served in the Northeast Chinese border area, and was ultimately repatriated in 1948. Although a work of historical fiction, *The Human Condition* reflects many of his experiences in Northeast China during and after the war.

In the first half of this epic novel, the protagonist, Kaji Daisuke—whose socialist ideals had led him to leave Japan for Manchuria, where ideological repression was much looser—faces the dilemma of being charged with improving the output of the mining company that employs him while wanting to provide humane labor conditions for its enslaved Chinese and Korean laborers. His moral dilemma results in his being stripped of the draft exemption to which he was entitled given his job in a vital industry, and he is sent to an army unit near the Soviet border. The rest of the novel tells of his often-horrific experiences in the army, his postwar captivity in a Soviet labor camp, and his eventual escape from the camp in a fatal attempt to return to his wife, Michiko, who has repatriated to Japan.

In his analysis of "Manchurian literature" after the demise of the Japanese Empire,[59] the Japanese literary critic Kawamura Minato locates the popularity of this novel not so much in its antiwar theme but more in its appeal to what Gluck calls "the middle-class postwar, or the postwar of private life."[60] Kawamura argues that another theme of the novel, the love between Kaji and Michiko, reflects the spirit of the era, which embraced the pursuit of happiness at the individual level in contrast to the collective ideology during the war (as exemplified, for instance, by the East Asia Coprosperity Sphere).[61] Only a few years later, the term *maihōmu-shugi* (my-home-ism) became a social phenomenon, illuminating the increasing number of men finding life's value not in work or social ideals but in their private world at home. Gomikawa's novel, which seems like an exception to the collective "amnesia" said to characterize the 1950s, functioned as a signifier of the postwar agenda—in particular, the idea of democracy built around personal life—while at the same time satisfying the conscience of the era's prevailing pacifist sentiments.

Exposing Japanese Atrocities in the 1970s

The high economic growth in 1960s Japan and the Cultural Revolution in China further pushed former Manchuria to the margins of history. Not until the early 1970s did violent images of Japanese imperialism in China surface within Japanese society.

After a forty-day investigative trip to China from June to July 1971, which took place prior to the unexpected normalization of Sino-Japanese relations the following year, journalist Honda Katsuichi wrote a series of essays for the major Japanese daily newspaper *Asahi shimbun*, published between August and December 1971 and later collected in book form.[62] Honda had been driven by his concern that, more than twenty-five years after the disappearance of the Japanese Empire, the Japanese remained ignorant about the brutality of the Japanese Imperial Army in China. Honda worried not only that the Japanese had been insensitive to the past in thinking about the developing relationship between China and Japan but also that they continued to misrecognize themselves as victims of the war while conveniently forgetting their role as perpetrators.[63] Graphic depictions of Japanese violence—mostly photographs of layers of human remains in old mines—accompanied his essays. These half-buried skeletal remains do not cry out; rather, they seem to be frozen in a land of aphasia. Honda's presentation of

Manchuria as a land of bloodshed and inhumanity inflicted by the Japanese shocked readers. Yet his publications failed to stir a wider public debate on Japanese guilt, as Honda had hoped.

Shortly thereafter, US President Nixon's visit to China in 1972 led to a sudden anticipation for the normalization of Sino-Japanese relations, resulting in a significant number of publications about the legacies of Japan's lost empire. The detailed data and narratives of these writings starkly contrast with the silence among Japanese intellectuals of the 1950s and 1960s on the former empire. Yet, in these numerous accounts of past violence, much like in Honda's pioneering work, the graphic images of the past violence were frozen in time, while survivors of these horrors depicted in images remained silent and thus publicly invisible. Although images of wartime violence were heavily circulated in the media during this period, they failed to spark public discussion.

Former Manchuria as Japan's Past and China's Present in the 1980s

The legacy of former Manchuria caught the Japanese popular imagination again in the 1980s, this time as the symbol of the past caught in underdeveloped China and as yet another site of Japanese victimhood. After the Japanese defeat, thousands of Chinese couples adopted Japanese orphans—*Chūgoku zanryū koji*, or simply *zanryū koji* in Japanese—who had been left behind in China.[64] Following the normalization of Sino-Japanese relations, the Japanese government invited *zanryū koji* to Japan to search for their biological parents and, if they wished, to (re)settle in Japan. In 1981, coverage of this new policy abruptly brought Manchuria back into Japanese living rooms.[65] Since then, a few times each year as new groups of orphans visit Japan, news programs on the public NHK television network broadcast head shots of *zanryū koji* with voiceovers describing their fragmented memories as clues about their Japanese parents and as signs of their Japaneseness. The programs then cut to footage of the teary-eyed *zanryū koji* with colorless Mao suits and similar haircuts stepping onto their "motherland" at the airport, followed by interviews with government officials (through translators) and their potential relatives. Throughout the 1980s and 1990s, and more sporadically in the 2000s, every time a new group visited Japan, national newspapers printed head shots of each visiting *zanryū koji* with summaries of whatever clues were available. Manchuria thus reappeared in Japanese discourses through these orphans, but their portrayal by the media accentuated their "Chinese" style and mannerisms.

These images of *zanryū koji* made visible to the Japanese public the divergent trajectories of China and Japan. The orphans' ordeals—starting with the Chinese civil war between the Guomindang and the Communists immediately after the Japanese surrender and followed by the brutal conditions during the Great Leap Forward and the turmoil during the Cultural Revolution—confirmed by contrast the consensus that postwar Japan had acquired not only peace and democracy but also economic prosperity. The images of Japanese orphans who carried with them Chinese style and mannerisms reaffirmed the foundation narrative of postwar Japan while adding another story to its victimization discourse. Wartime politics produced these war orphans, the narrative goes, and the politics of China exacerbated their misery. The "discovery" of forgotten children of past injustice highlighted the discourse of the war while omitting the discourse of imperialism that led to the war.[66]

The media coverage of their visits to Japan and the dramas that accompany them have become part of the seasonal scenery in now prosperous Japan, periodically reminding Japanese society of Manchuria. Since the orphans' initial appearance in 1981, popular culture concerned with Manchuria has flourished, as evidenced by numerous memoirs and television programs. A ten-hour-long television drama called *The Child of the Fatherland* (*Daichi no ko*), based on a multivolume novel of the same title by Yamazaki Toyoko,[67] has probably attracted the largest audience. NHK has broadcast this enormously popular television drama at least once a year over the past few decades. The book and the television adaptation illustrate the struggles of a Japanese orphan adopted by a Chinese couple in Changchun against the background of China's turbulent history and his unexpected encounter with his biological father through one of the first postwar Sino-Japanese joint ventures in Shanghai. These media images portrayed "former Manchuria" as a relic *and* as an example of China's backwardness in comparison to bubble-era Japan, then rapidly becoming a world economic power. In the Japanese imaginary of the 1980s, former Manchuria represented both Japan's past and China's backward present.

MISSING PAGES: FORMER MANCHURIA BETWEEN VICTIMHOOD AND PERPETRATION IN THE 2000S

Only after the increased popularity of former Manchuria tourism and Japanese investment in Northeast China in the mid-1990s did the reproduction of Manchuria in postwar Japan extend significantly beyond the media. This renewed interest turned this land of imagination into the site of encounters with landscapes of after empire.[68] The shift in the popular consumption of Manchuria from virtual to real has begun to disturb Manchuria's discursive location between the present and the future, where it shimmers just over the horizon as a saintly sanctuary for Japan's troubled history.

The early 2000s witnessed yet another surge of reflections upon former Manchuria in Japanese popular culture, adding another layer to the heated historians' debate that had peaked a few years earlier as the new cultural production of fiction, graphic novels, television dramas, and films defied a straightforward portrayal of Japanese victimhood and triggered strong revisionist responses. One example of this phase is *The Red Moon* (*Akai tsuki*), a semiautobiographical novel by popular author Nakanishi Rei that won the prestigious Naoki Literature Award.[69] In just a few years after its original publication in 2001, more than seven hundred thousand copies of the two-volume hardcover edition had been sold. Film and television adaptations came in 2004. In bringing individual desire to the fore and rejecting the simple narration of victimhood that had often characterized narratives of former Manchuria, it is similar to another very popular work of the period, *The Country Is Burning* (*Kuni ga moeru*) by Motomiya Hiroshi,[70] a graphic novel series originally published beginning in 2003 in weekly installments in one of the highest circulating weekly comic magazines, *Young Jump*.[71]

Both Nakanishi and Motomiya clearly portray those involved in Manchuria, be they military personnel or poverty-stricken farmers, as driven to a land of opportunity by personal desires; not all were passive executors of misguided government policies. At the same time, these works undeniably seek to elicit sympathy for those whose lives were torn apart by the nation-state. Through the exploration of this ambiguous space between the acknowledged sense of responsibility and that of victimhood, these works have captured the attention of younger readers. Manchuria, for this generation, may not even belong to history but serve as a fantasyland where they project their own desires. This mythical space is portrayed as having accepted and absorbed a wild energy rejected by tightly controlled Japanese society. Motomiya's graphic novel is highly popular among businessmen, who feel trapped within a rigid and repressive corporate culture in the seemingly permanent recession of contemporary Japan, with a diminishing sense of hope and purposefulness.[72]

In late 2004, threats by a group of right-leaning local assembly members who criticized *The Country Is Burning*'s depiction of history forced its discontinuation in the serial *Young Jump*, despite its popularity. Most major Japanese newspapers covered the incident, and a heated controversy followed. What triggered the violent reaction from the right was *not* Motomiya's overall interpretation of history, since eighty-seven installments of the story had already been published, but his graphic depiction in the eighty-eighth installment of Japanese brutality in the Nanjing Massacre, which critics claimed was not an accurate representation of the historical facts. All nineteen pages of the October 7 installment of *The Country Is Burning* were devoted to the 1937 massacre.[73]

In one scene over two full pages, Motomiya depicts the infamous killing competition (the so-called *hyakunin giri*, "one hundred beheadings") in which two soldiers were widely reported to have competed for the greatest number of beheadings with their Japanese swords.[74] Motomiya illustrates two Japanese soldiers beheading blindfolded Chinese with their swords, while fellow soldiers surrounding the spectacle cheer and bid for the winner as if watching a sporting match. Several pages illustrating the Nanjing Massacre follow. In these pages, through a confessional narrative of an anonymous former Japanese soldier, Motomiya relates various stories of cruelty, in part through graphic reproductions of widely circulated photographs of the Nanjing Massacre. He reproduces a photograph of a woman with her pants pulled down by a soldier; the picture appears in Iris Chang's *The Rape of Nanking*, where its caption reads, "Japanese soldiers sometimes forced their victims to pose in pornographic pictures, which were kept as souvenirs of rape."[75] In another panel, Motomiya reproduces a photograph of corpses covering the ground, many stripped down to their waists. The anonymous Japanese soldier's recounting of the massacre appears in typeface over several panels of illustrations filled with murder scenes and piles of corpses:

> At that time, I was stationed outside the walled city of Nanjing. I killed the Chinese one after another. I bound ten of them together with barbed wire, piled them up, poured oil over them, and burnt them alive. We used to call it bale binding at that time. It gave me a similar sensation to killing pigs. We killed prisoners of war as a way of warning others, and we cut off their ears and noses. We also inserted bayonets into their mouths and cut them out. When we stuck a bayonet under an eye, thick white bodily liquid came out. Women suffered the most of all. From small kids to the elderly, we raped everyone. We drove wood-burning trucks to villages, plundered, and every single soldier raped all the women under the sun. After raping them, we killed most of them. If they were alive, our acts were considered rapes, but if they were dead, our acts counted as those of wiping out enemies. We often conducted drawing and quartering by tying a woman to a willow tree with each of her ankles tied to a horse. When we whipped the horses, the woman's groin tore in two up

to her breasts. Everybody in the platoon watched it happened and our commander said nothing. Under the war situation, we had no choice.[76]

The right-wing critique of Motomiya's depiction of the massacre primarily revolved around the validity of original photographs that Motomiya used. On one of the several websites set up to criticize his work, his illustrative adaptation of the photograph of a woman stripped naked to the waist next to a soldier is posted side by side with the original photograph.[77] The website analyzes how Motomiya modified the original to create an impression that a Japanese soldier was raping a Chinese woman and argues that in the original it is not certain that the soldier is Japanese. Reframing the already framed photographic images in Motomiya's illustrative reproduction has become the site of double suspicion and interpretation. The seeming distance from the supposed original event, as the layers of framing suggests, disturbs the line between fiction and the real. Each weekly installment carries a footnote stating that it is a fictional story and bears no relation to actual characters, organizations, or incidents; however, his graphic copy of photographs, instead of illustrating the Nanjing Massacre through his own imagination, strongly hints at the presence of reality, which elicited a strong reaction from the right.[78]

When the series was republished in book format in 2006, the depiction of the Japanese invasion of Nanjing was reduced to three pages of images of bombing followed by a scene of triumphant soldiers with Japanese flags on top of the gate of Nanjing.[79] The book version simply omits the scene of the Nanjing Massacre that Motomiya originally illustrated elaborately over nineteen pages. These missing pages are analogous to the knowledge of "real history" that many younger generation Japanese visiting Changchun feel is absent in Japan. This widely shared sense that "we don't know the real history" drives many postwar-generation Japanese to former Manchuria in search of their missing pages.

IN SEARCH OF MISSING PAGES: MEMORY, POSTMEMORY, INHERITANCE

"Missing pages" represent not only the younger generation's perception of a lack of historical knowledge but also the radical discontinuity between war and postwar generations created by the traumatic past. In her study of the transmission of Holocaust memories to second-generation Holocaust survivors, Marianne Hirsch argues that postmemory—the "structure of inter- and trans-generational transmission of traumatic knowledge and experience"[80]—is an attempt to remedy this sort of generational rupture.[81] As she puts it, "Postmemory describes the relationship that the generation after those who witnessed cultural or collective trauma bears to the experiences of those who came before, experiences that they 'remember' only by means of the stories, images, and behaviors among which they grew up."[82] It is a form of mediated remembrance that is different from the memory of the first generation, those who experienced the Holocaust. Going against the widely shared assumption that memory signals continuity with the past, Hirsch sees the postmemory of the second generation as a remedy for the generational discontinuity that occurs as a result of traumatic events.[83]

While *hikiagesha* seek their own history in a former Manchuria that is literally absent from Japan, most other Japanese tourists to the region seek a "real" and "authentic" history (*honmono no rekishi*) of Japanese colonial violence that they feel is absent in Japan. Many postgeneration Japanese tourists to Changchun search for a postmemory in the form of "missing pages." Yet their encounter with "real" history in Changchun is a complicated one.

As we shall see, the generational transmission is not always linear, the mnemonic community is not always self-evident, and what is being transmitted is not always what one expects. What younger Japanese find in their search for missing pages is not so much postmemory that marks its deferred relation to the original event—in this case, Japanese imperialism in China. Rather, what they find instead is a form of inheritance, with layers of losses that unfold in the form of compounded debts as they acknowledge the receipt of a "gift" from the previous generation that they have no choice but to accept. The arrival of inheritance marks its presentness, its belonging to the now, presenting itself as the problem of the current generation. Unlike postmemory, there is nothing "post" about this inheritance, which, as these tourists discover, encompasses not only the losses incurred during the Japanese invasion of China but also the losses incurred *after* the demise of the Japanese Empire due to the lack of accountability for the original violence. We shall now turn to this shift—from postmemory to inheritance—that the younger Japanese tourists discover in Changchun.

Awase kagami: Refractive Structure of Generational Transmission

Predominantly in their twenties and thirties, younger Japanese visitors mostly study in China or are interested in historical issues between China and Japan. It is a self-selected group of tourists, and almost all of them carry a copy of *Chikyū no arukikata* (Walking around the Globe), the Japanese equivalent of *Lonely Planet*. In response to the growing interest among younger Japanese in Northeast China, the popular travel guide series produced its first edition focused solely on the region in 1998, with fifteen full-color pages devoted to Changchun. The section provides a historical tour of the city through Manchukuo's architectural remains, introducing readers to the Film Studio, the Palace Museum, the former State Council building and its Fake Manchukuo Museum, and the *Badabu*, the former Manchukuo ministerial buildings in the emperor's crown style, with color photographs of each building and close-ups of architectural details. The text explains the historical and current uses of each building and its architectural style, with commentaries such as "This ministry was in charge of collecting forced laborers, who were forced to serve Japan's war of invasion (*shinryaku sensō*) in China."[84] To complement their "former Manchuria" tour, many young Japanese tourists stay at Chunyi Hotel, formerly Yamato Hotel, the flagship Manchukuo hotel in front of the train station. This art nouveau building, once an embodiment of luxury, modern style, and Japanese colonial power, now houses a midrange three-star hotel. A shadow of its past glory, it features a dimly lit lobby, faded and shabby rose-colored carpets in the long corridors and staircases, and squeaky, lumpy beds. The younger Japanese encounter Changchun mostly through such architectural remains of Manchukuo.

Many Japanese tourists, especially postgeneration Japanese, express their encounters with the Changchun cityscape as "*usukimiwarui*" or "*odoro odoroshii*" (uncanny, ghostly), terms often used to describe anxiety caused by the anticipation of ghostly apparitions, or "*nama namashii*" (real, raw), a term used to describe a sighting of something whose existence is known to everyone but that is supposed to be hidden, covered, or disguised. A Japanese student studying in Changchun commented on the ministerial boulevard lined with the emperor's-crown-style structures: "When I first came to Changchun and saw these buildings, I found them very uncanny (*usukimiwarui*). It's right there, I mean, that history. It's so raw, unprocessed, and real (*nama namashii* and *egui*), right in your face. But now, after living in Changchun for nearly three years, I've gotten used to the sight and I don't get this kind of uncanny feeling anymore. These architectural remainders are part of my everyday scenery now." What struck him was twofold: the visual and tactile presence of history as well as how it felt real, as if what he saw was not a past entombed in architectural forms but something whose embodied power was very much present. He saw in the edifices not the trace of the past, as he had expected, but the past in the present tense. He found that his encounter with what he thought were material remains of the past was more like seeing ghostly apparitions—the appearance of that which is supposed to be dead and that has a power over the present.

The sense of the uncanny that many postgeneration Japanese visitors feel in Changchun expresses anxiety and fear caused by seeing what is supposed to be unseen, but it also points to the "real history" that they feel is missing in "amnesiac" Japan.[85] The lack of lack, the appearance of the unprocessed, not-quite-dead-yet past that is repressed and unseen back home in Japan, seems to trigger anxiety. The sense of the uncanny, then, is a reflection less of amnesia than of obsession in the form of this acknowledged lack, the missing pages. What Japanese tourists encounter in Changchun is the apparition of supposedly dead Manchukuo, which is both familiar and unfamiliar. On the one hand, Changchun presents a familiar landscape to the Japanese with its emperor's-crown-style architecture, especially the former State Council building that eerily echoes the National Diet Building in Tokyo. At the same time, its appearance is anachronistic, inducing a sense of unfamiliarity among the postgeneration Japanese. Manchukuo exists for those who grew up in the long Japanese postwar only in the realm of a distant past, yet in Changchun they encounter this distant history as real and alive. Here are the missing pages they sought: the "real" history in response to what is often concealed within Japan.

Yet the anticipated encounter with the absent past does not necessarily lead them to come to terms with the past, as they hope. Unlike *hikiage-sha,* who find closure in encountering the missing pages of their own pasts, many young Japanese tourists encounter a further opening, with layers of losses beyond the one they intend to see in the form of postmemory.

Although their initial reactions to former Manchukuo remainders result from projecting Japan's past onto these edifices, younger Japanese, after the initial shock of encountering the uncanny, project less the past than the present onto the Changchun cityscape. What many of them come to gradually acknowledge while walking around the city and visiting museums is more China's present than Japan's past. Kuroyagi Hiroshi, a man in his late thirties, wrote to me after his first trip to Northeast China, expressing sentiments similar to those that many Japanese tourists from his generation shared with me as I gave tours of the Palace Museum:

> To be honest, I was disappointed and a bit disturbed by the historical exhibitions in the museums I visited. I felt that they were less historical museums than political propaganda devices. There is no doubt that these exhibitions are based on historical "facts." Yet through re-presentations

> of these facts, they convey political messages. For us who go visit China with a keen awareness of Japanese historical responsibility, I felt that these historical exhibitions in China were counter-productive. I was turned off by the loud chorus of "Japan evil, Japan evil!" when I was seeking ways to come to terms with the past. But later, a young Chinese woman sitting next to me on my flight back to Tokyo told me that the Chinese government used these museums as leverage to "educate" its population and that those exhibitions were not intended for foreign visitors. Her interpretation made sense to me, that we were not exactly the targeted audience of this kind of historical exhibition. But it also made me think of how the Chinese government manipulates various images of Japan to control and manage its vast population. Yet we Japanese, who after all are the perpetrators, are not in a position to criticize their historical portrayal. If we did, the Chinese would regard us as right-wingers. The Chinese government is well aware of its structural position, and uses its moral superiority as the former victim to manipulate its domestic population as well as its diplomatic relations with Japan.

Kuroyagi's itinerary in Northeast China revolved around major remainders of Manchukuo, such as Changchun's Palace Museum, the 9.18 Museum (Manchurian Incident Museum) in Shenyang, and the Unit 731 Museum in Harbin. I accompanied him on his visit to the Unit 731 Museum, and he remained very quiet as we walked through the museum exhibition, which was housed in the former administrative building of the biological experimentation unit. When we arrived at the last hall, where they displayed publications about Unit 731, he finally murmured, "I need to study more." He continued, "I've read about Unit 731 before, but didn't realized that it was this terrible . . ." and fell silent again. During our long, bumpy bus ride back to downtown Harbin, he was absorbed in the material he had bought in the museum. Kuroyagi confessed later that the exhibition there, like those in the Changchun museums, had too strong a sense of political propaganda for an audience like him. The principal goal of these exhibitions, he felt, centered on the acknowledgment of Japanese atrocities during the war; the exhibitions were more propaganda than analysis, of which he wanted to see more.

His trip to trace Japan's imperial past yielded a glimpse of China and Japan *after* the demise of the Japanese Empire. He went back to Japan with no hope for possible reconciliation: "I've come to Northeast China to seek ways in which to come to terms with the past as a member of the postwar generation. But, to be honest, I feel that my very sincere desire is somewhat rejected from the Chinese side. Or to put it more bluntly, I now feel more confused about what it means to come to terms with the past, and what kind of actions from the Japanese side would be accepted and respected from the Chinese side as such."

With all the loud voices both at home and abroad claiming that Japan suffers from historical amnesia as evidenced by a failure to acknowledge past wrongs, and as part of the generation directly affected by the history-textbook controversy in the 1980s in which many descriptions of Japanese violence were diluted if not erased under pressure from the Ministry of Education,[86] Kuroyagi had drawn an equivalence between seeing the site of Japanese colonial violence (as a way of filling in the missing pages and thus seeing the historical Truth unavailable in Japan) and coming to terms with the past. His expectation reflects a widely held belief, in both Japan and China, that the Japanese inability to come to terms with its imperialist past is primarily due to Japanese misrecognition of the historical Truth. In other words, facing the missing pages by acknowledging and admitting the Truth is imbued with a promise of successfully coming to terms with Japan's problematic past. Yet Kuroyagi's experience in Changchun suggests that the crux of the issue may lie elsewhere.[87]

Uchida Hajime, in his twenties and carrying a copy of *Chikyū no arukikata*, articulated how he saw the postwar politics between China and Japan play out in Northeast China's urban landscapes. When I met him and his wife in the Palace Museum, they were going through the exhibition very carefully, reading every photograph caption. Both of them had been studying Chinese in Northeast China and were using their summer vacation to visit remainders of Manchukuo in various cities. To my question about what he thought of the historical museums in the Northeast, he immediately responded that they reflected the policies of the Chinese government. He observed how the exhibitions tend to be political instead of scholarly—how historical figures such as the number of war dead are not sourced, how photographs and artifacts are used to appeal to the emotions rather than the intellect, and how the narratives always start by demonstrating Japanese atrocities and end with praise for the anti-Japanese struggles of the Communist Party. He observed that the historical exhibitions such as the 9.18 Museum in Shenyang reflect the strong criticism from the Chinese leadership of the 1990s about Japan's inability to come to terms with the past. He did not hide his disappointment and frustration in encountering these presentations of the past.

Uchida's experience sums up the sentiments of disappointment and frustration I heard from many young Japanese tourists in Northeast China, many of whom belong to the self-acknowledged left-leaning postwar generation and yet who express their impression of their visits to historical museums in language that can be easily interpreted in China as a right-wing denial of Japan's historical responsibility. Writing about children of Nazi families in West Germany, Peter Sichrovsky finds an analogous sentiment, which he calls "disappointment over irreconcilability," to be widely shared among postwar-generation West Germans. He observes that many of them feel "that their hope for reconciliation is not respected or accepted by the victims and their descendants."[88] The letter to repay the debt is, so to speak, returned to sender.

For this generation of Japanese tourists, the Changchun cityscape vividly illuminates the double inheritance they encounter in the landscape of after empire: China's postcoloniality and their own postimperial positioning in relation to this space, as if seeing one's own back in the mirror arrangement known in Japanese as *awase kagami*. Their self-recognition is set in relation to the mirror that the Chinese are holding to create a twice-reflected image. One's figure becomes visible in the refracted reflection in the mirror; only this way can one see what one's naked optic vision fails to capture. The double mirror reflects one's otherwise invisible back, but it also reflects the one holding the second mirror—in this case, the Chinese. Through a reflection of a reflection, one's structural position within this mirrored environment is revealed. One is made keenly aware that what one sees is a product of a refracted image.

Through this mirrored vision, this generation of Japanese recognizes the *postimperial topography of guilt*. Since many young Japanese tourists to the Northeast study in and plan to engage with China both professionally and personally, they find their structural position within this moral topography frustrating because of the baggage they unavoidably inherit by virtue of their nationality. Many expressed that visiting Northeast China involved first psychologically preparing themselves for possible insults, aggression, and hatred, followed by comments such as, "Actually, I haven't received any insults yet." At the same time, they are cautious about expressing their frustration and disappointment in front of the Chinese for fear of being seen as right-wing. Their encounter with the Changchun urban landscape confirms their intuitive understanding of what they owe without their choosing. This strong sense of inherited moral debt was instantly shared by a group of high school students visiting Changchun even though many of them had not been aware of the presence of missing pages prior to their arrival.

We Were Born Guilty[89]

As part of an education program to spend one week with local Chinese high school students from the prestigious Changchun Foreign Language School, twenty Japanese students, selected from various public schools, visited the Palace Museum with their Chinese partners. The tour of the museum started cheerfully with forty teenagers who had just bonded by sharing meals and bedrooms at their houses. I walked them through the early development of Manchukuo and the life of Puyi. Their imagination was quickly captured by the exceptionally dramatic and turbulent life story of Puyi in the first photographic exhibition, which starts with an enlarged black-and-white photograph of him at age three in the Qing dynasty emperor's gown and ends with snapshots of his quiet final years as an ordinary citizen in Beijing after he was absolved of complicity during the Manchukuo period by the Chinese government. The restored quarters of Puyi's family and the palace administration followed. With wax figures posing in those rooms decorated with Qing-dynasty furnishings and colorful silk ornaments, this section of the museum has a strong resemblance to a historical theme park, and some students were particularly excited to see the original of what they had seen in Bernardo Bertolucci's epic movie *The Last Emperor*.

This chatty, cheerful, and excited group walked across a small courtyard, past where a museum vendor had set up a photo-shooting service offering a choice of Qing-dynasty costumes. I led them to the next section, the multiroom exhibition on Japanese atrocities during its fourteen years of rule in Northeast China. Using wax figures and photographs, this exhibit graphically illustrates violence committed by the Japanese. An uncomfortable and tense silence filled the small room, whose four walls were covered with blown-up black-and-white photographs of mutilated bodies and fear-struck faces of those whose lives were about to be ended violently. In front of a picture depicting Japanese soldiers slaying Chinese mothers and children, and shots of a pile of headless bodies, some Japanese students started to sob while holding their Chinese partners' hands tightly. Some completely lost their facial expressions and stood frozen like wax figures, consoled by their Chinese friends. A few could not remain in the room and stood outside on the balcony, their faces pale and expressionless, closing their lips tightly. "I had a lovely evening last night with my host family. My Chinese partner's grandmother was so sweet to me," one Japanese student started to tell me but suddenly couldn't continue.

I could clearly see that the Japanese students felt doubly uncomfortable. Facing these gruesome pictures was uncomfortable enough for anyone, but they were holding hands with their Chinese partners. Terror congealed in a photographic form was abruptly rendered less abstract through the presence of their new Chinese partner and by memories of dinner with their friend's parents and grandparents the night before. After their afternoon visit to the Palace Museum, they would go back to their host family's house, where they would share dinner once again with their partner's family members, who could have been some of the victims in the exhibition pictures.

The encounter with their unannounced inheritance, for many, came as a shock. They nevertheless did not question the sudden acknowledgement that they inherited the burden of history as Japanese. Not knowing how to respond to this new acknowledgement, many of them became motionless. Made keenly aware of being Japanese, they accepted the burden of the past and the responsibilities that accompanied it. Standing next to one female student with moist eyes and pursed lips, who had quietly stepped out of the room, I whispered, "It's not an easy exhibition to go through, is it?" To this, she replied without hesitation, "It's very, very tough. But as a Japanese, I have to see what the Japanese did in the past. I have to know."

Surrounded by panel after panel of photography of bodies mutilated during Japanese atrocities, the students' experience was intensified by the warmth of their Chinese partners' hands, which evoked the trauma of others, the others whose faces were no longer abstract. By tightly holding their Japanese partners' hands or shoulders, Chinese students participated in the Japanese students' unexpectedly difficult encounters with the burden that came with what they now saw as their scarred nationality.

Despite their physical expressions of despair at the site, however, many of these Japanese students seemed to come to a sense of closure—one that may lead to a new opening—a feeling that most Japanese tourists in their twenties and thirties did not attain in their active search. Having a recipient for their repayment letter, in the form of those Chinese students who were eager to reciprocate through their words and gestures, allowed these Japanese students to better face the double inheritance within the moral economy that both Chinese and Japanese students are born into.

In her exploration of the relationship between trauma and history, Cathy Caruth observes that "history, like trauma, is never simply one's own, that history is precisely the way we are implicated in each other's traumas."[90] History, she argues, emerges from trauma implicating each other in the act of understanding. The experiences of these high school students came close to this sense of history, through their encounters with the past in this environment in which both Chinese and Japanese students found themselves implicated in one another's understanding of the past.

Most of the Japanese students wrote letters to me a few days later, thanking me for the tour and telling me how much they were blown away by the experience. The following excerpts from these letters express how naturally they assumed their new role as bearers of inherited guilt.

> *Ishikawa Sachie, female sophomore*: Before visiting the Imperial Palace Museum, I didn't know much about it. I was taken aback to see so many pictures of heads without bodies and babies without heads. At first I didn't exactly know what these pictures were, and my Chinese partner told me that they were the babies killed by the Japanese Army. Without much thinking, I couldn't help but apologize to her. She replied that we were nice people. The Japanese did such terrible things to the Chinese, yet now the Chinese people not only accept us Japanese but also try to develop friendship. I never want to see something like this happen again in the future.

> *Yasuda Hiroshi, male sophomore*: As a Japanese, it was unbelievable to see what the Japanese did to China during the war. My heart is filled with sorrow and remorse when I think that it was indeed the Japanese who committed such crimes. I'm upset to see that a sense of responsibility for the past wrongs is wearing off in the Japanese society. It is selfish and irresponsible to say that these crimes were committed by earlier generations and that we are free from the accusations. As a Japanese, I feel terribly sorry for what happened, and I would like to apologize for these crimes committed in the name of Japanese. We should not forget that the current peaceful friendship between China and Japan is built upon uncountable sacrifices.

> *Tanaka Yumi, female sophomore*: I didn't have any background knowledge of the Imperial Palace Museum before visiting there the other day, and I was all curious and excited about this excursion. My excitement was crushed as I started to discover what this place was all about. There were numerous gruesome pictures, many of which I couldn't bear to look at. I had learned about the Manchurian Incident and known about Japanese atrocities during the war. But standing in front of these pictures in the very space where these things happened, the magnitude of cruelty and injustices blew my mind. Not as an individual but as a Japanese, I wanted to apologize to the Chinese people for what happened in the past. My new Chinese friend, Ms. Wu, held my hand throughout the tour of the museum, even in front of the most cruel pictures, and I was somewhat saved by her behavior. Even though those who started the Manchurian Incident were the previous generation of Japanese, it didn't

make it easier to face the history at all. I don't want to see those kind of pictures in the future. I don't want to create that kind of place in the future. It was a saving grace to know that the Chinese students looked at us as we are, instead of looking at us as the same as "those Japanese who killed our family members."

Hasegawa Mika, female junior: I thought that I had learned the history of this period before coming to China, but I was immobilized by a strong sense of fear after looking at the gruesome depictions of the war in the museum. I wanted to discuss so many things with my Chinese host sister, Ms. Jing, but my words got frozen in front of these portrayals of life in China during the war. Ms. Jing held my shoulders tightly in order to calm me down. It should have been my role to console her, but she told me again and again, "It's all right, it's all right," while patting my shoulder gently. "It's the past," she also added. Even though these things happened in the past, however, the fact remains. I feel quite ashamed and upset at myself for not being able to apologize to her and her family as a Japanese. Her grandmother was also very sweet to me. We cannot change the past, and I sincerely think that the Japanese did something very wrong. Now that we've learned the history, I hope that our generation will build a new friendship between China and Japan. Today is September 18, the day when the Manchurian Incident took place. I would like to reflect upon the fact that we are visiting Changchun on this very significant day in our history.

Takeda Hajime, male junior: I have been to Nanjing and am keenly aware of the horrible things done to the Chinese by the Japanese. I would like to apologize to the Chinese people for what happened during the war. When I stayed at my Chinese partner's house, his grandmother told me that we lived in the era of friendship between China and Japan. When I heard this, I couldn't help but cry uncontrollably. I truly believe that it is crucial for the Japanese government to acknowledge the past wrongs and contribute to world peace.

For these Japanese students, their encounter with Japan's imperial past was also an encounter with Japan's long postwar, in which they discover a lack of postimperial reckoning in their upbringing. Some angrily voiced in their letters how at school they had never learned the scope of the terror and violence committed by the Japanese. Through their trip to Changchun, and through their awakening acknowledgement of their postimperial inheritance, they *became* "born guilty" by their own will, although most seem to have perceived themselves to *have been* born guilty as Japanese. They consider historical responsibility and an accompanying sense of guilt an inheritance that they have no choice but to accept.

The Inverted Gaze

It is not the material remainders per se that arouse Japanese visitors' keen sense of their own postimperial presence within Changchun's landscape of after empire. What makes their experiences unique is what can be termed the *inverted gaze* that many of them express as an unnerving experience. In this urban space full of specters of Japan's imperialist past, Japanese visitors, the spectators of Manchukuo remnants, find themselves under the gaze—both real and imagined—of local Chinese. Instead of being viewing subjects, many Japanese tourists see themselves becoming the objects of the local Chinese gaze, which the Japanese imagine turns them into part of the "former Manchukuo" spectacle. Rather than seeing the Manchukuo remains in front of their eyes, Japanese tourists find themselves seeing themselves through the imagined gaze of local Chinese. In this theatrical space akin to a theme park, which nevertheless is the lived space of the everyday, the Japanese are constantly reminded of their national inheritance: their responsibility for the past violence, one way or another, as Japanese.

Colonial inheritance and accompanying moral debt in the name of the nation announce their arrival to Japanese visitors through the refractive transmission under the gaze of local Chinese. The inverted gaze thus creates unexpected sites of encounter *with* the gaze of the Other, however imagined these encounters may be, and these encounters reveal more than what meets the eye.

The inverted gaze is keenly felt by many in the Fake Manchukuo Museum, housed upstairs in the former State Council building, which mimics, often detail for detail, much of the architectural style of the Japanese Diet Building in Tokyo (figure 3.4). This small-scale historical museum occupies some hallway wall spaces and the office of the former prime minister of Manchukuo, exhibiting historical relics and enlarged photo panels portraying Japanese atrocities during its occupation. With the increase of Japanese visitors in recent years, the museum now has several Japanese-speaking tour guides, all Chinese women in their twenties. The museum guides, provided by the museum to all visitors, pause at each blown-up black-and-white photograph capturing the most horrendous violence committed by the Japanese and explain the image in heavily accented and not so fluent Japanese. By the time

3.4 The former State Council (currently Fake Manchukuo Museum): The former State Council building, whose architectural style resembles the Japanese Diet building in Tokyo, houses the Fake Manchukuo Museum today. Photo by author, 2002.

Japanese tourists reach the office of former prime minister Zhang Jinghui—appointed, as the guide explains, to disguise the fact that the Imperial Army wielded ultimate power—Japanese tourists are no longer spectators. They find themselves being looked at by the Chinese tour guide within this historically loaded space. The gaze of the Chinese makes them part of the exhibition of photographs, artifacts, and texts portraying the violence of the past, planned and directed from this very room. "Here is the balcony where the puppet prime minister saluted the public," announces the guide, leading the tourists to a large balcony overlooking the boulevard of ministry buildings and the site of what the Japanese had planned to be a new palace for the puppet emperor of Manchukuo, Puyi. In this very space where the prime minister once gazed, Japanese tourists uneasily shift their eyes, perhaps sheepishly take a few pictures (if any), and leave the museum without spending much time as if to escape the strong stares of their Chinese tour guides.

It is a space where many Japanese discover how the gaze of the Chinese defines who they are and makes them keenly aware of their national inheritance and moral debt.[91] The inverted gaze of the locals turns the Changchun cityscape into an urban theater for the visiting Japanese, who find themselves performing on stage. Spectators are thus turned into the spectacle: Japanese visitors, with the intention of "seeing history," find themselves an integral part of the history they expected to see. As impromptu actors, they project the moral economy between China and Japan onto this space and situate themselves within the *postimperial* topography of guilt.

Those who lived through the Manchukuo era, in particular, cannot hide their strong discomfort in being looked at by their Chinese tour guides. When I worked as a guide at the Palace Museum, many Japanese visitors did not hide their sigh of great relief when they found out that I was Japanese. Suzuki Sachio, a man in his sixties, often travels to Changchun on business, but his feeling of discomfort and uneasiness does not disappear, no matter how many times he visits the city. When Suzuki discovered that I, who appeared in front of him to lead a three-hour-long guided tour of the museum, was Japanese, he smiled weakly with a big sigh: "So you're actually Japanese? Thank goodness! To be honest, I was thinking that it would be quite uncomfortable to walk through this kind of history with a Chinese tour guide. Young people like you can probably face it objectively as historical facts. But for me, it's not that easy. After all, I spent my youth in the midst of this history—this history is part of my upbringing. It's really not that easy to face the past." Similar comments abound. Takeda Kazuo, a man born in the 1940s who was visiting Northeast China for the first time, told me,

> I felt quite uneasy when I visited the Fake Manchukuo Museum in the former State Council building. A Japanese-speaking Chinese tour guide accompanied me to explain the exhibit, which was so difficult to take. Especially when, standing in front of a photograph capturing the moment of a Japanese soldier about to cut off the head of a Chinese who knelt in front of a big hole, into which his decapitated head would fall, she proclaimed in broken Japanese, "This is a historical fact." It was uneasy enough to walk through these terrifying depictions of violence committed by the Japanese, and it was even worse to be in that position I was in, standing next to that young Chinese woman. I really didn't know how to respond.

The inverted gaze and the voice of the Chinese tour guide made Takeda keenly self-aware of his Japaneseness and national inheritance. Instead of seeing the atrocity exhibit in front of his eyes, he found himself seeing himself through the imagined gaze of his Chinese guide. In this shift from seeing to being seen, what he ended up "seeing" was not the representation of historical events captured in the exhibition but his own positioning within the Sino-Japanese moral economy. Cathy Caruth would describe Takeda's experience as "the betrayal of sight": the act of seeing atrocity photographs shifts the experience from seeing what actually happened through its photographic representation to seeing oneself in relation to that depicted past.[92] Yet Takeda's experience did not lead to what Caruth calls "*moral* betrayal within the act of sight."[93] Instead, it led to a betrayal of moral debt made visible through the workings of the inverted gaze. He was made aware of a latent sense of moral inferiority vis-à-vis his Chinese tour guide, who was his daughter's age and who seemed to be intently judging his response, as if he were a representative of the Japanese people. Similar to the experiences of the Japanese high school students, the primacy of visual experience in the idea of "seeing real history" quickly gave away to Takeda's social experience within the museum space, which positioned him within the postimperial topography of guilt.

Such social dynamics of "seeing real history" translate into a different mode of generational transmission of difficult pasts than that observed by Marianne Hirsch. Hirsch's study primarily involves the second generation's encounters with photographic representations of the Holocaust, often in isolation within a domestic space. In contrast, the experiences of Japanese tourists in Changchun take place in a public space, where the act of seeing atrocity photography itself becomes performative, in which the gaze of the audience—local Chinese, in this case—is an integral part of the theatrical act of transmission. Photography mediates this generational transmission in Changchun, as in Hirsch's study. But photography and other forms of representation (such as artifacts, wax figures, and restored buildings) are props within the larger theatrical setting where this transmission takes place.

These representations in themselves do not propel the transmission. It is the underlying moral debt (expressed in the form of felt lack, missing pages, and unaccounted-for losses)—which is articulated through the workings of the inverted gaze—that propels this generational transmission through the mediation of representational forms. It is this refractive structure of transmission in a manner of *awase kagami*, driven by the underlying moral economy, that characterizes the processes of inheritance of loss in Changchun.[94]

However, the accusatory gaze felt keenly by many Japanese tourists is partially imaginary. Many Japanese-speaking Chinese tour guides, of all ages, told me that they found it was not a simple task to give tours about the history of Manchukuo to Japanese visitors because they feared making the Japanese too uncomfortable. Tian Fei, a veteran tour guide in his midfifties who speaks near-perfect Japanese and who belongs to the first generation of Japanese-speaking tour guides in the People's Republic of China, told me that he did not want to emphasize the Japanese atrocities too much in a tour, "since those Japanese tourists are here on vacation, not for education or torture. I don't want them to feel uncomfortable." Then Tian recounted his initial visit to Japan in 1982 as part of the first group of Chinese tour guides invited by one of the largest Japanese travel agencies, Kinki Nihon Tourist. A group of thirty Chinese tour guides visited major tourist attractions all over Japan in a ten-day period: "It was shocking to be in Japan from totally underdeveloped China. I was particularly impressed by the bullet train, but also by the level of service and the general standard of living. Besides, the Japanese people were extremely nice to us Chinese. *I think that their sense of guilt was translated into their kindness* [emphasis mine]." Despite his claim of not emphasizing Japanese atrocities to elicit a sense of guilt during his tours, Tian's comment was framed within the assumed topography of guilt; that is, Japanese are indebted to Chinese within the Sino-Japanese moral economy.

A minority of tourists expressed frustration with what they saw as an attempt to tar all Japan's past actions with the brush of atrocity. Three men in their fifties and sixties, who were part of a tour organized by a local agricultural co-operative in Northeast Japan to visit Northeast China for the first time, drifted away from the other members of their group, who were nodding along to a Japanese-speaking Chinese guide's explanation of the life of Puyi. The three sat in a courtyard at the base of a stone memorial on which was inscribed, "Never Forget 9.18 (Manchurian Incident)," while looking at their group out of the corners of their eyes. Smoking cigarettes like delinquent teenagers sneaking out of school, they exchanged the following conversation in low voices:

MR. A: Manchukuo actually contributed a lot to the development of Changchun.

MR. B: After all, before Manchukuo, there was nothing here. No urban planning, no building whatsoever.

YK: (Here, I joined the conversation.) But many Chinese think that without the Japanese invasion, the Chinese economy would have developed much faster than it had.

MR. B: (taken aback by my sudden intrusion but quickly composing himself) That might be true. But even without the Japanese invasion, this country went through more than ten years of civil war between the Communists and the Guomindang, which totally ruined the country. The story is not that simple.

MR. C: In any case, the contribution of the South Manchuria Railway was enormous. Without the railway system, a city like Harbin would have remained a mere provincial city. Heilongjiang Province in particular would have missed the opportunity to be integrated into this new Chinese market economy without the railway connection. It's indeed the contribution of the South Manchuria Railway Company.

These Japanese men hoped that China would acknowledge Manchukuo's contributions to the development of infrastructure in Northeast China instead of looking only at the negative effects of the Japanese invasion. Their quiet utterances were made in private, out of earshot of the other Japanese tour members, not to mention their Chinese guide. Aware of their structural position as well as the behavior expected of them as Japanese, they released their frustrations with cigarette puffs. At the same time, their secretive sharing of their sentiments reflects and assumes the existence of their sense of moral debt as Japanese, despite their conspicuous sense of superiority over what they see as underdeveloped China.

In this simultaneous presence of moral inferiority and economic superiority the locals find the arrogance and irresponsibility of their former colonizer, often labeled as "right-wing." What this labeling often neglects is that an arrogant display of superiority can be a way of compensating for a sense of moral debt, driven by a strong desire to settle accounts. Many locals often ask why Japanese do not acknowledge past injustices or why they deny the history of atrocities. Yet these questions are usually misplaced precisely because the issue is not acknowledgement per se but rather the form that acknowledgement takes, which, as we have seen earlier, can take the shape of revisionism as much as memory work.

The urban space of Changchun forces Japanese visitors to face the difficult challenge of coming to terms with the past. Keenly aware of the gaze of the local Chinese, be it imagined or real, they face the question as *Japanese*, the inheritors of the past, caught in the moral economy of debt, which positions them structurally vis-à-vis Chinese. Under the shared assumption of their Japaneseness and the inheritance that comes with this scarred nationality, these tourists, the consumers of urban spectacles, find themselves turned into the object of the Other's gaze. They seek appropriate utterances and behaviors within unwritten scripts. In this anxiety-filled endeavor in this uncanny urban space, their reactions are easily absorbed into a relatively "safe" narration of the nation, which is to feel ashamed of the past as Japanese and to feel responsible for it.

For postgeneration Japanese, the sense of guilt therefore lies not in historical guilt itself but rather in its *lack*. Japanese experience in Changchun is a form of redemption for a primal lack in Japan's postwar—namely, the "historical amnesia" that has led to the inability to take responsibility for past violence. Their sense of moral inferiority ironically derives from their understanding that guilt is barely articulated back home. The missing pages are acknowledged as missing, which should imply a recognition of the moment when the pages disappeared. Yet Japanese visitors to Changchun do not know when the pages were cut out. It never came up in our conversations that Japanese society had actually been filled with the unarticulated guilt of the nation.[95]

THE DOUBLE INHERITANCE

What comes to light through these encounters is the structure of generational transmission of unaccounted-for pasts. Contrary to their expectations, Japanese postgenerations in Changchun encountered not so much a postmemory of the original violence in the form of missing pages but rather colonial inheritance, which announces its arrival through a refractive structure of transmission under the inverted gaze of local Chinese. In the manner of *awase kagami*, this refractive structure reveals more than the loss incurred through the original violence that Japanese visitors expect to find within the Changchun cityscape. Mirrored refractions display to the postgeneration Japanese what I call the *double inheritance* made visible within the landscape of after empire.

The double inheritance that emerges through this refractive structure encompasses at least two types of doubles: The first is temporal, because the confrontation with Japanese colonial violence evokes the politics of imperial amnesia *after* the demise of the Japanese Empire, what is often referred to in Japan as the question of "war responsibility" (*sensō sekinin*) that the postwar generation acknowledges in Changchun often reveals itself as "postwar responsibility" (*sengo sekinin*), indicating compounded debts accrued through after-empire inaction (i.e., the lack of postimperial reckoning).[96] Under the gaze of local Chinese, who hold the second mirror, the sense of moral debt arising from the original violence is compounded by the recognition of the lack of postwar efforts to account for it. In this process, the guilt of the war-generation Japanese is repackaged into a compounded moral debt inherited by the postgeneration. The generational transmission of the original loss thus reveals new forms of loss as part of the inheritance that postgeneration Japanese have no choice but to accept. The double inheritance in temporal terms thus challenges the assumed understanding of which loss is transmitted.

The second doubleness is expressed in geographic terms: Japanese and Chinese tasks of coming to terms with colonial modernity necessarily implicate each other, and dealing with one's own colonial inheritance inevitably requires dealing with the other's inheritance. The Japanese college students' encounter with Japanese inheritance was accompanied by their encounter with Chinese inheritance. Their search for missing pages led them to realize how their efforts to come to terms with the past were intricately linked to parallel Chinese efforts. Otherwise, as they discover to their disappointment, the letters to repay the moral debt are returned to the senders. Filling in the missing pages by seeing the historical Truth, they reluctantly fathom, is not sufficient for belated repayment of moral debt, as they had hoped.

While colonial inheritance arrives in the name of the nation, its arrival also suggests that a nation-based mnemonic community does not suffice to address deferred reckoning. The double inheritance in geographic terms makes apparent the mutually implicated nature of colonial inheritance and then questions the assumed mnemonic communities, separated in the name of the nation. On the one hand, the topography of guilt that becomes visible to Japanese tourists in Changchun reaffirms the nation-state-based mnemonic community in the form of the perpetrator's lineage. On the other hand, their experiences in Changchun expose the limits of such mnemonic communities' ability to address delayed reckoning while simultaneously suggesting the emergence of a different mnemonic community of postgenerations across national boundaries, as most evidently seen in the case of the high school students I have described. The dynamics among the Chinese and Japanese high school students at the Palace Museum suggest that the crux of coming to terms with the double inheritance precisely involves a challenge to the assumed mnemonic communities, separated by the lineage of perpetrator and victim nations. Their shared experience of facing their double inheritance starkly contrasts the shadowboxing of Japanese college students, whose letters to repay moral debts are returned to the senders.

What started as Japanese postwar generations' attempts to seek postmemory—the deferred arrival of the knowledge of past catastrophe no longer easily accessible to second- and third-generation Japanese—ends up revealing colonial inheritance: of losses sustained through colonial modernity, of losses incurred after the empire's demise, of Japanese and Chinese losses. The colonial inheritance, then, manifests itself to the postwar generations as *their* contemporary issue, rather than marking their delayed relation to the original events that took place before their time. In displaying the past through the touristic configuration of Manchukuo remnants, the Changchun cityscape reveals to postgeneration Japanese not so much their past but their future-oriented present.

RETURN TO SENDER

Postgeneration Chinese and Manchukuo Remnants

Even when material traces are present, the past can become invisible once its remainders become an integral part of everyday life. For many postgeneration local Chinese, the cityscape no longer symbolizes Japanese colonial power. During one cab ride to work at the Palace Museum, my conversation with the driver, in his midthirties, touched on the subject of history. As soon as he found out that I was Japanese and overcame his shock at finding out that a Japanese was employed at the Palace Museum as an official guide ("How did you get into *that* as a Japanese?"), his eyes started to sparkle. Talking to me without hiding his curiosity and excitement while navigating the morning rush-hour traffic with quick lane switches, he said, "So many things are much more advanced in Japan than China, aren't they? China is still so backward. It's all because of the corruption." Although corruption had been a persistent problem throughout Chinese history, he said, the Communist Party was particularly bad, and ordinary Chinese could do nothing about it. "For example, that's a government car in front of us. Even if they don't obey the traffic rules, the police won't say anything." Then, abruptly changing the subject, he said, "Many Chinese think that if Japan were to start a war again, it'll attack China." "But why? It doesn't make any sense that Japan would want to attack China now," I responded. He explained, "Well, what common people think often doesn't make sense. But in Northeast China, many Chinese, especially elderly people, hate Japanese, so they think that way, you know." He pointed at Renmin Street, the largest boulevard in the city, which stretches south from the train station: "These streets were designed by the Japanese, you know." I inquired, "When you see the buildings built by the Japanese, how do you feel?" He replied, "Japan is cool!" Taken aback, I had to ask him what he meant. "They built those buildings that last for decades. Look at the buildings built by the Chinese," he said, pointing at a group of gray, worn-down apartment buildings typical of the 1980s and 1990s, although they looked at least thirty or forty years older with their rusted balconies and cracked and stained façades. "They are in terrible shape, really awful, and without any style, you see." It had never occurred to me that some Chinese would think of historical structures from the "fake Manchukuo" era as embodying advanced technology and design in contrast to the local construction of a much more recent era. A moment later, he murmured, "Actually, I like Japan. So many things are advanced in Japan. For example, Japanese society has a functioning legal system." Then he resumed talking about corruption and how ordinary Chinese could not do anything about it.

That afternoon in the Palace Museum, I asked Li Min, one of my Chinese coworkers in his early twenties, what he thought of when he looked at the architectural remainders of fake Manchukuo. His answer, "China's backwardness," echoed what I had heard during my morning cab ride. He added, with a hint of embarrassment and uncertainty in his voice, "But China has been catching up very quickly in the past several years, hasn't it?" He had worked at the museum for five months, his first job after school. Though from Changchun, he had visited Puyi's Palace just once, on a school excursion, before taking the job. "Like many who never visit the touristy places of their hometown, I was never interested in these historical places in Changchun," he explained.

What young Chinese like Li and my cab driver project onto the material remains of Japanese imperialism is not necessarily Japan's colonial violence but Japan as a modern society and the future of China. It is the future that they project onto the same cityscape on which the Japanese project the past. A story that a Japanese woman studying in Changchun told me captures the sentiments of young Chinese. Her cab driver, who excitedly chatted with her about how advanced Japanese society was, told her with a sigh after complaining about the Communist Party, "If the Japanese had not been defeated in 1945, I would be a Japanese citizen now!" Surprised, she was not prepared to respond to such a comment, but she was struck by how seriously he seemed to have meant it.

After several similar encounters, I decided to meet more college-age Chinese. During discussions I had with students in both undergraduate and graduate seminars in the Department of History at Changchun's Jilin University, one of the top history departments in the nation, I was struck by how little they knew of the history of Manchukuo. This was a revelation, since the Chinese school curriculum stresses what it calls "patriotic education," which involves informing students about the anti-Japanese struggles of the early CCP through readings, films, and field trips. Many college students, who go through a grueling competition to get into universities, know very well the outlines of history, which are part of their examinations. Yet many of them know little about what happened in Changchun, Manchukuo's former capital, in part because local history has long been neglected in the curriculum. For these students, colonial-era architecture produces no special effect, and some of them are even unaware of its existence in the city. Yet many share a sense of intellectual superiority—claiming that they know history while the Japanese do not. Unsure if what I had heard was typical, I asked around among history professors and officials in the local government's Department of Education, and they confirmed my findings. The problems arising from this simultaneous excess and absence of "history"—on the one hand, a sense of interpretive privilege, and on the other, a lack of historical understanding due to standardization of historical interpretations—are now being acknowledged by Chinese intellectuals and government officials. In the fall of 2003, the Changchun municipal government established a planning committee for a new local-history curriculum.

As we have seen, some younger Chinese project the image of Japan as an advanced modern society onto the architectural remainders of Manchukuo and contrast them with China's underdevelopment. Their odes to Japanese progress referenced not only postwar Japan for its rapid recovery and economic development but also Japan during the Manchukuo era for its technological and managerial prowess. They often pointed to buildings built in the 1980s and 1990s, which looked even older, to illustrate China's backwardness in comparison with Japan, many of whose structures from the 1930s still look solid, even grand. Their comments reflected strong dissatisfaction with the authorities, and, as with the taxi driver, the conversation very often turned to the topic of political corruption in the Chinese government.[97]

Other young Chinese, meanwhile, expressed total indifference to the architectural inheritance from the Manchukuo era. They had, in the words of one, "no particular impressions of these edifices." A casual conversation with a local Chinese man in his thirties I had just met at a neighborhood market turned to my research in the city. He firmly stated, "I'm aware that Japan has problems with history textbooks and all that. But that's a problem at the government level. No matter how much money you put into it, and no matter how much energy you put into it, you can never know the real history." To my question about what younger Chinese thought of the remainders of fake Manchukuo, such as the ministry buildings and the Palace Museum, he replied, "I'm thirty-three years old. I was born in 1969. I tell you, our generation born after 1949, especially those of us in our twenties and thirties, don't know anything about history. For those in their sixties, seventies, and eighties, it's a different story, because they experienced the war. But for us, it's past, and besides, we really don't know anything. Even at school now, we don't really learn about that history much anymore.

Honestly, we don't care so much about it; it's not so important for us." One young Changchunite confessed even deeper ignorance to me: "Oh, those buildings were built by the Japanese? I used to think that they were ethnic Manchu architecture!" It is truly an irony of history that the emperor's crown style, which once symbolized the power and authority of the Japanese puppet state, is now often misinterpreted as indigenous. As if to reflect such perceptions, on Xinmin Boulevard, which is lined by emperor's-crown-style structures, stand two new buildings—one, the headquarters of a local newspaper, the other, a new high school—both echoing the motifs of the emperor's crown style (figure 3.5). There is a stark contrast here with the intense opposition triggered in Germany in the 1980s by a plan for a postmodern twist on designs of Albert Speer, Hitler's chief architect.[98]

At the Palace Museum, I often encountered Chinese tourists who seemed to see the palace as the remainder of the Qing dynasty instead of the Japanese puppet state. For instance, I overheard a young father explaining to his six- or seven-year-old son in front of the "Never Forget 9.18" memorial in the main courtyard, "This is the fake palace of the last emperor of China." To such Chinese tourists, the place symbolizes less the Japanese invasion of China than the vanished imperial Chinese culture—after empire of a different sort. Even though it has become easier for common people to travel, tourism remains a privileged activity in China. Most tour groups go to the Palace Museum not for education but for leisure, which takes the form of admiring the ornate culture of the Qing dynasty. When I shared this observation with my Chinese colleagues, they laughed at my puzzled expression and said, "Oh, yeah, these Chinese tourists don't care much about the history of Manchukuo. They did that stuff at school and that's that. You have to understand that many of them are here to see Qing culture. That photo stand where you can get a picture taken in a Qing costume is very popular, you see. We often skip the atrocity exhibition because many tourists don't care." The exhibition halls devoted to the fourteen years of Japanese rule were indeed usually empty except for Japanese and Korean tourists, while other sections of the museum, especially the restored living quarters of Puyi and his family and the special exhibit of the emperor's belongings ("The Historical Artifacts of the Imperial Palace of the Puppet State"), were flooded with Chinese tourists speaking many different dialects.

Local Perceptions of the Japanese Tourists

Despite apparent indifference to Manchukuo remainders, local Chinese are quite critical and skeptical of how the Japanese have dealt with the past.

3.5 A newly constructed high school building that echoes the emperor's crown style of the Manchukuo era: Some newly constructed buildings, such as this high school building, echo the emperor's crown style from the Manchukuo era. Photo by author, 2002.

Regardless of their status, educational level, or generation, many voice their dissatisfaction through comments such as "The Japanese know very little about the war" or "The Japanese people regard the war with China as a just war." My attempt to get a job as a museum guide at the Fake Manchukuo Museum located in the former State Council building gave me a glimpse of such sentiments. Unlike the Palace Museum with more than one hundred employees, the Fake Manchukuo Museum is a small-scale, less professionally curated museum, and it lacks the flamboyant flair of the Palace Museum. Walking through a grand, arched-stone entrance, a visitor steps into a dingy souvenir store, which also functions as the reception area, its walls covered with boxed ginseng root and powdered deer horn (for medicinal use), both regional specialties. As described earlier, a tour guide is automatically assigned to each visitor. Most of the guides, all young women, speak some Japanese or Korean in addition to Chinese. Seeing me chatting with my guide after a brief tour, a soft-mannered elderly man with thin white hair suggested that I join a group of guides who were hanging out in the souvenir shop, sipping herbal tea—another item on sale in the store—and looking quite bored (it was before the tourist season). It turned out that he was an advisor to the museum, a retired professor of history at Jilin University, and he spoke fluent Japanese because he had grown up in Changchun under Japanese rule.

Professor Wu happily agreed to ask the museum director on my behalf to see about working as a tour guide for the season. A few days later, he introduced me to the director, who was obviously reluctant to meet me. A standoffish man in his early fifties, he did not want to talk much and told me that my working at the museum would be "inconvenient" (*bufangbian*). I pressed him about what he meant by "inconvenient"—whether my being Japanese was an issue. But he simply repeated the same phrase, and our meeting ended. Later, when I visited the museum again, Professor Wu opened his arms and greeted me with a big smile. He was very apologetic about what had happened, telling me several times in a near-whisper how he felt upset by the director's behavior. Lowering his voice even more and switching to Chinese, he added that he was upset more generally about the attitude and management style of this museum. "I thought it would be a good thing for our museum if you worked with us," he continued, "but this place is very conservative." "Don't mention it," I replied. "I understand that some people are sensitive about foreigners, especially the Japanese, being involved in the issue of history in this country." He smiled weakly, responding, "But it's much better this way for you, now that you've arranged to work for the Palace Museum. It's a real museum, much more professional, and you will have access to much richer materials there. But again, our director's attitude is really regrettable. What's in his head are Japanese right-wingers." "It's sad that many Chinese think that most Japanese share a right-wing ideology," I said. To this, he replied with a sigh, "I know, I know, these right-wing people consist of only a small fraction of the Japanese population, but here in China, most people don't know this. Don't be hasty. Things like this need time, and you can't be impatient. Let's change the situation slowly, shall we?"

In a society where the majority sees the Japanese as supporters of right-leaning ideologies, the thousands of Japanese flocking to Changchun remain a mystery to those who have not had meaningful interactions with Japanese. Many locals, especially younger ones, did not hide their sense of skepticism about these visitors to Changchun: "I'm sure that they've never heard of these historical facts back in Japan," said one—a typical comment. Others expressed their pessimistic projection: "I'm afraid that those Japanese tourists don't believe in the historical facts portrayed in those museums even after visiting them." After hours of discussions with university students at

Jilin University, I concluded that these comments represented a widely held belief. As one student put it, "Since Japan is a democratic country, what is expressed by Japanese politicians who refuse to accept historical facts such as the Nanjing Massacre reflects what the majority of Japanese people think." For many Chinese, the fear they project onto the Japanese reflects a displaced distrust of their own government and media. The locals had little way of knowing how the Japanese visitors experienced confusion and guilt in their encounter with Changchun's urban space. Instead, the locals imagined that the Japanese saw the backwardness of Chinese society or the negation of Japan's colonial history, which often reflected the locals' own anxieties about Chinese society.[99]

CITY OF MONOLOGUES

The Changchun cityscape thus reflects not only the historical but also the moral topography of Sino-Japanese relations. Both Japanese visitors and Chinese locals project various images onto Changchun's urban space, yet their images rarely intersect. Rather, we find an anxiety-filled space in which the postgenerations of each country are full of unease about what the other is projecting. Former Manchuria's shift from virtual to real for postwar Japanese makes them keenly aware of their structural position within the Sino-Japanese moral economy. Yet absent a dialogue with the locals, who hold the refractive mirror for the visiting Japanese, the Japanese desire to come to terms with the past often remains a letter that is returned to the sender, while Japanese shadowbox with their own image of local Chinese. Due to the fundamental lack of shared understanding as to what it means to come to terms with their common past, what seemed like a unique space of (re) encounter with the past often ended up reinforcing stereotypes of the Other. What plays out in the urban space of Changchun is a theater of monologues.

The structure of generational transmission that we have seen in Changchun points to the intersection of Japanese and Chinese inheritances as the crux of the deferred reckoning for the postgenerations. Seen through the doubleness contained within colonial inheritance, attempts by postgenerations to come to terms with unaccounted-for pasts simultaneously reaffirm and defy assumptions about mnemonic communities and certainties about which past is being transmitted. The case of Changchun suggests how Japanese and Chinese attempts to come to terms with the past are intricately connected, implicated, and affected by each other—dynamics that are the subject of exploration in the next chapter. We shall see in Dalian what happens when generational transmission takes place within an actively dialogical economic environment in the context of rapidly growing Japanese direct investment. Whereas in Changchun the touristic consumption of preserved urban space became the site of this transfer, in Dalian the unfolding production relations in reconfigured urban and industrial space becomes the site for a different structure of generational transmission of loss.

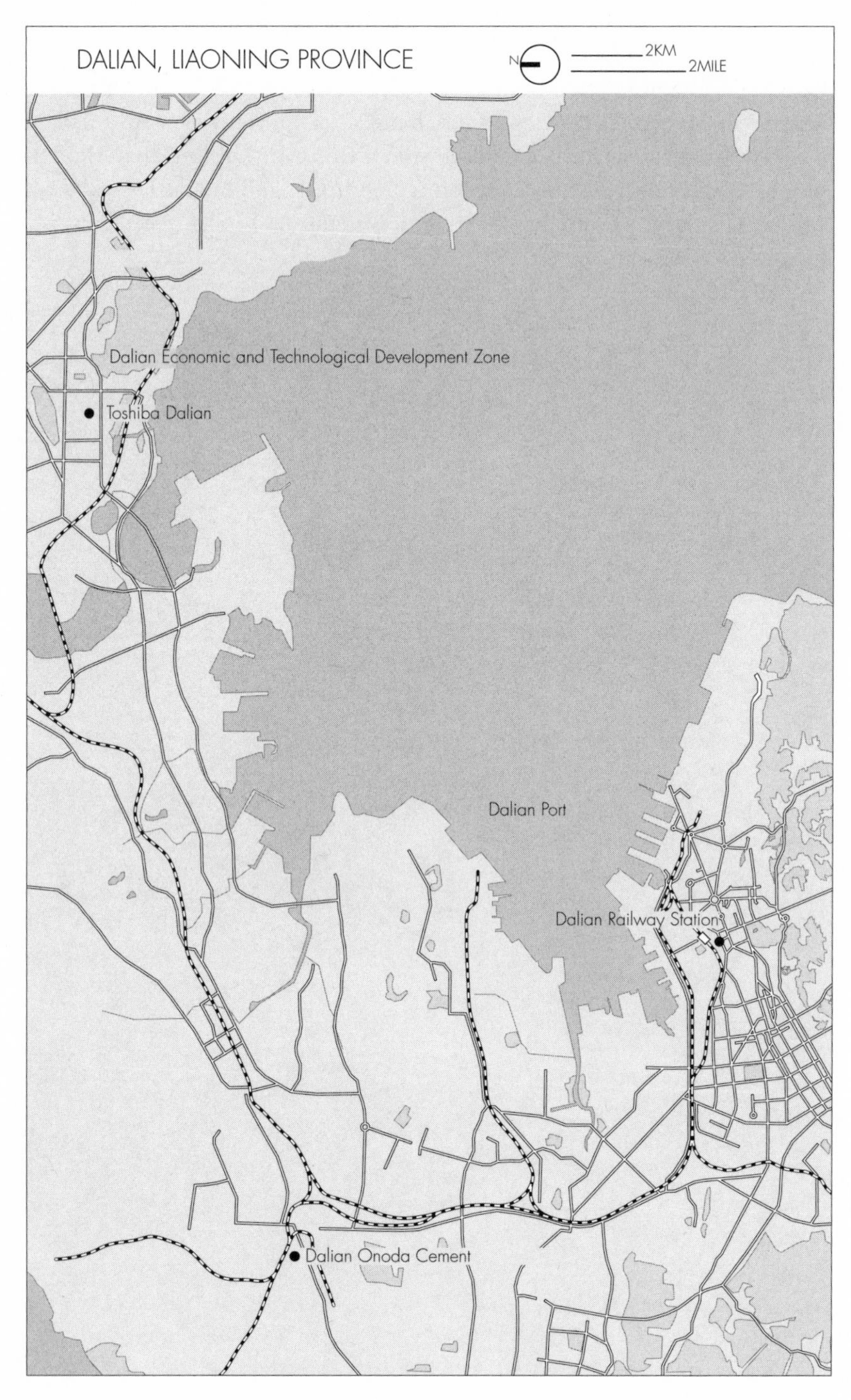

Map 6 Dalian, Liaoning Province

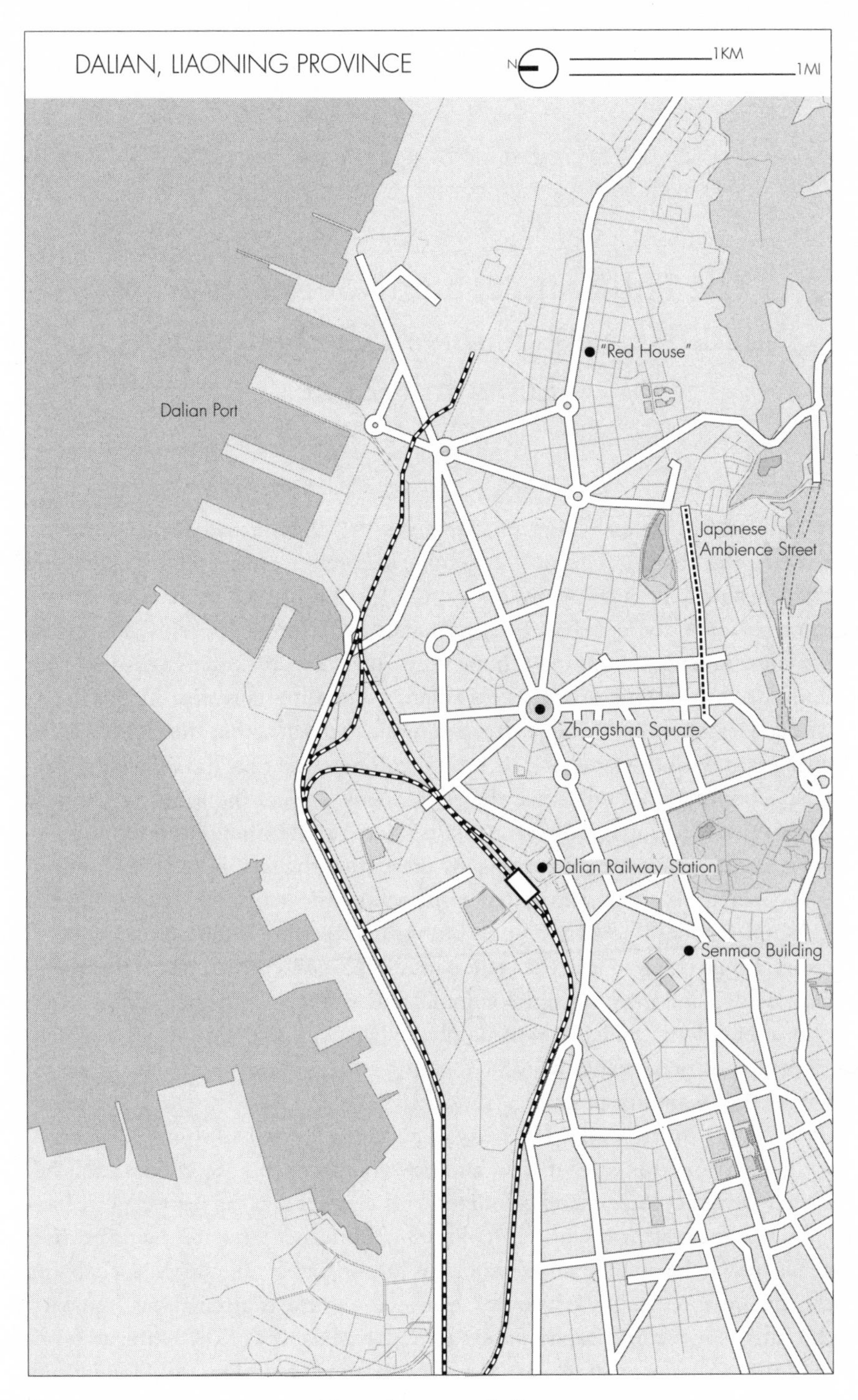

Map 7 downtown Dalian

CHAPTER FOUR

The Political Economy of Redemption: Middle-Class Dreams in the Dalian Special Economic Zone

"Dalian is neither China nor Japan, is it?" (*Dairen wa Chūgoku demo Nihon demo nai desho?*), Li Yanjie, a Chinese white-collar employee of a Japanese shipping company in her midthirties, uttered matter-of-factly in informal, friendly Japanese. Unconsciously switching between Chinese and Japanese, she was chatting with me while taking a break in a high-rise office building overlooking downtown Dalian, a booming port city in Northeast China. Her comment encapsulates a complicated dance that the city of Dalian engages in with the Japanese, its former colonizer, as they have developed robust economic relations since the early 1990s. One of the fourteen Chinese cities opened to foreign direct investment in 1984, Dalian has attracted predominantly Japanese corporations. By presenting the city as a "land of unlimited opportunity," a portrayal that eerily echoes the language once used by the Imperial Japanese government to promote investment and state-sponsored emigration to Manchuria, the Dalian municipal government has orchestrated a citywide capitalization of its colonial inheritance, from the incorporation of former colonial industries to supplying Japanese corporations with a high-quality and inexpensive workforce equipped with Japanese-language skills. Under the banner of pursuing "modern life" (*xiandai shenghuo*), such concerted efforts have resulted in a cityscape suffused with all things Japanese.

Set within this site of new and developing economic cooperation between former colonizer and colonized, this chapter and the next explore how Dalian's engagement with its colonial inheritance and its capitalization sheds new light on China's economy. While speculation, which has become the driving force behind the new Chinese economy, is often associated with the future, my ethnography points to a pivotal aspect of the Chinese economy that speculates on its past. On questions of colonial history or relations

4.1 Zhongshan Square, the central square in downtown Dalian, with colonial-era buildings: Photo by author, 2003.

with Japan, Dalian positions itself differently than the other cities we have examined; it uses its self-described exceptional status to explain its vibrant economy, which relies heavily on its ties with Japan. This produces a moral economy symbiotic with the formal economy—I call this symbiosis a *political economy of redemption*—that achieves a level of reconciliation between Japan and China seemingly beyond reach in Changchun (chapter 4). This reconciliation, however, is premised on a selective use of the past that does not acknowledge colonial violence—a tactic that ends up highlighting the very past it seeks to elide (chapter 5).

This chapter examines how Dalian seeks to turn its colonial inheritance into capital not only though the reclaiming of colonial-era architecture, as in Harbin and Changchun, but also through incorporating colonial industries and narratives allowing its people to capitalize on their skills in the new global marketplace. Where in Changchun we have seen the touristic consumption of reconfigured space, in Dalian we shall explore production relations unfolding in reconfigured space (figure 4.1). We will see how the city's use of Japan through urban renewal to showcase "modern life," local historiographical debates on the city's "colonial" history, the narrative of Dalian exceptionalism and the discourse of *suzhi* (quality), and the aggressive incorporation of Japanese corporations into Dalian's special economic zone all point to how the everyday pursuit of middle-class modern life, from factory floors to karaoke clubs, has become a primary site for coming to terms with the city's colonial history.

The case of Dalian demonstrates that the *political economy of redemption* is a critical yet underexplored site of reckoning, made visible through the lens of after empire. Dalian's future-oriented economy is in fact infused with desires for redemption of inherited losses. We shall see how the supposedly rational formal economy has become a constant reminder of the underlying moral economy and accompanying unpaid debts, propelling desires from both Chinese and Japanese sides to reckon with what remains unaccounted for through day-to-day economic activities.

INCORPORATING JAPAN: "MODERN LIFE" AND CHINA'S NEW URBAN MIDDLE CLASS

High levels of energy, excitement, and expectation filled the fourth Dalian Housing Fair in 2004, held in a modern convention center and crowded like a rush-hour subway. More than thirty developers lured potential buyers with meticulously prepared scale models, glossy brochures, and promotional videos portraying the sophisticated life of the urban middle class. Phrases like "urban ambience" (*dushi fengqing*) and "urban life" (*dushi shenghuo*) danced on banners and colorful brochures. The cover of the full-color official housing-fair brochure made the promise of "Leading you into a new modern life." On display was not just the life of a newly emerging urban class but also a life elsewhere, outside of China, as the names of these large-scale housing complexes attested: Nanshan Japanese Ambience Street, European Village, and Italian Manor, complete with the Little Oxford international bilingual kindergarten.[1] One exhibition for a development called Singapore Garden was especially crowded with people eager to get the information package, which came with a fake passport with an inset picture of the apartment and a colorful brochure cheerfully encouraging "emigration to Singapore Garden."

With their careful composition, these brochures define, articulate, and encapsulate the lifestyle of the new urban middle class. The amenities—such as gyms, conference and recreational rooms, underground parking, and twenty-four-hour security—define the material standards of this coveted class. Each apartment's floor plan and description articulates a new and expected form of family life. With the advertising slogan, "The new coordinate of urban life," one developer claims to set "a model for the new urban lifestyle." A 1,800-square-feet three-bedroom apartment that sold for $93,000 consisted of a spacious kitchen, an enormous dining room and living room, a large library/guest room, a master bedroom as large as the living room with floor-to-ceiling curved windows overlooking a garden, a spacious master bathroom with a Jacuzzi and a walk-in closet, and a second bedroom with a full bathroom.

Private life being as important as work life, the home is a space for enjoying the pursuit of culture, creativity, and family life. One developer advertises its apartment layout as a "refined white-collar condominium," and the brochure appeals in poetic language to those who have succeeded in China's new economic system. The description eschews the image of the socialist worker and cherishes those who appreciate luxury, creativity, freedom, leisure, and private life. Another developer trumpets that its service "exempts you from wasting your energy by worrying about daily chores." Its new development, European Village, provides residents with a cleaning service for "hygiene, security, and maintenance." The brochure proclaims, "You realized one day that 'life can actually be this beautiful!'" The brochure's inset photograph is of a family dining room where two uniformed young concierges have just brought a cake and flowers for the resident's daughter's birthday. The young girl is dressed in a pink satin dress, while the father greets the concierges in his pajamas. At the dining table sit likewise nicely dressed small girls with beautifully wrapped presents. It portrays a family-oriented lifestyle of a leisure class, who are served by others so they might direct their creative energy into cultural and economic activities.

As in Harbin, Dalian's urban landscape is dominated by European-style structures from the early twentieth century, most of which were built by the Russians and the Japanese as a way of demonstrating their modernity during their successive periods of control over the city between 1899 and 1945. While prominent colonial-era structures have been restored and landmarked in recent years, many dilapidated structures are rapidly being torn down and replaced by housing developments and office buildings for the new middle class. The vibrant housing market provides a site for the domestic and spatial instantiation of emergent desires and aspirations and goes hand in hand with the new corporate workspaces. On weekends in downtown Dalian's pedestrian-only commercial district, local bank employees in uniform, often accompanied by loud music, hand out flyers for mortgage and other loan programs offering the promise of "modern life." Advertisements for new residential developments adorn the pages of local daily newspapers, which devote considerable space to columns on interior decoration, communicating that owning a tastefully decorated apartment is a marker of culture and civilization (*wenming*).

Japan as Style

The hot housing market is an integral part of the efforts by the Dalian municipal government to foster an urban middle class through citywide urban renewal. With tax revenue from foreign investment in the Dalian Economic and Technological Development Zone (*kaifaqü*, or Zone, for short), which was created in 1985 as an experiment in a market economy, the Dalian municipal government carried out an aggressive urban-renewal program, creating a space that would attract global capital as well as nurture the new middle class. They relocated old state-run factory units from the city to the suburbs and sold these plots of land to developers, who turned them into new commercial and high-end residential districts. The government used the revenue from the land sales for relocating and updating the state-run factories, renovating dilapidated colonial-era structures, and creating parks and greenery. With this well-thought-out mechanism for utilizing foreign investment, most of which came from Japan, Dalian succeeded in drastically renewing its cityscape, creating an urban theater for newly defined consuming and producing subjects. The municipal government of Dalian turned ghosts from the past into fantasies for modern life.

Incorporation of Japanese capital into the citywide celebration of modern life has been accompanied by the incorporation of modernity in the image of Japan. A Japanese-owned and -styled department store in front of the train station is one of the city's most popular, and it adds an international flair by using Chinese, Japanese, and English for in-store announcements. In the packed basement food court, families and couples enjoy Japanese foods, from sushi to curry rice to eel rice bowls, for the price of a McDonald's Happy Meal (17 RMB, approximately $2)—not cheap, but something they can afford once in a while as a special treat. The city now has many fashionable cafes, some of which closely resemble those in Tokyo. In many of these cafes, young Chinese waitstaff greet you with a chorus of "*irasshaimase!*" (Welcome!) in heavily accented Japanese, a sign of contemporary cool, despite the fact that (or maybe because) many of the cafes are actually owned by Taiwanese.[2] At lunchtime, office workers in fashionable suits pour out from the Senmao Building, one of the upscale office buildings in downtown Dalian, where most of the tenants are brand-name Japanese corporations. One after another, members of the new middle class are picked up by a prized Japanese or European car with either a chauffeur or their partner in the driver's seat. Chinese editions of Japanese fashion magazines such as *Oggi, CanCam*, and *Ray* are featured at bookstands and set fashion trends for the emerging class of *bailin* (white-collar workers). These Chinese editions often carry feature articles on successful Chinese businesswomen, portraying them as intelligent, sophisticated, and beautiful cosmopolitan globetrotters who boost their careers by studying abroad, mostly in Japan and the United States.

The large presence of Japanese corporations in Dalian has resulted in what is known as "Tokyo Street," lined with Japanese restaurants and bars. One can mistake it for a side street in downtown Tokyo catering to worn-out corporate warriors, in which alcohol, home-style comfort food, and attentive service by young female companions and a mother-figure owner provide alternatives to the salarymen's alienated home lives at a fraction of what they would pay in Tokyo. At lunchtime, Chinese and Japanese employees from nearby office buildings pack these establishments; the sounds of both languages mix with the sound of chopsticks busily shuttling down now enormously popular Japanese food. The popularity of things Japanese in Dalian goes far beyond the cuisine and the young women who mimic Tokyo fashion and lifestyles. Stepping into the Senmao Building is like stepping into a skyscraper in the Tokyo business district.

Outside the city, the Zone—originally developed to accommodate *waizi*, a neologism for foreign corporations in China (the term literally means "foreign capital")—has the feel of a late-modern incarnation of a foreign concession. As one young Chinese employee in his twenties working for a Japanese bank in the Senmao Building succinctly put it, "Dalian looks as if it has become a Japanese colony." Now that the Beijing government has decided to allow foreigners to build railroads in China, it may not be too far in the future when a foreign company will build a new railway to Dalian, an eerie echo of the way the foreign occupation of the city began at the end of the nineteenth century with the arrival of the Russians. Even the term *wenming*, civilization, itself is among the numerous concepts imported from the Japanese language in the nineteenth century, and its colloquial use today epitomizes the high stakes of the Dalian government's urban and economic policies.

Refracting Modernity along Japanese Ambience Street

Nothing epitomizes the complex role of Japan in Dalian's pursuit of modern life more than "Japanese Ambience Street," one of the new housing developments clamoring for attention at the Dalian Housing Fair. Located in the upscale Nanshan district, it is the only development that is a restored

4.2 "Japanese Ambience Street," an upscale housing district for Dalian's new middle class: "Japanese Ambience Street" is one of the upscale housing districts in downtown Dalian. The area was originally developed in the late 1910s to provide luxury houses with gardens for Japanese as well as wealthy Russians, Europeans, and some Chinese. Today, to signal its longstanding ties to Japan, the newly restored district for upper-middle-class Chinese has public statutes of Japanese women in traditional kimonos. Photo by author, 2003.

historical area of European-style houses built by the Japanese early in the twentieth century. The developer's brochure proudly proclaims that it offers the "atmosphere of a foreign country" (*yiguo qingdiao*) while noting the development's Japanese-style planning and infrastructure. Located on a sunny hillside within walking distance of downtown, the neighborhood's main street is adorned with trees and life-size statues of smiling young Japanese women in traditional kimonos, placed in front of the restored European-style houses to greet visitors and residents alike (figure 4.2). These doll-like statues mark the site's historical connection to Japan.

Apart from these statues, nothing marks the Japaneseness of the Nanshan Japanese Ambience Street, because all the buildings are European in style, despite the brochure's claim that the district "emphasizes typical and historical Japanese characteristics and culture." The same is true in other parts of the city built by the Japanese, for unlike Changchun, where the ubiquitous emperor's-crown-style architecture marks the trace of Japan's empire, in Dalian the Japanese built authentic-looking European-style structures to demonstrate their modernity to the Western imperial powers. The absence of identifiable "Japanese" architectural styles in Dalian and the presentation of modernity in the Nanshan Japanese Ambience Street, with smiling Japanese women-dolls installed to convey Japaneseness, capture the triple refractive structure of Dalian.

The image of modern life in contemporary Dalian is a product of multiple refractions, much as was the case in the early twentieth century, when, with eyes toward Europe, Russians and Japanese covered the cityscape with European-style architecture and urban planning. That Dalian's urban space was conceived as a modern showpiece from its inception attests to how externality not only is translated into newness but also seeks recognition in the gaze of others. Walking through Japanese Ambience Street, the externality in architectural style signals modernity, and the statues of Japanese women stand as if to give a nod of recognition to the modernity the residents have achieved. Modern life does not float in an abstract space but is rather enacted in an "elsewhere" that in Dalian often takes the form of the "West" refracted through the mirror held by the Japanese. Although in Changchun it was the local Chinese who held the second mirror of *awase kagami*, in Dalian we shall see another refractive image created through the mirror held by the Japanese living and working there, who in turn find themselves in the reflection of a mirror held by the Chinese. To understand these entwined refractive structures in Dalian, we have to trace its history as a city and its relationship to imperialism.

LOCATING "COLONIAL" DALIAN

The 1999 Dalian Centenary Celebration

During the buildup to its centenary celebration in 1999, the Dalian municipal government carefully observed the failure of similar centenary plans in Harbin. As I illustrated in chapter 2, the Harbin municipal government got caught up in the so-called historians' debate surrounding the city's colonial origin and ended up canceling the planned centenary celebration at the last minute in 1998. Unlike in Harbin, where the debate took place through widely publicized symposia and heated exchanges among local intellectuals in daily newspapers, the debate about the centenary preparation in Dalian took place behind closed doors within the municipal government.

Zhao Wenjun, born in 1943, is a relaxed man with the air of an intellectual rather than a government official. As a high-ranking official of the Dalian Communist Party, he took part in a committee to decide the birth date of the city. He cheerfully and lightheartedly recounted the process through which the committee members came up with a date that would exempt them from repeating the embarrassment that the Harbin municipal government went through. "In brief, the Dalian municipal government rejected the idea that Dalian was a colonial city," Zhao began.

> We investigated the cases in Shanghai, Guangzhou, Qingdao, and Harbin, and discussed when exactly the birth date of the city should be. We ruled out August 11, 1899, when Russian Emperor Nicholas II decided to make Dalian a Russian city. That was unacceptable (*shoubuliao*). So we decided to focus on when the actual construction of the city started—September 15 was when the ground was broken for the construction of the Dalian port. Then Mayor Bo Xilai—he was the mayor at that time—suggested September 19, 1899. This date sounded like a good day for the Chinese. We Chinese love the number nine, you know. This is how we set September 19, 1999, at 9:00 a.m. as the time for the centenary ceremony.

Despite Zhao's claim that the notion of Dalian as a colonial city was swiftly rejected, an internal government report on the decision-making process, circulated months before the planned centenary celebration in 1999, tells a slightly different story. It shows that the concern for the "colonialist historical perspective" (*zhimin zhuyi lishiguan*), which was the central issue in the historians' debate in Harbin, did not enter the discussion until the Dalian municipal government started looking into the cases of other cities, Harbin in particular. According to this report, the city gazetteer office began to investigate archival materials in 1995 and came up with a suggestion two years later that the construction of the Dalian port should mark the city's origin. Upon deciding the exact date, however, the office noted that it would be inappropriate to use August 11, 1899, which is when Tsar Nikolai II ordered the construction of both the Dalian port and the city. Another internal report from the spring of 1998 summarized three competing perspectives: (1) the founding date should be August 11, 1899 (although some suggested avoiding the date); (2) setting the founding date before August 1945 is unacceptable, as Dalian was under colonial rule by the Russians and the Japanese and "this period was the disgraced history of the Chinese people"; and (3) the origin of Dalian dates several hundred years further back. These perspectives corresponded to those presented in the historians' debate in Harbin, yet in Dalian, the final decision concluded that marking the city's origin as a colonial city would highlight "the nature of colonial aggression by the Russians," "the anti-imperialist spirit of the Chinese people," and "the history of how Dalian was built with difficulties and sufferings of the Chinese people." The centenary celebration thus became an official acknowledgement of Dalian's colonial roots.

In sharp contrast to Harbin, the Dalian municipal government held the city's centenary celebration with great fanfare. Despite the report's references to the colonial struggle, the decision-making process indicates that they were little more than an afterthought to justify the celebration while avoiding potential blame for holding an inappropriate historical perspective. The ceremony itself was as lighthearted as the discussion; if anything, it was not backward-looking but future-oriented. "On the day of the celebration, it rained in the morning but cleared up by ten o'clock," he recalled. "The city organized an exhibition entitled 'Overview of the Dalian Centenary' (*Dalian bainian zhanlan*) and other events for the celebration. We lined up one hundred and one local Dalianites whose age ranged from zero to a hundred years old. We also buried a time capsule containing local products. I feel that it all went pretty well."

From "Dalini" to "Dairen" to "Dalian"

As part of the centenary celebration, the municipal government published a multivolume history of Dalian under the title *Collected Works on the History of the Imperialist Invasion of Dalian* (*Diguo zhuyi qinlue Dalian shi congshu*). Its 1,700-page, two-volume centerpiece, *A Hundred-Year Modern History of Dalian* (*Dalian jin bainianshi*), carefully examines the role of colonialism in Dalian's development into a modern city.[3] In portraying its trajectory from Russian Dalini in 1899 to Japanese Dairen in 1905 to Chinese Dalian after the Japanese defeat in 1945, the authors of *A Hundred-Year Modern History of Dalian* ask, "How do we interpret the imperialist invasion?"[4] The posing of this question itself is a departure from conventional historiographical practices in Northeast Chinese cities, which often do not leave any room for interpretation but start with the assumption that imperial invasion was negative. In the preface, the authors express their concerns over revisionist history (*fandong shiguan*) in Japan, which seeks to justify colonial rule in China by arguing for the "contribution of colonialism" (*zhimin yougong*) to the country's development.[5] The book is set against this revisionist historical perspective in Japan and instead depicts Dalian in the first half of the twentieth century as a colonial city that suffered tremendously from colonial violence and exploitation.

"Colonial Dalian," however, is by no means a straightforward concept. Zhao Wenjun's recounting of the municipal government's rejection of "the idea that Dalian was a colonial city" echoes vernacular conversations among the locals, who often invoke Dalian's "special" relationship with Japan by pointing out how the city was technically a leased territory and never officially colonized, unlike other cities in Northeast China.[6]

Yet *A Hundred-Year Modern History of Dalian* takes pains to document the period of colonial rule. Although it begins with a consideration of the nature of leased territory, which was Dalian's legal status from the arrival of the Russians up to the Japanese defeat, it goes on to illustrate how Dalian nonetheless became a de facto colonial city. After the First Sino-Japanese War ended with Japanese victory in 1895, the Treaty of Shimonoseki granted the Liaodong Peninsula, where Dalian is located, to Japan. European imperial powers immediately protested through the Triple Intervention of Russia, France, and Germany, each with its own designs on China. Japan, as an aspiring imperial power, agreed to withdraw from the peninsula in exchange for a payment from the Qing government. In 1898, Russia made an agreement with the Qing government to lease the southern part of the peninsula, the Kwantung Leased Territory, for twenty-five years and started to construct the Chinese Eastern Railway to Harbin and to build a modern city, Dalian (*Dalini* in Russian), at the location of a deep, ice-free port. Under the Treaty of Portsmouth in 1905, following the Japanese victory in the Russo-Japanese War, the Japanese took over the Russian-leased territory and *Dalini* became *Dairen* (in Japanese). In 1915, as a result of the Twenty-One Demands, Japan forced the Chinese government to extend the lease to ninety-nine years. Following the establishment of the Japanese puppet state of Manchukuo in 1932, the Kwantung Leased Territory was officially transferred to Manchukuo, from which Japan subsequently leased it. *A Hundred-Year Modern History of Dalian* shows how Dalian was turned into a de facto colony by Russia and Japan despite the fact that the sovereignty over the leased territory legally belonged to China.

The major publications on the post-Liberation history of Dalian portray the city's development in accordance with the nationwide process of socialist building and transformation.[7] The conversion to a socialist economy in the 1950s, the Great Leap Forward and its failure in the late 1950s, the tremendous damage caused by the Cultural Revolution, and finally the rapid economic development since the late 1970s culminated in the 1984 decision by the Beijing government to designate Dalian as one of fourteen cities open to foreign investment. The Zone came into being in 1985. With this new phase in the city's development, one author wrote, "the half-century history of turmoil finally came to an end."[8] Yet the ambiguous and ambivalent positioning of "colonial" Dalian expressed through the city's self-portrayal reflects multiple conundrums involved in the inheritance of colonial modernity, with its attendant risks and opportunities, as we shall see next.

EMBODYING COLONIAL INHERITANCE

Dalian Exceptionalism

Locals and Japanese alike, regardless of generation, frequently told me how Dalian had a "unique relationship" to Japanese colonial aggression in China. "Actually, not everything was all that bad during the war," people of the older generation often said, recounting their personal interactions with Japanese friends or neighbors. "Because the Japanese didn't do bloody things in Dalian during the war, we Dalianites have a different attitude to Japanese than people in other parts of Northeast China, say, Changchun or Harbin," was a sentiment locals repeatedly conveyed to me, trying to explaining why "Dalianites are much friendlier to the Japanese than people in other parts of China." "And that's what we heard," confirmed Japanese working in the city, regarding this particular attitude toward them as a form of absolution for any nagging sense of moral inferiority they might feel as a result of Japan's lack of accounting for its historical responsibility.

This narrative of Dalian exceptionalism appeared over and over again in my conversations with locals. The narrative is accompanied by a sense of historical continuity, from the colonial period to the Mao era to the present, in notable contrast to Chinese national narratives, which draw a radical discontinuity either from the era of colonialism or from the Mao era. Professor Li Liangfeng at Liaoning Normal University in Dalian vividly illustrates this prevailing narrative of continuity in Dalian in his account of its history. Professor Li emphasizes how Chinese collaborators in the city during the Japanese colonial period mostly avoided persecution after the Liberation, unlike other places in China: "In Dalian, we had a rule that anyone who explained clearly (*shuo mingbai*) was pardoned for their acts during the Japanese rule. This was not the case in many other places in Northeast, where those people who had worked for the Japanese were often executed or purged. At the most pragmatic level, we couldn't have done that in Dalian, because so many people had some connection to the Japanese."

Professor Li's life trajectory is a microcosm of Dalian's unique relationship to Japan in the post-Liberation period, when the connection to Japan persisted even before the city's opening to foreign investment in 1984. He was born in 1930 to a Korean family living in Korea under Japanese rule. The family had owned a fish store in Seoul for generations but moved to Dalian for better economic prospects with the help of a relative already in the city. His father's uncle, who grew up in Osaka, Japan, and worked for the South Manchuria Railway Company, arranged for Li to attend Japanese schools in Dalian. Li's friendship with his former Japanese classmates continues even today, and after so many years of living in Dalian, he still seems more at ease in expressing himself in Japanese than in Chinese. "I cried at the news of the Japanese defeat," Professor Li recalled in his elegant Japanese, explaining how he had considered himself a loyal imperial subject during the war. "I was planning to join the Japanese Army after attending a university in Japan."

When the Japanese in Northeast China were repatriated, Japan's former Korean colonial subjects were left behind in China. From 1945 to 1946, Korean ships illegally brought salted fish to Northeast China and secretly repatriated Koreans on the way back, but Li's family remained in Dalian. Li started selling salted fish with his Japanese classmates, but the business ended when his classmates were repatriated to Japan, leaving Li behind. He went through a succession of odd jobs, from playing the drums in a dance-hall band to serving as an interpreter for Russian engineers; eventually, in the 1950s, he found work as an engineer himself. When private-sector exchanges between China and Japan resumed in 1960,[9] the Public Security Bureau sought people with Japanese proficiency to train their officers and customs officials. Li was one of three chosen to teach Japanese, which he did for five years. The three teachers were then transferred to Liaoning Normal University to start a Japanese studies program. Except during the Cultural Revolution, when he was sent down to rural Dalian to manage a factory for six years, Professor Li has been teaching Japanese at the university ever since. Many locals fluent in Japanese whom I met in Dalian were either his students or students of his students.

"I'm going to Japan next month to attend a reunion of my school," Professor Li told me excitedly at one of our meetings over coffee in a sleek Japanese-owned downtown cafe in the Senmao Building, his favorite cafe in the city. "The Dalian China-Japan Alumni Association, which consists of us graduates from Japanese schools during the Manchukuo era, now has a few hundred members, and many of us have played a significant role in municipal government, business, and academia in Dalian. Many of us reconnected with our old Japanese classmates in the 1970s, when they came back to Dalian as tourists." Professor Guo Rongji, the chairman of the alumni association and five years Li's senior, had joined us that day; he nodded at Li's account and told me how he had reconnected with his old classmates the same way. Professor Guo continued, "Because Dalian was a Japanese-leased territory, we are different from other parts of Northeast China, which became a Japanese colony."

As we have seen, this distinction between leased territory and colony, often used to explain Dalian's uniquely friendly relationship with Japan, was de-emphasized in favor of highlighting colonial violence in the official history published as part of the city's centenary celebration.[10] Yet in Professor Li's account, this distinction sets the stage for post-Liberation Dalian's sustained relationship with Japan, which came to fruition, as the narrative goes, with China's open economic policy.

What the narrative of Dalian exceptionalism produces is a sense of continuity from the era of colonialism to the present, including the Mao era. This stands in contrast to Harbin, where its "exceptional" cosmopolitanism in the early twentieth century is used to bracket the Mao era by associating the city's past glory with its future—the less said about the recent socialist past, the better. While the sense of continuity in Dalian seems to put the city more at ease with its own past, its incorporation of its colonial history also creates an odd disjunction with China's national narrative.[11]

Wang Zhaowen, the vice president of Dalian Onoda Cement, one of the prewar Japanese corporations that "returned" to Dalian after the city was opened to foreign investment, described Dalian's relationship to Japan in the language of Dalian exceptionalism and historical continuity. Born in 1953, he graduated from Beijing's elite Tsinghua University and joined a major Dalian chemical company, which became one of the investors in Dalian Onoda Cement. Wang joined Onoda Cement in 1995 and spent a year in Japan in 1997 for further training. Speaking of Dalian's relationship to Japan, he stressed how unique it was:

> Dalian has a special relationship to Japan. During the war, for example, my father worked for a Japanese shipbuilding factory in Dandong [in Northeast China]. Because he worked with the Japanese for many years, he understands some Japanese. After the war ended, in 1948, he became the factory manager. But the factory was bombed by the US during the Korean War, and he moved to Dalian, where I was born. In Dalian, most people over seventy speak some Japanese. I don't think that people in Dalian have particularly bad feelings toward Japanese. In this sense, Dalian

> is very different from other parts of China. The fact that no fighting took place in the city must explain this special situation in Dalian. Also, since the 1980s, many Japanese businesses and corporations have come to Dalian, and a widely shared understanding here is that Japanese corporations obey the law and respect individuals. I never thought twice about working with the Japanese. In addition, many families in Dalian raised Japanese orphans left behind at the end of the war. Although many of these Japanese orphans returned to Japan in the 1980s, most of us played with these Japanese kids as we grew up, so we share a sense of familiarity as well. The only thing I'm concerned about working for a Japanese corporation is that the Japanese management style is very strict, and I often worry that Chinese employees would find it difficult to adapt to that system. But other than that, I actually have nothing against working for a Japanese corporation.

What comes through in his illustration of Dalian's "special relationship to Japan" is a familiarity with Japan that has persisted throughout Dalian's history after the demise of the Japanese Empire. This example of the prevailing narrative of Dalian exceptionalism relies on *shinnichi*, a Japanese term for foreigners who possess an intimate understanding of Japan based on familiarity with the culture. *Shinnichi* does not preclude a critical stance; on the contrary, a foreigner to whom *shinnichi* applies is accorded the honor of being able to offer criticism. In this vein, many Dalianites, both older and younger, proudly proclaim that the city provides rich human resources with a high level of Japanese-language proficiency, familiarity with Japanese culture, and a friendly attitude toward Japanese. Altogether, they emphasize their high level of Japaneseness, of considerable value in a city where the majority of foreign investment comes from Japan. Many locals reason that this derives from the fact that Japan-related *rencai* (talent, human resources) was consistently appreciated in post-Liberation Dalian, in contrast to the situation in much of the rest of China during the Mao era, where it was often punished.

Nonetheless, the municipal government's initiative to invite Japanese corporations to invest in the city in the early years of the Zone was not without resistance from the local population. As Lisa M. Hoffman notes, the government decision "produced many tensions within the local population, reflected in a common saying that the municipal government was better at selling the country (*maiguo*) than at loving the country (*aiguo*)."[12] This initial resistance to the return of the Japanese and its erasure in present-day Dalian suggests that the narrative of Dalian exceptionalism itself is a product of the era. How did the city and its people make the transition from considering the citywide welcoming of Japanese corporations as "selling the country" (*maiguo*) to perceiving it as "loving the country" (*aiguo*)? What was the mechanism through *maiguo* was turned to *aiguo*? As we shall see next, one of the key mechanisms is the Chinese concept of *suzhi* (quality), which allows the embodiment of colonial inheritance in the figure of the urban middle class in the rhetoric of economic rationality.

Embodying Colonial Inheritance in *Suzhi* (Quality)

With his fluent Japanese and intimate familiarity with the Japanese corporate culture, Wang Zhaowen epitomizes the quality (*suzhi*) of local human resources that the municipal government advertises to potential Japanese investors. Song Xiaotao, the deputy director of the Dalian Foreign Trade and Economic Cooperation Bureau, captured the currency of *shinnichi* when, in flawless Japanese, she related the history of Sino-Japanese economic relations in the city during our first meeting in her office:

> Because 260,000 Japanese lived in Dalian during the Manchukuo era, Dalian has a deep relationship with Japan. When Dalian became open to foreigners in 1984—originally aimed at encouraging tourism for the purpose of acquiring foreign currencies—anti-Japanese sentiments were indeed present also in Dalian. But because the idea that it was the Japanese government that started the war and that the Japanese citizens were also victims had penetrated into our society through education, such sentiments didn't turn into actions to expel the Japanese from Dalian. Furthermore, because Japanese culture had already penetrated our everyday life, the return of Japanese culture in the 1980s was smoothly and quickly incorporated into the everyday. . . . The first Japanese corporations to invest immediately after the opening of Dalian to foreigners were mostly those returning companies that used to operate in Dalian before 1945, such as Onoda Cement and Nisshin Oil Refinery. Japanese banks also started to invest in Dalian, mostly through personal connections—many CEOs of these banks were born and raised in Dalian during the war, and they introduced other Japanese corporations to the city. In the early 1990s, we saw a big boom in Japanese investment in Dalian, and most large Japanese corporations started their investment during this period. Now one tenth of the Japanese investment in China is in Dalian, and the success rate of Japanese corporations in Dalian is much higher than that of Korean corporations, the other major investors

> in the city. *I believe that this is because Japanese investors understand Dalian due to its history*. (emphasis mine)

In Song's narrative of *shinnichi*, the Japanese—widely considered by Chinese to have failed to recognize their historical responsibility—are portrayed as "understanding Dalian [better than other foreigners] due to its history." Her comment echoes similar sentiments expressed by other locals, especially among the older generation.

Shifting to the domestic sphere, she added, "If you look at words we use and things we like to eat, you can see how much we have internalized Japanese culture. In Dalian, we use borrowed words from Japanese, such as *tatami*, *shōji* (window covering of wood and paper), *waishatsu* (shirts), and *mochi* (rice cakes), in our everyday speech. Also, Japanese food culture such as eating *sashimi* (raw fish) was accepted in Dalian from early on." Song points to spoken words and ingested foods to show the corporeal embodiment of the colonial inheritance in the form of *suzhi* (quality).[13] Her narrative naturalizes colonial inheritance by presenting it as if it were part of the natural metabolism.

The recent nationwide hype about this Chinese concept of *suzhi* as a signifier of one's marketability is based on a merging of the three dictionary definitions of the term: inherent psychological traits, original quality, and accomplishment.[14] The character *su* refers to the original, natural, or essential quality, and *zhi* refers to character, nature, or quality. *Suzhi* has come to refer to the values one should cultivate in order to become a suitable subject in the newly available global economy. This discourse flourishes in the education and labor market; university websites attract prospective students and their parents by demonstrating how they emphasize *suzhi* education.

The discourse of *suzhi* in Dalian, often framed within the narrative of its exceptionalism due to its colonial history, provides a historical dimension that illustrates how *suzhi* illuminates embodied inheritance.[15] When locals talk about Dalian's unique *rencai* (talent, human capital), they often talk about cultivating their inherent familiarity with Japanese language and culture through education and training. As Wang Zhaowen's account of his family history and his own career path illustrates, Japaneseness—which is to say, the intimate understanding of Japanese culture that qualifies a foreigner as *shinnichi*—is an integral part of the local conception of *suzhi*, or inherent quality, that is now cultivated through education and training as exchange-value to be circulated in the Dalian labor market.[16]

Market forces thus co-opt and internalize history through the valuable currency of *suzhi*, which brings the rhetoric of market rationality and legitimacy to a potentially problematic colonial inheritance. Unlike Harbin, where the colonial origin of the city often generates anxiety, as we have seen in the charged historians' debate, Dalian's municipal government and Dalianites are busy turning the city's inheritance into capital-generating assets within a newly configured urban theater that celebrates modern life. *Suzhi* has come to signify both the depository of colonial inheritance and the fruit of its contemporary manifestations. It is a form of coming to terms with the past in the economic realm through modern workers who embody the past as a form of capital accumulation.

The prevailing narrative of Dalian exceptionalism has thus allowed the city and its people to capitalize on its particular colonial inheritance through the language of economic rationality. In doing so, this discourse reinforces colonial reference as a way of thinking about being modern,[17] including measuring progress. A nod of recognition from the life-size Japanese statues in kimonos on Japanese Ambience Street epitomizes this framework.

The exceptionalism narrative, then, potentially conflicts with the Chinese national discourse of anticolonialism. Yet it nevertheless conforms to the new Chinese socioeconomic discourse that embraces a new national identity based on middle-class modernity. The narrative of Dalian exceptionalism and the discourse of *suzhi*, which enable the incorporation of colonial inheritance in the bodies of modern workers, have generated an inverted discourse on surplus value that is now sanctioned by the Communist state: it is the urban workers who produce surplus value, while the farmers embody the lack of it.[18]

Chinese society now locates value not in class but in desire—it is the desiring subject who produces surplus value.[19] The narrative of Dalian exceptionalism, the discourse of *suzhi*, and the shift in organizational principles of society from class to desire all converge in the Zone, which was created by expropriating land from those who are lacking in *suzhi* (farmers) for the creation of those with a surplus of *suzhi* (the urban middle class). The Zone epitomizes the inversion of class narrative through its spatial effacement of class within its immaculate urban-industrial landscape. In the Zone, to which we now turn, dreams, pleasure, guilt, and money all collide to generate wealth and the political economy of redemption.

THE ZONE AS AN URBAN MIDDLE-CLASS FRONTIER

Buses to the Zone leave from the back of the newly renovated Dalian train station built by the Japanese. Outside the station is a cityscape reminiscent of the one before the recent urban renewal: an uneven dirt lane crowded with hawkers winds through a maze of streets lined with dingy eateries and stores housed in dilapidated colonial structures. Two types of buses idle next to each other. One type are large buses with cushioned seats, in which well-dressed men and women sit apart from each other, avoiding unnecessary contact. The others are dented microbuses of the sort often seen in major Chinese cities. On the microbus, the driver calls out for more passengers and often stops at unmarked locations to pick up passengers. Everybody on board holds on to anything they can to avoid being thrown from their seats as the bus speeds through a sea of cars, trucks, and motorcycles. The bumpy forty-minute ride passes by industrial areas, sprawling housing complexes, and wholesale stores, all in shades of muted gray concrete. Crossing the bridge to the Zone, the road suddenly becomes smooth and the buildings one now passes are all brand-new, made of glass and steel. The gate to the Zone closes at night except for those with residency permits.

Unlike downtown, which trumpets its distinctive Dalianness with its European-style colonial structures, urban planning, and new buildings that echo design elements from the bygone era, the Zone is physically nondescript, filled with the kind of characterless glass-and-steel contemporary architecture found elsewhere in China. And unlike downtown Dalian, bustling with people, sounds, and flashing neon, the Zone is orderly, quiet, and sparsely populated. Everything looks and feels new, from the anonymous buildings, new signs, disproportionately large streets, and long city blocks with young trees by the sidewalks to the total absence of elderly people and migrant workers on the streets.

From its inception in 1985, the Zone provided a demarcated experimental space for the introduction of a new economic system to a society still deeply embedded in the socialist economy. A special set of legal arrangements were administered in the Zone: the income-tax rate for foreign corporations was set at 15 percent, while those located elsewhere in Dalian were taxed at 24 percent.[20] The low tax rate and other measures, such as the preferential allocation of infrastructure and resources along with low-cost labor, created an attractive investment environment for foreign corporations.[21] At its inception, this exceptional space had the image as well as the physical reality of an "other space" that would embody the future modern. In this sense, the Zone was an archetypal Foucauldian heterotopia—an external articulation of a utopian future by early reform-era China.[22] The narrative of Dalian exceptionalism finds a spatial manifestation in the Zone, which functioned as a clearly marked space of exception during China's transition to a market-oriented economy. Both Chinese and Japanese take advantage of this space in pursuing their versions of modernity.

The Zone was, and still is, an instance of what Michel Foucault calls *heterotopias*—external countersites or exceptional "other spaces," which are neither essentialist nor hybrid locales but can be described as external interiority.[23] While special economic zones are quintessential examples of heterotopias in the contemporary era, the use of "other spaces" in constructing modernity can be traced back to colonialism. For example, Louise Young's account of the making of Japan's Manchuria demonstrates the workings of heterotopias in Japanese colonial endeavors.[24] Her study shows that one of the powerful mechanisms of colonial modernity was to use "other places"—Manchuria, in this case—to work through aspirations, ideals, and phobias held by Japanese society as a result of modernization efforts. Under the banner of "the land of unlimited opportunity," Manchuria became the site of not only the articulation of modern ideals but also the displacement of the margins of Japanese society.

The following ethnographic exploration of the Zone, from factories to nightclubs, illustrates what happened to this powerful underlying mechanism of colonial modernity that shaped the early development of Dalian, now at the crossroads of postsocialism, postcolonialism, and postimperialism.

A Very Modern "Japanese Colony"

"Dalian looks as if it has become a Japanese colony." This statement by a young Chinese employee of a Japanese bank in downtown Dalian captures the prominent presence of Japanese corporations in the city's commercial districts, especially the Zone. A walk around the Zone's central business district reveals factories of brand-name Japanese corporations lined up one after another. Across the street is a popular cafe owned by a Japanese woman. The interior is Tokyo-style casual-chic, and they serve home-style Japanese dishes along with freshly ground coffee. At a table on one early afternoon sat a group of four Japanese businessmen. One was telling the others how he had spent the previous Sunday at an aquarium with a Chinese *xiaojie* (a derogatory Chinese term for a club hostess) from a karaoke bar. Unlike Beijing or Shanghai, where infrastructure for the Japanese business community (such as Japanese-language schools for business men's children) is well established, Dalian still lags in this regard; many Japanese businessmen live alone in Dalian, leaving their families back in Japan. As a result, the city's Japanese business community is almost exclusively male, encouraging the sort of corporate culture that Japanese society once embraced many years ago. Accompanying this business environment is a proliferating sex industry catering to this predominantly male Japanese population. The prevailing practice of "buying *xiaojie*" is a public secret in Dalian, creating a weekend spectacle in the Zone's housing complexes, which are specially designated for the Japanese business community. On weekend mornings, the tennis courts are crowded with Japanese businessmen playing mixed doubles against their colleagues, each with their favorite *xiaojie*. The conversation I overheard in the café provided a glimpse of such established practices. As much as Japanese corporations take advantage of Dalian's low-cost labor, land, and natural resources, Japanese businessmen take advantage of the economic and temporal disparity between China and Japan to "buy" these young Chinese women at a bargain price.

At another table, a young Chinese couple in their twenties ate lunch without exchanging any words or glances, completely absorbed in comic books. The café stocked the latest Japanese magazines—fashion, gossip, literary—as well as comics and newspapers. A party of four, two Japanese and two Chinese, occupied another table. It sounded like the Chinese were showing the Zone to the Japanese, who had just arrived in Dalian. The only woman in the group, a Chinese lady in an elegant gray pantsuit with a starched white shirt (just as might be found in a Japanese fashion magazine), spoke Japanese. She had an air of confidence and authority, which likely derived from her being the only one in the group who understood both Chinese and Japanese. Her forceful and determined tone of voice was louder than necessary, as if to show off her power to the other Chinese in the café, who either dined or worked there.

From Japanese businessmen who seek "manliness" through the readily available and inexpensive sex industry, to the young Chinese couple absorbed in the latest pop culture from Japan, to Chinese and Japanese business partners, to young Chinese women working at nightclubs that cater to Japanese businessmen, the Zone is the new frontier for the urban middle class and those who aspire to it.

From "Empty Land" to New Frontier

In the late 1980s, the first cluster of foreign corporations started constructing factories in the Zone, which was then sparsely populated farmland. Ogawa Akira, the CEO of Mabuchi Motors Dalian, one of the first Japanese corporations to operate in the Zone, recalls how empty it was in 1990: "I still can't believe how much has changed in the past fifteen years. When the Zone started, there was really nothing here, just the land." He paused, as if transported back in time for a moment, and then continued: "What struck me the most was how dark it was at night—it really felt like a frontier. The supply of water and electricity was extremely unreliable, which was a killer for running a factory, you know. The Dalian municipal government put all of us Japanese into one designated housing compound, which felt like a camp. Every day was a struggle and a new learning."

The Japanese in Dalian often invoke the image of "empty land" when describing how it was before the first wave of large-scale construction was completed in the early 1990s. The advancement of this perspective makes them complicit in the municipal government's attempt to efface widening class disparities in the efforts to nurture the new urban middle class. In the Japanese recollection of the early years of the Zone, farmers, whose land was expropriated by the government, and migrant workers, who laid the bricks for the factories, are absent. Instead, the image many Japanese (and middle-class Dalianites for that matter) project onto the Zone is that of a wild frontier, a no-man's-land waiting to be conquered.[25] The Zone thus epitomizes the inversion of China's class narrative through its spatial effacement of the new class disparity.

Even though more than twenty years had passed since the inception of the Zone, many Japanese CEOs shared with me their sense of being on a frontier, which they expressed with a combination of apprehension and boyish excitement for adventure. Their favorite topic of conversation over our numerous dinners was the difficulty of running a business in China, which was often accompanied by humorous, seemingly never-ending tales of being cheated and cutting corners. Yet despite abundant obstacles, and possibly because of them, almost without exception, their eyes sparkled when they shared their adventurous business practices in navigating what many of them described as a lawless frontier where one could more or less do whatever one wanted (*yaritai hōdai, rūru mo nanimo attamon ja nai*). Tanaka Yōji, the president of a major Japanese shipping corporation and a mischievous man in his midfifties, his face red from excitement and alcohol, grew louder and louder as he recounted how many business deals fell through because his Chinese counterpart "cheated" him behind his back and how his Chinese employees keep cutting corners while constantly asking for raises. After draining his third glass of beer, his face turned serious, and he spoke with feeling:

> When I was back in Japan, I felt that I was simply a wheel in a large corporate machine, which didn't even promise a better future, as it once did to our parents' generation. Here in Dalian, even though I always complain about business practices, it's really exciting to take part in this amazing transformation that Chinese society is going through. I can see the

> difference I make, and that's something I never really felt in Japan. It's quite something to see how I can make a difference, and how the life of the people improves year after year, day after day.

Kinoshita Keisuke, the president of Mizuho Bank Dalian, had spent many years in the bank's branches abroad; he shared with me the freedom and adventure he had found in China while expressing great disappointment in Japan's corporate culture: "Being in China, I've come to realize how socialist Japanese society is and how deeply capitalist the Chinese are. I keenly feel that what's lacking in Japan is the spirit of capitalism, which is abundant in China. This is where you can do what you can't do in Japan now." Kinoshita, like most Japanese CEOs in Dalian in their late forties or fifties, is part of a generation that grew up during Japan's period of high economic growth. They joined the workforce in the midst of the bubble economy in the 1980s and then experienced the economic recession of the 1990s. For them, it is no longer a given that hard work translates into more pay, a larger house, and a better life, as their parents' generation assumed. "Japan is stuck, it's not going anywhere," Tanaka declared gravely, echoing Kinoshita's sentiments. "Being in China, I realize how deeply socialist the Japanese society is, and how deep into the skin, deep in their bones, the Chinese are capitalists. It's absolutely crazy but thrillingly exciting here, I admit, despite my daily complaints." This self-portrayal as a socialist citizen who has discovered the true spirit of capitalism in China is an oft-heard sentiment among the Japanese executives. This external countersite exposes Japan through revealing its inversion. It serves, at the same time, as a locale for the enactment of middle-class dreams and aspirations, which are disappearing rapidly in a Japan stuck in a prolonged recession since the early 1990s.

The idea of middle-class modernity—involving the identification of the middle class with modernity itself—was the hallmark of postwar Japanese recovery and prosperity until the recession, which came along with a major structural shift in the Japanese economy. The drastic reorganization of society around the neoliberal economy—most notably through the deregulation of various economic sectors as well as the collapse of the lifetime employment system and accompanying corporate welfare system—fundamentally shook the long-held conviction in middle-class modernity as the central organizational principle in Japan's long postwar.[26] The growing use of the term *kakusa shakai* (society with disparity) in the news media—an annual media survey listed it as one of the top ten buzzwords in 2006[27]—is but one indication of how the middle class no longer functions conceptually to magically unite and drive Japanese society. The fact that such a concept as "society with disparity" has emerged as a notable new phenomenon itself demonstrates how the idea of the homogeneous middle class has penetrated the postwar Japanese psyche. Now, instead, Japanese public discourse is flooded with terms describing the newly emerging underclass, such as "Internet cafe refugees" (*netto kafe nanmin*) and "working poor" (*wākingu puā*), as well as "destitution business" (*hinkon bujinesu*), a growing business sector catering to and perpetuating such populations.[28] The collapse of middle-class modernity as a nationally embraced aspiration thus also involves the demystification of the economy, as the link between economy and modernity is no longer a given in the form of promised growth for the nation and a better life for every individual. In recessionary Japan, people are becoming disillusioned by projects of modernity.

The perception of the Zone as an urban middle-class frontier by Japanese businessmen is an expression of their process of disenchantment and re-enchantment with modernity. The speed at which the Chinese economy has expanded, as many commented, reminds them of Japan's high-growth period (*kōdo keizai seichō ki*) in the 1960s, when the society fully embraced the pursuit of modern progress with a shared belief that growth meant a bigger slice of the pie even for the lowest strata of society. Often invisible to many Japanese businessmen in the Zone is the rapidly expanding class disparity in China, which is on full display in downtown Dalian, where migrant construction workers and street vendors cross paths with well-dressed upper-middle-class achievers in brand-new foreign cars. Despite the top-down call in China to build a "harmonious society" (*hexie shehui*), itself an acknowledgment of how the widening socioeconomic gap is visibly exacerbating social tensions, very few Japanese businessmen saw any parallel between Japan and China in terms of a growing wealth disparity connected to the dismantling of long-held socialist organizational principles. Instead, most Japanese seem to be dazzled by the overall economic growth in Dalian, which they believe will benefit even the most disadvantaged in the society. Seen in this manner, the Japanese characterization of the Zone as a frontier is a quintessentially modern form of nostalgia for the eager pursuit of progress.

Zone of Aspiration

Like the Japanese businessmen, local Chinese also see the Zone as a new frontier in which to pursue urban middle-class modern aspirations. Li Hui, a factory-line worker in Mabuchi Motors in her midthirties, recalled how she decided to take the job at Mabuchi instead of at a state-owned enterprise, the standard choice for high school graduates in 1991:

> I didn't want to work for the state-owned work unit, where you just sit around and do nothing all day. I had just graduated from a high school in rural Dalian, where my parents had been "sent down" during the Cultural Revolution. I wanted to continue the mode of life with a busy schedule I had at high school. You know, at school, your life is busy all day, full of things to do, and I wanted that. But in a state-owned unit, life is very predictable, and I was looking for a different kind of lifestyle—something new and challenging.[29]

For many, working for a foreign corporation in the Zone promised excitement, expectations for better future, and a clear break from the past and the familiar. Wu Jianxin and Yang Xianggao both left their promising careers in state-owned enterprises and joined Toshiba Dalian in 1992, one of the most coveted foreign corporations among high school and college graduates in Dalian. Wu, born in 1963, received his master's degree in political science and law from prestigious Jilin University in Changchun, became a member of the Politburo of the Dalian Communist Party, a very elite career path, and joined a state-owned enterprise in Dalian before joining Toshiba. Yang, born in 1967, received his master's degree in engineering from the highly regarded Harbin Engineering University and then worked for the prominent state-owned Dalian Shipbuilding Company before his move to Toshiba. Each said they joined the Japanese-owned firm to learn more advanced management and technology skills at a company they—and many others—admired. According to Yang, in the mid-1980s, the theme song of a Toshiba television commercial became so popular that he, like many others, used to hum it often. "We all knew that song very well, and Toshiba symbolized the future, something new and exciting, and a new life," he told me, stressing the impact of the commercial on a society recovering from the Cultural Revolution.[30] It presented new possibilities in a world that seemed totally different from what they knew. He joined Toshiba Dalian despite protests from his relatives, who, due to bitter memories of the war against Japan, found it unthinkable that a family member would work for a Japanese corporation. More than a decade has passed since Wu and Yang made the big leap to the land of opportunity in the Zone, and they have internalized this once-foreign otherness. Both of them laughingly expressed how they had already been "Japanized" (*Ribenhua*) to the extent that when, for instance, city officials visited the factory, they could not help but feel foreign in contrast to the officials' "Chinese" mannerisms. "I was looking at them from a Japanese perspective," Yang explained with a wry smile.

Despite the growing class disparity in both societies, within the sanitized space of the Zone, where the weak, the poor, the elderly, and the floating population are invisible, those employed in the Japanese corporate space—Chinese and Japanese alike—embrace their own version of modernity as they engage in the production of commodities that have become markers of the urban middle class in today's China. Construction of urban middle-class modernity in the Zone—through both the production of middle-class consumer commodities and the accession of Chinese employees into the new urban middle class—becomes a common project for Chinese and Japanese. The Zone as a heterotopic site allows both Chinese and Japanese to project their versions of modernity through their production relations.

But it is more than the common pursuit of middle-class modernity that oils the machinery of production in the Zone. Similar to the embedded historicity in the cherished attribute of *suzhi*, the shared pursuit and celebration of modernity in the Zone is driven by underlying forces with a pivotal historical dimension. As the following ethnography illustrates, individual desires to be modern have become a site not only for future-oriented aspiration but also for redeeming the past. It is these dynamics beneath the celebration of middle-class modernity that we shall explore next.

THE POLITICAL ECONOMY OF REDEMPTION

Toshiba Dalian, which in 1991 was among the first Japanese corporations to operate in the Zone, now employs 1,800 Chinese and 11 Japanese.[31] Takeda Fumitaka, the president, showed me around the factory, located within a large walled compound, which included multiple factory and administrative buildings as well as living quarters and recreational facilities for employees. We walked through the austere administrative building, where a conversation in Chinese spilled into the hallway from one conference room while from another came a heavily accented Japanese conversation mixed with Chinese phrases. At the entrance to one of the factory buildings, we put on protective shoe covers and hats. Inside the climate-controlled, spotless television factory, geometric beauty created through carefully prescribed and choreographed positioning and movements of workers and machines produced a sense of calm amid the sound of machines moving rhythmically (figure 4.3). Women in pastel uniforms color-coded according to their skill levels were putting computer chips onto the logic boards of television sets as the belt conveyer slowly moved past. They placed millimeter-size pins onto maze-like boards with machine-like precision and concentration—or that's what

4.3 Dalian Toshiba factory in the Special Economic Zone: Dalian Toshiba is one of the most sought after companies for young Dalianites seeking both white- and blue-collar jobs. Inside the spotless and quiet factory, line workers, many from rural Dalian, wear color-coded caps to indicate their skill levels. Photo by author, 2003.

I thought. Takeda whispered to my ear with unconcealed pride in his voice, "You see these ladies, many of them come from rural Dalian. Their nimble fingers and their stunning vision—nobody wears glasses, you see—allow them to accomplish what the latest state-of-the-art machines cannot do."

Takeda's comment made me realize that at the core of this high-tech, state-of-the-art factory space was the line workers' highly skilled labor and acute senses. This realization brought a sudden reversal of imagery in my mind—as if I discovered that what I had thought was a positive photographic image turned out to be a negative—and my thoughts were transported to the opening chapter of Adam Smith's *Wealth of Nations*.[32] Smith described a pin factory in eighteenth-century England, in which the accumulation of seemingly simple, machinelike movements of factory workers led to a much higher level of productivity for the nation as a whole.[33] He illustrated how under certain circumstances the individual pursuit of self-interest collectively leads to moral good—in his case, the wealth of the nation (a bigger pie for the society). Although Smith was here making a point about the power of the modern division of labor to generate wealth, his work more broadly points to the sort of convergence of the formal and moral economies that captures forces at work in the Japanese corporate zone in Dalian.[34]

What Smith left out in his analysis of the junction between the formal and moral economies is the role of historicity embedded in the individual pursuit of self-interest, which is key to understanding the economic dynamics in Dalian. As we shall see, "self-interest" in Dalian is partially fueled by a strong desire on the part of the Japanese to repay the moral debt arising from Japan's unaccounted-for colonial violence. The moral good that is produced is not only wealth—as generated by Dalian's booming economy—but also a sense of redeeming the past. In economic language, self-interest is something that emerges in the present and is projected toward the future, yet the case of Dalian shows how self-interest is articulated in relation to the past and the present. Self-interest, in the form of aspirations and desires that bear a historical burden, is often expressed through moral debt. It is this dynamic created by the *political economy of redemption* to which we shall now turn.

Kobayashi Takeshi, a Japanese midlevel manager in his fifties at Toshiba Dalian, recounted how he faced his structural position as a Japanese at the workplace within the moral economy between China and Japan. In the factory one day, a Chinese colleague came up to him and said point-blank, "I don't like the Japanese." In response to this out-of-the-blue provocation, he "really didn't know what to say." Kobayashi, who had lived in Dalian for five years and traveled extensively all over China, continued, "But then, these incidents are exceptional moments when deeply ingrained hard feelings burst out. The difficulty is that I don't know exactly what to do." Our conversation reminded him of another experience of a similar nature when he visited the Memorial Hall of the War of Resistance against Japan on the outskirts of Beijing (where the Marco Polo Bridge Incident took place in 1937): "Noticing that I was Japanese, a man came up to me and told me quite bluntly, 'Now Japan is invading China in the economic sphere.' I understand the sentiment, given what Japan did during the war, but then I didn't know how to respond to a comment like that." A Japanese colleague of Kobayashi's who had been listening in on our conversation nodded knowingly and added how he had had a similar experience.

Beyond being a space for displaced dreams of entrepreneurship and the promise of social mobility embodied by the frontier imagery, the Zone also reveals *and* accommodates a latent sense of moral debt in the name of the nation, which is often invisible within Japan and finds expression elsewhere, as it does in Changchun. "Well, actually I haven't visited Puyi's Palace Museum in Changchun yet," Kawada Tōru, an employee of Toshiba Dalian in his fifties, said sheepishly, as if not having visited this historical site made him a bad citizen. "You know all these displays about Japanese atrocities during the war," Kawada continued. "My brain understands that I should just face it, but then my mind hesitates to go through such a predictably uncomfortable experience on vacation." Whereas Japanese tourists to Northeast China may brush away their moral debt as they return to their daily lives in Japan, Japanese businessmen in the Zone work amid constant reminders of it.

The Zone as a heterotopic site thus exposes the nagging guilt among Japanese that arises from Japan's unaccounted-for historical responsibility. In Changchun, we saw how tourist sites of Manchukuo remnants illuminated the topography of guilt for Japanese visitors. In Dalian, this underlying moral economy is highlighted in the realm of daily workplace activities. Corporate space in the city establishes a refractive structure—*awase kagami*, as discussed in chapter 3—in which both Chinese and Japanese see themselves in a mirror held by the other, mutually reflecting their respective national inheritances in the common pursuit of wealth accumulation. Japanese corporate space in Dalian has become a performative space not only for pursuing formal economic productivity but also for both parties to perform according to their respective national inheritances within the moral economy of after empire. For the Japanese, as the inheritors of moral debt, the keen recognition of that inheritance, prompted by the perceived gaze of the other, underlies the future-oriented pursuit of economic production in the Zone. Japanese desires to repay their moral debt, therefore, are an integral part of their renewed pursuit of modernity.

The sense of moral debt shared among the Japanese in Dalian is brought out by the very economic activities that are eagerly orchestrated by the municipal government to incorporate Japanese interests and to orient people away from the past and toward the future. The speculative logic of capitalism, which operates on the basis of financial debt as the source of wealth, intersects with the moral economy of debt, which is brought to light by face-to-face encounters between Chinese and Japanese in the workspace. Within this economic realm, reminders and enactments of nationality in adjectives such as "Chinese" and "Japanese" are an integral part of daily negotiations in the workplace, from the choice of language to work ethics.

Despite or perhaps because of the welcoming gestures and various legal measures granting a special preferred status to Japanese corporations in Dalian, the Japanese in Dalian feel a sense of moral indebtedness. Their work becomes a way of channeling this underlying anxiety. Many Japanese CEOs in particular feel the need to redeem Japan in the eyes of the Chinese. Tanaka

Yōji, the president of a shipping company, bluntly situated Japanese corporations in China within the moral economy: "The Japanese economy won't be able to compete with China for a long time. The Japanese government doesn't have any strategy whatsoever. But look at the Chinese government; they are different and very strategic. In the form of 'luring' foreign investment, they plan to learn everything they can and then throw us away. Because the Chinese government didn't receive any postwar reparations from Japan, I suspect that they are trying to milk Japanese corporations in the name of welcoming Japanese investment. *Well, the bottom line is that we Japanese are indebted to the Chinese*" (emphasis added).

Tanaka was referring to the Chinese government's decision not to pursue reparations from Japan when the two countries normalized diplomatic relations in 1972. In their Joint Communiqué, the Japanese received a "gift" from the Chinese—the renunciation of reparations—on the implied condition that Japan not forget its past and not resort to militarism.[35] Tanaka's comment underscores how he saw the Chinese renunciation of its claim for war reparations as a generous gift, in which the Japanese incurred a debt.[36] Japanese were not forgiven with the Chinese renunciation of reparations. Rather, as I argued in chapter 1, Japanese were *given time* to repay the debt, which the Japanese were almost certainly bound to be unable to repay, since it was measured in their attitude toward the past rather than in currency or concrete demands.[37] This historic 1972 agreement, which officially marks Japanese indebtedness to China, made the standing of the Japanese government's Official Development Assistance (ODA) to China, which began in 1979, ambivalent within this gift economy. As the dollar value of Japan's direct investments has surpassed that of the ODA, the range of meanings given to the ODA, from a form of displaced reparation to a tool of Japanese neocolonialism, has come to be seen in a new light. When the Japanese government considered discontinuing the ODA in 2004, Chinese Premier Wen Jiabao remarked that the Chinese government considered the ODA as a form of reparation.[38] Japanese money invested in China, either in the form of the ODA or foreign direct investment, is embedded in the gift economy—*(for)given time*—with a punctuated reminder of Japanese indebtedness.

The rapid increase in Japanese direct investment in Dalian is indeed infused with discourses of debt—both the financial debt upon which the specular economy operates *and* moral debt—as if the specter is conjured up as a logical consequence of the gift of time, reminding the Japanese of the unpaid debt. Japanese money has become a sign of these two forms of debt that circulate in Dalian. Hence the Zone, the site for an emphatically future-oriented, specular economy, has also become the site of retrospection about the past.

In the Zone, the economic aspirations of Chinese and Japanese converge: Chinese aspiring to middle classes embrace the new economy while Japanese businessmen attempt to recuperate the middle-class dreams that are rapidly disappearing in a Japan mired in recession. In the Zone, this economic logic also converges with the logic of time set forth by the moral economy of debt marked with the Chinese gift of (for)giving Japanese aggression in exchange for the prospect of future investment.

In this convergence of financial and moral economy, the *political economy of redemption* emerges: China's growing economy channels contradictory impulses toward erasing, confronting, or capitalizing on the past into new forms of production, consumption, and accumulation. Ogawa Akira, president of Mabuchi Motors in Dalian, who has lived in the city since the early years of the Zone, spoke about practical steps he has taken to address this sense of indebtedness and stigma attached to Japanese nationality:

> There are things I emphasize during the training period of my Japanese employees. You really need to be sensitive to the feelings many Chinese have toward the Japanese because of our history. For example, I repeatedly tell my colleagues not to use the Japanese word *baka* (idiot, stupid) at work. In Japan, we use it often and lightly in the normal course of work-related conversations, but the Chinese get really insulted when they hear this word directed at them by Japanese. As you know, this is probably the most well-known Japanese word in China. All the anti-Japanese war movies always highlight this word while everything else they speak as Japanese soldiers is nonsensical Japanese. Also, our company takes community relations very seriously. We have already built three subsidized schools, and there are other smaller local activities all year round. In addition to creating attractive jobs—we employ more than six thousand people here—I want the locals to feel that they benefit from more than having additional jobs and that Mabuchi is part of their community. We Japanese corporations have to work extra hard to gain confidence and trust from the local community because of history, and these are the things I hope help ease the tension. I've heard so many stories about how they often beat up workers in Korean corporations in Dalian. But if something like that would happen in a Japanese corporation, there would be a big anti-Japanese demonstration.

As I listened to him talk calmly with an unconcealed passion for his work and a strong sense of personal investment in Dalian, I recalled how some Chinese workers at the Mabuchi Motors factory had fondly described him.

"He is really fun," one told me. "He often takes us out to karaoke bars, and he sings Chinese songs pretty well." "Actually his Chinese is quite good," another chimed in. It is this new image of Japan, which stands in opposition to the portrayal of Japanese atrocities in Chinese war movies, that many Japanese CEOs value as a product no less important than the physical output of their factories.

Setting higher standards for employees and expressing a strong commitment to community-outreach programs are some of the ways in which Japanese corporations hope to redeem Japan's negative image in the eyes of the local Chinese public. Takeda Fumitaka, the president of Toshiba Dalian, proudly noted during our first meeting that the company procured all the furnishings for its offices locally, an uncommon practice among foreign corporations, especially when the Chinese market was just beginning to shift from a socialist economy. Other CEOs of Japanese corporations in Dalian also emphasized their similarly conscious efforts to contribute to the local economy through means other than the direct creation of jobs and tax contributions. Many talked about increasing the local procurement rate to boost the local economy.

And these efforts seem to work. The eyes of the line workers at Mabuchi Motors brightened when they told me about the company's community-outreach programs, including one to build elementary schools. "These social activities make us feel very proud of being members of Mabuchi Motors," Li Hong, a woman in her midthirties, told me in a sincerely excited tone. "Yes," her colleague said, nodding in strong agreement, "it makes me feel really good about having chosen to work for Mabuchi. My relatives in rural Dalian, who were originally ambivalent about my working for a Japanese corporation back then, now look up to me." Redeeming Japan through respectable corporate practices is important to the Chinese as well as the Japanese.

The renewed image of Japan, distinct from the blood-soiled image of Imperial Japan, is a much-needed confirmation of the "newborn" Japan for both Japanese and Chinese. This image also serves to affirm the long-held, Communist Party–endorsed interpretation of Japan's historical responsibility. In this official interpretation, the fascist Japanese government and military led the powerless Japanese people into a reckless war, and the Japanese, as much as the Chinese, were victims of state irrationality. I encountered this narrative numerous times, every so often accompanied by a sense of relief from my Chinese hosts after finding out that my grandfather lived in Northeast China for nearly a decade as a civilian, which seemed to further justify their sharing meals with me. Nevertheless, a widespread, deeply felt anxiety attaches to this narrative, as the Chinese news media never fail to report incidents that affirm the right-leaning tendencies of Japanese society. Expressions of anxiety about Japanese remilitarization are something I heard often, especially from younger Chinese. The image of a new and moral Japan that many Japanese corporations in Dalian attempt to portray serves to assuage this simmering anxiety. As much as Japanese society has sought to affirm again and again a radical discontinuity from its imperial past, the Chinese have long yearned to be convinced that this discontinuity is real, and the deeds of the Japanese corporations thus anchor a sense of redemption for both parties in need of visible signs of closure.

As a result, efforts to redeem Japan are well covered by the local media. For instance, during the SARS epidemic in the spring of 2004, Japanese corporations were the first to donate emergency funds to the municipal government, which was favorably reported on the front page of the leading local newspaper, *Dalian ribao* (Dalian Daily). The paper devotes considerable space to a long-running and widely popular biweekly column, written by senior journalist Zha Jinfeng. Since 1983, the column has introduced socioeconomic and cultural aspects of contemporary Japanese society to the paper's readers. Zha's vivid ethnographic accounts of life in Tokyo while she was stationed there in 1999 portrayed a modern, rational, and humane society—in effect, a new Japan. Born in 1953 and having experienced the Cultural Revolution in her formative years, like many intellectuals of her generation she is driven by a strong sense of justice. Passionate, direct, and a woman of action, she is constantly on the move to spread the gospel of this transformed neighbor to emulate, and her columns have triggered equally passionate responses from readers. When I asked her about the Japanese invasion of China, she untypically interrupted me, saying firmly, "Let's not bring up the past again, OK? We've already reconciled, right?" (*Yiqian de shi women buyao zai ti le, haoma? Women yijing hejie le ba?*), as if talking about it would conjure up unnecessary ghosts. Redeeming Japan in her positive portrayal in her essays seemed to be her way of coming terms with the past. Belief in postwar Japan's radical discontinuity from its imperial past, as epitomized by the Japanese term *newborn Japan* (*shinsei Nihon*), is just as important to the Japanese as it is to the Chinese. Redeeming Japan within the corporate zone in Dalian has hence become a common project.

As much as both Japanese and Chinese feel the need for the redemption of Japan, Chinese employees in Japanese corporations seek another form of redemption: the redemption of their pride and honor through becoming modern to dispel the image of being a "backward" Asian Other—an image that the Japanese, in both prewar and postwar eras, have often projected onto them. Many young Chinese I encountered in Dalian often emphasized how China remained "backward" (*luohou*) but how it was nevertheless catching up rapidly. I was struck by how such proclamations were often followed by their anxious question to me, "isn't it?" as if my affirmation was crucial for them to feel truly modern. Another comment I heard more than once from Chinese employees in Japanese corporations, "The Japanese don't look down upon us, but they have a sense of superiority" (*meiyou kanbuqi de ganjue, ke Ribenren you youyuegan*), also mirrors a sense of inferiority vis-à-vis the Japanese on the scale of modernization. In a corporate setting in which evaluation by Japanese bosses matters, Chinese workers' desire for recognition from the Japanese is magnified. This self-consciousness of how they appear in the eyes of the Japanese reflects their perception that overcoming backwardness by becoming modern is a way of redeeming the "Chinese," which is distinct from making money or ascending in social status. Dalian native Wang Zhirong, a mild-mannered elite banker born in 1962, expressed this sentiment in fluent Japanese: "When I left the Bank of China to take a position at a Japanese bank, many wondered why I would give up a very elite career with a bright future. But it gives me great pleasure when my Japanese boss trusts me."

The psychology of the Japanese corporate zone in Dalian is strongly tinted and fueled by redemptive desires from all sides, which feed into production relations. It also shows how mutual recognition is the key to the fulfillment of redemptive desires. What we have observed in Dalian contrasts sharply with the dynamics in Changchun, where each party's redemptive scenery includes the Other only as external spectator; there, Chinese and Japanese alike are self-conscious about the refractive mirror arrangement in which they are enclosed, yet both end up shadowboxing due to the lack of direct encounters.

In Dalian, the Other functions as an external interiority—as a *recognizing* Other. As if an invisible hand is at work, this political economy of redemptive desires has generated forms of coming to terms with the past at the personal and societal levels alike. This process has become possible only through a system of interdependency of recognition in the workplace. Economic operations in Dalian's corporate zone revolve around feeding off others' desires and anxieties in the everyday work environment. Chinese and Japanese employees project various images onto their counterparts, and the results include exchanges of moral and psychological indebtedness, processes of settling accounts, and the creation of more wealth, which in turn produces spaces for more dreams, fantasies, and money. We now turn to a space where dreams, pleasure, guilt, and money converge again, this time to the accompaniment of karaoke tunes.

JAPAN FANTASIES IN THE KARAOKE BAR

"What do you think about going to a karaoke bar with some young members of our company tonight? We've been busy and haven't done this for a while, so it's about time, I'd say," Takahashi Kenji, the president of a Japanese freight company, whispered in my ear one afternoon when I dropped by the company's main facility, located near the Dalian port, to chat with some Chinese employees. "There is a nice club owned by an interesting Japanese lady that I would like you to meet," he continued. I jumped at this opportunity, since these karaoke bars—or "clubs," as they are often called—are meant to entertain businessmen, not women, and I would be an awkwardly uninvited customer if I were to go to such an establishment alone. After dinner at a nearby Japanese restaurant with Wang Yu and Li Peng, recent college graduates and the company's two youngest employees, we took a short cab ride to the central commercial district in downtown Dalian. Neon signs glittered, and the sidewalks were full of couples, friends, and colleagues out for dinner, looking into illuminated fish tanks of different restaurants. On an old-fashioned side street, something out of a 1920s silent-movie scene, incandescent lamps shed warm light upon lively exchanges in a tiny enclave of old Dalian surrounded by a forest of high-rise buildings. We walked down the street, crowded with stalls full of fish, meat, vegetables, tofu, and dried nuts as well as a cart with steaming food in Styrofoam boxes, and came to a small steel door next to a bustling restaurant.

Beyond the door, a narrow, steep, dimly lit staircase led up to a large room divided into several booths with cushy benches and a plain but well-stocked bar behind which pink and purple neon lights twinkled. It was still early for club going, but there were already a few Japanese businessmen quietly sitting, pressed up against young hostesses, or "*xiaojie*," as they are often referred to by their customers. "*Irasshaimase*," a petite woman in a muted navy kimono greeted us in Japanese. "It's been a while, so good to see you, Mr. Takahashi." She was the owner of the club—"Mama," as female club owners are usually called by Japanese businessmen, who seem to seek an idealized mother or wife figure outside of their own homes. Mama, in her late fifties, had a rough, square face. Alongside her stood a young Chinese woman, Zheng Wei, in an identically patterned kimono. She was second in command at the club. Mama and Zheng Wei led us to a reserved private room in the back. It was equipped with a fancy karaoke machine, a big screen, and long couches along two walls on either side of a table in the middle. "I requested the 'number one' *xiaojie* tonight," Takahashi whispered into my ear, not hiding his excitement. "She is very pretty and 'safe,' perfect for this kind of occasion." By "safe," he meant that her presence would remain at the level adequate for entertainment, not overtly and embarrassingly sexual, and thus appropriate for an after-work outing with his young colleagues and a female friend. His phrasing implied that there were other ways to have fun with *xiaojie* on different nights.

Shortly after the table was covered with small home-style Japanese dishes and the young Chinese employees began flipping through the karaoke song book in a very accustomed manner, the "number one" *xiaojie* came in. A slender young woman with a very fair complexion, beautiful eyes, and long, flowing hair, she was dressed in a pastel *qipao,* a tight-fitting traditional Chinese dress with deep slits along the sides of the legs. She was charming and full of spirit. "My name is Sakura ("cherry blossom" in Japanese), very nice to meet you," she said, smiling at me with an unconcealed mixture of curiosity and apprehension at this unusual guest. The slightly awkward moment of our introduction was immediately swept away by the sound of karaoke. Sakura prepared drinks for Takahashi and the rest of us, sang some songs, and then prepared some more drinks, clapping and smiling. Wang and Li, the two Chinese employees fresh out of college, were having a good time, singing the latest Chinese hits one after another, while Takahashi, in his early fifties, sang some Japanese songs from the 1970s.

We spent three hours singing and playing games in the dimly lit, windowless room. Takahashi filled me in on what he described as the "shameful" stories of Japanese businessmen in Dalian, such as those who "buy" *xiaojie* for 10,000 RMB ($1,200) per month. "I don't do this," he said. "When I take her to go shopping or for dinner out, I'd pick her up at this club and send her back here again, and pay for her service here at the club. Hmm, I see, you wouldn't like this either, would you?"

Most Japanese in Dalian agree that a certain type of sex industry is unusually well developed in the city, which heightens its attraction to Japanese businessmen. Free monthly Japanese-language publications, distributed in hotels and Japanese restaurants and read by local Chinese as well as Japanese businessmen, are filled with columns and essays on the daily experiences of Japanese businessmen, along with practical information about living in Dalian, new places to visit, and news on culture, society, and the economy. In a column series called "Mystery Japanese Goes to Dalian: The Japanese View" (*Nazo no nihonjin dairen e: Nihonjin no me*) that appeared in *Bipure: Business and Play*, for example, the anonymous author recounted how he was first attracted to Dalian in part by the wonderful experiences he had at its nightclubs, where "pure, innocent and beautiful young ladies introduced me to delicious food and beautiful scenery."[39] In the following issue, he described in adoring detail the considerate service he received from a Chinese mama at one club.[40]

As much as Japanese corporations are taking advantage of the time lag in economic development between Japan and China in the form of low-cost labor, property, and natural resources, these businessmen are also taking advantage of this time lag in their private lives—their behavior is something that was popular and reluctantly accepted in Japan twenty years ago but no longer, as more and more women have joined the workforce.[41] Yet in Dalian, this public secret remains "secret," as it has become an integral part of the redemptive economy that fuels desires to emulate Japan.

This pervasive practice is also a form of guilty pleasure, a mirrored double of the inherited guilt many Japanese businessmen feel in the eyes of their Chinese colleagues. Their commonly shared feeling of moral indebtedness to the Chinese and of the need and perceived pressure to acknowledge their inherited guilt through their socially responsible work efforts, combined with their nagging sense of betrayal—*we work hard and conscientiously, yet the Chinese cheat us because they hate the Japanese anyway*—have found expression outside of their workspaces, in night clubs. The rampant practice of "buying *xiaojie*" often takes the form of providing a hostess a monthly allowance large enough that she does not to have to work at a club, in exchange for her complete attention to her "buyer." By playing the role of both benevolent gentleman (rescuing a *xiaojie* from her degrading job by virtue of a financial power that derives from economic disparity between China and Japan) and delinquent (enjoying extramarital relationships away from home), the practice confirms the businessman's financial superiority, compensating for the moral inferiority and humiliation he may feel in daily life in Dalian. It is an effort at balancing through inversion of the disparity between financial economy and moral economy, both of which turn the wheels of political economy in Dalian.[42]

This perverse redemptive structure is reinforced by the strong desire shared by many young Chinese women to "marry up." Many Chinese hostesses expressed to me that marrying a Japanese man means a better life and more opportunities, a not-uncommon view in the larger Dalian population. *Xinshengbao* (New Business News), a major local newspaper, for example, published a full-page article, "The Reality of Happiness of Dalian Brides in Japan," indicating significant interest in this issue.[43] Several women were interviewed, describing their lives after wedding Japanese men. The article ended with a quotation from one, whose job in Japan was not as good as what she had had in Dalian but who was happy with her marriage: "I'm very happy with my marriage and life. I guess that's because I didn't marry my husband for any reason other than love."

In Dalian, the desire for all things Japanese, including the quality of life with which the country is identified, thus feeds into the redemptive economy. When I first went to the aforementioned karaoke club, I had a preconceived image of club hostesses that had been shaped by images from 1990s Japan. Chinese hostesses who were sent to Japan through agencies connected to organized crime networks became a social issue during that time, and the Japanese media repeatedly reported on the deplorable situations of hostesses from rural China. These agencies often confiscated women's passports upon their arrival in Japan, and the women had no choice but to work as prostitutes until they earned enough to pay off their large debt. As I spent more time with young women in Dalian, I realized that many of them were part of the new wave of those aspiring to the new urban middle class, who, with the spirit of capitalism, saw Japan as a land of opportunity.

"I took this job because I wanted to improve my Japanese conversational skills," Sun Lili, the youngest hostess at the karaoke club, told me matter-of-factly. And it turned out that this was the reason almost all the women at the club said they chose the job. They have several preconceived images of Japan, from the extreme brutality depicted in war movies to the world of Japanese television drama series such as *Oshin* in the 1980s[44] (a story of rags to riches through hard work) and *Tokyo Love Story* in the early 1990s (a more recent and fashionable portrayal of sleek modern life in Tokyo). Then there are their direct interactions with their Japanese businessmen customers, whom they describe with Japanese adjectives ranging from *sukebe* (lecherous; having excessive interest in women as sexual objects) to *yasashii* (gentle and kind), and their suspicion of being "not modern enough" in the eyes of the Japanese. These visions cast Japan as the land of opportunity elsewhere—a zone of dreams, escape, and a better life. The following portraits tell stories of two hostesses at the club, whose voices echo those of many other women I met in their profession.[45]

Dreamworld Japan

Sun Lili's Encounters with Japan

Born in 1983, Sun Lili was the youngest *xiaojie* at the club, outside of which, in her plain clothes, she looked like a student. Her parents were originally from Inner Mongolia, but she grew up in the city of Lüshun (Port

Arthur), not far from Dalian. After graduating from a vocational high school in design, she had been on her own, with various jobs. She took Japanese classes at Lüshun Central Middle School, which was established with money from a Japanese donor, and her love for the language grew. She enrolled in a part-time Japanese-language course at Dalian Foreign Language University in October 2002 in the hope of going to Japan for further study. To improve her conversation skills, she took a job at the club in December 2002: "I had no idea what kind of job it was. All I knew was that at this kind of club I would have a lot of opportunity to practice Japanese. I also wanted a rather relaxed job. I don't really like to work. I found it really exhausting to work at stores."

I asked about her impressions of Japan, to which she hesitantly answered,

> Please don't get upset. Because of the history, you know, like these war movies—have you seen those? My image of the Japanese was pretty bad, that they were all bad people. But after interacting with Japanese customers at the club, I've come to realize that there are all kinds of Japanese, some good and some bad. But in general, Japanese women are very nice, very kind. Actually even in these war movies, women are *yasashii* [gentle and caring—she used a Japanese word here]. Our mama is also very *yasashii*, unlike Chinese bosses, who would just yell at you. Mama doesn't yell at us even when we make mistakes; she just tells us what we should have done.
>
> But, you know, Japanese men are *sukebe*. There are also customers who don't talk with us, just sit quietly without any interactions with us, and that's really annoying. But still, in general, Japanese customers are better than other customers, since they do what they promise us to do, like going shopping with us, or taking us out for a nice dinner and things like that. Some Chinese customers just make these promises and never follow through.

I asked if she ever felt that Japanese men looked down on her.

> Oh, yes, Japanese do look down on us Chinese. For instance, my customers often ask me if I have a bath at home, which upsets me quite a bit. They think that China is still a developing country. So do Mama and her daughter. I feel that they also look down on Chinese. They often tell us that we don't clean the bathroom well or we don't do this or that properly in a way that indicates that they see China as still an underdeveloped, low-culture place.

> Actually, I don't like this work. When I first started, for the first month, I really enjoyed it. It was much more relaxed than any other work I had done before, just drinking and chatting basically, and I also felt that my Japanese conversation skills improved. But now, I feel that this kind of environment is not necessarily the best one for learning Japanese, since all the talk is quite similar, like where you are from, what do you do, and all sex-related things, not much else. So I don't know, I originally wanted to go to Japan this spring, but my friend in Tokyo told me that it was impossible to earn enough money to cover tuition and living expenses and that she was coming back to Dalian, so I guess I can't go now. I really don't know, I don't really like to work so much, although I don't like to just stay at home either. I wish I could find a nice husband. Now, you know, when I have money, I just spend it. Like if I get a 100 RMB tip [approximately $12, about one eighth the average monthly wage in Dalian] from my customer, I would just buy this and that small thing at the store, like earrings and clothing, not so expensive, but I like to buy this and that all the time, and I end up throwing them away in a few months and then buying another one, and I can never save money with this kind of work. You see, I don't see tips from customers as money to be saved—I just use it as soon as I get it. So I want to get a different kind of job, but I don't know what.
>
> I don't particularly like most girls who work at the club. They are always scheming, and they kind of look down on me because I'm young and don't have much experience. I can't really open up with them. They are not thinking much about their future. They just want to have a comfortable life on a daily basis. They just want to get more money, want their customers to buy them a car, nice clothes, or send them to Japan to study Japanese. They really don't have any plans for the future. Those *fuwuyuan* ["service personnel," a politically correct way of referring to *xiaojie*] who have been in this business for a long time, like Zheng Wei, behave very differently from me, this you can tell.

Sun Lili had recently started dating a young man in his twenties, a hair stylist. "A job that's not so great, cannot earn much money," she added. "I want to find a husband with money. You can't be happy without money, you see. I don't want to get married without buying an apartment or having enough savings. It would be so miserable to get married without these. How can you get married without a house—totally unthinkable!" With this, she left, saying that she had to do some shopping for her boyfriend's birthday party.

Zheng Wei's Zone of Escape and Hope

Zheng Wei, who is second in command, manages more than twenty *xiaojie* at the club. Born in 1977, she is slightly older than the other hostesses. Originally from a rural village near Jiamusi in Heilongjiang Province, she dropped out of middle school when she was in the second year, not because her family could not afford it, but because she "had a real headache whenever I studied." After she quit school, her relatives, many of whom were school teachers, gave her home tutorials, while she supported herself taking all kinds of odd jobs, such as working in a restaurant and selling vegetables at a market. Then she decided to come to Dalian because she saw more opportunities with its open economic policy. A woman who was slightly senior to her took her under her arm and gave her Japanese-language lessons at home. Encouraged by this, she borrowed money from her relatives to enroll in a Japanese-language course at Dalian Foreign Language University for six months. But with six-month-level Japanese, it was impossible to find a job, and she ended up working for a karaoke club. She eventually switched clubs to the one at which I met her and was promoted to her current position.

"I haven't told my parents what I do in Dalian, since they would feel ashamed of my job," she told me gravely.

> What I want is to save some money and go to Japan. I want to study Japanese, enroll in school, and hopefully find a better job, and, if possible, find a nice Japanese man to marry. Dalian is too small, and I need to get out of here to start a new life. Even if I get some more education here, people will know what kind of job I did in the past, and it's difficult to find a different kind of job. But when I tell my customers about my dream of studying in Japan, they don't take it seriously. They think that we just want their money and that we're not interested in improving our lives by ourselves. They would often tell me that I should just marry a nice man with money.
>
> I've been feeling quite depressed these days, thinking about my future. I can't see clearly what exactly I want. But I want to be financially independent no matter what. I'm also certain that I want to go to Japan to study Japanese and change my life. The other *xiaojie* at the club are still really young and their lifestyle is quite messy, no responsibilities or plans for the future. But I'm already twenty-six years old, and I know that I neither want nor can maintain this kind of lifestyle, and I've been feeling quite anxious. I want to educate myself in order to land a better job. I've gone through so many financial problems—at one point I didn't have four jiao [approximately five US cents] to use a beeper. Luckily, I

have a lot of friends and was able to get through these crisis moments, but I really need to change my lifestyle.

I haven't had the opportunity to talk like this before. When I'm with other younger *xiaojie*, they like to play mah jong, so there is not much space for having this kind of conversation. I talk with my customers about my dream of going to Japan and all that, but they don't believe me. They don't take me seriously. They often think that what I'm expecting is their money.

Anxious Accumulation

What comes through these strikingly similar narratives, variations of which I heard from many other women working at the club, is the idea of Japan as "elsewhere," a place onto which visions of escape can be projected. They are aspiring to join the middle class, and without a college degree that opens up doors to white-collar jobs, they see Japan as a shortcut to a desired lifestyle. Many of them expressed to me their dreams of someday owning their own karaoke club or a store, as some former *xiaojie* have succeeded in doing. "Do you know that karaoke club, Kitashinchi? The owner used to work in a karaoke club, and one of the Japanese customers helped her open her own club. Well, it was 'given' to her by one of her customers," Zheng Wei told me, and others filled me in with other examples of successful *xiaojie* who became small-business owners. In their eyes, Japanese customers are potential husbands or investors.

Yet, as Zheng Wei most explicitly put it, these young women are also aware of their social status. Their anxiety is apparent in their contradictory declarations, "I like this easygoing lifestyle" and "I hate this job." This anxiety is channeled into their desire for Japan and, in the end, their image of themselves as Japanese-speaking subjects who use acquired *suzhi* to generate wealth and status and become modern, thus redeeming China's reputation as not-yet-modern. These sorts of Japan fantasies are not unique to karaoke hostesses; they are also echoed by those who have already achieved the coveted middle-class status, and their fantasies further fuel the redemptive economy in Dalian.

Middle-Class Fantasies of Japan

Wang Jie, a chatty woman in her early thirties, has been working for Toshiba Dalian for eleven years. Her husband, Dai Lisheng, also works for the company, and together they share many tangible markers of their newly acquired middle-class status, such as a foreign car, a brand-new apartment in an upscale neighborhood, highly desirable investment property in downtown Dalian's Manhattan Building, and a large stock portfolio. The couple invited me over for dinner. They came to pick me up in their shiny white Toyota SUV, a prime object of envy. A brief ride took us to a newly constructed apartment complex near Xinghai Park, now turning into an upscale residential area. While Dai Lisheng put the car in the building's underground parking garage, Wang Jie showed me around their spacious three-bedroom apartment, filled with modern furniture. Dai joined us. "I was in charge of designing the interior," he said with pride in his cheerful voice. "Come, what do you think?" he asked, pointed to niches in the living-room walls that displayed colored vases and decorative glass tiles. With ambient incandescent lighting (fluorescent is the household norm in China), a sleek leather sofa in the middle of the sunken living room, and a dark wood dining-room cabinet with beveled glass doors showing off bottles of cognac and other European liquors, the apartment was a realization of the images of "urban life" and "modern life" promoted at the Dalian Housing Fair.

After an elaborate dinner in their elegantly appointed dining room, Dai suggested that we go out for drinks with some of their friends. In a sleek bar in downtown Dalian, Dai and his friends ordered a bottle of Jonny Walker Black—which cost nearly one third of his monthly salary—and started singing karaoke.[46] Wang Jie sat next to me and told me about her plan to go to a Japanese-language school in a Tokyo suburb for one year and then apply to a Japanese university. Since she already had an associate's degree, all she needed was another two years of university education to receive a bachelor's degree.

> My mother doesn't support my plan of going to Japan. She doesn't understand why I have to give up my great job at Toshiba. My salary is very high by Dalian standards [she earned 1,200 RMB, about $150, a month], and I have a very comfortable life here. My husband and I bought two nice apartments, one for investment and another for ourselves, both with a mortgage from the bank. We don't have any financial problems with our cushy double income now. But if I quit my job, it won't be as easy as it has been. . . . But I've been working for Toshiba for eleven years, and I feel I've had enough of it. Since I'm already thirty-three years old and my husband is thirty-four years old, my mom wants to see a grandchild, but that's not what I want now.
>
> What am I going to do after coming back from Japan? This, I don't know. I will have to look for a new job, but I'm not worried. There are so

> many Japanese corporations in Dalian. Also I'm actually thinking about opening my own store, maybe a karaoke bar for Japanese businessmen or a Japanese restaurant. There is one Japanese man who is willing to invest 600,000 RMB [$75,000] in opening a karaoke bar—I'll only have to invest 100,000 or 200,000 RMB [$12,500 or $25,000] to get it started. And I think that this business will be very lucrative. I've been to many of these places with my Japanese colleagues, and the ways in which they spend money is quite unimaginable. They can easily spend 10,000 RMB ($1,250) per night!

She told me about her friends and relatives who had studied in Japan to improve their career opportunities when they returned to Dalian. Japan has become the land of opportunity for many young Dalianites.[47] Through language study and a university degree from Japan, Wang Jie hopes to equip herself with *suzhi* (quality) and become more marketable to generate further wealth. Wang Jie's aspiration aims at better positioning herself within an economy that cherishes certain forms of consuming and producing subjects.

Her aspirations, expressed—like others in Dalian—through fantasies about Japan, underlie and fuel the political economy of redemption by coopting the heterotopic mechanism, which articulates sites of possibility for what seems impossible and invisible at home in a spatial elsewhere. Various mechanisms for capitalizing on colonial inheritance—from urban renewal to the narrative of Dalian exceptionalism to the discourse of *suzhi*—underscore this mechanism, which greases the wheels of the redemptive economy. Japan as a newfound heterotopia for younger Chinese is an extension of this economy.

"THE LAND OF UNLIMITED OPPORTUNITY"

The recent incorporation of Japan into Dalian's economic life has thus generated a political economy of redemptive desires, in which narratives of Dalian exceptionalism play a significant role in imagining oneself in relation to the Other, be it temporal or geographical. Some versions of this narrative see Dalian's past—both under the Japanese occupation and post-Liberation under Mao's leadership—as exceptional in China in that the city has maintained its unique relationship to Japan, while other versions characterize contemporary Dalian as an "elsewhere" that is "neither China nor Japan," as many put it. Within this political economy, acting out modernity "elsewhere" has generated a certain form of coming to terms with the past for both Chinese and Japanese, as if an invisible hand were at play.

Adam Smith observed in eighteenth-century England how morality and economy intersected and, as an unintended effect, produced the common good. For him, the common good was the growth of a national economy through a harmonious system for efficient allocation of resources through the division of labor. This organic linkage between individual interests and the national interest described by Smith illuminates the historicity embedded in those interests in the case of Dalian.

In Dalian today, the common good for Chinese and Japanese is coming to terms with the past and redeeming modernity's promise while, at the same time, growing the city's economy. This linkage between individual and national redemptive desires fuels this economy. Dalianites' pursuit of middle-class desires accords with the Chinese national project to redeem itself as a modern state,[48] and the narrative of Dalian exceptionalism and the discourse of *suzhi*, two of the principle mechanisms behind the local version of the invisible hand, have justified and reproduced this particular form of redemptive political economy.[49] Japanese businessmen in Dalian project modernity's promise, disappearing in recession-struck Japan, onto the Zone. Their search for modernity's promise—lost in Japan but rediscovered in Dalian—is met with modernity's failure, Japanese colonialism. Through their pursuit of modernity's promise, and by co-opting the colonial logic of heterotopia, they attempt to redeem both modernity's promise and its failure.

The double inheritance at work in this political economy of redemption reveals how modernity's loss is redeemed by modernity's promise and how the redemption of Japan's past failure and contemporary disillusionment feeds off the Chinese sense of inherited loss (from being colonized due to not being modern enough) and newly articulated aspirations as a result of the transition to a market-oriented economy. Seen in this manner, the landscape of after empire in the Zone fuels the political economy of redemption and wealth accumulation through the mediation of middle-class aspirations and fantasies as a form of modernity.

Foreign investment in Dalian's economy continued to grow in the early 2000s, reaching $2.245 billion in 2006, a 124.1 percent increase from the previous year.[50] In 2006, a total of 853 more foreign corporations, an increase of 19.3 percent, joined the Dalian market. With the recent increase of foreign investment from other countries, the ratio of Japanese investment to total foreign investment has decreased; however, Japan remains the major investor in Dalian.[51] Of all new foreign investment in Dalian in 2006, Japanese investment was the largest, with $615 million and 302 corporations, followed by South Korea ($189 million, 167 corporations), the United States ($162 million, 68 corporations), and Hong Kong ($24 million, 123 corporations).[52]

Reflecting the growing importance of the relationship, in 2003 the two major Japanese passenger airlines, Japan Airlines (JAL) and All Nippon Airways (ANA), started daily flights between Tokyo and Dalian. There are daily cargo flights as well to Japan, which continues to be Dalian's top trading partner even as other countries have vied for a larger slice of the pie. In 1988, 58 percent of Dalian's exports and 59 percent of imports were with Japan. As South Korea, the United States, and Hong Kong entered the market, in 2003 the Japanese share of exports and imports fell to 45 percent and 39 percent, respectively. The comparable rates were 39 percent and 34 percent in 2004, and 37 percent and 29 percent in 2005.[53]

As Dalian's labor force maintains a high level of Japanese-language proficiency, the city continues to provide an attractive investment environment for Japanese corporations. In 2005, 48,433 people in China took the highest-level Japanese proficiency exam administered by the Japanese government (*Nihongo nōryoku shiken ikkyū*); Dalian ranked second in the number of people who took this exam (12.4 percent), following Shanghai (16.9 percent), whose population is more than forty-six times greater than Dalian's, with Beijing (10.2 percent) and Changchun (5.6 percent) coming in next.[54] Given the population disparity among these cities and the fact that some of those who took exams in Shanghai and Beijing were originally from Dalian, it is clear that Dalian plays an unusually important role in producing a work force with a high level of proficiency in Japanese. Meanwhile, the municipal government is ever more eager to highlight Dalian's unique inheritance, and it organized its second annual "Japan Week" in May 2007 with great fanfare.

The narrative of Dalian exceptionalism seems to have functioned as a self-fulfilling prophecy. Even during the tide of anti-Japanese demonstrations that swept China for a few weeks in April–May 2005, Dalian remained calm, while only four hours away in Shenyang, the capital of Liaoning Province, more than a thousand people took part in anti-Japanese rallies and the Japanese Consulate was attacked with stones. While other parts of China responded to the failure to come to terms with the past through these demonstrations, it appears that the political economy of redemption in Dalian allowed its population to focus on the growth of wealth within its realm of "elsewhere." The attempt to capitalize on Dalian's colonial inheritance is hence not limited to incorporating Japanese capital. It also involves taking advantage of the logic of heterotopia—a logic that contributed to the creation of Manchukuo itself—co-opted into the new machinery of the market economy in the pursuit of modern life in the early twentieth-first century.

In the past, the Japanese government presented Manchuria to the Japanese as a frontier,[55] and now Dalian again appears as a newly discovered frontier for a Japan mired in recession. Japanese businessmen are not drawn to today's Dalian by nostalgia for the colonial era: they long instead for the period of Japan's postwar economic prosperity, when the achievement of one's middle-class dreams was only a matter of time. In this sense, Dalian provides Japanese corporate workers with a space to redeem modern dreams that they feel are lost in Japan. The municipal government eagerly activates these desires by promoting Dalian as the land of unlimited opportunity.

Nowhere was this more apparent than at an event in Tokyo in 2004. In a reception hall on the ground floor of an elegant four-star hotel, a crowd of nearly four hundred participants in dark suits gathered for the third annual Northeast Investment Promotion Policy Seminar (*Tōhoku chihō shinkō seisaku seminā*). Approximately eighty delegates from municipal governments in Northeast China and more than three hundred Japanese businessmen were busily exchanging business cards at the booths set up for each municipality, which were filled with brochures and promotional DVDs. I spotted Song Xiaotao, deputy director of the Dalian Foreign Trade and Economic Cooperation Bureau, accompanied by several young staff members, who eagerly handed me a colorful, glossy brochure and DVD.

The main event was the speeches by the governors of the three provinces of Northeast China and Inner Mongolia. The Japanese businessmen who filled the large banquet hall listened attentively on headphones to simultaneous translations of the speeches. Fang Wenjie, governor of Liaoning Province, where Dalian is located, came to the stage and launched into a PowerPoint presentation. Confident, articulate, and constantly citing statistical data, he repeatedly emphasized that his province offered an ideal investment climate for Japanese corporations: "Liaoning Province provides wonderful resources and opportunities for Japanese investors. . . . We have excellent infrastructure, rich natural resources and human resources, in particular high-quality labor with Japanese and technological fluencies." Painting a picture of a land of seemingly unlimited opportunities, he "welcomed Japanese friends to invest in Liaoning Province" more than ten times during his twenty-minute speech. Listening to him, I could not help but note the similarity between his pitch and that of the Imperial Japanese government.[56] Fang closed his spiel with an avid invitation: "We welcome Japanese corporations to come invest and develop the industries in Liaoning Province. . . . We welcome Japanese friends to lead Liaoning Province to build modernization (*jianshe xiandaihua*)." This ghostly echo of earlier Japanese modernizations hints at another layer of the politics of colonial inheritance, where anxiety lurks beneath the well-manicured cityscape.

CHAPTER FIVE

Industrious Anxiety: Labor and Landscapes of Modernity in Dalian

The March 2003 issue of the Chinese edition of *Oggi*, a Japanese fashion magazine, devotes four pages to successful Chinese women who have returned from Japan and the United States.[1] A beautiful full-page portrait accompanied by three attractive snapshots introduces a woman who has recently returned to Shanghai, after studying and working in Japan, to start her own business. Under the headline "Conscientious (*renzhen*) women are the most beautiful," the text describes her: "It is not difficult to figure out that she studied in Japan from her appearance—dyed long hair, simple yet fashionable outfit, subtle smile that is as if permanently engraved on her lips, all of which give you the sense of a spring breeze." The article portrays her as a conscientious, sincere, elegant, calm, and thoughtful person. The article's use of *renzhen*, which is often used by the Chinese in Dalian to describe the Japanese work ethic in a half-respectful and half-critical way, gives it a certain cachet, marking it as a value leading not only to success but also to physical beauty.

Most of the Chinese employees in Japanese corporations I spoke with used *renzhen* to describe their Japanese colleagues. Their use of *renzhen* captures their ambivalent feelings toward the Japanese. On the one hand, it expresses their awe and respect for how their Japanese colleagues work conscientiously and diligently—and their recognition of how such hard work led Japan to become an economic power in the postwar years. This recognition that being *renzhen* could potentially lead to success in the new social order is precisely what has led people to cherish *renzhen* as a value. On the other hand, there exists a pervasive cynicism that hard work is not always equally rewarded in a society suffering from the malaise of corruption. Thus the use of *renzhen* invokes an ideal society where hard work is rewarded, an image often projected upon Japanese society.

Not only associated with positive aspects of Japanese society, *renzhen* is also used to tease: "Why always be so serious? Come on, relax!" as one employee in a Japanese corporation in the Dalian Economic and Technological Development Zone (*kaifaqü*, the Zone hereafter) put it after expressing his sincere respect for the Japanese work ethic. Usually implicit, though occasionally explicit, this use of *renzhen* draws a connection between conscientiousness and Japanese militarism and how, in prewar Japan, the former led to the latter. This linkage between *renzhen* and prewar militarism suggests the danger within the machinery of the modern work ethic, which creates a structural gap between conscientiousness and good conscience. This chapter looks into this simmering anxiety expressed in the double usage of *renzhen* through the figure of Japanese workers to explore what is at stake in the otherwise robust political economy of redemption in Dalian.

The anxiety expressed through this double usage of *renzhen*, which casts doubt on the assumed radical discontinuity between prewar and postwar Japan, echoes the question posed by Theodor Adorno more than half a century ago, in the aftermath of the Holocaust in Europe, in his eponymous essay "What Does Coming to Terms with the Past Mean?"[2] Observing postwar West Germany in the 1950s, Adorno expressed his concern that the national calls for "coming to terms with the past" had become less about "working through" a difficult past than merely turning the page to forget about it.[3] He argued that a sense of redemption acquired through postwar economic prosperity gave Germans the illusion that they were different from their countrymen under National Socialism. Germans, he observed, continued to fail to see themselves as agents of history; they considered themselves not as the subjects but rather the objects of an abstract structure called society. He argued that this mentality, in turn, could be easily manipulated to serve another manifestation of totalitarian politics. Adorno thus questioned the assumed radical discontinuity at Germany's zero hour and warned against what he saw as an unchanging national tendency toward totalitarianism.[4]

Decades since Adorno made this observation about West Germany, we have seen that there is no real "turning the page" in order to forget about the past. Through the dynamics of *inheritance and betrayal*, what was erased comes back to remind the current generation of unaccounted-for losses. The political economy of redemption itself is a manifestation and acknowledgement of what resists erasure in the form of accrued moral debt. While robust economic activities have indeed made invisible certain pasts, as Adorno warned, the same process works simultaneously to reveal the very thing that the economic rationality aims to hide, as we have seen in the cases of the capitalization of colonial remnants in Northeast China. Dalian's well-manicured urban and industrial landscape, so accommodating to returning Japanese, is built upon a selective use of the past that does not acknowledge colonial violence—a tactic that ends up, in spite of itself, highlighting the very past it seeks to elide through economic activities. Counter to the general perception that economic rationality masks unaccounted-for pasts, this chapter further looks into the vigorous Sino-Japanese economic activity in Dalian as a key site to explore the longstanding question of what it means to come to terms with the past.

A pressing question for postgenerations today, then, is not whether economic prosperity masks the lack of coming to terms with the past, nor is it about the erasure of a difficult past. Rather, what is troubling is the smoldering sense of not having come to terms with the past *despite* the newly acknowledged losses (new historical knowledge) revealed through the capitalization of colonial remnants. Not only are more pasts made visible to postgenerations than before but what is being erased—the missing pages of history—are also becoming more visible to them. Furthermore, the political economy of redemption in Dalian brings out, rather than represses, the underlying moral economy and desires to reckon with inherited losses. And yet, beneath Dalian's beautified landscape, which welcomes returning Japanese and celebrates "modern life" often through a refraction of Japanese modernity, lies a tension between Japan as a model to emulate and Japan as the object of suspicion and often hatred, instantiating a simmering sense of failed reckoning, epitomized in the double usage of *renzhen*. Acknowledgement of losses (the "Truth") and accompanying moral debt, a model for coming to terms with the past often evoked among both Chinese and Japanese publics, does not seem to deliver the desired effect.

This chapter examines this latent anxiety that persists *despite* such knowledge of the past as I look at robust economic relations built through face-to-face encounters among Chinese and Japanese postgenerations. My use of the phrase "despite such knowledge" echoes the evocative title of Eva Hoffman's *After Such Knowledge: Memory, History and the Legacy of the Holocaust*.[5] "Despite such knowledge" references the multiple levels of anxiety contained within the postgenerations' deferred reckoning that I will explore in this chapter. First, despite the knowledge of the past catastrophe, postgeneration Chinese and Japanese are building robust economic relations, as we have seen in the preceding chapter.[6] Second, despite the knowledge of the past catastrophe, which has become more visible than before, there remains a nagging sense of not having reckoned with the past.

Dalian offers a unique window through which to explore the crux of this question, precisely because the city of Dalian seems to offer opportunities for Chinese and Japanese postgenerations to come to terms with the past through their new economic relations, yet at the same time the city is full of smoldering anxiety over the lack thereof. This chapter suggests that while the political economy of redemption channels accrued debt into productive redemptive relations, enough remains to stir the latent anxiety of postgenerations. This chapter looks into this excess that escapes the redemptive mechanism in the economic sphere through the concept of *renzhen*, which allows for the presence of the past in the vision of the future.

This chapter brings this latent anxiety encapsulated by *renzhen* into focus by examining the capitalization of colonial inheritance (or lack thereof) at two major industrial sites in Dalian. The first is the current Dalian Onoda Cement plant located on the outskirts of the Zone. One of the prewar Japanese corporations that returned to the city, Onoda resumed operations in 1989 as one of the first foreign companies to invest in Dalian after the opening. The municipal government boasts this former colonial industry as one of the origins of Dalian's modern industry—as an integral part of the city's history of modernization since the beginning of the twentieth century.[7] But capitalization of colonial inheritance in Dalian goes beyond reincorporating former colonial industries through tax incentives and preferential allocation of resources. It extends to embodying Japaneseness in the bodies of workers, in the form of linguistic and cultural fluency expressed in *suzhi*, as we saw in the previous chapter, or in acquiring a "Japanese" work ethic as modern workers, as we shall see in this one. Dalian Onoda Cement's current factory grounds provide a glimpse of the landscape of after empire, which incorporates colonial remnants through the rhetoric of economic rationality while eliding colonial violence.

The second site, on the former grounds of the Fukushō Chinese Labor Company near the city's port, instantiates the state's refusal to capitalize on particular forms of colonial remnants. Fukushō, established under Japanese rule and called "Fuchang" in Chinese, both directly enslaved Chinese workers and was also in charge of "procuring" forced laborers for other companies during the war. Despite the municipal government's reluctance to mark its violent history at this site adjacent to the Dalian port, the ghostly resonance of the wartime use of forced labor became reified through national media heroine and celebrated activist Wang Xuan's weeklong visit to Dalian in May 2003 as part of her sustained effort to investigate wartime biological human experiments by the Imperial Japanese Army.

At these two ethnographic sites, linked through the concept of *renzhen*, we shall see how capitalizing on colonial inheritance—or the avoidance of such capitalization—provides a locale where generational transmission of colonial remnants reveals the underlying anxiety surrounding the rhetoric of "not enough apology." Anti-Japanese sentiments in China are supplemented by a deep if unarticulated anxiety toward modernity that evades individual accountability and good conscience while celebrating the diligence and conscientiousness of modern workers. The double usage of *renzhen* further suggests the simmering anxiety about the lack of accountability of the modern state, not only the Japanese, but also the Chinese. The case of Dalian illustrates a delicate articulation of Chinese society's ambivalent impulses toward modernity. Beneath the cityscape full of celebrations of the modern in fashion, beauty, and lifestyle lurk unresolved tensions contained within pursuing modernity. Through the celebrated figure of urban middle-class workers, the capitalization of colonial inheritance comes back to question the accountability of the modern state and workers.

INCORPORATING COLONIAL INDUSTRY

"They are doing very well—a good company," a middle-aged cab driver commented with pride when I asked him to take me to the Dalian Onoda Cement factory in a remote location forty-five minutes outside the city. As we left downtown Dalian behind and drove past rows of new apartment developments on the outskirts of the city, the road quickly became deserted, and soon the driver made a sharp turn onto a narrow dirt road leading to what seemed like a no-man's-land. A long, bumpy ride along a narrow lane eventually opened onto a desolate plain of reddish-brown earth and occasional cornfields. In the distance, something resembling an abandoned battleship, the faint shape of a factory, came into view (figure 5.1).

Onoda Cement dates back to the Meiji era in Japan. It was founded in 1881 as the country's first privately owned cement company (its original name was *Semento Seizō Gaisha*, literally Cement Production Company), producing materials for a nation in the midst of aggressive modernization.[8] The Dalian factory operated for nearly forty years, from 1908, soon after the Russo-Japanese War (1904–5) and the establishment of the South Manchuria Railway Company (1906), until the Japanese defeat in 1945. Although the company changed its name to Taiheiyō Cement Corporation in 1998 as the result of a merger with two other firms, its factory in Dalian retains its old name, Onoda Cement, to signal its longstanding presence in the city.

"Oh, is that what your cab driver told you about our company?" asked Sasaki Susumu, the president of Dalian Onoda Cement, without concealing his joy and excitement about the company's reputation among the locals. "But it was very rough for the first decade here in Dalian. It's only in the

5.1 The new "returning" Onoda Cement plant on the outskirts of Dalian: Onoda Cement was one of the first Japanese companies to "return" to Dalian in the late 1980s when the city became open to foreign investment. The history of Onoda Cement in Dalian dates back to 1908, immediately following the Russo-Japanese War and the establishment of the South Manchuria Railway Company, and the Dalian factory operated for nearly forty years until the Japanese defeat in 1945. Today, the state-run Dalian Cement operates the original Onoda Cement plant from the prewar era, while the returning Onoda Cement Company built the state-of-the-art new plant that overlooks the original. Photo by author, 2003.

past few years that we started to make a profit," he continued. Today Dalian Onoda Cement employs four hundred full-time and one hundred temporary Chinese employees and seven Japanese managers. Sasaki is a reserved and laconic man in his late fifties, and a silent pause followed his every sentence. "When we started in the early 1990s, we exported more than 70 percent of our product to the United States and Southeast Asia. But after the Asian economic crisis in 1997, the price of cement went down so much that export didn't make sense any longer, and since 1998, we have produced primarily for the Chinese domestic market. It was really tough, and we almost withdrew from Dalian. Well, you see, it means a lot to hear that locals consider us a good company." Then he suggested that I meet employees of different ages and in various positions to get a better sense of the company.

Handing me a heavy book on the hundred-year history of Onoda Cement, he arranged for my return to the factory several days later.

Almost none of the employees I met at Dalian Onoda Cement, Chinese or Japanese, were aware of the ongoing lawsuit against its parent company filed on October 4, 1999, in Los Angeles Superior Court by a naturalized Korean-American demanding compensation for wartime slave labor at an Onoda Cement plant located in Japanese-occupied Korea.[9] The case is based on the Hayden Act (an amendment to California Code of Civil Procedure section 354.6), which not only removed the statute of limitations for forced labor cases but also extended the scope of liable perpetrators to include Nazi allies and businesses operated within the territories of Nazis and their allies and sympathizers. What is now Taiheiyō Cement has a Los Angeles–based subsidiary, which enabled the plaintiff to file a lawsuit against the parent company in Japan, and Jae Won Jeong thus became the first Asian-American to bring a Japanese corporation to a US court for wartime compensation claims.[10] The lawsuit was widely covered in the Western media as the first case to take advantage of this new legal opportunity.[11]

When asked whether they had heard of the lawsuit, the Chinese employees, mostly in their late twenties and midthirties, said "no" and were indifferent to the issue. The response from the Japanese employees, mostly middle-aged, was usually an embarrassed grin. One younger Japanese employee in his midthirties, however, had learned about the case when he was first assigned to the Beijing office a few years earlier. Speaking about the indifference of the Chinese employees, he observed, "I don't think that they get that type of information. The Internet has become more available, but still the information from abroad is limited and selective here. Besides, they might be thinking that it wouldn't be advantageous for China to pursue compensation lawsuits against Japan, given the economic relationship between the two. Another factor is that many Chinese draw a clear line between prewar and postwar Japan."

The corporate history compiled in preparation for the company's centenary in 1981 makes no mention of using forced labor during the war.[12] Yet the description of the factory operation in Dalian in the first half of the twentieth century does portray a factory with a constant labor shortage, especially after the outbreak of the Pacific War in 1941. As the war effort on all fronts demanded more industrial output even as conscription depleted the labor force, the Japanese government started to aggressively mobilize Chinese and Koreans for industrial production in Japan and its colonies.[13] The "rabbit hunt operation" (*usagi gari sakusen*) to capture Chinese was carried out by a number of organizations in both China and Japan.[14] The North China Labor Association (*Kahoku rōkō kyōkai*) administered the capture and transportation of 34,000 out of the approximately 40,000 Chinese brought to Japan.[15] Other "Chinese" organizations involved—all controlled, in fact, by the Japanese—were the Sino-Japan Labor Association (*Nikka rōmu kyōkai*), the North China Transportation Corporation (*Kahoku unyu kabushiki gaisha*), and the Fukushō Chinese Labor Company (*Fukushō Kakō gaisha*), known as Fuchang Company. Headquartered in Dalian as a subsidiary of the South Manchuria Railway Company, Fuchang "procured" 1,020 Chinese, mostly in Manchukuo, 2.6 percent of the total Chinese forced laborers sent to Japan.[16] In addition to these China-based organizations, the Japanese Great East Asia Ministry (*Daitōashō*), the Army Ministry (*gunjushō*), the Ministry of Transportation (*unyushō*), the Ministry of Welfare (*kōseishō*), and the Home Ministry (*naimushō*) took part in the project, evidence of the systematic nature of the operation.[17] Despite the lack of conclusive evidence, it is thus not hard to imagine that Onoda Cement—which was recognized as vital to the war effort and received preferential allocation of resources, including the use of Chinese forced labor in its factories in Japan—would also have used forced laborers in Dalian. The pervasive indifference to this aspect of the corporate history among younger Chinese who would otherwise be the first to express anti-Japanese sentiments was somewhat puzzling.

My unsettled feeling acquired visual and spatial reinforcement when President Sasaki showed me around the factory grounds. As we walked through the enormous cement-processing plant, what had looked like an abandoned battleship from the distance now appeared like something out of Fritz Lang's *Metropolis*. Enormous dark-gray metal tubes went up and down and across, and our words were lost amid the constant, deep, and loud sounds of the plant. Sasaki was proud of the state-of-the-art facility, which was built on what used to be a cornfield. I asked him what had happened to the original, prewar Onoda Cement plant. "Come, I'll show you," he said, and he led me out to his car. After a couple hundred yards, a gentle white hill covered with pebbles, reminiscent of a Zen garden, began to fill the view, while the powerful modern machinery I had just seen faded away in the background. In striking contrast to the relentless activity of the plant, this was a site of tranquility. "Have you seen a lime mountain before?" asked Sasaki, grabbing pebbles from the earth with the affection only a cement man could have. He continued, "This is what we do, and this is everything. This mountain will let us produce cement for the next thirty to forty years, at least." He urged me to walk over to the far side of the mountain. All of a sudden, a vista opened up. Down below, I saw some factories, cornfields, and more factories, and in the distance, I recognized the faint silhouette of downtown Dalian. "You see the factory down there?" Sasaki asked, pointing toward the factory beneath their lime mountain. "That's the original Onoda Cement plant from the prewar era. Now it's operated by the state-run Dalian Cement, but their mountain will end its life within ten years."

I looked down again to see the decaying colonial inheritance below, and then I looked back to where we'd come to see the bustling reincarnation of this fading physical remainder of the past. The capitalization of colonial industry visible in this landscape reveals Chinese society's complex relationship to colonial modernity, which cannot be reduced to contemporary manifestations of Chinese nationalism that often take the form of anti-Japanese or anti-Western sentiments. *Dalian Fifty Years* (*Dalian wushi nian*), a Communist Party–endorsed history of Dalian since the Liberation in 1949, portrays the development of the city's cement industry as a seamless transition from colonial industry to post-Liberation nationalization to the successful reincorporation of a returned Onoda Cement under the open economic policy.[18] There is no room in this description for the abuse of Chinese laborers under Japanese colonial rule. Instead, Dalian's industrial development is a narrative of a smooth and continuous modernization from the colonial period through today.

In the industrial landscape of Dalian Onoda Cement, literally overlooking its prewar past, traces of colonial violence are abstract if not altogether invisible. What is more—as the spatial juxtaposition of the old Onoda Cement plant, now a state-owned operation with a soon-to-be exhausted lime mountain, and the new Onoda factory, with its pristine lime mountain, epitomizes—it is the "returning" Japanese corporation that is given the rightful lineage within Dalian's industrial modernity. Similar to how the rhetoric of inheritance allowed the Harbin municipal government to claim an otherwise problematic "tradition" (colonial-era edifices built mostly by Russians and Japanese) as its own, the same rhetoric allows Dalian to locate the colonial industry *and* its contemporary reincarnation as the rightful origin and heir to the city's successful industrialization over a century.

While Dalian's industrial landscape may appear to confirm Adorno's concern that economic prosperity obscures historical scars, we shall see how the wealth accumulation through the political economy of redemption fails to assuage deep-seated anxieties. While such anxieties often remain latent under the rhetoric of Dalian exceptionalism, *suzhi* (quality), and inheritance, these anxieties resurface in disguised or displaced forms, often triggered by what Carol Gluck calls "memory activists"[19] such as Wang Xuan, a national media heroine widely known for mobilizing Chinese victims to sue the Japanese government for its wartime biological experiment on Chinese civilians. Her visit to Dalian, which gave a face to wartime slave labor within this otherwise future-oriented cityscape, provides a window through which to examine these anxieties that escape the redemptive economy.

ENCOUNTERS WITH A SCARRED LANDSCAPE[20]

On the front page of *Dalian ribao* (Dalian Daily) on April 23, 2003, a large and eye-catching bordered column called for information: "Wang Xuan to arrive in Dalian for an evidence-gathering trip: investigating evidence of the crimes of Japanese biological warfare in order to extend justice to innocent victims—informants and victims please contact."[21] In the following week, the city was swamped with Wang Xuan fever: a troop of various local media crews covered her activities day and night; ordinary citizens called in with information; people rushed to shake hands with her to show their support; and a restaurant patron rushed out to get a large bouquet of flowers upon recognizing her.

An activist who led 180 Chinese plaintiffs in their suit against the Japanese government in the "Unit 731 Germ Warfare Trial" (*731 butai saikinsen kokka baishō seikyū soshō*),[22] Wang Xuan was chosen by the national television network CCTV as one of the "top ten great people who moved China" (*gandong Zhongguo shi da renwu*) in 2002.[23] The plaintiffs, from Zhejiang and Hunan Provinces, demanded financial compensation and an official apology for their sufferings from plague and cholera bacilli dispersed by the Japanese Army, developed by the infamous Unit 731 biological human experimentation site located on the outskirts of Harbin. Although Wang Xuan was brought up in Shanghai and had followed her husband to Japan, the case brought this cosmopolitan woman back to her ancestral village south of Nanjing, which had suffered a sudden plague epidemic during the war.

Wang Xuan is a passionate and sharp woman in her early fifties. Like many intellectuals of her generation, her drive to fight injustice seems to come from her family's experience during the Cultural Revolution. Over dinner, she explained to us that her father was a high government official in the Public Prosecutor's Office and was labeled as a "rightist" (*youpai*). He passed away in 1985 without having had his reputation rehabilitated. Every time our conversation turned to personal matters, Wang Xuan would talk with bitterness about how the Communist Party had treated her father.

Wang Xuan had come to Dalian to investigate her suspicions that the Japanese Army had conducted biological experiments there during the war. Earlier that year, she had interviewed Song Chengli, a seventy-four-year-old man in Shandong Province, whose father she suspected was a victim of Japanese biological experiments. Song's father, along with Song, was abducted in 1942 by a group of Chinese serving under the Japanese to work for the Fuchang Company at the Dalian port. Born in Dandong near the Korean border, Song's father was a man of culture—he was very good at calligraphy, Song repeatedly told us with pride. His father had moved to Shandong Province, where he ran a small business. After the Manchurian Incident in 1931, Song's father gave up the business and started working as a load bearer in Shandong. When agents of the North China Labor Association captured his father, they roped him and branded four marks on his torso. Since Song's elder brother was sick at that time, his father told Song, then just twelve years old, to accompany him. Together with his father at Fuchang Company in Dalian, where they were transported, Song would carry extremely heavy disks of dried soybeans.

In the fall of 1943, a Chinese guard at Fuchang told Song that his father had suddenly taken ill. In the "clinic" at Fuchang, he found his father, uncle, and his friend Shi Zaizi's father dying one next to another. Song's father, barely able to speak, could only tell him that he had received two shots and two white pills and had felt terribly sick immediately afterward. Four days after falling ill, Song's father died at the age of forty-eight. After Shi was told about his own father's death, he went to see the corpse. His father was forty-five years old, but he had weighed a mere hundred pounds at the time of his death. After the sudden deaths of their fathers, Song and Shi worked and ate together constantly. They even escaped the company three times but returned on each occasion, "since we didn't have any job to support ourselves outside of Fuchang Company." After the war ended, Song joined the Chinese Liberation Army and later, in 1978, a state-owned company, and he played a role in the Chinese Communist Party (CCP). After the war, he never returned to Dalian, until Wang Xuan suggested that they come back together to investigate whether his father was a victim of a Japanese biological experiment.

While Wang Xuan, Song Chengli, and a troop of journalists were visiting the former Japanese-Russian Prison in Lüshun (Port Arthur), Guo Lingmei, the director of CCTV, who had accompanied Wang Xuan and Song to Dalian, received a phone call from a journalist at the *Dalian Daily*. A man named Shi Shutian had contacted the newspaper claiming that he was the very person that Song had mentioned as his childhood friend during his years at Fuchang Company. Wang Xuan and Guo decided to arrange a meeting at the man's apartment that afternoon—with some reservations, as his name was not exactly what Song remembered. At the news, Song became overwhelmed with emotion, but he was instructed by the CCTV director to ask certain questions to confirm that this person was indeed who he claimed to be.

A large group of television crews and newspaper journalists went along with Wang Xuan and Song to the meeting. It took us a while to find the apartment, which was located on the former grounds of the Fuchang Company. Finally we ran into a tall man in his late forties, who turned out to be the son of the man we were looking for. His father lived on the first floor of a typical 1980s apartment. The director set up chairs right outside of the apartment entrance for filming.

A tall figure appeared at the dimly lit front entrance of the dilapidated apartment building. Song stared intently at the figure, his ailing body expressing his anxious expectation. Both men's desperate eyes examined each other in silence while we onlookers held our breath, every bit as anxious as they were. "Are you Shi Zaizi?" Song slowly asked, his voice trembling. "Do you remember me?" he continued now in haste. "I'm Song Chengli, from Fuchang." "Yes, I'm Shi Zaizi," the other man answered firmly. With this, the two men tightly held each other without further words. Camera flashes enveloped them, and the young television crew eagerly captured the tearful reconnection of the long-lost childhood friends from the wartime enslavement (figure 5.2).

The two men held hands tightly throughout their brief, sudden, and unexpected reunion. Little by little, they pieced together their shared memories of the alleys they used to run through together and of the places where they lived. They recalled their living quarters with narrow wooden bunk beds. Then Song took out some black-and-white postcards of old Dalian. One of them showed a hill covered with shanty houses. It was a slum area next to Fuchang Company, and Shi Zaizi (who had changed his name to Shi Shutian after the war) stared at the photograph, gasping at the flood of memories, and tears streamed again from his eyes. The faded postcard captured where they used to live—the so-called red houses (*hong fangzi*), two-story brick residences on the company grounds. As the two old men reflected for a while on their memories of the red houses, Song raised his voice, tears welling in his eyes, and firmly proclaimed, "This is where our fathers died. We have to tell the younger generation what happened here, let them not forget, let them learn from history!" He continued, "What I want to ask [the Japanese government] through my fight in the court is 'Why won't you admit it?' (*Wei shenme bu chengren?*)."

Here, Song evoked the literal meaning of the two Chinese characters that make up the term *renzhen*—to recognize, acknowledge, and admit (*ren*) the

5.2 **Reunited former "coolies," enslaved by Fuchang Company at Dalian Port in the 1940s:** Song Chengli and Shi Zaizi, former "coolies" enslaved by Fuchang Company, reunited in front of Shi's apartment building. Both of them were teenagers when they were captured along with their fathers. They worked, ate, and slept together, and both of them lost their fathers to what is suspected to have been a biological human experiment conducted at the company as part of the Imperial Japanese Army's development of biochemical weapons. Photo by author, 2003.

truth (*zhen*)—signaling how Song considers *renzhen*, in the sense of seeking and admitting historical truths in a conscientious manner, to be at the crux of coming to terms with the past. Following this rhetorical question, Song emotionally began to sing a song about the Nanjing Massacre that an old *laogong* ("coolie," or unskilled laborer) had sang for him at night. With its reference to one of the most contested historical issues between China and Japan, this song, which none of the young journalists recognized, underscored the centrality of *renzhen* as seeking Truth. Prompted by his singing, everybody around him started discussing a plan to write a letter to the Dalian municipal government to request protection of the last remaining red houses and to turn them into a historical museum. The ensuing discussion revolved around the vanishing traces of the past in Dalian's cityscape and the concerns felt by many about losing connection with historical truth. This view—that the recognition, or lack of recognition, of truth is at the center of the longstanding "history problem" with Japan—echoes a similar recognition described in chapter 3 among younger Japanese tourists in Changchun.

"Red houses," known as *hekizansō* (blue mountain houses) in Japanese, were originally built to showcase Japan's modern labor management. Established in 1909, Fuchang Company built a sprawling housing complex to accommodate the so-called coolies in 1911.[24] Equipped with hygienic living space and recreational facilities, the homes were considered by Japanese as ideal, state-of-the-art residences for Chinese workers, and the complex became a destination for Japanese tourists and school-sponsored trips.[25] During a school trip to Manchuria in 1939, a student from Nara Women's University in Japan wrote in her diary, "*Hekizansō* are primarily for the coolies working at the Dalian port, and they accommodate 20,000 workers. Managed by Fukushō Chinese Labor Company, the facility is well thought through for taking good care of their everyday life and in case of sickness. For most coolies from Shangdong Province, I've heard, this is a place they yearn for. I guess it is important for the Japanese to extend warm hands to those people."[26]

Fuchang Company proudly produced a brochure about the *hekizansō* to be distributed to Japanese visitors. The cover of the twenty-page *hekizansō* brochure features a sweeping photographic view of the housing complex overlooking the Dalian port (figure 5.3).[27] The bird's-eye view of the geometrically aligned rows of houses symbolized modern order, hygiene, and control. The brochure trumpets Fuchang Company's modern labor management by first proclaiming its decision not to use the expression *kuli* (coolie), which they found derogatory, to refer to their Chinese laborers and instead to refer to them as *kakō* (Chinese laborers) "in order to express a sense of respect."[28] It claims that "they have made this place [*hekizansō*] a safe haven (*anrakukyō*) for a kind of life unimaginable in their hometowns in Shangdong Province."[29] With statistical data, the booklet boasts of the loyalty of the company's workers and their high rate of retention. It explains how "they consider *hekizansō* as their own homes to the extent that they beg to be sent back to the 'red houses' even when they are recovering from illness in the luxurious and beautiful South Manchuria Railway Company hospital" and how they see the *hekizansō* as "the extension of their hometown, home, grave, and refuge."[30] Pointing to the crucial importance of the labor management of Chinese workers for the success of Japan's Manchurian policy, the booklet ends by soliciting visitors' criticisms and suggestions.

In his detailed account of the development of labor relations in Fuchang Company, Japanese historian Yanagisawa Asobu traces the transformation

5.3 The cover illustration of *hekizansō* (red houses) in the 1929 Fuchang Company brochure: The cover of the 1929 brochure of Fuchang Company illustrates the panoramic view of the housing complex called *hekizansō* (or "red houses," as the workers called them) that accommodated Chinese workers. The brochure boasts of the company's state-of-the-art facilities and modern labor management.

of Fuchang's prized modern labor-management system into a site of colonial exploitation when the company struggled to adapt to rapidly changing socioeconomic relations as Japan deepened its involvement in war efforts.[31] In earlier years, because of its welfare package—the promise of clothing, food, and housing in *hekizansō*—Fuchang Company enjoyed a high labor-retention rate compared with other Japanese companies in Dalian despite its relatively low wage level. But with the outbreak of war against China in 1937 and against the United States in 1941, the demand for labor increased while its supply declined. Procurement of Chinese labor became more difficult and costly, and competition for the limited number of available workers grew as shortages of food and everyday goods became a serious issue. As a result, the labor conditions at Fuchang Company deteriorated rapidly in the late 1930s, and the company lost workers through escape and pirating by other companies in the 1940s.

The historical transformation of *hekizansō* to "red houses"—from a model modern housing facility for workers to the symbol of Japanese colonial violence—illuminates not only the different positionalities of Japanese and Chinese but also the transformation of Manchuria, in both image and reality, from an idealized land of opportunity to a colonial dystopia. It also highlights the location of colonial inheritance within the topography of after empire in contemporary Dalian. The visit to the red houses with former "coolies" opened a space where young Dalianites encountered the colonial history invisible beneath the city's beautified downtown. In the presence of two former forced laborers who had lost their fathers, quite likely to Japanese biological experiments, colonial violence was no longer an abstract trace. Rather, the occasion provided a locale for the younger Chinese to acknowledge their colonial inheritance, which had been made invisible to them within a cityscape full of celebrations of "modern life."

But Wang Xuan's visit did not stop at reversing the invisibility of the deep scars in Dalian's landscape. Her investigative trip further exposed what was behind this invisibility. In a similar manner to how colonial inheritance betrayed unexpected losses, as we have seen in other cities, the acknowledgement of colonial inheritance was accompanied by yet another betrayal of losses: those sustained by the CCP due to its inaction and complicity.

Wang Xuan's cell phone kept ringing as locals offered to provide her with information. On the second night of her visit, a local man who remained anonymous contacted *Dalian Daily* saying that he had important information regarding the Japanese biological warfare site near Dalian. After several phone calls, she learned that the former Imperial Japanese Army Hospital (now the People's Liberation Army Hospital) in the suburb of Dalian had also once been the headquarters of Imperial Japanese Army Unit 693, which was linked to Harbin's Unit 731. A *Dalian Daily* article reported that an informant who worked for the Dalian railway had discovered a mass grave on the grounds in 1968.[32] According to the article, the hospital was meant to be used for producing the plague bacillus but was incomplete at the time of the Japanese defeat. To conceal evidence of their plans, the Japanese spent three days burning documents. An astonishing number of Chinese workers—eight thousand—died mysteriously during the hospital's construction, the article reported.

In the early 1990s, Zhao Wenjun, who later took part in planning Dalian's centenary celebration in 1998 (as described in the preceding chapter), started investigating the biological human experiments in Dalian. His study indicates that the Sanitation Department of the South Manchuria Railway Company was the first to plan biological experiments in Northeast China, and Unit 731 was later established in Harbin as part of a larger project designed by the Sanitation Department. According to Zhao, Unit 319 was established in Dalian in 1939 as a branch of Unit 731. The Army Hospital was the home of Unit 693, which, along with Unit 319, was an integral part of the Japanese germ-warfare infrastructure.[33]

With this information, Wang Xuan was eager to investigate the former site of the Army Hospital. Yet, despite her passion, she could not break through the state bureaucracy. The People's Liberation Army Hospital rejected her repeated requests to visit the site for reasons of security and confidentiality as an army hospital. Likewise, her request for access to the archive at the Dalian port to seek evidence of Fuchang Company's possible involvement in Japan's germ-warfare operations was denied. Since Song Chengli's father suddenly took ill immediately after he was given white pills, Wang Xuan suspected that the pills were part of a human experiment. In spite of the intense interest among ordinary citizens in her investigative trip, Wang Xuan fever did not force open long-unaccounted-for moments of history closed off behind state power. "You see, this is typical China. We Chinese blame Japan for not dealing with the past, but look at this. They don't care about war victims," Wang Xuan snapped, disgust and fatigue on her face.

Wang Xuan's comment points to the Chinese state's complicity in deferred reckoning, and she mentioned privately that her activism was actually directed at changing Chinese society more so than changing Japanese society. The difficulty in achieving that was exemplified by the actions of the young journalists who had followed her with such excitement—the detailed reports they ultimately filed about the day's events did nothing to problematize the inaction and complicity of the Chinese state and its lack of *renzhen* in seeking the truth.

SEEKING TRUTHS BY EMBODYING *RENZHEN*

We went back to Wang Xuan's hotel late at night, frustrated and exhausted. As I was talking with Zhao Wenjun, I heard Wang Xuan's high-pitched voice from a room next door. She was yelling at an old man in his sixties. He had come to Wang Xuan to discuss his wife's case. His wife was a survivor of the 1932 Pingdingshan Massacre, the first large-scale massacre that took place after Manchukuo was established. Approximately three thousand people were killed on September 16, 1932.[34] He was telling Wang Xuan that he wanted to go to Japan to attend the court ruling scheduled for just two weeks hence—May 9, 2003. In response, Wang Xuan kept telling him to drop it: "How can you go to Japan? Do you have a passport? What will you do if you go to Japan?" She interrogated him with a sharp edge in her voice. "Have you contacted someone there?" "No," he replied, "but I have this document." He handed her a piece of paper. "This has nothing to do with this court ruling on May 9," she said with unmasked anger. "But, here, I signed it," he pleaded, "and here are the names of the Japanese lawyers."

I looked at the document. It was a petition organized by a group of Japanese lawyers asking the Japanese government to apologize to the victims of the Pingdingshan Massacre. They had gathered the signatures of these victims' relatives, including this man. I attempted to explain the specific purpose of the petition to him and that it was not a legal document or related to the lawsuit. He looked puzzled. Growing angrier, Wang Xuan said to him, "You see, this is not a legal document for compensation. That's why it's no use for you to go to Japan for this trial, since you are not one of the plaintiffs." Clearly, this man was under the impression that he was among the plaintiffs of this case because he had signed a document with Japanese lawyers whose names were on it. Wang Xuan continued to argue with him: "Do you understand how to sue in Japan? Do you even understand how to sue in China? Have you ever investigated it by yourself? If you want to do something for your wife, instead of going to Japan, you'd better ask the local court and local lawyer how they can help you." At this point, she was screaming. The old man shrunk and started apologizing to her.

When we finally sat down for dinner past ten o'clock, Wang Xuan told us how she had encountered similar situations so many times in the past (figure 5.4). She was deeply frustrated by the widespread attitude that, as she put it, "someone will help me" or "someone will give me money." At the same time, she was personally embarrassed by the situation. All the postwar compensation lawsuits filed in Japan against the Japanese government or Japanese corporations, she explained, were supported by Japanese volunteers and pro bono Japanese lawyers. Her trip to Dalian was financed by her former boss in Japan, where she used to teach English. Wang Xuan told me later, "I feel it's wrong that Chinese expect all this support from Japanese who volunteer to do so from a strong sense of justice and for whom it is a redemptive act for what their parents' or grandparents' generations did in the past. My goal is not to be the leader of these victims. My goal is to encourage these people to take their own action."

Here, Wang Xuan underscored what she perceives as a problematic asymmetry in the moral economy: it is actually the Japanese who are overpaying

5.4 Searching for the traces of the biochemical experiments conducted by the Imperial Japanese Army: Wang Xuan, Song Chengli with his son, and a television crew discussed that week's media reporting of themselves while finishing a late-night dinner after a long day of tracing the biochemical experiments directed by the Imperial Japanese Army. Wang Xuan suspects that Song's father was one of the victims of the biological experiments conducted in the "red houses." Photo by author, 2003.

in their eagerness to redeem their moral debt. But what she considers the skewed balance sheet in the moral economy also suggests something else. Her agitated interaction with the husband of a Pingdingshan Massacre victim points to the absence of the Chinese state in addressing the needs of victims and their families. The elderly man was on his own, looking helpless and lost, with a newspaper clipping of the article reporting on Wang Xuan's visit to Dalian clutched in his hand. The years-old document he presented, which he thought was a contract with the group of Japanese lawyers representing Chinese war victims, had been carefully folded in an envelope in a manner that shows how he had treasured this piece of paper as a sliver of hope in the dark. Wang Xuan's exasperated response to this frail man was, in part, a reflection of her own experience of loss and anger at having been left in the dark for many decades about her own family's victimhood.

Wang Xuan's deeply ingrained suspicion toward the Chinese state since the Cultural Revolution has found an outlet in her crusade on behalf of the victims of Japanese colonial violence, who have been overlooked not only by the Japanese government but by the Chinese government as well, despite its anti-imperialist rhetoric. Until 1995, when she learned from an article in the English-language newspaper *Japan Times* (Tokyo) about the Japanese germ-warfare attacks in her ancestral home, Wang Xuan herself had not been aware that her uncle was one of the victims. "The Chinese government is anxious about all citizens' organizations, and these victims have been neglected in China," she explained bitterly. I recalled a comment made by a local man in the housing complex where Song Chengli and Shi Zaizi had their dramatic, tearful reunion. As we were packing up to leave, a neighbor told us that during the Cultural Revolution schools in this neighborhood used to invite former coolies to share their stories of life under Japanese rule, and that that was how he had learned about the history of the neighborhood as a small child. But with the end of the Cultural Revolution and the establishment of diplomatic relations between China and Japan, the tables had turned. Now China looks forward, leaving the past within an encapsulated space of anti-Japanese war movies and historical museums, carefully choreographed and prescribed by the party-state.[35] As a result, the contemporary Chinese landscape displays the simultaneous omnipresence and absence of Japanese colonial violence.

For the young journalists reporting on Wang Xuan's visit, the figures of Song Chengli and Shi Zaizi as speaking subjects mediate between the Japanese invasion as historical relic and the Japanese invasion as conveyed through intimate family tales of terror. For many younger Chinese, the recent surge of postwar compensation lawsuits in Japan against the Japanese government and corporations is a wake-up call to unearth remnants of the colonial violence long unacknowledged despite their omnipresence. As young journalists discovered scarred landscapes within their familiar modern Dalian cityscape, they became aware of their own status as inheritors of victimhood. Wang Xuan's visit also filled a blank space—the Chinese version of "missing pages"—between national history and family history in a society where local history education is little emphasized, as we have seen in chapter 3. The journalists' participation in Wang Xuan's investigative trip also confirms their preconceived understanding that it is the missing pages—the absence of Truth—that sits at the core of deferred reckoning.

But Wang Xuan's importance goes beyond her role in seeking truth (*renzhen*) and finding the "missing pages." Her crusade to link the present to colonial-era violence itself has also become a way of filling the gap between Mao-era and postreform China. Portraying Wang Xuan as a much-needed moral figure, the local media drew a sharp contrast between her and the members of the new middle class, with their self-indulgent lifestyles. An article written by a journalist in her twenties portrayed Wang Xuan as a stern and austere yet approachable individual.[36] She described how Wang Xuan modestly ate stir-fried tomatoes and eggs for dinner, how she doggy-bagged her leftovers, and how plainly and practically she dressed, without suits or high-heeled shoes, which had become the attire of choice among the professional class. In short, she was portrayed as a present-day reincarnation of a mythologized figure of the People's Liberation Army, Lei Feng, who died young battling a flood in the 1960s. The idealized embodiment of national morality and loyalty to the party, he has legendary status in contemporary China. Only a few months before Wang Xuan's visit, *Dalian Daily* had printed a weeklong special feature on Lei Feng, revisiting his greatness and encouraging others to follow his example. Now with the official endorsement of the pursuit of wealth, China is in desperate need of a new Lei Feng, someone who devotes his or her life to the good of society despite the general exaltation of individual gain.

Wang Xuan fits perfectly into this role, and the media treats her like a star. A self-centered, money-making mode of thinking and living now pervades society, and the sentiment that those who remain poor are deserved losers, either stupid or lazy, is widespread. The show windows of Dalian bookstores feature books with titles like *Why You Are Poor*, *Why You Are Rich*, and *Why You Remain Poor*, reflecting the spirit of the era.[37] Wang Xuan—who wears worn-out jeans, T-shirts, and sneakers everywhere; eats at dingy local restaurants; and stays in dilapidated hotels—is a perfect antidote to the new religion of money. But she is more than a modern-day Lei Feng, an exemplary applicant of *renzhen* (work ethic) for the good of the society. In her conscientious pursuit of justice, she embodies the other salient meaning of *renzhen*, which is to recognize and admit (*ren*) the truth (*zhen*). Her relentless pursuit of truth through her conscientious work ethic makes her a comprehensive icon of Chinese conscience.

She is the anachronistic yet contemporary embodiment of the complex values cherished in both old and new China—true to the anti-imperialist struggle with her strong sense of moral justice and a selfless and modest lifestyle, yet also a cosmopolitan globetrotter with impressive linguistic and cultural fluency in English and Japanese, a true exemplar of the cherished concept of *suzhi* (quality). At the same time, as a descendent of a family of Japanese germ-warfare victims, she is seen as the legitimate inheritor of Chinese victimhood. The figure of Wang Xuan thus personifies the link between China's past and present as she unearths neglected postcolonial landscapes in Dalian.

THE DOUBLE LABORS OF *RENZHEN*

Reporting on Wang Xuan, local newspaper articles emphasized how her actions had brought respect from a Japanese (me), a signal and marker of redemption. As part of their eager coverage of her visit, reporters noted in earnest how a young Japanese was getting involved and how Wang Xuan and I "hit it off even though [we] met only yesterday."[38] Yet it was not a straightforward process for them to quote me describing Wang Xuan in positive terms and to describe me as a Japanese scholar "investigating the Japanese invasion in China."[39] Upon discovering that I was Japanese, several reporters quickly surrounded me and started asking questions with notepads in their hands. "Have you heard of the Rape of Nanjing?" a man in his late twenties immediately asked in a strongly suspicious tone. He looked surprised at my affirmative answer. Another asked, "Have you heard of Unit 731?" When I said I had visited the site several times, there was again a moment of pause and puzzlement. After a series of "have you heard of" questions, they accepted that my research was well intentioned and finally relaxed their guard. These questions reflect how, for these young journalists, the crux of the deferred reckoning is the acknowledgement of Truth (*renzhen*). Yet my further conversations with members of this generation led me to suspect that their identification of the crux of the longstanding "history problem" may be misplaced.

As I answered their test questions, I recalled a conversation I had had with some young Chinese employees at Onoda Cement I had met for the first time only a few days earlier. They were all in their midthirties, and our discovery that we were all born in the year of the rooster had quickly broken the ice. They told me how they had decided to take a job at a Japanese corporation, some despite opposition from their relatives, and our conversation was relaxed and friendly. We talked about the difficulties and excitement of crossing cultural boundaries and about negotiating generational gaps. When I asked them how the history between China and Japan might have influenced their career choice and their interactions with their Japanese colleagues, one of them, Li Lin, responded, "Work is work, and history is history," with a tone of "why are you still talking about the past?"

As I told them about my plan to accompany Wang Xuan, the atmosphere in the room suddenly grew tense. Li Lin became visibly agitated, and without hiding the suspicion and discomfort in his voice, he asked me in an interrogating tone, "Why are you joining her investigation?" Unclear what he was getting at, I expressed my puzzlement. Seeing this, he rephrased his question in an unambiguously hostile tone: "Are you trying to disprove her findings?" At this point, I realized what was happening. It was not the first time that I had encountered such a question from a member of this generation wondering if the intention of my research was to disprove Japanese war atrocities. As exemplified by the reactions of both Li Lin and the young journalists covering Wang Xuan, the deeply ingrained suspicion of Japanese historical consciousness resurfaces like a reflex as it is again and again confirmed by media reports of Japanese politicians' "slips of the tongue" or outright denials of Japanese atrocities. This revelation of the young Onoda employees' latent anxiety over Japanese inability to come to terms with the past—epitomized by the rupture of their otherwise rational rhetoric of "work is work, and history is history"—is revealing precisely because they are typical members of Dalian's new middle class, who take full part in the political economy of redemption.

How, then, can we understand this seemingly contradictory attitude among younger Chinese, in which Japan and the Japanese are the object both of desire and of distrust and hostility? My conversation with the young employees at Onoda Cement about Japanese politicians' official apologies for imperialist aggression hinted at how this question might be explored. Li Lin summarized the consensus in the room: "Despite the repeated official apology by Japanese politicians, it lacks good conscience (*renzhen*)." *Renzhen*, so often used in Dalian to describe the diligent and conscientious Japanese work ethic, was here repurposed to point to a lack of good conscience, in that the official apologies by Japanese politicians lack sincerity and seriousness of heart. Others used the related terms *chengshi* (honest) and *chengxin* (sincerity, honesty) to indicate the gap between words and thought.

Renzhen is thus used to describe both the excessive work ethic and lack of good conscience that they see in the Japanese. With this double usage, *renzhen* illustrates Japan's ambiguous place within the contemporary Chinese imaginary as the object of both emulation and resentment. The employees' use of *renzhen* and their shifting attitude when they suspected my motive was to disprove the "Truth" excavated by Wang Xuan point to how Truth claims remain central to their thinking about the difficult past.

The double usage of *renzhen* also captures unresolved anxieties about the machinery of the modern work ethic. The seemingly arbitrary link between the work ethic and moral aptitude that appears in the term's double meaning of conscientious/conscience started to make sense as I talked with Zhang Yong, a banker born in 1978 who now works for a major Japanese bank in downtown Dalian. He spoke fondly about contemporary Japanese popular culture, including books by Murakami Haruki and trendy TV dramas, one of which, starring Kimura Takuya and Matsu Takako, he described as "very romantic" with a shy smile. After sharing his observation of and respect for how a conscientious work ethic and cooperative spirit had led to Japan's rapid economic growth, he commented, "But such disposition could also lead to militarism. There is something scary about the Japanese spirit (*Riben de jingshen tai kepa*)."

The connection he was making between the work ethic and moral disposition points to two levels of anxiety expressed through the use of *renzhen*. One is deep suspicion toward the assumed radical discontinuity between prewar and postwar Japan. While the belief that a latent and persistent fascistic tendency is a national trait of the Japanese is frequently evoked in public discussions in both China and Japan, the second point that Zhang suggested is articulated much less often: how a conscientious work ethic does not always translate into good conscience at the collective level but rather can potentially contribute to state violence. The conscientious Japanese work ethic once led Japan to fascism, an extreme manifestation of the lack of good conscience.[40] Zhang's observation of the "scary" Japanese spirit captures an ambivalent location of Japanese modernity within the contemporary Chinese imagination.

The gap that many Chinese see in the Japanese character—excess *renzhen* at work and a lack of *renzhen* when it comes to apologizing for past violence—lies in this discrepancy *and* the linkage between the two in modern society.[41] This link Zhang drew between the *renzhen* work ethic and the image of Japanese imperialism hence expresses the unresolved anxiety contained within modernity, an anxiety that has slipped out of most discussions of war responsibility between the two countries in their primary focus on truth claims. The double usage of *renzhen* substantiates this tension in modernity by illuminating the link—and the gulf—between conscientiousness and conscience within banal everyday deeds in the realm of beauty and labor, from fashion magazines to the work ethic.[42]

This fundamental anxiety about the dangers inherent in the "force of the collective"[43] in modern society was rarely articulated by most Chinese I encountered—many of them insisted that all they want is a sincere apology and acknowledgement of historical truths from the Japanese, echoing the aims of Song Chengli's postwar compensation lawsuit. The double usage of *renzhen* to express both excess and lack captures what is at stake in their persistent dissatisfaction and anxiety with the Japanese efforts (and lack of them) to come to terms with the past. The double usage of *renzhen* suggests that through "apology" Chinese hope that the Japanese (and themselves, too) can come to terms with the modern paradox contained within the term—the perverse combination of conscientiousness and lack of conscience that once led Japan to its violent colonial aggression. The Chinese want to believe as much as the Japanese in a radical break between prewar and postwar Japan to give assurance and confirmation that what exists now is indeed a "newborn Japan." Zhang's words, however, betray a lingering anxiety that recognizes continuity between past and present Japans, but more important, it is also an anxiety about the role of individuals within the modern state and how they can potentially become the willing executioners of state violence.

Renzhen thus functions as a hinge, whose double usage belies the illusion of postwar Japan's radical discontinuity from prewar Japan and further exposes even deeper anxiety about modern state–society relations. The Communist Party narrative that ordinary Japanese were also victims of Japanese militarism remains dominant in China. This narrative, however, avoids addressing the accountability of ordinary citizens by displacing the issue of accountability and responsibility to abstract structures (in particular, the state). It fails to provide a clear picture as to how such passively victimized ordinary citizens even unwillingly contributed to the destructive fascist machinery. An uneasy and unaddressed anxiety thus haunts the society in the form of a continuous chorus of "not enough apology," despite the repeated apologies by Japanese politicians over the years.[44]

The ethnography in this chapter directs attention to how the perceived lacks—of acknowledgment of Truth (i.e., *renzhen*) and of accompanying apology—may be misplaced as the crux of failed reckoning. Anxiety projected onto the figure of Japanese workers epitomizes what remains unassuaged *despite such knowledge* and despite the political economy of redemption. This anxiety suggests instead that, for the current generations, the crux of the issue is less the question of seeking Truth and apology than the question of accountability within the topography of after empire.

RENZHEN AND ANXIOUS STATES

As epitomized by the historical trajectory of Dalian Onoda Cement, which is seamlessly incorporated into the narrative of the city's industrial modernization process, Dalian's urban landscape has ingested its colonial past as inheritance and turned it into capital. The gleaming plant of the new Onoda Cement factory and its majestic lime mountain preside over its prewar remainder down below, now taken over by the state-run Dalian Cement

Company with its dwindling lime mountain that will be entirely gone within a decade. Nothing marks this piece of history within the industrial landscape. Onoda Cement employees are concerned about their jobs and families, not the ongoing lawsuit against their parent company for wartime forced labor in a distant California court. Likewise, the last remaining "red houses" bear no markers of colonial violence. The "red house" area appears as nothing more than a tight-knit, family-oriented, and lively neighborhood, where make-shift stalls in the courtyard sell everything from vegetables to steamed buns to newspapers, while the elderly sit on stools for an evening chat (figure 5.5).

Despite this beautified cityscape geared toward a prosperous future, the concept of *renzhen* allows us to see that behind the rhetoric of "not enough apology" and repeated surges of anti-Japanese sentiment lies a deep and unarticulated anxiety about modernity that sets aside individual accountability and good conscience while celebrating diligence and conscientiousness as modern workers. Even with "enough apology" in good conscience from the Japanese, that apology could never satisfy the anxiety generated by Japan's violence in the name of the modern state.

The anxious state that emerges through the double usage of *renzhen*, then, has implications beyond Japanese historical responsibility. The official resistance that Wang Xuan and the former forced laborers met during their investigation hints at the Pandora's Box that the Chinese state holds tightly shut. Squarely addressing the double meaning of *renzhen* could potentially lead to a reevaluation of individual responsibility in cases of state violence, bringing up taboo questions such as those concerning collaborators during Japanese rule[45] or the role of ordinary citizens during the Cultural Revolution. Chinese society's anxieties about modernity become particularly visible through the way "modern life" is often refracted through Japanese modernity with corresponding images of fashion and work ethic. *Renzhen* is a signifier of these anxieties, whose displacement onto legitimate criticisms of Japan's lack of sincere apology for its colonial violence compounds an already difficult task of coming to terms with the past. Through this displacement, *renzhen* is a constant reminder of how the Chinese state slips between good conscience and complicity in making scarred landscapes invisible.

There is a crucial gap between the excess that capitalization of colonial inheritance produces (in the form of double inheritance, which extends the scope of responsibility and mnemonic communities across time and space) and the public discourse in both China and Japan on the issue of coming to terms with the past, which focuses on the lack of historical recognition and

5.5 Former site of "red houses," originally built by the Japanese to accommodate Chinese workers at the Fuchang Company, which was in charge of "procuring" Chinese laborers by force or deception: Memory activist Wang Xuan suspects that the Japanese conducted biochemical experiments on Chinese laborers housed in these dormitories, disguised as medical treatment. Today, the site does not bear any markers of wartime forced labor or the alleged human biochemical experiment. Photo by author, 2003.

apology. While the public discourse tends to approach the longstanding question of coming to terms with the past as an unchanging and deferred task, this chapter suggests that the nature of this task itself is changing as a result of the passage of time since the original violence. *Renzhen* in its doubleness calls attention to the entagled tasks postgeneration Chinese and Japanese face in inheriting accrued losses across time and space.

CHAPTER SIX

Epilogue: Deferred Reckoning and the Double Inheritance

They were a small group, exhausted after thirty hours of travel and displaying the disorientation of visitors experiencing their first trip abroad. For some, it was their first time away from home. The eleven-year-old boy and the three young adults, two men and one woman, were victims of exposure to mustard gas from chemical weapons abandoned by the Imperial Japanese Army at the end of the Second World War, which were accidentally unearthed in August 2003 in the Qiqihar construction site that I described in the prologue. It was now May 2004, and a select group of survivors were visiting Tokyo in preparation for their lawsuit against the Japanese government.

During a welcome dinner at a small Chinese restaurant, they repeatedly expressed their gratitude to the assembled Japanese lawyers and supporters, who far outnumbered them. Anxious and uncertain, they began to recount their experience. They would tell their stories many times in the ensuing week, which was packed with meetings from morning till night with lawyers, NGOs, and politicians. As the week progressed, the fragments they presented turned into narratives and vivid images of excruciating pain and fear.

The Japanese lawyers, whom the victims revered, encouraged them to punctuate their narratives by exposing their scarred bodies. Whenever they displayed their burnt skin, still painfully raw months after the accident, all present gasped. Their bodies became monuments of victimhood in this effort to highlight the colonial inheritance that haunts both China and Japan almost sixty years after the war.

Later, while sending them off to the airport, I recalled how much had changed since we first met several months earlier in Qiqihar. When the Japanese lawyers investigating the incident initially sought them out in December 2003, the victims had refused to meet with them despite repeated phone calls. High-level negotiations between China and Japan were under way at the time, and the victims were afraid of antagonizing the Chinese government by initiating anything on their own. To this was added an instinctive fear of discrimination due to their disfigured bodies and a lack of understanding of the lawyers' intentions, compounded by the fact that they were still simply too weak and sick to leave their homes.

Yet most of the victims owed enormous sums of money to the hospital for their difficult and continuing treatment, and desperation drove the father of one small injured girl to meet the lawyers literally at the last minute, at the station just as they were about to leave Qiqihar. Like a scene out of a movie, the father and daughter hid behind a tall stone column in the dimly lit Manchukuo-era train station to avoid attracting attention. Holding his little daughter under his arm as if to shield her from public exposure, the father emerged swiftly and quietly, exchanging furtive words through an interpreter. The father handed the Japanese lawyers a sheet of paper with contact information for some of the other victims, his nervous, desperate eyes seeking signs of hope and trust. I remained in Qiqihar after the Japanese lawyers left, and in the following days I came to know some of the other victims, all under terrible financial strain and struggling with recurrent medical problems and ceaseless discrimination.

For the victims, Tokyo at the time seemed much more than a thousand miles away. Now, in the sleek meeting rooms of the Japanese Lawyers Association's high-rise headquarters, the four delegates were faltering at the lawyers' questions about details. Fragmented words came out of their tight mouths to be woven by the lawyers into sentences and then supplemented by the victims with more words. The sessions revolved mostly around the same fact-finding questions, starting with "Where were you when the accident took place?" The victims squeezed out terse answers, each one adding a little more detail.

By the third day, each victim was narrating his or her own story again and again to different audiences and again and again revisiting their trauma. Or perhaps it was not so much revisiting as recognizing their trauma *as* such through the force of narrating and being listened to. Liu Wenshu, a twenty-four-year-old construction worker with a shy smile and friendly demeanor, broke down in tears on the third day while recounting his ordeal for probably the tenth time since he arrived in Tokyo. It was, it turned out, the first time that he had cried over his catastrophic misfortune, which would haunt him for the rest of his life. He had traveled over a thousand miles from home to encounter his own trauma.

The trip also led the Chinese victims to discover the wounds of others.

The adult delegates, Liu Wenshu, Zhao Liangjie, and Wang Nanying, all in their twenties and thirties, were eager to learn more about the Japanese lawyers who had sought them out in a freezing northeastern city near the Russian border, a twenty-four-hour train ride from Beijing, and who had paid for the victims' trip to Japan out of their own pockets. Repeatedly expressing their deep gratitude and indebtedness, these Chinese victims wondered why the lawyers would devote so much time, money, and emotion to people to whom they had no relation whatsoever.

Tanaka Mikio, a passionate, articulate lawyer and a man of action, was the locomotive leading the nearly three-hundred-member Japanese legal team, which had worked pro bono on various postwar compensation lawsuits representing, among others, so-called comfort women and victims of wartime forced labor. Tanaka explained how he felt the need to repay the debt that he had inherited from the previous generation:

> When I started working as a lawyer many years ago, I was not interested in Japan's imperial past. But the news about the discovery of human remains [suspected to be those of victims of wartime human experiments] at the former site of the Japanese Army Medical College near Shinjuku [a downtown Tokyo skyscraper area] led me to start interviewing the surviving families of the victims of human biological experiments at Unit 731 in Harbin, which shocked me tremendously.[1] Since then, I have strongly felt the weight of the perpetration (*kagai no omosa*). As the postwar generation, we inherit the burden of the past. This is my lifework, and I cannot simply consign these events to the past.

The young victims from Qiqihar leaned forward, hanging on Tanaka's every word. Wang Nanying, a charming twenty-seven-year-old woman, later expressed to me how deeply touched she was to know what was driving these Japanese lawyers, mostly born after the war, who had extended their hands to the victims as no one else had, and to understand the pain they harbored in having inherited the burden of the past. As the negative inheritance of the Japanese Other became implicated in the process of sharing the victims' trauma,[2] both sides moved toward a collective sense of closure, and their farewell dinner was also a new beginning for them. Nevertheless, sharing was itself a torturously painful process for the victims, who again and again revisited their trauma. But their (re)encounter with their trauma was accompanied by their encounter with the Japanese lawyers' inheritance of the burden of the past, which the lawyers felt they had no choice but to accept. The lawyers saw this process as reciprocal. As Tanaka put it, "Learning about and working with the Other's trauma inflicted by their and our parents' or grandparents' generation is the only way for Japan to recover from its own trauma."

Here we find two transformations emerged from the interactions between the Japanese lawyers and those affected by the Qiqihar incident: the silent survivors were turned into speaking victims, and their injured bodies were transformed from personal bodies into symbolic bodies of national suffering and redemption.

In her exploration of the relationship between trauma and history, Cathy Caruth observes that "history, like trauma, is never simply one's own, that history is precisely the way we are implicated in each other's traumas."[3] Her insights into the role of the Other in understanding catastrophic historical events speaks to what I observed during the Qiqihar victims' visit to Tokyo, where Chinese victims and Japanese lawyers came to acknowledge their double inheritance through refractive transmission. What Caruth does not bring out, but what stands out in the interactions between the Qiqihar victims and the Japanese lawyers described above, is how a political economy of redemption, in addition to history, emerges from this process of mutual implication. A strong sense of indebtedness arising from the acknowledgment of *(for) given time* and the attendant national debt—both moral and monetary—is what drives the Japanese lawyers to seek redemption and make repayment in their pro bono work for the Chinese plaintiffs. The Japanese lawyers' sense of inherited debt elicits in turn the survivors' moral and financial sense of debt to the lawyers for their pro bono work. This indebtedness, however, is not unproblematic, for it replicates asymmetrical power relations and provokes performative obligations on the survivors' side, as expressed in their hesitant willingness to play the role of the victim, including publicly displaying their scarred bodies. The unspeakable pains that the victims labored to convey to their Japanese lawyers, their supporters, and the general public were very personal ones, at the cusp of being incommensurable. Yet, at the point of their enunciation in the form of individual narratives, they turned into narratives of national suffering that framed the very personal dimension of their ordeal.[4] The victims' personal pain represents the suffering inflicted by the Japanese on the Chinese nation. When victims' narratives are framed within the narrative of national suffering, their double suffering—from their original pain and from their recounting of it—finds a heroic space within this narrative. In this process, victims' injured bodies are transformed into iconic bodies that serve as symbols of the moral and financial debts of the nation. What emerges is a political economy of redemption in the name of the nation.

Within this theater framed through national losses, both Chinese and Japanese participants assume their respective roles as inheritors of debts from previous generations. In this inheritance of loss, victims' bodies and voices circulate as the symbolic currency for redemptive exchanges.[5] Victims' bodies, whose traumatic inscriptions bear the link between the past and the present, have become the currency within this political economy of redemption.

THE POLITICS OF ABANDONMENT

The story of the inheritance of loss and its redemption through the lens of colonial inheritance begins with the story of abandonment. The *politics of abandonment*—leaving people and things unaccounted for, and without assigning responsibility—is the silent underlying mechanism of after empire in East Asia. As described in the introduction, the diplomatic framework of *(for)given time*—deferral of repayment of moral debt by prioritizing formal economy over moral economy—was formally acknowledged in the 1972 Joint Communiqué, which normalized diplomatic relations between China and Japan and in which the former renounced its reparation claims. Beneath the agreed-upon *(for)given time* between the two states lies the politics of abandonment, of chemical weapons and their victims, and of victims of Japanese imperial violence in China, in pursuit of wealth accumulation.[6]

Abandonment is an integral and problematic aspect of after empire, which acknowledges particular forms of material remnants, labor, and productivity while the rest are left abandoned to decay. Inheriting itself is accompanied by losses and debts; abandonment is an often overlooked form of inheriting, which points to losses incurred *after* the empire's demise. Despite its social invisibility in many contexts, abandonment accrues debts and becomes an integral part of what postgenerations inherit. Belying the inclination to think of abandonment as a state of being, the Qiqihar case directs our attention to abandonment as an action, which can sometimes take the form of inaction.[7]

In this closing chapter, I will focus on this dimension of colonial inheritance—abandonment as an action—by following the Qiqihar victims, who find themselves shut out of the formal economy due to the effects of their victimization. Whereas the preceding chapters on the capitalization of colonial remnants revolve around repossession, capitalization, and reincorporation, the Qiqihar case revolves around dispossession, abandonment, and inaction. They are both stories of after empire in East Asia, where the underlying moral economy plays a key role in the transgenerational processes of redeeming accrued losses stemming from colonial modernity.

THE INHERITANCE OF LOSS AND ITS REDEMPTION

The ethnographic journey through the urban landscapes in Northeast China in this book has revealed the tangled and often double-edged relationship that formed between market and history as China transitioned to a market-oriented economy at the turn of the twenty-first century. The cases of Harbin, Changchun, and Dalian demonstrate how the moral economy of seeking redemption for colonial modernity's losses (as inheritors of either victimhood or perpetration) is inexorably linked to a formal economy of wealth accumulation through exports, consumption, and the pursuit of middle-class dreams. This book explored this linkage—the *political economy of redemption*—and how it structures the generational transfer of colonial remnants.

Colonial inheritance is something more than the classical economic conception of the circulation of property. As the metaphor of *awase kagami* illustrates, the effectiveness of colonial inheritance goes beyond the simple transfer of remainders of the past from one generation to another; through refractive transmission, in which acts of inheriting involve all three common usages of the term *betrayal*, as I explored in chapter 2.[8] The first usage is the primary meaning of *betrayal* as an act of treason and disloyalty. The second refers to the act of revealing, disclosing, showing, or exhibiting. The third refers to the disclosure or revelation of what should be kept secret. Since what one inherits is often murky and secret-laden, making colonial remnants visible could reveal what is supposed to be unseen and therefore become a betrayal in all three senses. By exposing what has long been invisible through historical restoration, tourism, and foreign direct investment, the capitalization of colonial inheritance becomes burdened by an unexpected excess that disturbs long-maintained narratives of the past. It is through this dynamic of *inheritance and betrayal* that unexpected losses and debts are transmitted across generations. Just as debts and losses are unexpected by-products of colonial inheritance, so are new forms of unexpected value. The doubled nature of colonial inheritance, revealed through the refractive structure of generational transmission, is one such significant new value.

THE WORKINGS OF DOUBLE INHERITANCE

The double inheritance at work in Harbin, Changchun, and Dalian makes visible a topography of after empire where formerly and formally defined categories such as colonizer/colonized and perpetrators/victims become fluid, contested, and conflated over decades, while simultaneously exposing the mutually implicated and deeply intertwined nature of these historical relations. This generates three kinds of doubles: The first is primarily temporal—the generational transmission of the original loss reveals new forms of losses incurred *after* the demise of the Japanese Empire. The double inheritance points to the elusiveness of inheritance's origins and the layers of sediments that make each act of inheritance temporally double: confronting the unaccounted-for pasts from the era of colonialism brings the politics and complicity of after empire into question. Inheriting involves layers of losses and compounded debts, and the double inheritance in temporal terms thus challenges the certainty about which past is transmitted.

The second manifestation is geographical—the double inheritance exposes the mutually implicated nature of colonial inheritance and thereby calls into question the widely accepted frame of analysis of mnemonic communities, separated by the lineage of perpetrator and victim nations. Rather, my ethnography suggests that Chinese and Japanese tasks of coming to terms with colonial modernity necessarily implicate each other, as dealing with one's own colonial inheritance inevitably requires dealing with the other's inheritance.

In its third manifestation, the double inheritance brings to the fore modernity's promise and its self-destructive potential, which turned the project of colonial modernity simultaneously into an object of desire and of disavowal. Inheriting itself involves navigating the space between these poles. In effacing, rejecting, and redeeming each other, these two faces of modernity produce the political economy of redemption, in which participants attempt to redeem colonial modernity's failure through the pursuit of "modern life" and middle-class dreams. At the same time, as the double usage of *renzhen* (conscientiousness/conscience) indicates by describing the Japanese work ethic with both admiration and skepticism, this redemptive economy simultaneously exposes unresolved anxieties arising from modernity's historical record of (and future potential for) violent destruction and the lack of accountability at both the individual and state levels.

In Harbin, an attempt to capitalize on colonial inheritance has resurrected an uncanny inheritance from the Cultural Revolution era, a past that exceeded its narrative the moment it seemed to be under control. Changchun illustrated how the Other's inheritance is implicated in one's own attempts to face the past and how the tenacious misrecognition of this dynamic generates the frustration and anxiety experienced by Japanese tourists and local Chinese alike, despite their respective desires to come to terms with the past. Other than the visit of the Qiqihar victims to Tokyo, it was the group of Japanese and Chinese high school students in Changchun who most directly confronted the double inheritance through their encounters in front of the photographs of Japanese atrocities. Confronting what was not visible in Japan unveiled a new difficulty of what it means to come to terms with the past for the Japanese students. Yet the generosity of their Chinese host families opened new redemptive possibilities. For the Chinese students, it was also a process of learning about the burden that comes through sharing inherited loss. The nature of colonial inheritance demands more than filling the missing pages of history by seeing the historical Truth. It demands recognition from the other with whom one is placed in a moral economy of debt. Without this recognition, any attempt to repay the debt is marked "return to sender."

Dalian complicates Theodor Adorno's observation about postwar West Germany that economic prosperity can minimize and obscure past violence.[9] The city's growing economy routinely channels Japanese and Chinese desires to come to terms with the past into production, consumption, and accumulation. Within this political economy of redemption, the Japanese desire to make up for the broken promise of Japanese modernity and the Chinese desire to redeem their perceived lack of modernity feed off one another in generating more wealth. But colonial inheritance comes back to haunt the very activity that sought to make good on its inheritance. The cherished value of *renzhen*, the conscientious Japanese work ethic that Chinese both esteem and critique, brings up the specter of Japanese fascism, where conscientiousness led to a collective lack of conscience. The political economy of redemption, therefore, operates upon the perpetual deferral of the debt in a typically late-capitalist manner. Debt is not something to avoid but something upon which to build new relations of production and wealth generation—until, as Japanese know all too well, the bubble bursts.

THE CHANGING GEOPOLITICAL LANDSCAPE IN EAST ASIA

In 2008, an economic bubble did burst, but this time starting in the United States, led by the collapse of the housing market and the Lehman Brothers bankruptcy. While the US economy was thrown into panic at the prospect of a decades-long recession like that of Japan, the Chinese economy flourished, with a spectacular show of its potency through the 2008 Beijing Olympics. Chinese capital flowed out to every corner of the globe, fueling purchases of resources from rare metals to farm lands to water resources. As the US empire seems to wane, China has emerged as a new economic empire, with its capital both visibly and invisibly pervading the global economy.[10]

China's ascendance as a global power coincides with a major shift in the political landscape in East Asia. China has had less need of Japan's financial assistance, while increasing nationalism, both within and outside China, has prompted the Chinese to be more strident about the unpaid moral debt. In Japan and South Korea, politicians with direct lineage to Japan's imperial history came to power in 2012 and 2013, respectively: Japanese Prime Minister Abe Shinzō is the grandson of Kishi Nobusuke, an architect of Manchukuo and class-A war criminal who himself became prime minister in the late 1950s, renewed the controversial US-Japan Security Treaty in 1960, and normalized diplomatic relations with South Korean President Park Chung-hee in 1965; and South Korean President Park Geun-hye is the daughter of Park Chung-hee, whose career took off when he served as an officer in Imperial Japan's elite Kwantung Army while Korea was under Japanese rule and who led South Korea as military chief and president from 1961 until his assassination in 1979. Abe has sought to reclaim Japan as a "normal nation" by remilitarizing the country, while Park has sought to undo her collaborator lineage by appeals to Korean nationalism. The Chinese government—now led by Xi Jinping (son of Communist revolutionary figure Xi Zhongxun), who became general secretary of the Chinese Communist Party in 2012 and president of the People's Republic of China in 2013 with a public display of his ambition for China's reemergence as an imperial power—has played on the way Abe and Park have fanned nationalism in their countries to its own political gain.

The so-called island problem surrounding what are called the Diaoyu Islands in Chinese and the Senkaku Islands in Japanese that escalated in 2012 brought to a halt not only diplomatic relations between the two countries but also mutual economic and cultural activities, culminating in the cancellation of official and unofficial celebrations of the fortieth anniversary of the normalization of diplomatic relations with the signing of the Joint Communiqué. Ignited by the Japanese government's sudden decision to nationalize the islands on September 11, 2012, the territorial dispute has led to an unprecedented level of street demonstrations against and violent destruction of things Japanese, from cars to stores to the Japanese embassy and consulates across China, as well as open-sea confrontations, cancellation of formal and informal events, and a heightening of hysterical nationalist discourse in both societies.

Facing this crisis, Zhu Jianrong—a professor of political science, the then-president of the Overseas Chinese Professors Association in Japan (*Nihon kajin kyōju kaigi*), and a well-respected and influential public intellectual in both countries—choked up in front of the assembled members of the association at its annual meeting in November 2012: "We have devoted the past forty years of our careers to building the new Sino-Japanese relationship, which came to fruition in robust and interlocking relations between the two societies. Or that's what I thought. Now, facing the rapid crumbling of what we built in the past forty years, I begin to wonder what we did wrong." He had to stop for a moment to regain his composure as the audience in the large auditorium fell silent. Subsequent symposium speakers, all prominent Chinese intellectuals teaching at various Japanese universities, spoke of the "negative inheritance" of Japanese imperialism in China, which, despite the development of relations in the preceding four decades, had been left unaccounted for.

Seen through the lens of high politics, Sino-Japanese relations are on the brink of a schism primed by increased militarization and nationalist discourse on both sides. The economic activities between the two countries are at the lowest level in recent years. According to the recent statistics published by the Chinese Commerce Department, total Japanese direct investment in China during the first half of 2014 dropped to nearly 50 percent of that in the previous period.[11]

Yet, through the lens of the inheritance of loss and its redemption, we see a different dynamic at play. While the heightened nationalism of recent years has raised the stakes in acknowledging the doubled nature of colonial inheritance, at the same time the double inheritance is now calling into question the long-maintained topography of after empire and the diplomatic framework of *(for)given time*. Deferred reckoning is starting to challenge the underlying politics of abandonment itself. The rest of this epilogue looks at recent developments in the Qiqihar case, which epitomizes what is at stake in postgenerations' attempts to reckon with colonial inheritance and hints at a new direction impelled by the working of double inheritance within the emerging geopolitical landscape.

DEFERRED RECKONING AND THE POLITICS OF ABANDONMENT

Overshadowed by the confrontation between the two countries over the "island problem," the Tokyo High Court on September 21, 2012, handed down a significant decision in the Qiqihar victims' lawsuit.[12] That morning, one by one, the Japanese lawyers and citizen supporters of the victims gathered outside the gates of the Tokyo High Court building. They set up a banner and a loudspeaker and took turns appealing to passers-by while other members of the group distributed flyers with information about the

6.1 In front of the Tokyo High Court on the day of the decision on the abandoned-chemical-weapon case in 2012: Qiqihar victims of mustard gas exposure, their lawyers, and citizen supporters marched in front of the Tokyo High Court in 2012 before entering the court to hear the ruling on the abandoned-chemical-weapon case. Photo by author, 2012.

accident in 2003 that immediately killed one person and severely injured forty-three others, two of whom had died during the appeals process. As two of the victims from China joined the group later, the pace of entreaties to the busy Japanese public coming in and out of the nearby subway station picked up pace. The mood was upbeat, especially among the lawyers, who had high hopes for what one of the lead lawyers described as "a uniquely liberal bench, not just one judge but all three." A sudden rain led the group to seek shelter temporarily in a nearby subway station. As the heavy rain came to a brief halt, the group of approximately sixty people marched in formation behind a banner, carried by the two victims and their lead lawyers, back toward the courthouse, as Chinese and Japanese television crews vied to capture their entrance (figure 6.1).

Room 101, one of the largest in the Tokyo High Court, was full with nearly seventy people, including a dozen reporters from the two countries. The right side of the bench was packed with victims' lawyers while the left side, reserved for the lawyers representing the Japanese government, had only three lawyers occupying a small corner of their allocated space. The room quieted down as the three judges entered, and everyone stood up to bow. As everybody sat back down, the court announced that the media would be allowed to videotape the courtroom scene for two minutes. Movement ceased with this announcement, and everyone froze as if posing for a still photograph. The judges looked uncomfortably stiff as they faced the cameras filming their frozen faces, motionless and emotionless. This awkward two-minute interval signaled to all present that they had entered a special space demarcated from the everyday.

Japanese court rulings consist of two parts: "facts and reasons" and "judicial decisions," or *shubun*. Ōhashi Hiroaki, the presiding judge, opened his heretofore tightly shut mouth and pronounced, "*Shubun*." Upon hearing this one word, both the victims' lawyers and their seasoned citizen supporters tensed up, as such an abrupt conclusion with no explanation of "facts and reasons" beforehand was not a sign of good news for the plaintiffs. After a brief pause, Ōhashi declared the following two points, "First, the court rejects the appeal. Second, the appellants pay for the legal costs." As the lawyers and supporters waited now for "facts and reasons" to explain this *shubun*, the judges stood, turned, and exited. This almost scandalous behavior of the judges, leaving the court without a word of explanation for their decision, broke the stillness of the room. Unrest quickly spread, with some in the audience leaping up and shouting angrily at the retreating judges to explain their decision. This thirty-second drama left the room full of supporters speechless. The two Chinese plaintiffs, who did not even have the chance to get any of the judge's words translated into Chinese by their court interpreter, were left in a state of anxious disappointment upon seeing the reactions of their trusted lawyers and supporters. The lawyers were at a loss for words, just staring at one another as if having lost the ability to process information, while the supporters turned to one another in disbelief, asking aloud, "How could they possibly do this?"

In strong contrast to the well-organized march into the court, the group of supporters dispersed in a state of confusion and despair, waiting for the lawyers to appear at the courthouse gates. When they had marched in less than an hour earlier, the lawyers carried a pair of banners written in traditional brush and ink at the ready—one for "victory" and the other for "unjust ruling" (*futō hanketsu*). Normally, the lawyers would rush out to the gate of the courthouse right after the ruling to display one of the banners to the assembled media and supporters who could not fit into the courtroom. But this time, none of the lawyers appeared with the expected sign that signals a sense of closure to the case to the waiting supporters. Nearly an hour passed before the lawyers and the victims finally emerged, dazed and with deep fatigue carved into their faces. As Lawyer Hotta took a loudspeaker to explain the ruling to the assembled supporters, Lawyer Sasaki, whose youthful face bore the trace of tears, was urged by the supporters to raise high the banner for "unjust ruling." Senior lawyers surrounded the young lawyers and victims with exhausted and emotionally blank faces, and the victims looked down with their tight bodies expressing deep disappointment, disbelief, and confusion. Feng Donghong, one of the two victims visiting Tokyo for this occasion, looked particularly fragile, his shoulders bent inward, his head down, and his hands ice cold. He later explained at the press conference that he almost fainted upon hearing the court decision.

At the packed press conference, Liu Wenshu, who was one of the first Qiqihar victims to visit Tokyo in 2004, as we saw in the opening of this chapter, looked straight into the assembled reporters and the telephoto lenses set up by the television crews. In marked contrast to Feng Donghong, who kept looking down and avoiding eye contact, Liu maintained his composure throughout, until he started describing the hardships that the victims and their families had gone through in the past nine years since the accident. As he recounted the families broken apart, children dropping out of school, and the seemingly endless new and recurring medical difficulties and uncertainties for the future, his deep emotions dissolved his composure, with his eyes becoming moist and his voice trembling, which the media eagerly captured and broadcast on the evening news.

Duplicity and the Doctrine of "Foreseeability"

While the terse, blunt oral delivery of the Tokyo High Court's ruling stunned even the most seasoned lawyers and citizen supporters, the written text of the ruling, distributed to the lawyers immediately afterward, made a momentous argument. A close reading of the text reveals a nuanced approach to colonial inheritance that marks a significant departure from the long-held approach to the "history problem" in East Asia, which starts with unquestioned categories of perpetrators and victims. The court in effect signaled that it is crucial to see colonial inheritance as the double inheritance of Japan and China, involving the wartime and postwar actions and inactions of both states.

The court thus suggests the centrality of seeing double in colonial inheritance for deferred imperial reckoning. At the same time, the internal tension and contradictions within this text indicate how such an approach raises the stakes for all the parties involved. We have seen how the generational transmission of colonial remnants in the economic sphere revealed doubles within colonial inheritance. In the High Court decision, we now see this same process in the legal sphere. Whereas the anxiety contained within double inheritance remained latent in the economic sphere, the Tokyo High Court ruling exposes the political stakes in seeing double.

The judges devote more than half of the eighty-one-page document to reiterating the appellants' argument concerning how the Japanese government, from 1945 to the present, systematically concealed the wartime use of the chemical weapons.[13] Through one piece of historical evidence after another, the court presents—through the voice of the appellants—how the Japanese government repeatedly attempted to avoid addressing the abandoned chemical weapons within China, even after an official request from the Chinese government in 1990, while systematically collecting information on the same issue within Japan, where the Imperial Japanese Army also developed chemical weapons at various sites. The court's recapitulation of the appellants' argument highlights this deliberate *inaction* by the Japanese state even though they had not only the opportunity but also diplomatic obligation to do so.

After a comparatively brief presentation of the state's argument,[14] which revolves around a challenge to the appellants' legal standing, the court presents its own argument.[15] What is notable is how the court mentions on multiple occasions the difficulty of attaining information from the former Imperial Japanese Army officers and soldiers involved in the production, deployment, and disposal of chemical weapons.[16] On one occasion, the court describes in detail how the former officers refused to talk frankly about the chemical weapons and especially about circumstances of their abandonment and that the former soldiers deferred to their former officers in interviews commissioned by the Japanese Ministry of Foreign Affairs. The way in which the court describes this unwillingness to share information suggests the presence of secrets that they refuse to make public.[17] It also indicates that the court did not exercise its judicial power to demand disclosure of more information. Yet, at the same time, the court acknowledges that

> had the Japanese government conducted interviews with former Imperial Japanese Army personnel before this accident [in Qiqihar], it would have been possible to identify the locations where the abandoned chemical weapons were buried, and such identified locations could have included the location of the accident, which was a former Japanese military facility. Part of the reason why the defendant [the Japanese government] did not pursue more information by conducting further interviews is due to

> budgetary and personnel constraints. But part of the reason is because the government was aware of its lack of legal responsibility regarding the abandoned chemical weapons in China, and this reason is inappropriate (*datō dewa nakatta*).[18]

The court contextualizes the resulting lack of information about the whereabouts of chemical weapons within the legal doctrine of "foreseeability" (*yoken kanō-sei*): it argues that the Japanese government did not have adequate information to foresee the Qiqihar accident and thus rejects the appellants' claim by stating that the defendant was devoid of legal responsibility. While the court deploys the foreseeability doctrine as a rationale for its decision, the text of the ruling effectively documents the Japanese government's willful evasion of responsibility. Furthermore, in its admission that the accident might have been avoided had there been more conscientious efforts by the Japanese state to account for its actions, the court bespeaks its own complicity through its inaction.

Seen in this light, the curt oral delivery of the ruling—the proclamation of *shubun* without "facts and reasons"—encapsulates the court's inability to speak. Despite the court's rejection of the appellants' claims, the court document, through the voice of the appellants, effectively expresses what the court itself cannot speak. In the classic manner of how colonial inheritance betrays, the court "speaks" the Japanese government's responsibility and its deliberate evasion of that responsibility through the verbatim reiteration of the appellants' argument.

But it is not only the Japanese government's role that the court highlights in its decision. The court also introduces the role of the Chinese state and brings the Chinese government's responsibility to the table.[19] Pointing out the trajectory of the accident site—from its original use during the war as an Imperial Japanese Army airfield arsenal to its postwar use as an arsenal by the People's Liberation Army and, ultimately, to its designation as a housing construction site sold to a developer in the early 1990s by the Chinese government—the court argues that the Chinese government was no less aware than the Japanese of the site's former use before the accident took place and that the Chinese government was therefore responsible for alerting the developer and the local population of possible danger when the construction of a housing development began (figure 6.2).

Describing the mutual evasions and inaction of both the Japanese and Chinese governments, the court thus presents the abandoned chemical weapons as the double inheritance of the two countries. Through foregrounding the double inheritance in geographical and temporal terms, the court thus

6.2 The site of the 2003 mustard gas exposure from the chemical weapons abandoned by the Imperial Japanese Army in Qiqihar at the end of the war: Beijiang Flower Garden, a new housing development in Qiqihar, became the site of the 8.4 Incident in 2003, in which mustard gas, abandoned by the Japanese Imperial Army at the end of the war, killed and injured forty-four Chinese civilians. The ground was originally used as an arsenal for Imperial Japanese Army Unit 516, which was linked to the infamous Unit 731 on the outskirts of Harbin. Photo by author, 2003.

hints at another form of doubleness—the duplicity of the Japanese and Chinese governments. By publicly hinting at the evasion and displacement of accountability, the text of the ruling betrays the duplicity contained within this double inheritance in the form of action, inaction, cover-ups, and the lack of accountability by the states involved—the *politics of abandonment* that underlies the topography of after empire. In a similar manner to the dynamics of *inheritance and betrayal*, which evades political attempts to harness the past, as I have illustrated, colonial inheritance betrays and exposes the very structure of this politics of abandonment.

It might well be that what many legal commentaries describe as the "strange" and "incomprehensible" ruling of the Tokyo High Court on the Qiqihar case, both in its abbreviated oral delivery and its rich textuality, especially coming from "an unusually liberal bench," reflects the historically unprecedented tension between the two countries triggered by the "island problem" and the political pressure from the Japanese government. In fact, after careful analysis of the text, the lawyers representing the victims suspected that the foreseeability doctrine was inserted in the already-prepared ruling *after* the then-recent eruption of the "island problem" became a major political impasse, which the lawyers speculated had led to political pressure on the judges. The remarkable gap between the court's oral performance and written text, and the way the latter highlights the inability to speak enacted in the former, would seem to underscore the high political stakes in any public acknowledgement of the double in colonial inheritance.

The presiding judge was not the only one who saw high stakes in recognizing the double. While the Japanese lawyers representing the victims recognize that abandoned chemical weapons are the double inheritance of both Chinese and Japanese, their deep-seated sense of inherited moral debt to China prevents them from recognizing another aspect of double inheritance: the duplicity of the Japanese *and* Chinese governments in their postwar inaction to address the abandoned chemical weapon issue. It is the role of the Chinese state that the Japanese lawyers refused to acknowledge. Put differently, the lawyers refused to acknowledge the issue as a question of after empire by insisting on seeing it as a question of Japan's postwar. It was the appellants' lawyers' turn to display their inability to speak.

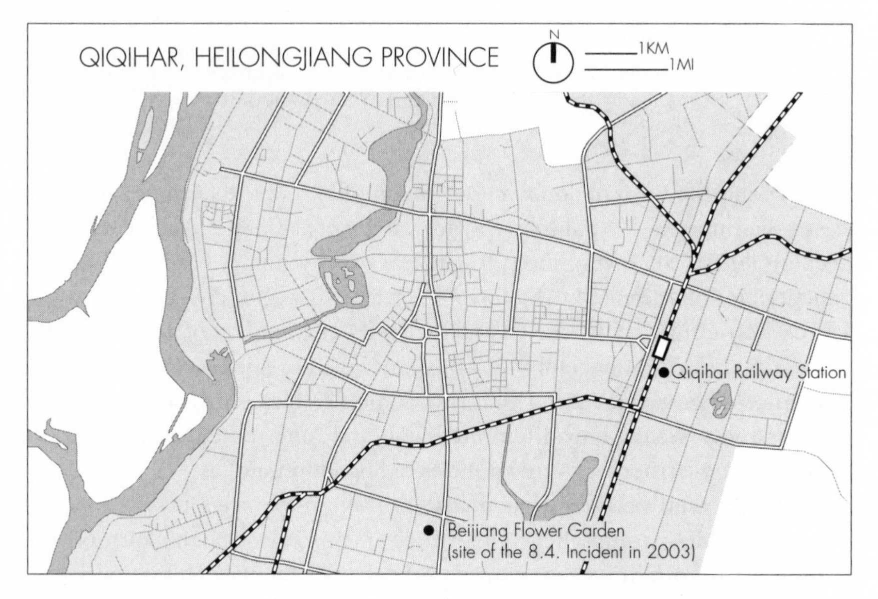

Map 8 Qiqihar, Heilongjiang Province

The legal documents submitted to the court by the plaintiffs' lawyers are the product of considerable legwork piecing together disparate and fragmented historical traces to demonstrate not only the Japanese government's involvement in the development and use of chemical weapons during the war but also their postwar cover-ups of such wartime acts and their inaction to address the risks arising from abandonment. The voluminous historical data presented to the court embodies a form of sweat repayment by these lawyers and citizen supporters-turned-historians, who persistently tracked down buried, forgotten, or hidden historical traces. However, despite the fact that accidental exposures to abandoned chemical weapons persisted throughout the decades since the Japanese defeat and that the recent construction boom in China only increased the frequency of encounters with these deadly colonial remnants, these legal documents, otherwise rich with historical revelations, are silent about the Chinese government's role.[20] My discussions with the lawyers underscored their strong resistance to considering the accountability of the Chinese state. As one reluctantly put it, "In our minds, the Japanese are the perpetrators and the Chinese are the victims. And it is very difficult for us to place blame on China."

The high stakes in acknowledging the doubled nature of colonial inheritance are an issue for not only the right-leaning actors but the left-leaning ones such as the Qiqihar victims' lawyers as well. Seeing double without sounding like apologists for the Japanese state is a sensitive issue for the Japanese, who bear the scars of their country's imperialist past,[21] especially against the backdrop of heightened nationalism in East Asia. Yet the unwillingness to acknowledge the mutual duplicity contained within this double inheritance also risks leaving unquestioned the underlying politics of abandonment through which Sino-Japanese relations have operated since the demise of the Japanese Empire.

Confronting Losses after Empire

We have seen in Dalian that behind the citywide wealth accumulation lurks anxiety over modernity, seen through the celebrated yet despised Chinese concept of *renzhen* (conscientiousness/conscience) and its ambivalent connotations when used to describe the conscientious Japanese work ethic, on the one hand, and Japanese lack of conscience in repenting their imperialist past, on the other. The double usage of *renzhen* points to the double face of modernity: the way a conscientious modern work ethic can lead to a lack of conscience, as in the case of Japanese fascism.

How the High Court addressed the accountability issue arising from inaction in the Qiqihar case points to this modern structure of eluding accountability: the court's unwillingness to make those who were involved in the use and abandonment of chemical weapons accountable for their actions, its unwillingness to account for the Japanese state's postwar inaction through deployment of the foreseeability doctrine, and its displacement of the burden of accountability to the Chinese state. It is no coincidence that the English translation of *fusakui* (the Japanese legal term for "inaction") is "omission," whose antonym is "conscientiousness" (i.e., *renzhen*). Yet the more the court decision evades accountability, the more it betrays the duplicity of the states involved, whose lack of *renzhen* expresses itself in their inaction, dispossession, and abandonment. The politics of abandonment thus sits at the core of the anxiety expressed through the double usage of *renzhen*.

As this book has shown, the dynamics of *inheritance and betrayal* undermine attempts to harness the past through the capitalization of colonial remnants. The various doubles exposed through the generational transmission of these remnants are a form of betrayal, revealing secrets contained within colonial inheritance. The preceding chapters highlighted three types of double inheritance (geographical, temporal, and modernity's doubled face), and the Qiqihar case exemplifies a fourth: the duplicity—lack of *renzhen*—of the Japanese and Chinese governments through their politics of abandonment and attendant lack of accountability. Ironically, the manner in which the court publicly revealed this duplicity was itself a display of its own duplicity. On the one hand, the High Court decision indicates to the public that lack of accountability is emerging as a political liability for both the Japanese and Chinese states. Yet, at the same time, the ruling exploits the geographical double inheritance to avoid dealing with the responsibility of the Japanese government and instead displaces it onto the Chinese.

The High Court decision thus directs us to the possibilities and perils of seeing double in colonial inheritance and to attendant responsibilities for postgenerations. The crux of deferred reckoning is seeing double without evading accountability through deflection, displacement, and disengagement—in short, to be *renzhen*. As evidenced by the different but parallel silences of the presiding judge and the Japanese lawyers representing the Chinese victims, however, seeing double in colonial inheritance is delicate and sensitive, if not controversial, especially in the current political climate of heightened nationalism. Their silences point to the fundamental tension contained in being *renzhen* in acknowledging double inheritance.

As noted in chapter 5, the Chinese characters for *renzhen* literally mean to recognize, acknowledge, and admit (*ren*) the truth (*zhen*), raising the question of how truth claims, which play a central role in the "history problem," relate to the multiple forms of doubleness and attendant responsibilities that span space and time.[22] We have seen how the Japanese lawyers representing the Qiqihar victims, for example, feel that acknowledging the postwar responsibility of the Chinese state would be a betrayal of their expected role as the inheritors of perpetration. We have also seen how these Japanese lawyers cannot speak about this duplicity of Japanese *and* Chinese governments for the fear of becoming seen as apologists for the Japanese state. How about the presiding judge's silence—his inability to speak of any of the "facts and reasons" that supported the court's final judgment? Does it indicate his inability to betray his own government by publicly exposing the duplicity of the Japanese state? Or, alternatively, does his silence indicate his sense that he is betraying *himself*, as one of the most liberal judges in the country, in displacing the Japanese government's responsibility onto the Chinese government via the foreseeability doctrine? What does it mean for these postgeneration Japanese to be *renzhen*, and for whom? As inheritors of perpetration, is it a form of betrayal—lack of *renzhen*—for Japanese to acknowledge doubleness in colonial inheritance? And for the Qiqihar appellants, as the victims of Japanese violence and as symbolic figures of the Chinese national injury, is it a form of betrayal for them to see double and to recognize the duplicity of the Chinese state?

The Qiqihar case raises the question of what it means to be *renzhen* as postgenerations face complex dimensions of colonial inheritance, which carries with it layers of losses, actions, and inactions across time and space beyond the original losses. Throughout this book, we have seen how unsettling it is when layers of doubleness emerge through the act of inheriting colonial remnants. For one, exposed doubles challenge the assumed mnemonic communities of postgenerations—lineages of perpetration and victimhood in the name of the nation. For another, these doubles challenge assumptions about what is being transmitted through inheriting; where losses originate and end is not as clear as the conventional understandings would have it. The landscapes of responsibility that emerge out of this refractive transmission complicate not only the expected narratives of victimhood and perpetration but also how loss is recognized and articulated as loss. While the anxiety contained within colonial inheritance remained largely latent in the cases dealt with in the preceding chapters, the Qiqihar case lays bare the political stakes and immediate consequences for the victims in being *renzhen* by acknowledging doubleness in colonial inheritance.[23]

Seeing double, through the refractive transmission of colonial remnants, is thus a mechanism that allows postgenerations to see the very means by which accountability for colonial modernity's violence is evaded. The lens of double inheritance directs us to see structures of violence and injustice after empire as an integral part of the colonial inheritance that the postgenerations have no choice but to inherit. We have seen in the Qiqihar case how refusing to acknowledge double inheritance by faithfully playing the expected role of inheritor of either perpetration or victimhood comes at a price.

The inability or unwillingness to see double in colonial inheritance perpetuates the structure of abandonment and silencing and provides alibis for the Japanese and Chinese states for their inactions, further delaying an already deferred reckoning. The lens of double inheritance shifts our understanding of what constitutes the most crucial truth claims from historical facts (i.e., the Chinese or Japanese version of the truth) to the structural forces that obscure, obstruct, and oppose the postgenerational pursuit of those historical facts and accountability for them.

More than anyone else described in this book, the Qiqihar victims experience the effects of the politics of abandonment by both the Japanese and Chinese states. The political economy of redemption, generated in this example through the interactions of the victims and their Japanese lawyers, itself reflects this underlying politics of abandonment. Almost all the plaintiffs, mostly in their thirties and forties, lost their jobs after the accident and suffer from a deep sense of failure due to their inability to support their families. As a result of losing the ability to work, they have difficulty recognizing their own labor as plaintiffs, which leads to their strong sense of indebtedness to the Japanese lawyers who represent them pro bono.

How do you attach value to this kind of labor, in which bodies are literally at work as legal objects? The victims' testimonies are the product of their painful and laborious process of weaving their unspeakable pains into recognizable and communicable sentences. They stand up in front of cameras while their bodies itch like mad—"including in the inside of my head," as Dong Fenhong once put it—while pains shoot through their mustard gas scars and deep fatigue leads to nausea after even a few minutes of standing. Despite all their labor as plaintiffs, their enunciation of suffering in the form of testimonies and interviews and their display of their scarred bodies in public, the victims recognize only the labor of their attorneys. Why do the Chinese victims feel indebted to the Japanese lawyers? What is behind this appearance of the economy of debt, in which the Japanese lawyers attempt to repay their moral debt, which in turn incurs a sense of debt on the part of the victims, which they in turn attempt to repay through their performance as plaintiffs?

Due to their inability to work, the victims often feel left outside of the formal economy; compounding their sense of abandonment, they receive little assistance from either government. "We are also war victims" is a common refrain among them, and many liken themselves to those who were directly affected by colonial modernity's violence, like the so-called comfort women and the victims of wartime forced labor, who have long been silenced and shunted to the margins of society—in sum, those known in Japanese as *kimin*: abandoned people. The Qiqihar victims' inability to recognize their own labor directs our attention to the question of *kimin*, whom the state deems invisible and thereby outside the purview of its responsibility.

The politics of abandonment and the attendant diplomatic framework of *(for)given time* is a structural mechanism of after empire that has made certain forms of economy (most especially, moral economy) and labor (such as the Qiqihar survivors' labor as victims) publicly "invisible" while giving the state an alibi for its lack of accountability. Looking through the lens of the political economy of redemption, by contrast, we see different dynamics at work: the victims' otherwise unrecognized labor is productive in generating the redemptive economy by turning their bodies into symbolic currency and their experiences into the conduit for generational transmission. In doing so, the political economy of redemption produces social forces that challenge the taken-for-granted political framework. The Qiqihar case points to a new locale for labor, production, and exchange left unacknowledged within the formal economy. Those who have been abandoned at the margins of both Chinese and Japanese societies, those who have been left behind in the frantic pursuit of wealth in recent years, are now at the center of this increasingly significant redemptive economy, which has made the double inheritance both an issue of political accountability for the respective states and a task for the postgenerations.

As we have seen, the activation of colonial remnants through generational transmission turns loss/debt into gain/capital, a process fueled by the debt itself. And the dynamics created through this redemptive economy come back to challenge the very structure that produced the loss and the debt on which interest has accrued. The result is a new topography of after empire and possibilities for deferred reckoning at the crossroads of the moral and formal economies.

THE NEW TOPOGRAPHY OF AFTER EMPIRE

The Qiqihar accident took place in 2003 amid the height of Japanese direct investment in China, which went hand in hand with the aggressive capitalization of colonial remnants. The accident struck both Chinese and Japanese societies as if time were out of joint with a ghostly and anachronistic apparition of the long distant past. As much as the Chinese public was enraged by the *delayed violence* inflicted, yet again, by the Japanese, they were also quick to either forget the victims or discriminate against and marginalize them within their own communities. The Japanese public was even quicker to push the news from the front pages into the dust bin and return instead to looking at the rapidly ascendant Chinese society as the displaced future for their lost modernity.

Now, more than a decade after the peak of economic courtship between the two countries, national sentiments have soured on both sides. The marginalized, the forgotten, and the seemingly anachronistic are now casting new light on the double inheritance—the duplicity of abandonment and the lack of accountability across space and time—as the key question of after empire for the Chinese and Japanese postgenerations. The dynamics created by the recognition and redemption of colonial modernity's losses through the Qiqihar victims and many others subjected to Japanese colonial violence, whose voices had been marginalized even within China, are now putting pressure on the political sphere. These processes are shifting the focus of dealing with the imperial legacy from apology/reparation to accounting for this doubled structure of abandonment/duplicity, hidden behind the diplomatic framework of *(for)given time* between the two countries while simultaneously providing an excuse for their lack of *renzhen*.

In a notable political move, the Chinese state decided in 2014 to hear a legal case filed by victims of Japanese wartime use of forced labor[24] after years of refusing to accept such lawsuits within Chinese jurisdictions out of fear of opening a Pandora's Box.[25] The Chinese state is belatedly addressing its longstanding inaction and abandonment, although the consequences of such action are yet to be seen. This tectonic shift in the transnational legal landscape in East Asia—allowing victims to seek legal redress for Japanese imperial violence in their own national jurisdiction, rather than in the perpetrator's jurisdiction, beginning with a series of compensation lawsuits filed in the mid-1990s—signals that the Chinese state may be preparing to dismantle *(for)given time*. The legal frontier, it seems, is starting to unsettle the structure of abandonment and duplicity.[26]

Through the story of the inheritance of loss and its redemption, we have seen how colonial remnants, the very products of the politics of abandonment that have framed Sino-Japanese relations since the demise of the Japanese Empire, are being reincorporated into the social fabric of everyday urban life in Northeast China. Long-abandoned remnants, activated through newly available economic relations, mark the generational transmission of colonial inheritance. Physical scars of Japanese imperialism in China—the urban landscapes bearing material traces of colonial modernity and the injured bodies of victims of Japanese imperial violence—are made publicly visible and put into circulation to generate redemptive economies.

The political economy of redemption is a site where the entangled processes of postcolonial and postimperial reckoning, which may remain latent or seem separate, are made visible at the intersection of the moral and formal economies. While East Asian studies has been on the sidelines of postcolonial studies, I hope this book has persuaded readers to see how it is not the degree or length of the formal history of colonialism that calls for postcolonial analysis. Rather, it is the relationship of people's experiences to what the Chinese call the era of colonialism—in which societies were entangled in and transformed through colonial modernity, either as imperial powers, the colonized, or in between these two poles—that invites us to explore the often invisible, displaced, or seemingly discrete processes of *after empire*, of the afterlife of losses and their redemptions, of envisioning the present and the future in relation to what remains, and of renewed desires for going after empire.

NOTES

CHAPTER ONE

1. In her study of postsocialist transition in East Central Europe, Katherine Verdery observes that physical remains of socialism—in this case, dead bodies—function "as political or symbolic capital" (33) against a background of the shortage of financial capital. See Katherine Verdery, *The Political Lives of Dead Bodies: Reburial and Postsocialist Change* (New York: Columbia University Press, 1999). In contrast, the capitalization of colonial inheritance in Northeast China has turned colonial remnants into sites of economic accumulation, even at the risk of losing political legitimacy.

2. This book engages with what Lieba Faier and Lisa Rofel call "encounter approaches to (a) transnational capitalism, (b) space and place, and (c) human-nonhuman relations" (363) by exploring how the capitalization of colonial inheritance has opened up sites for second- and third-generation Chinese and Japanese to encounter not only what remains but also one another in the everyday, as well as the political economy that emerges from these encounters. See Lieba Faier and Lisa Rofel, "Ethnographies of Encounter," *Annual Review of Anthropology* 43 (2014): 363–77.

3. The English-language literature on Japanese and Russian imperialism in Northeast China and Japan's Manchukuo set against the competing Chinese nationalist movements in the region is abundant. See, for example, James H. Carter, *Creating a Chinese Harbin: Nationalism in an International City, 1916–1932* (Ithaca, NY: Cornell University Press, 2002); Blaine R. Chiasson, *Administering the Colonizer: Manchuria's Russians under Chinese Rule, 1918–29* (Vancouver: UBC Press, 2010); Daqing Yang, *Technology of Empire: Telecommunications and Japanese Expansion, 1883–1945* (Cambridge, MA: Harvard University Press, 2011); Prasenjit Duara, *Sovereignty and Authenticity: Manchukuo and the East Asian Modern* (Lanham, MD: Rowman and Littlefield, 2003); Peter Duus, Ramon H. Myers, and Mark R. Peattie, eds., *The Japanese Informal Empire in China, 1895–1937* (Princeton, NJ: Princeton University Press, 1989); Joseph W. Esherick, ed., *Remaking the Chinese City: Modernity and National Identity, 1900–1950* (Honolulu: University of Hawai'i Press, 2000); Chong-Sik Lee, *Revolutionary Struggle in Manchuria: Chinese Communism and Soviet Interest, 1922–1945* (Berkeley: University of California Press, 1983); Yoshihisa Tak Matsusaka, *The Making of Japanese Manchuria, 1904–1932*

(Cambridge, MA: Harvard University Asia Center, 2001); Janis Mimura, *Planning for Empire: Reform Bureaucrats and the Japanese Wartime State* (Ithaca, NY: Cornell University Press, 2011); Rana Mitter, *The Manchurian Myth: Nationalism, Resistance, and Collaboration in Modern China* (Berkeley: University of California Press, 2000); Emer O'Dwyer, *Significant Soil: Settler Colonialism and Japan's Urban Empire in Manchuria* (Cambridge, MA: Harvard University Asia Center, 2015); David Wolff, *To the Harbin Station: The Liberal Alternative in Russian Manchuria, 1898–1914* (Stanford, CA: Stanford University Press, 1999); and Louise Young, *Japan's Total Empire: Manchuria and the Culture of Wartime Imperialism* (Berkeley: University of California Press, 1998).

4. For an overview of the wartime use of "comfort women" in English, see, for example, C. Sarah Soh, *The Comfort Women: Sexual Violence and Postcolonial Memory in Korea and Japan* (Chicago: University of Chicago Press, 2008); and Yoshiaki Yoshimi, *Comfort Women: Sexual Slavery in the Japanese Military During World War II*, trans. Suzanne O'Brien (New York: Columbia University Press, 2000). On the Nanjing Massacre, see Joshua A. Fogel, ed., *The Nanjing Massacre in History and Historiography* (Berkeley: University of California Press, 2000); and Takashi Yoshida, *The Making of the "Rape of Nanking": History and Memory in Japan, China, and the United States* (New York: Oxford University Press, 2006). On the issue surrounding the Japanese involvement in the development of biochemical weapons, see Jing-Bao Nie, Nanyan Guo, Mark Selden, and Arthur Kleinman, eds., *Japan's Wartime Medical Atrocities: Comparative Inquiries in Science, History, and Ethics* (New York: Routledge, 2010); and Sheldon H. Harris, *Factories of Death: Japanese Biological Warfare, 1932–1945, and the American Cover-Up* (New York: Routledge, 1994).

5. On Japan's "history problem" in English, see, for example, John Breen, ed., *Yasukuni, The War Dead and the Struggle for Japan's Past* (New York: Columbia University Press, 2008); Alexis Dudden, *Troubled Apologies among Japan, Korea, and the United States* (New York: Columbia University Press, 2008); Joshua A. Fogel, ed., *The Nanjing Massacre in History and Historiography* (Berkeley: University of California Press, 2000); Yinan He, *The Search for Reconciliation: Sino-Japanese and German-Polish Relations since World War II* (New York: Cambridge University Press, 2009); Laura Hein and Mark Selden, eds., *Censoring History: Citizenship and Memory in Japan, Germany, and the United States* (Armonk, NY: M. E. Sharpe, 2000); Akiko Takenaka, *Yasukuni Shrine: History, Memory and Japan's Unending Postwar* (Honolulu: University of Hawai'i Press, 2015); and Yoshida, *The Making of the "Rape of Nanking."*

6. Veena Das, *Life and Words: Violence and Descent into the Ordinary*, foreword by Stanley Cavell (Berkeley: University of California Press, 2007). In contrast to how memory studies generally approach catastrophic events by making trauma visible, Das suggests we look into "what happens to the subject and world when the memory of such events is folded into ongoing relationships" (8), which she calls "the recesses of ordinary" (1). She directs our attention to the passage of time since the original violence formally ended (what she calls the "work of time" [16]). My exploration in this book examines this work of time for those with no direct experience of the catastrophe.

7. Tani E. Barlow, "Introduction: On 'Colonial Modernity,'" in *Formations of Colonial Modernity in East Asia*, ed. Barlow, 1–20 (Durham, NC: Duke University Press,

1997), 12. See also Tani E. Barlow, "~~Colonialism~~'s Career in Postwar China Studies," *positions: east asia cultures critique* 1, no. 1 (1993).

8. For an overview of these cities' historical development, see Joseph W. Esherick, ed., *Remaking the Chinese City: Modernity and National Identity, 1900–1950* (Honolulu: University of Hawai'i Press, 2000). For an overview of colonial-era architecture in Northeast China, see Fujimori Terunobu and Wan Tan, eds., *Zenchōsa higashi Ajia kindai no toshi to kenchikū, 1840–1945* [A comprehensive study of East Asian architecture and urban planning, 1840–1945] (Tokyo: Chikuma Shobō, 1996).

9. Quoted in Koshizawa Akira, *Manshūkoku no shuto keikaku: Tokyo no genzai to mirai o tou* [The urban planning of the Manchurian capital: Questioning the present and the future of Tokyo] (Tokyo: Nihon keizai hyōronsha, 1988), 188.

10. For the architecture and urban planning of Shinkyō, see Koshizawa, *Manshūkoku no shuto keikaku*. For the major architectural remainders of Manchukuo in Changchun, see Shen Yan, *Changchun weiman yizhi daguan* [An overview of the architectural remainders of fake Manchukuo in Changchun] (Changchun: Jilin sheying chubanshe, 2002).

11. Shenyang also retains colonial-era urban planning and architecture similar to Dalian; however, this study focuses on Dalian, which eagerly capitalizes on its colonial remainders. Unlike Harbin, Changchun, and Dalian, which were developed primarily by Russia and Japan in the early twentieth century as colonial cities, Shenyang has several thousand years of history as a city, including being the capital of the Manchu dynasty (Later Jin dynasty) in the seventeenth century. For the Manchu dynasty and the role of Shenyang, see Mark C. Elliott, *The Manchu Way: The Eight Banners and Ethnic Identity in Late Imperial China* (Stanford, CA: Stanford University Press, 2001); and Qinghua Guo, "Shenyang: The Manchurian Ideal Capital City and Imperial Palace, 1625–43," *Urban History* 27, no. 3 (2000): 344–59.

12. For an insightful analysis of public debates surrounding apology, see, for example, Dudden, *Troubled Apologies*; and Norma Field, "War and Apology: Japan, Asia, the Fiftieth, and After," *positions: east asia cultures critique* 5, no. 1 (1997): 1–49.

13. For the construction of Japanese victimhood in postwar Japan and the attendant imperial amnesia, see John W. Dower, *Ways of Forgetting, Ways of Remembering: Japan in the Modern World* (New York: New Press, 2012); Yoshikuni Igarashi, *Bodies of Memory: Narratives of War in Postwar Japanese Culture, 1945–1970* (Princeton, NJ: Princeton University Press, 2000); Ian Jared Miller, *The Nature of the Beasts: Empire and Exhibition at the Tokyo Imperial Zoo* (Berkeley: University of California Press, 2013); James Joseph Orr, *The Victim as Hero: Ideologies of Peace and National Identity in Postwar Japan* (Honolulu: University of Hawai'i Press, 2001); and Lisa Yoneyama, *Hiroshima Traces: Time, Space, and the Dialectics of Memory* (Berkeley: University of California Press, 1999). Victim narratives in Japan generated various interest-based politics. For the development of memory politics among civic organizations in postwar Japan, see Franziska Seraphim, *War Memory and Social Politics in Japan, 1945–2005* (Cambridge, MA: Harvard University Asia Center, 2006). For an analysis of postwar narratives of Japanese victimhood/perpetration within a global context, see Fogel, ed., *The Nanjing Massacre in History and Historiography*; Hein and Selden, eds., *Censoring History*; Yoneyama, *Hiroshima Traces*; and Yoshida, *The Making of the "Rape of Nanking."*

14. In fact, to describe this process as imperial *amnesia* is misleading. It is the act of *erasure* that created the public disappearance of empire in postwar Japan. Lori Watt's historical study, for example, documents the repatriation of Japanese nationals from Japan's former empire in the 1940s and 1950s, which was one of the most publicly visible displays of the afterlife of the Japanese Empire. See Lori Watt, *When Empire Comes Home: Repatriation and Reintegration in Postwar Japan* (Cambridge, MA: Harvard University Asia Center, 2009).

15. Since the early 1950s, Mao Zedong had expressed the view that a small number of militarists led Japan to war and that ordinary Japanese were also victims of the war. Mao's viewpoint became an official policy in March 1955 under "Zhong Gong Zhongyang guanyu dui Ri zhengce he dui Ri huodong de fangzhen he jihua" [The Politburo of the Communist Party of China policy toward Japan and the plan and direction of activities toward Japan].

16. Through his analysis of the changing commemorative practices for Chinese General Zhang Zizhong, who was killed by the Japanese in 1940, Arthur Waldron traces how the war has been remembered in China and shows a major shift in the discourse from anti-Guomindang to anti-Japanese. This shift, he argues, signals the shift from "utopian communist ideas toward nationalistic and patriotic themes" in organizing the legitimacy of the party-state. See Arthur Waldron, "China's New Remembering of World War II: The Case of Zhang Zizhong," *Modern Asian Studies* 30, no. 4 (1996): 869–99. Rana Mitter illustrates such a shift in the national discourse in his analysis of the exhibition at the Beijing War of Resistance Museum. See Rana Mitter, "Behind the Scenes at the Museum: Nationalism, History and Memory in the Beijing War of Resistance Museum, 1987–1997," *The China Quarterly* 161 (2000): 279–93. See also Parks M. Coble, "China's 'New Remembering' of the Anti-Japanese War of Resistance, 1937–1945," *The China Quarterly* 190 (2007): 394–410; James L. Hevia, "Remembering the Century of Humiliation: The Yuanming Gardens and Dagu Forts Museums," in *Ruptured Histories: War, Memory, and the Post-Cold War in Asia*, ed. Sheila Miyoshi Jager and Rana Mitter, 192–208 (Cambridge, MA: Harvard University Press, 2007); He Yinan, "Remembering and Forgetting the War: Elite Mythmaking, Mass Reaction, and Sino-Japanese Relations, 1950–2006," *History and Memory* 19, no. 2 (Fall 2007): 43–74; and He, *The Search for Reconciliation*.

Through his analysis of the BC class war tribunals in mainland China and Taiwan after the Japanese defeat, Barak Kushner locates the seemingly magnanimous attitude toward the Japanese in these trials within the competing attempts by the Guomindang and the CCP to gain legitimacy within the new international legal structure under the Cold War. See Barak Kushner, *Men to Devils, Devils to Men: Japanese War Crimes and Chinese Justice* (Cambridge, MA: Harvard University Press, 2015).

17. In her anthropological study of Dalian, Tiantian Zheng points to how "political leaders [in Beijing after the establishment of the PRC] eliminated the crucial function of Dalian in the battle [against Japanese] because Dalian used to be a colony" and that "most Chinese were eager to forget Dalian's tarnished history as a colony" to explain the rapid decline of the economy in Northeast China despite the presence of a solid industrial base. What is indicated here is how the post-Liberation CCP attempted to erase China's postcoloniality through the marginalization of the former Japanese colonial region. See Tiantian Zheng, *Red Lights: The Lives of Sex Workers in Postsocialist China* (Minneapolis: University of Minnesota Press, 2009), 49.

18. Mao Zedong's position exempting ordinary Japanese from war responsibility was confirmed and widely publicized during the negotiations leading to the signing of the Joint Communiqué. In his speech delivered at the banquet held in Beijing on September 25 of that year to welcome Japanese Prime Minister Tanaka Kakuei, Chinese Premier Zhou Enlai stated, "As the Japanese militarists invaded China, Chinese people suffered tremendously, but Japanese people also became victims. . . . Following the teachings of Chairman Mao Zedong, Chinese people strictly distinguish a small number of militaristic factions from the vast majority of Japanese people." Zhou's speech was incorporated into an editorial of the *People's Daily* a few days later to reiterate the longstanding official view at this historic moment. See "Zhou Enlai zongli de zhujiu ci zai huanying Tianzhong shouxiang yanhui shang" [Premier Zhou Enlai's speech at the banquet to welcome Prime Minister Tanaka], *Renmin ribao* [People's Daily] (Beijing), September 26, 1972, 3; and "Zhong Ri guanxi shi de xin pianzhan" [A new chapter to the history of China and Japan], *Renmin ribao* [People's Daily] (Beijing), September 30, 1972, shelun [editorial], 2.

19. The Chinese renunciation of reparation claims in the Communiqué was prefaced by and framed within the proclamation of Japanese responsibility for Chinese losses sustained during the war, effectively presenting China's waiver as a generous gift to Japan. The preamble of the Joint Communiqué of the Government of Japan and the Government of the People's Republic of China states that "the Japanese side is keenly conscious of the responsibility for the serious damage that Japan caused in the past to the Chinese people through war, and deeply reproaches itself." Having said that, article five of the Communiqué reads, "The Government of the People's Republic of China declares that in the interest of the friendship between the Chinese and the Japanese peoples, it renounces its demand for war reparation from Japan." By linking its renunciation of reparation claims to the promise of good deeds in the future ("in the interest of the friendship between the Chinese and the Japanese peoples"), the Chinese side expresses its expectation for reciprocity from the Japanese government, in the form of a return gift of friendship built on a deep sense of repentance.

20. Marcel Mauss, *The Gift: The Form and Reason for Exchange in Archaic Societies*, trans. W. D. Halls, foreword by Mary Douglas (New York: W. W. Norton, 1990 [1924]).

21. I owe my reading of Mauss here to Rosalind Morris, who points to the play of memory and economy that is mediated with gift and debt through her reading of Jacques Derrida's observation on the gift: "For Derrida, the recipient's recognition of the gift constitutes the moment in which it is transformed into debt. Hence, a true gift would rest upon the forgetting of the gift and, moreover, a forgetting of the act of forgetting." If both the gift giver and the recipient recognize the gift as such, it ceases to be a gift at the moment of its announcement. Since this paradox structures an economy of the gift, the words that declare its arrival mark contractual relations in this economy of debt. See Jacques Derrida, *Given Time: I. Counterfeit Money*, trans. Peggy Kamuf (Chicago: University of Chicago Press, 1991), especially chapters 1 and 2; and Rosalind C. Morris, *In the Place of Origins: Modernity and Its Mediums in Northern Thailand* (Durham, NC: Duke University Press, 2000), 33.

22. In his critical reading of Mauss's exploration of gift, Jacques Derrida points to how a gift, which always incurs debt, is a gift of time for future repayment. Here, Derrida points to how what is given is not the thing itself but time for future repayment of the debt incurred from this gift. See Derrida, *Given Time*.

23. An explosion of heated discussions in China, which was triggered by the Japanese government's announcement in 2007 of its plan to end the ODA to China, highlighted this enigmatic location of the Japanese ODA in relation to Japanese moral debt to China. See, for example, Cao Haidong and Huang Xiaowei, "Riben Dui Hua Yuanzhu San Shi Nian" [Thirty years of Japan's aid to China], *Nanfang Zhoumo*, February 20, 2008, http://www.infzm.com/content/7707.

24. For a concise historical overview of the political use of war memory in China, see He, "Remembering and Forgetting the War" and *The Search for Reconciliation*. On the Chinese Communist Party's use of war memory, see Zheng Wang, *Never Forget National Humiliation: Historical Memory in Chinese Politics and Foreign Relations* (New York: Columbia University Press, 2012). For an analysis of these historical museums, see Kirk A. Denton, *Exhibiting the Past: Historical Memory and the Politics of Museums in Postsocialist China* (Honolulu: University of Hawai'i Press, 2014), and "Horror and Atrocity: Memory of Japanese Imperialism in Chinese Museums," in *Re-envisioning the Chinese Revolution: The Politics and Poetics of Collective Memories in Reform China*, ed. Ching Kwan Lee and Guobin Yang, 245–86 (Stanford, CA: Stanford University Press, 2007); Hevia, "Remembering the Century of Humiliation"; and Rana Mitter, "Behind the Scenes at the Museum" and "China's 'Good War': Voices, Locations, and Generations in the Interpretation of the War of Resistance to Japan," in *Ruptured Histories: War, Memory, and the Post-Cold War in Asia*, ed. Sheila Miyoshi Jager and Rana Mitter, 172–91 (Cambridge, MA: Harvard University Press, 2007).

25. The use of "invasion" sent signals to the Japanese government, since this term was the point of contestation in the 1982 textbook controversy. The Ministry of Education revised the expression "invasion (*shinryaku*) of north China" into "advance (*shinshutsu*) into north China." For a concise overview of the Sino-Japanese contention over historical issues in the 1980s, see Arif Dirlik, "'Past Experience, If Not Forgotten, Is a Guide to the Future'; or, What Is in a Text? The Politics of History in Chinese-Japanese Relations," in *Japan in the World*, ed. Masao Miyoshi and H. D. Harootunian, 49–78 (Durham, NC: Duke University Press, 1993).

26. On Unit 731 in English, see, for example, Nie, Guo, Selden, and Kleinman, eds., *Japan's Wartime Medical Atrocities*; and Harris, *Factories of Death*. A recent addition to the large body of literature in Japanese and Chinese is Aoki Fukiko, *731* (Tokyo: Shinchōsha, 2005), which traces the creation of Unit 731 and its postwar history through an examination of recently discovered notebooks written by Unit Chief Ishii Shirō immediately after the Japanese defeat.

27. Morimoto Seiichi, *Akuma no hōshoku: Dai 731 butai no senritsu no zenbō!* [Devil's gluttony: The chilling reality of Unit 731!] (Tokyo: Kadokawa Shoten, 1983). This controversial publication, which originally appeared in the Japan Communist Party newspaper *Shinbun Akahata* (The Red Flag), unleashed subsequent publications on Unit 731 in both China and Japan.

28. Traveling in China never fails to make you aware of its history with colonial modernity. Many cities have museums or historical sites that illustrate the era of colonialism, built mostly in the 1980s. These sites are often designated as "patriotic education bases." Anticolonialist and anti-imperialist rhetoric (often used interchangeably) is omnipresent in school textbooks, films, and historical relics. At the same time, the state

tightly controls the interpretation of the era of colonialism. The discourse of the "New China" under the CCP marks 1949 as its zero hour, and China's modern history before the establishment of the PRC is treated as a relic, consigned to the demarcated space of historical sites. As a result, China contains both omnipresent remnants of colonial modernity *and* erased traces of them.

29. Andreas Huyssen, *Twilight Memories: Marking Time in a Culture of Amnesia* (New York: Routledge, 1995), 15.

30. Ann Laura Stoler, "Preface" and "Introduction: 'The Rot Remains': From Ruins to Ruination," in *Imperial Debris: On Ruins and Ruination*, ed. Stoler, ix–35 (Durham, NC: Duke University Press, 2013); and "Imperial Debris: Reflections on Ruins and Ruination," *Cultural Anthropology* 23, no. 2 (2008): 191–219.

31. See Rubie S. Watson, "Memory, History, and Opposition under State Socialism: An Introduction," in *Memory, History and Opposition under State Socialism*, ed. Rubie S. Watson (Santa Fe, NM: School of American Research Press, 1994), 1–20; and Søren Clausen and Stig Thøgersen, *The Making of a Chinese City: History and Historiography in Harbin* (Armonk, NY: M. E. Sharpe, 1995), 199–217.

32. Unlike other "posts" that are marked with publicly recognizable events as "ends," such as post-postwar and post–Cold War, or postsocialism in Eastern Europe and the Soviet Union, China's postsocialism lacks a recognizable marker for an "end." In fact, postsocialism in the case of China refers to a metamorphosis of socialism through China's transition to a market-oriented society, which has yet to be given a proper name. My usage of *postsocialism* here, then, highlights less the temporality of afterness (and the accompanying afterlife of what ended formally) than the anticipatory sense of yet-to-come.

33. For an overview of the changing memory landscape in East Asia, see Sheila Miyoshi Jager and Rana Mitter, eds., *Ruptured Histories: War, Memory, and the Post-Cold War in Asia* (Cambridge, MA: Harvard University Press, 2007).

34. Elsewhere, I have explored the new dynamics generated by the public appearance of long "invisible" Chinese war victims and the subsequent development of a series of compensation lawsuits filed by the victims against the Japanese government and corporations. See Yukiko Koga, "Accounting for Silence: Inheritance, Debt, and the Moral Economy of Legal Redress in China and Japan," *American Ethnologist* 40, no. 3 (2013): 494–507; and "Between the Law: The Unmaking of Empire and Law's Imperial Amnesia," *Law and Social Inquiry*, 41 issue 2 (Spring 2016): 402–34.

35. On the global context in which postwar compensation for Japanese war crimes is motivated by the Holocaust compensation attempts, see Lisa Yoneyama, "Traveling Memories, Contagious Justice: Americanization of Japanese War Crimes at the End of the Post-Cold War," *Journal of Asian American Studies* 6, no. 1 (2003): 57–93.

36. See, for example, Ackbar Abbas, *Hong Kong: Culture and the Politics of Disappearance* (Minneapolis: University of Minnesota Press, 1997), 65–69. Writing on Hong Kong, Abbas warns that the historical preservation of colonial-era architecture and resultant aestheticization turn these edifices into kitsch by reducing historical site to historical sight.

37. Arif Dirlik provides a concise overview of the term *postcolonialism*. He mentions three prominent uses of the term: (a) "as a literal description of conditions in the formerly colonial societies"; (b) "as a description of a global condition after the period of

colonialism"; and (c) "as a description of a discourse on the above-named conditions that is informed by the epistemological and psychic orientations that are products of those conditions." See Arif Dirlik, "The Postcolonial Aura: Third World Criticism in the Age of Global Capitalism," *Critical Inquiry* 20 (Winter 1994): 328–56, 332.

While the definition of postcolonialism that Dirlik spells out (and is shared by many others) is useful, this book suggests that such a definition has limited the scope of our understanding of colonial modernity's extended reach and its aftereffects.

38. For example, Prasenjit Duara argues against the relevance of the postcolonial lens for analyzing post-Liberation China because of China's short history of semicolonial status compared with the experiences of colonial India, although he employs a postcolonial approach to bring to light competing narratives—subaltern voices silenced under the dominant national narrative—in his analysis of early twentieth-century China. Comparing the role of colonialism in shaping the narrative of the nation in India and China, Duara observes that the lack of postcoloniality in China stems from a relative lack of a colonial mindset among Chinese. This, he argues, derives from the fact that the influence of imperialism in China was contained within the political and economic spheres while the cultural domain remained relatively free of it. See Prasenjit Duara, *Rescuing History from the Nation: Questioning Narratives of Modern China* (Chicago: University of Chicago Press, 1995), 224. See also Prasenjit Duara, "Introduction: The Decolonization of Asia and Africa in the Twentieth Century," in *Decolonization: Perspectives from Now and Then*, ed. Prasenjit Duara, 1–18 (New York: Routledge, 2004).

It should be noted that China studies is not the only area studies that is reluctant to employ the postcolonial lens. Fernando Coronil lamented how the narrow scope of postcolonial studies has led some scholars to claim that Latin America is not postcolonial, unlike India or Indonesia. See Fernando Coronil, "Editor's Column: The End of Postcolonial Theory? A Roundtable with Sunil Agnani, Fernando Coronil, Gaurav Desai, Mamadou Diouf, Simon Gikandi, Susie Tharu, and Jennifer Wenzel," *Publications of the Modern Language Association* 122, no. 3 (2007): 633–51, 637.

39. Barlow, "Introduction: On 'Colonial Modernity.'"

40. See Barlow, "~~Colonialism~~'s Career in Postwar China Studies" and "Introduction: On 'Colonial Modernity.'" For the development of debates over colonial modernity in the past decade, see also Tani E. Barlow, "Debates over Colonial Modernity in East Asia and Another Alternative," *Cultural Studies* 26, no. 25 (2012): 617–44.

41. The reluctance to analyze contemporary society's relation to colonial modernity is not limited to China studies but is also found in studies of South Korea, despite its history of formal colonialism over nearly half a century. In her richly nuanced study of colonial literature in Korea under Japanese rule, Nayoung Aimee Kwon intervenes in this absence by exploring the delicate and politically sensitive space between modernity's lure and its devastation through the lens of "intimacy," which captures "a 'shared but disavowed' *conundrum* of modernity experienced in colonial subjection." See Nayoung Aimee Kwon, *Intimate Empire: Collaboration and Colonial Modernity in Korea and Japan* (Durham, NC: Duke University Press, 2015), 9. See also Tani E. Barlow, ed., *Formations of Colonial Modernity in East Asia* (Durham, NC: Duke University Press, 1997); and Gi-Wook Shin and Michael Robinson, eds., *Colonial Modernity in Korea* (Cambridge, MA: Harvard University Press, 1999).

Kuan-Hsing Chen points to how the double process of decolonization and deimperialization in East Asia was suspended by the Cold War and shows that the region is experiencing the delayed process after the end of the Cold War. See Kuan-Hsing Chen, *Asia as Method: Toward Deimperialization* (Durham, NC: Duke University Press, 2010).

42. See, for example, Peter Zarrow, *After Empire: The Conceptual Transformation of the Chinese State, 1885–1924* (Stanford, CA: Stanford University Press, 2012); and Odd Arne Westad, *Restless Empire: China and the World Since 1750* (New York: Basic Books, 2012). As Mark Elliott demonstrates, in the late nineteenth century Chinese intellectuals came to refer to the Qing dynasty as an "empire" (*diguo*), which is a term they imported from Japan (*teikoku*), an aspiring imperial state. Mark C. Elliott, "Chuantong Zhongguo shi yi ge diguo ma?" [Was the traditional China an empire?], *Dushu* (Beijing), January 2014, 29–40.

43. On the use of *guochi* in Chinese politics, see Wang, *Never Forget National Humiliation*.

44. On China's recent global expansion, see, for example, Elizabeth C. Economy and Michael Levi, *By All Means Necessary: How China's Resource Quest Is Changing the World* (New York: Oxford University Press, 2014); Howard W. French, *China's Second Continent: How a Million Migrants Are Building a New Empire in Africa* (New York: Knopf, 2014); Kevin Gallagher and Roberto Porzecanski, *The Dragon in the Room: China and the Future of Latin American Industrialization* (Stanford, CA: Stanford University Press, 2010); Ching Kwan Lee, "Raw Encounters: Chinese Managers, African Workers, and the Politics of Casualization in Africa's Chinese Enclaves," *The China Quarterly* 199 (2009): 647–66; Barry Sautman and Hairong Yan, "African Perspectives on China-Africa Links," *The China Quarterly* 199 (2009): 728–59; David Shambaugh, *China Goes Global: The Partial Power* (New York: Oxford University Press, 2013); and Westad, *Restless Empire*.

45. This book thus builds on works that trace contemporary China's relation to, and perceived lack of, modernity back to its encounters with Western imperial forces. See, for example, Ann Anagnost, *National Past-Times: Narrative, Representation, and Power in Modern China* (Durham, NC: Duke University Press, 1997); and Lisa Rofel, *Other Modernities: Gendered Yearnings in China after Socialism* (Berkeley: University of California Press, 1999). Within the realm of politics and diplomacy, recent works by political scientists have demonstrated how the CCP has deployed a sense of national humiliation and historical memory in solidifying its power. See Wang, *Never Forget National Humiliation*; and He, *The Search for Reconciliation*. Historian James L. Hevia examines the centrality of humiliation expressed in museums in his "Remembering the Century of Humiliation."

46. The dynamics of *inheritance and betrayal* that the following chapters bring to the fore are akin to the betrayal of tradition that Marilyn Ivy analyzes in her ethnography of modern Japan. Ivy illustrates the emergence of the Japanese nation-state at sites where what became marginal and exotic as Japanese society embraces modernity has come to be "re-discovered" as authentic tradition within the Japanese national-cultural imaginary. Chinese municipal governments' deployment of the rhetoric of "inheritance" to reincorporate exotic and foreign colonial remnants—enigmatic "tradition" of some sort, which had been long-neglected until China's transition to a market-oriented society—

has produced similar dynamics to those generated through "tradition" analyzed by Ivy: while both "tradition" and "inheritance" claim and capitalize on the exotic/foreign on the margin by locating it in the proper lineage of "Japan" or "China," the process of this transmission produces excess that betrays the past. On betrayal of tradition, see Marilyn Ivy, *Discourses of the Vanishing: Modernity, Phantasm, Japan* (Chicago: University of Chicago Press, 1995).

47. Marianne Hirsch, *The Generation of Postmemory: Writing and Visual Culture after the Holocaust* (New York: Columbia University Press, 2012).

48. Eva Hoffman, *After Such Knowledge: Memory, History and the Legacy of the Holocaust* (New York: Public Affairs, 2004).

49. Michael Rothberg, *Multidirectional Memory: Remembering the Holocaust in the Age of Decolonization* (Stanford, CA: Stanford University Press, 2009). Similar attempts within memory studies to question the widely assumed link between memory and original trauma include such concepts as "prosthetic memory" and "knots of memory." On prosthetic memory, see Alison Landsberg, *Prosthetic Memory: The Transformation of American Remembrance in the Age of Mass Culture* (New York: Columbia University Press, 2004). On knots of memory across transnational milieus, see Michael Rothberg, "Introduction: Between Memory and Memory: From Lieux de mémoire to Noeuds de mémoire," *Yale French Studies* 118/119, *Noeuds de mémoire: Multidirectional Memory in Postwar French and Francophone Culture* (2010): 3–12. Through a lens of migration, Michael Rothberg and Yasemin Yildiz challenge the assumed mnemonic community in "Memory Citizenship: Migrant Archives of Holocaust Remembrance in Contemporary Germany," *Parallax* 17, no. 4 (2011): 32–48.

50. In the East Asian context, Lisa Yoneyama's *Hiroshima Traces* and Mariko Asano Tamanoi's *Memory Maps: The State and Manchuria in Postwar Japan* (Honolulu: University of Hawai'i Press, 2009) are notable works that capture the multidirectionality of memory. Unlike Rothberg, both Yoneyama and Tamanoi locate the origin of memory in the respective original traumas of the atomic bomb in Hiroshima and Japan's Manchuria.

51. Rothberg, *Multidirectional Memory*, 5.

52. Rothberg, *Multidirectional Memory*, 35–36.

53. Rothberg, *Multidirectional Memory*, 5.

54. Arthur Kleinman et al. explore the new moral landscape that has emerged through China's transition to a market-oriented society in *Deep China: The Moral Life of the Person: What Anthropology and Psychiatry Tell Us about China Today* (Berkeley: University of California Press, 2011). *Inheritance of Loss* expands the scope of this landscape to illuminate the moral landscape that has emerged through transnational encounters.

55. In her ethnographic analysis of post-Pinochet Chile, Clara Han examines how the new regime employed the rhetoric of moral and social debts and corresponding political and social projects to account for the past violence. At this intersection of moral and formal economies, Han observes how the debt-inflicted economic precariousness of the present has made many victims of the Pinochet violence perceive these repayment projects *not* as the markers of radical discontinuity from the past, as intended by the state, but rather as the continuation of state violence now in the name of care. In contrast, as we shall see in the following chapters, the intersection of formal and moral economies can

become a site of redemption. See Clara Han, *Life in Debt: Times of Care and Violence in Neoliberal Chile* (Berkeley: University of California Press, 2012).

56. In his analysis of German society's coming to terms with its Nazi past, A. Dirk Moses explores the concept of "redemption" through the lens of Christianity, as he finds limits to the term's secular use. In the East Asian context, redemption is primarily a secular term, and my use of it in the concept of the political economy of redemption highlights the word's dictionary meanings in Chinese and Japanese (to pay off debt, to salvage, to compensate, or to satisfy obligation). I situate the oft-stated economic rationality within the workings of the exchange economy that the term *redemption* implies. See A. Dirk Moses, *German Intellectuals and the Nazi Past* (New York: Cambridge University Press, 2007), and "Stigma and Sacrifice in Postwar Germany," *History and Memory* 19, no. 2 (2007): 139–80.

57. Didier Fassin and Richard Rechtman, *The Empire of Trauma: An Inquiry into the Condition of Victimhood*, trans. Rachel Gomme (Princeton, NJ: Princeton University Press, 2009). See also Didier Fassin, "Compassion and Repression: The Moral Economy of Immigration Policies in France," *Cultural Anthropology* 20, no. 3 (2005): 362–87.

58. In his critical overview of the genealogy of the concept of "moral economy," Marc Edelman laments how appropriations of this concept in recent anthropological studies tend to eviscerate the core class tension that E. P. Thompson highlighted through moral economy as an analytical tool. Edelman underscores how, for Thompson, "markets" consist of "moral economy" and "political economy" surrounding monetary transactions. My ethnographic analysis of moral economy in this book demonstrates how the separation of the moral and formal economies is itself a historical product sanctioned by the framework of *(for)given time*. See Marc Edelman, "E. P. Thompson and Moral Economies," in *A Companion to Moral Anthropology*, ed. Didier Fassin, 49–66 (Oxford: Wiley-Blackwell, 2012); and E. P. Thompson, "The Moral Economy of the English Crowd in the Eighteenth Century," *Past and Present* 50 (February 1971): 76–136.

59. Akin to the political economy of redemption in Northeast China, David Scott observes the redemptive nature of generational transmission of the unaccounted-for past stemming from the failed Grenada Revolution. Yet whereas in Scott's analysis the mnemonic community is assumed through this transmission, my ethnography illustrates how newly available face-to-face encounters between ordinary Chinese and Japanese sets in motion a mode of generational transmission that challenges this assumed mnemonic community and opens up new terrain for relating to unaccounted-for pasts. See David Scott, *Omens of Adversity: Tragedy, Time, Memory, Justice* (Durham, NC: Duke University Press, 2014).

60. Ray Chow introduces the concept of "entanglements," which is useful for thinking about the working of double inheritance here. Borrowing from quantum physics to refer to connections not based on proximity, Chow extends the concept of entanglement from the conventional usage to also refer to linkages "through partition and parity rather than conjunction and intersection, and through disparity rather than equivalence" (1–2). She encapsulates this concept as "the linkages and enmeshments that keep things apart; the voidings and uncoverings that hold thing together" (12). Rey Chow, *Entanglements, or Transmedial Thinking about Capture* (Durham, NC: Duke University Press, 2012).

61. Through the concept of "imperial debris," Ann Laura Stoler directs us to explore sites of "imperial formations" that the existing postcolonial studies fails to see as objects

of study. These are imperial ruins and sites of ruination, where lasting effects of imperialism/colonialism are often effaced, dislocated, and disguised. Stoler approaches these sites not as monumentalized objects of imperial nostalgia but as lived experiences of those people who have no choice but to live with. In so doing, she questions the assumptions of existing postcolonial studies and calls for analyses of remainders that have escaped postcolonial studies and often been analyzed instead through the lenses of modernity, capitalism, or globalization. Colonial inheritance in my study is a form of imperial debris, and my book suggests a new direction in postcolonial studies and much less discussed postimperial studies in a spirit similar to Stoler's intervention.

Parallel to Eric Santner's analysis of the Germans' inability to mourn in postwar Germany, the pronoun *we* bears the scars of history here. Adjectives such as *Chinese* or *Japanese* carry the inherited scars of colonial modernity's violence as former victims and former perpetrators. Recognizing this perceived inseparability and inherited burden allows me to examine the afterlife of the "national thing," which itself is a form of colonial remainder—the thing that remains and reminds. Instead of consigning the metropole/colony duality to the past, I integrate this duality and its afterlife into my analysis through the lens of after empire. See Ann Laura Stoler, "Preface" and "Introduction: 'The Rot Remains'"; and Eric L. Santner, *Stranded Objects: Mourning, Memory, and Film in Postwar Germany* (Ithaca, NY: Cornell University Press, 1990). On the "national thing," see Slavoj Žižek, "Eastern Europe's Republic of Gilead," *New Left Review* 183 (September/October 1990): 50–56.

62. Recent studies of colonialism have brought to the fore the intertwined nature of colonial relations. See, for example, Jean and John Comaroff, *Of Revelation and Revolution: Christianity, Colonialism, and Consciousness in South Africa* (Chicago: University of Chicago Press, 1991); Nicholas B. Dirks, *Castes of Mind: Colonialism and the Making of Modern India* (Princeton, NJ: Princeton University Press, 2001); Caroline Elkins and Susan Pedersen, eds., *Settler Colonialism in the Twentieth Century: Projects, Practices, Legacies* (New York: Routledge, 2005); Ann Laura Stoler, *Carnal Knowledge and Imperial Power* (Berkeley: University of California Press, 2002), and *Race and the Education of Desire: Foucault's History of Sexuality and the Colonial Order of Things* (Durham, NC: Duke University Press, 1995); Michael Taussig, *Shamanism, Colonialism, and the Wild Man: A Study in Terror and Healing* (Chicago: University of Chicago Press, 1987); Jun Uchida, *Brokers of Empire: Japanese Settler Colonialism in Korea, 1876–1945* (Cambridge, MA: Harvard University Press, 2011); Gary Wilder, *The French Imperial Nation-State: Negritude and Colonial Humanism between the Two World Wars* (Chicago: University of Chicago Press, 2005).

63. For example, Caroline Elkin shows how decades of erasure and silencing of the victims of the Mau Mau Uprising ensued after Kenya's independence from Britain, not only in Britain but also in post-independence Kenya, while it was the British who recognized their own victimhood in this war that led to decolonization. See Caroline Elkins, *Imperial Reckoning: The Untold Story of Britain's Gulag in Kenya* (New York: Henry Holt, 2005).

64. The Japanese concept of *kimin* (abandoned people), which I discuss in chapter 6 through the case of victims of abandoned chemical weapons, is one such example of losses incurred *after* the end of empire through inheriting processes. The optic of after

empire casts light on those who fell through the cracks that opened up in the formal transition from empire to nation-states and are left abandoned by postcolonial and postimperial states, such as those who suffered from the forced migration and repatriation of people and human remains as a result of an empire's end, including the contested legal status of former colonial or imperial subjects (such as the case of resident Koreans in Japan after the empire's demise). On the question of citizenship after the demise of the Japanese Empire, see, for example, Asano Toyomi, *Sengo Nihon no baishō mondai to Higashi Ajia chiiki saihen: Seikyūken to rekishi ninshiki mondai no kigen* [Japanese postwar reparation and reconfiguration of the East Asia region: The right to claim reparation and the origin of the historical consciousness problem] (Tokyo: Jigakusha shuppan, 2013); and Ōnuma Yasuaki, *Tan'itsu minzoku shakai no shinwa o koete: Zainichi Kankoku Chōsenjin to shutsunyūkoku kanri taisei* [Beyond the myth of a single ethnic society: Koreans in Japan and the emigration and immigration administration] (Tokyo: Tōshindō, 1986).

The topography of after empire, then, is a space that challenges the perceived radical discontinuity between empire and nation-states by exposing what becomes invisible through this perception. On landscapes of after empire seen through the lens of citizenship in other empires, see, for example, Michelle U. Campos, *Ottoman Brothers: Muslims, Christians, and Jews in Early Twentieth-Century Palestine* (Stanford, CA: Stanford University Press, 2010); and Frederick Cooper, *Citizenship between Empire and Nation: Remaking France and French Africa, 1945–1960* (Princeton, NJ: Princeton University Press, 2014).

65. I use the term *delayed violence* to highlight the temporal linkage with the distant past that the victims subjected to such violence feel, as expressed in their proclamation, "We are also war victims!" This perceived temporal aspect—felt proximity to the distant original violence—differentiates delayed violence from what Rob Nixon calls "slow violence," which is "a violence that occurred gradually and out of sight, a violence of delayed destruction that is dispersed across time and space, an attritional violence that is typically not viewed as violence at all" (2) and "is decoupled from its original causes by the working of time" (11). Although these two forms of violence are intricately intertwined, delayed violence underscores the eventfulness of such violence to the victims themselves even when such violence may appear slow or dispersed from afar. Nevertheless, as I discuss in chapter 6, the structure of abandonment that is an integral part of the economy of inheriting makes the catastrophic eventfulness for the victims socially invisible to others and turns these events into what Elizabeth A. Povinelli calls "quasi-events," which are "ordinary, chronic, and cruddy rather than catastrophic, crisis-lade, and sublime" (13). See Rob Nixon, *Slow Violence and the Environmentalism of the Poor* (Cambridge, MA: Harvard University Press, 2011) and Elizabeth A. Povinelli, *Economies of Abandonment: Social Belonging and Endurance in Late Liberalism* (Durham, NC: Duke University Press, 2011).

66. An example of new debts incurred through the transition from empire to nation-state is the approximately fifty-seven million Japanese yen compensation that the Japanese government paid in 1946 to the Japanese corporations that had engaged in wartime use of Chinese forced labor for the "loss" of their laborers at the end of the war. This *inverted compensation*—in which the involved corporations were rewarded against the

background of unpaid wages and compensation to the victims, who were shipped back to civil-war-torn China without a penny—instantiates the compounded debts made visible through the lens of after empire. A similar imperial debt is found in Britain. From 1834 to 1845, the British government paid approximately twenty million pounds to former slave owners as compensation for the loss of their slaves after emancipation. On the Japanese case, see Koga, "Accounting for Silence" and "Between the Law"; on the British case, see Nicholas Draper, *The Price of Emancipation: Slave-Ownership, Compensation and British Society at the End of Slavery* (New York: Cambridge University Press, 2013).

67. According to the data compiled by JETRO (the Japan External Trade Organization), the Chinese share of total Japanese imports became 18.3%, compared to the US share of 17.1%.

68. See, for example, Maki Yōjirō, "Chūgoku ga kushami o suruto . . . : Shudōken o ubawareta nihon keizai" [When China sneezes . . . : Japanese economy without hegemony], *Ekonomisuto* [Economist], extra edition, July 11, 2004, 46–49.

69. In the early 2000s, the expression "*chūgoku kyōi-ron*" (threat of China) was common in the Japanese media when portraying China's emergence as an economic superpower. In the past few years, however, "*chūgoku tokuju-ron*" (special procurement boom with China), an expression that has a historical resonance to the special procurement boom during the Korean War, has captured the optimism in Japan that the Chinese economic boom is beneficial to the Japanese economy.

70. The landscape of after empire in East Asia in this book broadens and complicates the European-centered understanding of imperialism and its aftermath, similar to Fernando Coronil's plea in his essay, "After Empire: Reflections on Imperialism from the Americas," in *Imperial Formations*, ed. Ann Laura Stoler, Carole McGranahan, and Peter C. Perdue, 241–71 (Santa Fe, NM: School for Advanced Research Press, 2007).

CHAPTER TWO

1. The transcript of his speech is found in Haerbinshi jianzhu weiyuanhui, *Sheng Suofeiya jiaotang* [St. Sophia Cathedral] (Harbin, China: Haerbinshi jianshe weiyuanhui, 1997), 38–42, see 40.

2. At a fund-raising meeting on June 13, 1997, Yue Yuquan, the deputy mayor of Harbin and the director of the St. Sophia Cathedral restoration project, emphasized that the project would raise the level of civilization in Harbin: "Building a civilized city is a centuries-long process and is a necessary direction to take if Harbin is to flourish. Building a civilized city requires a combination of material and spiritual civilization, which will influence each other to raise their levels of achievement. The restoration of St. Sophia Cathedral . . . will increase civilizational awareness and public ethics among citizens, and turn this area into a showcase of Harbin's efforts to build a civilized city." See Haerbinshi jianzhu weiyuanhui, *Sheng Suofeiya jiaotang*, 50–51.

3. On railway imperialism and settler colonialism in Harbin and how the Chinese co-opted these two forms of colonial modernity for their pursuit of nationalism before the establishment of Manchukuo, see Herbert P. Bix, "Japanese Imperialism and the Manchurian Economy, 1900–31," *The China Quarterly* 51 (July–September 1972): 425–43; James H.

Carter, *Creating a Chinese Harbin: Nationalism in an International City, 1916–1932* (Ithaca, NY: Cornell University Press, 2002); Blaine R. Chiasson, *Administering the Colonizer: Manchuria's Russians under Chinese Rule, 1918–29* (Vancouver: UBC Press, 2010); Shun-hsin Chou, "Railway Development and Economic Growth in Manchuria," *The China Quarterly* 45 (January–March 1972): 57–84; Søren Clausen and Stig Thøgersen, *The Making of a Chinese City: History and Historiography in Harbin* (Armonk, NY: M. E. Sharpe, 1995); Prasenjit Duara, *Sovereignty and Authenticity: Manchukuo and the East Asian Modern* (Lanham, MD: Rowman and Littlefield, 2003); Peter Duus, Ramon H. Myers, and Mark R. Peattie, eds., *The Japanese Informal Empire in China, 1895–1937* (Princeton, NJ: Princeton University Press, 1989), especially Ramon H. Myers's chapter, "Japanese Imperialism in Manchuria: The South Manchuria Railway Company, 1906–1933," 101–32; Yoshihisa Tak Matsusaka, *The Making of Japanese Manchuria, 1904–1932* (Cambridge, MA: Harvard University Asia Center, 2001); Lori Watt, *When Empire Comes Home: Repatriation and Reintegration in Postwar Japan* (Cambridge, MA: Harvard University Asia Center, 2009); and David Wolff, *To the Harbin Station: The Liberal Alternative in Russian Manchuria, 1898–1914* (Stanford, CA: Stanford University Press, 1999), and "Harbin and Manchuria: Place, Space, and Identity," *South Atlantic Quarterly* 99, no. 1 (2000), special issue.

4. On imperial debris, see Ann Laura Stoler, "Preface" and "Introduction: 'The Rot Remains': From Ruins to Ruination," in *Imperial Debris: On Ruins and Ruination*, ed. Stoler, ix–35 (Durham, NC: Duke University Press, 2013), and "Imperial Debris: Reflections on Ruins and Ruination," *Cultural Anthropology* 23, no. 2 (2008): 191–219.

5. Observing the reform-era China of the 1990s, in which the discourse of *wenming* replaced that of class struggle, Ann Anagnost shows how the *wenming* discourse allows the party-state to become a "pedagogical state" and exert control over the newly emerging market. Anagnost lays out three meanings of *wenming*: modernization (*xiandaihua*), Westernization (*xifanghua*), and civilization (*wenming*). In *wenming*'s original usage as "civilization," *wen* refers to written tradition, culture, or refinement, and *ming* refers to brightness, clarity, or openness, invoking China's glorious past as one of the world's oldest civilizations. In the late nineteenth century, *wenming* came to mean modernization and Westernization. In reform-era China, *wenming* has resurged as an organizing principle, a semiotic fulcrum for leveraging the past, even as it represents "a discourse of lack, referring to the failure of the Chinese people to embody international standards of modernity, civility, and discipline." The discourse of *wenming* gives the party-state legitimacy to become a pedagogical state that prepares the "backward" (*luohou*), "uncultured" (*meiyou wenhua*) peasant population for the global market. As she puts it, newly emerging productive energies in the reform-era "cannot be allowed to signify the economy as a zone of autonomous action but must be harnessed by the party for its self-representation" (95). See chapter 3, "Construction of Civility in the Age of Flexible Accumulation," in Ann Anagnost, *National Past-Times: Narrative, Representation, and Power in Modern China* (Durham, NC: Duke University Press, 1997), 75–97.

6. Wang Yulang, "Du 'Haerbin chengshi jiyuan de qisuan shijian'" [Reading the 'historical origin of Harbin'], *Xinwanbao* [New Evening News], April 3, 1992; Wang Yulang, "Zaidu 'Haerbin chengshi jiyuan de qisuan shijian'" [Rereading the 'historical origin of Harbin'], *Xinwanbao* [New Evening News], April 6, 1992.

7. Wang Dexin, "Haerbin de chengshi qiyuan yu chengshi jiyuan (1)" [The origin of the city and the historical beginning of the city of Harbin (1)], *Xinwanbao* [New Evening News], April 10, 1992.

8. Wang Dexin, "Haerbin de chengshi qiyuan yu chengshi jiyuan (2)" [The origin of the city and the historical beginning of the city of Harbin (2)], *Xinwanbao* [New Evening News], April 13, 1992.

9. Feng Hui, "Zhuanjia wei wo shi bainian qingdian xianji" [Experts offer advice on our city's centenary celebration], *Xinwanbao* [New Evening News], December 14, 1994; Lu Xiangdong, "Hashi zhaokai Haerbin chengshi jiyuan lunzhenghui" [Harbin city organizes Harbin city origin conference], *Shenghuobao* [Life Daily], December 14, 1994; Yu Wenxiu, "Sheng cheng xuezhe yantao Haerbin jianchengri" [Experts discuss Harbin's birthday], *Heilongjiang chenbao* [Heilongjiang Morning News], December 14, 1994.

Thomas Lahusen offers a detailed analysis of a parallel discussion that took place within the internal government publication, *Haerbin shizhi* [Harbin city gazetteer], around the same time as this public discussion. See Thomas Lahusen, "A Place Called Harbin: Reflections on a Centennial," *The China Quarterly* 154 (June 1998): 406–10.

10. Yuan Xiaoguang, "Haerbin, natian shi nide shengri" [Harbin, when is your birthday], *Shenghuobao* [Life Daily], March 17, 1996.

11. The labor force for citywide construction consisted predominantly of workers from Shangdong Province. Many of them remained in the region and, in Harbin, formed the old Chinese district of Fujiadian in Old Harbin (currently the Daowai district), where they covered their neighborhood with what some call "Chinese Baroque" buildings. Many of them resemble European-style edifices they built elsewhere for Russians and Japanese, but a close look reveals that detailed motifs were taken from materials familiar to their daily life. For Chinese Baroque architecture in Harbin, see Nishizawa Yasuhiko, *"Manshū" toshi monogatari: Harubin, Dairen, Shinyō, Chōshun* [The tales of "Manchurian" cities: Harbin, Dalian, Shenyang, Changchun] (Tokyo: Kawaide shobō shinsha, 1996), 38–42. For an overview of the great migration of twenty-five million Chinese from Shangdong and Hubei Provinces to Northeast China from the 1890s to the Second World War, see Thomas R. Gottschang and Diana Lary, *Swallows and Settlers: The Great Migration from North China to Manchuria* (Ann Arbor: University of Michigan Press, 2000).

12. This contrasts sharply with Korea, where the former Japanese colonial headquarters building in Seoul was demolished in the mid-1990s after a long debate. See Hashiya Hiroshi, "Sōru no kenchiku: shokuminchika to kindaika" [Architecture in Seoul: Colonization and modernization], in *Kindai Nihon to higashi Ajia: Kokusai kōryu saikou* [Modern Japan and East Asia: Reconsidering international exchange], ed. Yūzō Katō (Tokyo: Chikuma shobō, 1995), 209–34.

13. For the privatization of the state-run heavy industry in Northeast China, see Antoine Kemen, "Shenyang, Privatisation in the Vanguard of Chinese Socialism," in *Privatizing the State*, ed. Béatrice Hibou, 11–94 (New York: Columbia University Press, 2004). For an ethnography of laid-off workers in Harbin, see Mun Young Cho, *The Specter of the People: Urban Poverty in Northeast China* (Ithaca, NY: Cornell University Press, 2013).

14. For the recent surge of protests in Northeast China, see Ching Kwan Lee, *Against the Law: Labor Protests in China's Rustbelt and Sunbelt* (Berkeley: University of California Press, 2007), and "The 'Revenge of History': Collective Memories and Labor Protests

in Northeastern China," *Ethnography* 1, no. 2 (2000): 217–37. See also Timothy B. Weston, "'Learn from Daqing': More Dark Clouds for Workers in State-Owned Enterprises," *Journal of Contemporary China* 11, no. 33 (2002): 721–34.

15. Gao Ling, Xiao Shuyuan, and Shi Fang, *Lishi huimou: Dongfang zhenzhu Haerbin* [Glancing back at history: Harbin, the pearl of the East], 3 vols., vol. 2 (Harbin, China: Haerbin chubanshe, 1998).

16. Upon the commencement of the restoration of St. Sophia Cathedral in downtown Harbin, a local newspaper front-page article sensationally reported how this beauty has long been "invisible" from the streets. Zheng Min, Wen Ting, and Liu Jingsong, "Ta fang sheng Suofeiya dajiaotang" [Investigation of St. Sophia cathedral], *Shenghuobao* [Life Daily], January 5, 1997.

17. For the construction of "Chinese" history at the expense of silencing non-Han ethnic groups, see Clausen and Thøgersen, *The Making of a Chinese City*, 215–16.

18. Ackbar Abbas, *Hong Kong: Culture and the Politics of Disappearance* (Minneapolis: University of Minnesota Press, 1997), 65–69.

19. The case in Harbin is not unique in drawing out dynamics that defy the transformation of "site" into "sight" through historical preservation, as suggested by Ackbar Abbas. John Collins, for example, shows how the UNESCO World Heritage Program in Brazil exposes racialized sedimentation of history rather than naturalizing and taming historical contestation. See John Collins, "Ruins, Redemption, and Brazil's Imperial Exception," in *Imperial Debris: On Ruins and Ruination*, ed. Ann Laura Stoler, 162–93 (Durham, NC: Duke University Press, 2013).

20. The government publication on the restoration of St. Sophia Cathedral explains that the cathedral became a target of destruction during the Cultural Revolution because it embodied "culture." See Haerbinshi jianzhu weiyuanhui, *Sheng Suofeiya jiaotang*, 135.

21. Zheng, Wen, and Liu, "Ta fang sheng suofeiya dajiaotang."

22. Li Debin, *Lishi huimou: Ershi shiji de Haerbin* [Glancing back at history: Twentieth-century Harbin], 3 vols., vol. 3 (Harbin, China: Haerbin chubanshe, 1998), 263.

23. Liu Jingsong and Zheng Min, "'Suofeiya' bu hui wangji: Harbin Suofeiya jiaotang guangchang zonghe zhengzhi zhuiji" [Unforgettable 'Sophia': A follow-up report on the comprehensive restoration of Harbin St. Sophia cathedral square], *Shenghuobao* [Life Daily], September 7, 1997, 1 and 15.

24. Haerbinshi jianzhu weiyuanhui, *Sheng Suofeiya Jiaotang*, 98.

25. Li, *Lishi huimou*, 262.

26. Nishizawa, *"Manshū" toshi monogatari*, 32.

27. It reads, "Glancing back at history, Harbin was originally the headquarters for the Imperial Russian invasion of China and later housed an exile community of White Russians. From the Qing Dynasty to the Republic of China, and from the puppet government controlled by the Japanese colonists to the periods before Liberation, Harbin experienced decades of social upheaval. During these years, invasion and resistance persisted, and oppression and struggle never ceased."

28. From the introduction to Section Three, "Quotidian Vignettes: The Early Twentieth Century."

29. Due to the current political climate, Zhao Yihong and Liu Jun are pseudonyms. For this reason as well, bibliographical citations for their publications are omitted.

30. On *guanxi*, see Mayfair Yang, *Gifts, Favors and Banquets: The Art of Social Relationships in China* (Ithaca, NY: Cornell University Press, 1994).

31. In a society in which losing face is more than just an embarrassment, the cancellation was not an easy decision to make. Other cities in Northeast China, which share similar historical trajectories to Harbin, carefully watched the unfolding of the political drama. After a close examination of the case in Harbin, the city of Dalian decided to forego its plan to celebrate its centenary in 1999, as we shall see in chapter 4.

32. Haerbinshi jianzhu weiyuanhui, *Sheng Suofeiya jiaotang*, 41.

33. Haerbinshi jianzhu weiyuanhui, *Sheng Suofeiya jiaotang*, 41.

34. The mayor justified the city's decision to preserve a material witness to imperialism: "This way, we have attained cultural dignity and a break point for patriotic education and economic development. Some claimed that the cathedral was a material witness to imperialist invasion, and I also feel that it is a reasonable argument. But what is more important is to sum up history [*zongjie lishi*], develop oneself, and bring Harbin a new spiritual power." See Haerbinshi jianzhu weiyuanhui, *Sheng Suofeiya jiaotang*, 40.

35. In contrast to what Mayfair Mei-Hui Yang observes in rural Southeast China, where religion has become a key site for the state's suppressive spatial politics, diverse religious practices are an integral part of the daily rhythms of life in Harbin. Not all religious structures were destroyed during the Cultural Revolution, and those remaining edifices now house ardent worshippers. For instance, along Dongdazhijie Street, which stretches east from Red Flag Square (where St. Nicholas Church used to be), lies a Catholic church, a Protestant church, and a Ukrainian Russian Orthodox church, all next to one another. On weekends, the Protestant church becomes packed with worshippers, while a small number of Russian and Chinese with Russian ancestries gather quietly in the Orthodox church. If you walk farther down the street, you will find a Buddhist temple next to a Confucian temple. In the center of the Daowai district (former Fujiadian in Old Harbin) stands a beautiful mosque, which offers a serene communal living space for the Muslim population in the city. A few blocks down stands a Protestant church, which is always lively with more than one hundred ethnic Korean Chinese packed in the small space, cheerfully singing carols. This building was originally a synagogue in the early part of the twentieth century, and although they put a wooden cross in front of the building, the remaining Star of David motif speaks of its former life. See Mayfair Mei-Hui Yang, "Spatial Struggles: Postcolonial Complex, State Disenchantment, and Popular Reappropriation of Space in Rural Southeast China," *Journal of Asian Studies* 63, no. 3 (August 2004): 719–55.

36. The general distrust of the government exacerbated the sense of panic and the circulation of rumors when Harbin suffered the stoppage of its water supply in November 2005 as a result of a chemical-factory explosion along the Songhua River, which became heavily polluted with toxic benzene.

37. On the newly-emerging class distinction and how ordinary people—from the new middle class to laid-off urban workers to migrants from the rural areas—make sense of the new social reality in Harbin, see Carolyn L. Hsu, *Creating Market Socialism: How Ordinary People Are Shaping Class and Status in China* (Durham, NC: Duke University Press, 2007); and Cho, *The Specter of the People*.

38. As Susan Stewart puts it, "Nostalgia, like any form of narrative, is always ideological: the past it seeks has never existed except as narrative, and hence, always absent, that past continually threatens to reproduce itself as a felt lack. . . . nostalgia wears a distinctly utopian face, a face that turns toward a future-past, a past which has only ideological reality." See Susan Stewart, *On Longing: Narratives of the Miniature, the Gigantic, the Souvenir, the Collection* (Durham, NC: Duke University Press, 1993), 23.

39. Old Harbin nostalgia is not alone within China to express such losses in the present. Old Shanghai nostalgia in recent years has produced an equally if not more vibrant nostalgia cultural industry. See, for example, Jie Li, *Shanghai Homes: Palimpsests of Private Life* (New York: Columbia University Press, 2014), and Mark Swislocki, *Culinary Nostalgia: Regional Food Culture and the Urban Experience in Shanghai* (Stanford, CA: Stanford University Press, 2009). Colonial nostalgia within former colonized societies as a reflection of longing and loss in the present is not limited to China. See, for example, William Cunningham Bissell's exploration of colonial nostalgia in Zanzibar city, which he contrasts with imperial nostalgia in the former metropole, in "Engaging Colonial Nostalgia," *Cultural Anthropology* 20, no. 2 (May 2005): 215–48. On imperial nostalgia, see Renato Rosaldo, "Imperialist Nostalgia," *Representations* 26 (Spring 1989): 107–22.

40. A notable exception is the collection of photographs taken by photojournalist Li Zhensheng for *Heilongjiang Daily*, which was published as *Red-Color News Soldier*, with an introduction by Jonathan Spence (London: Phaidon Press, 2003). But this publication remains unavailable in China.

41. Takahashi Tetsuya, *Sengo sekinin ron* [On postwar responsibility] (Tokyo: Kōdansha, 1999), 64–74. Here, Takahashi is alluding to Derrida's work on mourning. See Jacques Derrida, *Specters of Marx: The State of the Debt, the Work of Mourning, and the New International*, trans. Gayatri Chakravorty Spivak, corrected ed. (New York: Routledge, 1994).

42. David J. Davies, "Old Zhiqing Photos: Nostalgia and the 'Spirit' of the Cultural Revolution," *The China Review* 5, no. 2 (Fall 2005): 97–123; Jennifer Hubbert, "Revolution *Is* a Dinner Party: Cultural Revolution Restaurants in Contemporary China," *The China Review* 5, no. 2 (Fall 2005): 123–48; Guobin Yang, "China's *Zhiqing* Generation: Nostalgia, Identity, and Cultural Resistance in the 1990s," *Modern China* 29, no. 3 (July 2003): 267–96; Guobin Yang, "Days of Old Are Not Puffs of Smoke: Three Hypotheses on Collective Memories of the Cultural Revolution," *The China Review* 5, no. 2 (Fall 2005): 13–41; and Ming-Bao Yue, "Nostalgia for the Future: Cultural Revolution Memory in Two Transnational Chinese Narratives," *The China Review* 5, no. 2 (Fall 2005): 43–63.

43. Guobin Yang, for instance, demonstrates how the recent proliferation of Cultural Revolution nostalgia among ordinary people and former Red Guards, especially in cyberspace, is a form of protest of the recent drastic socioeconomic change that has made this generation feel as if it has been left behind. See Yang, "China's *Zhiqing* Generation" and "Days of Old Are Not Puffs of Smoke."

44. Xue Yanwen and Zhang Xueshan, eds., *Zhiqing lao zhaopian* [Old zhiqing photos] (Tianjin, China: Baihua wenyi chubanshe, 1998).

45. Davies, "Old Zhiqing Photos."

46. Davies, "Old Zhiqing Photos," 106.

47. Davies, "Old Zhiqing Photos," 106–8.

48. Marilyn Ivy, *Discourses of the Vanishing: Modernity, Phantasm, Japan* (Chicago: University of Chicago Press, 1995), 95, emphasis in original.

49. The destruction of St. Nicholas during the Cultural Revolution was followed by the construction of a "Working-Class Cultural Revolution" memorial, which gained the nickname "ice candy tower," as it was in the shape of Harbin's famous ice candy. This political memorial, on which Lin Biao inscribed "Always keep in mind," was hurriedly destroyed overnight and replaced by a small hill covered with trees and flowers upon Zhou Enlai's visit to Harbin in 1972. This small hill, which Harbinites nicknamed "big grave," was later covered with metal sheets as part of the roof for the three-story underground shopping mall. See Ji Fenghui, "Chengshi guangchang" [City square], *Heilongjiang chenbao* [Heilongjiang Morning News], May 8, 2002.

50. Harbin is not exceptional in "erasing" the Mao era from its official discourse. For example, the *New York Times* reported on the absence of Mao in the new history textbook that was experimentally introduced in Fall 2007 in Shanghai. The article describes a drastic change in the portrayal of history: "Socialism has been reduced to a single, short chapter in the senior high school history course. Chinese Communism before the economic reform that began in 1979 is covered in a sentence. The text mentions Mao only once—in a chapter on etiquette." See Joseph Kahn, "Where's Mao? Chinese Revise History Books," *New York Times*, September 1, 2006, A1.

51. Observing the demise of socialism in Europe, Jacques Derrida wrote, "The most familiar becomes the most disquieting. The economic or egological home or the *oikos*, the nearby, the familiar, the domestic, or even the national (*heimlich*) frightens itself. It feels itself occupied, in the proper secret (*Geheimnis*) of its inside, by what is most strange, distant, threatening." See Derrida, *Specters of Marx*, 144–45. Derrida alludes to Freud's essay "The 'Uncanny,'" in *The Standard Edition of the Complete Psychological Works of Sigmund Freud*, vol. 17, ed. James Strachey, 217–56 (London: Hogarth Press, 1955), 241.

52. Jacques Derrida's search for the specters of Marx at the demise of socialism in Europe hints at a possible direction for thinking about colonial inheritance in Northeast China. My thinking about colonial inheritance is inspired by Derrida's understanding of inheritance. See Derrida, *Specters of Marx*, especially chapters 1 to 3.

53. Duan Guangda and Ji Fenghui, *Lishi huimou: Dongfang zhenzhu Haerbin* [Glancing back at history: Harbin, the pearl of the East], 3 vols., vol. 1 (Harbin, China: Haerbin chubanshe, 1998); Gao, Xiao, and Shi, *Lishi huimou*; Li, *Lishi huimou*; and, Zhang Fushan, *Lishi huimou: Haerbin shihua* [Glancing back at history: A narrative history of Harbin] (Harbin, China: Haerbin chubanshe, 1998).

54. Clausen and Thøgersen, *The Making of a Chinese City*, xii–xiii, emphasis original.

55. These volumes portray Harbin in the 1920s as a very cosmopolitan city and claim that in recent years it has regained its past glories, drawing a link between the pre-1949 past and the present. We can see the institutional constraints in choosing the "right" discourse here, since some of the authors of these volumes are among the intellectuals who are behind the nostalgia industry. The 1920s was an ambiguous period in terms of political control of Harbin. Despite the official reversion of sovereignty to the Chinese as a result of the Russian Revolution that led to fragmentation of the Russian society, so-

called warlords staked various claims while collaborating with foreign forces. As James H. Carter observes, "'Chinese' rule in Harbin was a changeable patchwork of regional authorities rather than a centralized state bureaucracy." See Carter, *Creating a Chinese Harbin*, 79. Chinese workers remained exploited by foreigners, as Chong-Sik Lee describes: "The Chinese workers were severely discriminated against by both the Japanese- and Russian-operated industries, the pay of a Chinese worker being not one-tenth that of a Japanese." See Chong-Sik Lee, *Revolutionary Struggle in Manchuria: Chinese Communism and Soviet Interest, 1922–1945* (Berkeley: University of California Press, 1983), 71. In one of the major protests that took place in 1928, students, workers, and merchant groups marched through the streets of Harbin carrying "banners and placards that read 'Down with Japanese Imperialism!' and 'Down with Warlords!'" (Carter, *Creating a Chinese Harbin*, 172).

56. The ensuing production of nostalgia took the form of historical publications, glossy multilingual books, photo exhibits, and newspaper series devoting columns to Old Harbin, all of which sought to portray Old Harbin as a uniquely cosmopolitan and culturally rich city in an era of turmoil and strong exclusionist sentiments. Part of the photography exhibition was turned into a book in three languages (Chinese, English, and Japanese), nostalgically illustrating the glorious days of the city on glossy pages. See Li Shuxiao, ed., *Haerbin jiuying* [Old photos of Harbin] (Beijing, China: Renmin meishu chubanshe, 2000). The Heilongjiang Province Academy of Social Science held an extensive photography exhibit titled "Jews in Harbin," a bilingual (Chinese and English) book version of which followed. See Qu Wei and Li Shuxiao, eds., *Youtairen zai Haerbin* [The Jews in Harbin] (Beijing, China: Shehui kexue wenxian chubanshe, 2003). Details of daily life in Harbin are vividly described in Ji Fenghui, *Huashuo Haerbin* [Talk about Harbin] (Harbin, China: Heilongjiang renmin chubanshe, 2002). See also Ji Fenghui, *Haerbin xungen* [The roots of Harbin] (Harbin, China: Haerbin chubanshe, 1996), and Zeng Yizhi, *Cheng yu ren: Haerbin gushi* [The city and the people: Stories of Harbin] (Harbin, China: Heilongjiang renmin chubanshe, 2003).

57. Recent works by Western scholars interrogate the assumption of "colonial" Harbin. David Wolff poses this question by exploring the form of colonialism that Tsarist Russia adopted in shaping its colonial desire in the Far East. Despite the appearance of Russian colonial Harbin to casual observers at that time, what Wolff describes as a "liberal" colonial policy created a multiethnic society where integration rather than exclusion became the name of the game. James H. Carter, through his analysis of Chinese materials, shows how Harbin after the Russian Revolution in 1917 became the playground for bubbling Chinese nationalism of all sorts, all aimed at creating a Chinese Harbin through modernization efforts in cooperation with foreigners in the city. The eventual clash and fragmentation among Chinese nationalists even resulted in some factions collaborating with the Japanese in promoting a new form of nationalism around Manchukuo. See Wolff, *To the Harbin Station*; and Carter, *Creating a Chinese Harbin*. See also Chiasson, *Administering the Colonizer*. For an overview of the recent scholarship on the history of Harbin, see Mark Gamsa, "Harbin in Comparative Perspective," *Urban History* 37, no. 1 (2010): 136–49.

58. Song Hongyan, *Dongfang xiao Bali* [Paris of the east] (Harbin, China: Heilongjiang kexue jishu chubanshe, 2001), 3.

59. The case of Harbin thus shows how the postsocialist moment and analysis, in their critique of the socialist past, have unexpectedly brought out postcolonialism. Therefore, instead of thinking *between* the posts (as Sharad Chari and Katherine Verdery suggest), today's Harbin, which stands at the crossroads of postsocialist and postcolonial, presents layers of posts that have come to converge. It is the dynamics of this layering and convergence that demonstrate the power of thinking "between the posts." See Sharad Chari and Katherine Verdery, "Thinking between the Posts: Postcolonialism, Postsocialism, and Ethnography after the Cold War," *Comparative Studies in Society and History* 51, no. 1 (2009): 6–34.

60. Svetlana Boym, *The Future of Nostalgia* (New York: Basic Books, 2001), 130.

CHAPTER THREE

1. On Manchuria tourism in the 1930s and 1940s, see Kō En, "'Rakudo' o hashiru kankō basu: 1930 nendai no 'Manshū' toshi to teikoku no doramaturugī" [A tour bus in 'paradise': 'Manchurian' cities in the 1930s and the dramaturgy of the empire], in *Iwanami kōza kindai nihon no bunka shi 6: Kakudai suru modanitī*, ed. Yoshimi Shunya, et al. (Tokyo: Iwanami shoten, 2002), 215–53; and Kenneth J. Ruoff, *Imperial Japan at Its Zenith: The Wartime Celebration of the Empire's 2,600th Anniversary* (Ithaca, NY: Cornell University Press, 2010).

2. On former Manchuria tourism, see Kō En, "Kioku sangyō to shite no tsūrizumu" [Tourism as memory industry], *Gendai shisō* 29, no. 4 (2001): 219–29; and Sakabe Shōko, *"Manshū" keiken no shakaigaku: Shokuminchi no kioku no katachi* [Sociology of "Manchuria" experiences: Forms of memory of the colony] (Tokyo: Sekai shisōsha, 2008), and "'Manshū' keiken no rekishi shakaigaku teki kōsatsu: 'Manshū' dōsōkai no jirei o tōshite" [A sociohistorical analysis of "Manchuria" experience: The case of "Manchuria" reunion associations], *Kyoto shakaigaku nenpō* 7 (1999): 101–20. See also Mariko Asano Tamanoi, *Memory Maps: The State and Manchuria in Postwar Japan* (Honolulu: University of Hawai'i Press, 2009).

3. Disagreement exists on the name of the style of these ministerial buildings in Changchun. In popular literature such as travel guidebooks, they are described as emperor's-crown-style architecture. Against this, Koshizawa Akira regards the ministerial architecture in Changchun as a developmental form of the emperor's-crown-style architecture in Japan. Due to its style that expresses the ideology of "coprosperity of ethnic groups" (with roofs with a slight Chinese touch), he calls the style of these ministerial buildings "*kōa* style" (literally, building Asia style) and distinguishes it from the emperor's-crown-style architecture in Japan. I use the term *emperor's crown style* to describe the architectural style of the ministerial buildings, partly because this naming itself is what captures the imagination of Japanese tourists to Changchun, and partly because it illuminates the continuity and developmental form of ideas that this architectural style embodies. See chapter 7 of Koshizawa Akira, *Manshūkoku no shuto keikaku: Tokyo no genzai to mirai o tou* [The urban planning of the Manchurian capital: Questioning the present and the future of Tokyo] (Tokyo: Nihon keizai hyōronsha, 1988).

4. In his evocative exploration of twentieth-century architectural history in Japan through close examination of four generations of prominent Japanese architects, Iijima

Yōichi persuasively demonstrates how the seemingly amnesic postwar architectural landscape is full of corporeal metaphors of the Showa Emperor. Arguing against the assumed radical discontinuity between the prewar and postwar Japan, Iijima points to the persistent presence of the imperial tendency in Japan despite the visible absence in the Tokyo cityscape. See Iijima Yōichi, *Ō no shintai toshi: Shōwa tennō no jidai to kenchiku* [The city as the Emperor's body: The era of the Showa Emperor and its architecture] (Tokyo: Seidosha, 1996).

5. Marianne Hirsch, *The Generation of Postmemory: Writing and Visual Culture after the Holocaust* (New York: Columbia University Press, 2012), 5. See also Marianne Hirsch, "The Generation of Postmemory," *Poetics Today* 29, no. 1 (2008): 103–28, 106, and "Surviving Images: Holocaust Photographs and the Work of Postmemory," *The Yale Journal of Criticism* 14, no. 1 (2001): 5–37.

Art Spiegelman's two-volume graphic novel, *Maus*, which is based on his father's account of his experience in Auschwitz, is one such example of postmemorial work that Hirsch discusses in her book. See Art Spiegelman, *Maus I: A Survivor's Tale: My Father Bleeds History* (New York: Pantheon, 1986).

6. Eva Hoffman, *After Such Knowledge: Memory, History and the Legacy of the Holocaust* (New York: Public Affairs, 2004).

7. Gu Wanchun and Li Rongxian, *Changchun chengshi bianqian* [The transformation of Changchun urban space] (Changchun, China: Changchun chubanshe, 1998), 146–56.

8. For the urban planning of Shinkyō, see Koshizawa, *Manshūkoku no shuto keikaku*. For an overview of the historical development of Changchun in English, see David D. Buck, "Railway City and National Capital: Two Faces of the Modern in Changchun," in *Remaking the Chinese City: Modernity and National Identity, 1900–1950*, ed. Joseph W. Esherick, 65–89 (Honolulu: University of Hawai'i Press, 2000); and Qinghua Guo, "Changchun: Unfinished Capital Planning of Manzhouguo, 1932–42," *Urban History* 31, no. 1 (May 2004): 100–117.

9. Although the Japanese did not destroy the physical landscape of the city at the end of the war, they destroyed the archival traces of their puppet state. When the Japanese officials and the Army evacuated Changchun before the impending Soviet advance at the end of the war, they destroyed a large number of official documents by burning them in the swimming pool on the palace grounds.

10. Huo Liaoyuan and Cui Guoxi, *Cong lunxian dao jiefang: 1931 nian dao 1948 nian de Changchun* [From surrender to liberation: Changchun from 1931 to 1948], Changchun wenshi ziliao vol. 47 (Changchun, China: "Changchun wenshi ziliao" bianjibu, 1995); Tang Jige et al., *Changchun erbai nian* [Two-hundred-year history of Changchun] (Changchun, China: Changchunshi Zhengxie, 2000).

11. For a detailed account of this period, see Huo and Cui, *Cong lunxian dao jiefang*. In English, see Andres Jacobs, "China Is Wordless on Traumas of Communists' Rise," *New York Times*, October 2, 2009, A4.

12. Tang, et al., *Changchun erbai nian*, 181.

13. Gu Wanchun and Li Rongxian, *Changchun chengshi bianqian* [The transformation of Changchun urban space] (Changchun, China: Changchun chubanshe, 1998), 161; Xinhua meiri dianxunshe, *Jizhu Changchun* [Remembering Changchun] (Beijing: Xinhua chubanshe, 2000), 132.

14. Gu and Li, *Changchun chengshi bianqian*, 156–59, 161–62.

15. On the Chinese Communist Party's use of war memory through the concept of national humiliation, see Zheng Wang, *Never Forget National Humiliation: Historical Memory in Chinese Politics and Foreign Relations* (New York: Columbia University Press, 2012).

16. For an overview of the remaining colonial architecture in Northeast China, see Fujimori Terunobu and Wan Tan, eds., *Zenchōsa higashi Ajia kindai no toshi to kenchiku, 1840–1945* [A comprehensive study of East Asian architecture and urban planning, 1840–1945] (Tokyo: Chikuma Shobō, 1996). On the architecture and urban planning of Shinkyō, see Koshizawa, *Manshūkoku no shuto keikaku*. On the major architectural remainders of Manchukuo in Changchun, see Shen Yan, *Changchun weiman yizhi daguan* [An overview of the architectural remainders of fake Manchukuo in Changchun] (Changchun, China: Jilin sheying chubanshe, 2002).

17. Quoted in Koshizawa, *Manshūkoku no shuto keikaku*, 188.

18. The architectural culture in Changchun evoked lively discussions on architectural styles and expressions of political ideology among architectural critics in Japan in the 1930s and 1940s. See, for example, Kishida Hideto, "Manshū kenkoku jisshūnen to sono kenchiku" [The tenth anniversary of Manchukuo and its architecture], *Manshū kenchiku zasshi* 22, no. 11 (1942); and Satō Takeo, "Shina tairiku ni okeru gaikoku kenchiku to sono seiji hyōgen" [Foreign architecture in China and its political expression], *Kenchiku zasshi* 691 (1942).

19. As I discussed in chapter 1, these postwar narratives led to what I call the *inversion of victimhood*, in which the perpetrator Japan became the victim. On the construction of these postwar narratives, see, for example, Yoshikuni Igarashi, *Bodies of Memory: Narratives of War in Postwar Japanese Culture, 1945–1970* (Princeton, NJ: Princeton University Press, 2000); Lisa Yoneyama, *Hiroshima Traces: Time, Space, and the Dialectics of Memory* (Berkeley: University of California Press, 1999); and James Joseph Orr, *The Victim as Hero: Ideologies of Peace and National Identity in Postwar Japan* (Honolulu: University of Hawai'i Press, 2001).

20. This is what Yoshikuni Igarashi describes as the process of naturalizing forgetting. See Igarashi, *Bodies of Memory*.

21. This acknowledged absence of consciousness can be seen as part of imperial debris, which often disguises itself. In this case, obsession expresses itself in amnesia.

22. During the Japanese economic boom in the 1980s, foreign observers coined the term "Japan, Inc.," to describe the entwined relations between the Japanese government and business. The economic bubble burst in the early 1990s dismantled this interlocking system behind the Japanese postwar economic reconstruction, recovery, and emergence as a world economic power. See, for example, Peter F. Drucker, "The End of Japan, Inc.? An Economic Monolith Fractures," *Foreign Affairs* 72, no. 2 (Spring 1993): 10–15. On the societal responses to the demise of Japan, Inc., see Anne Allison, *Precarious Japan* (Durham, NC: Duke University Press, 2013).

23. Harry Harootunian, "Japan's Long Postwar: The Trick of Memory and the Ruse of History," *The South Atlantic Quarterly* 99, no. 4 (Fall 2000): 715–40; and Marilyn Ivy, "Revenge and Recapitation in Recessionary Japan," *The South Atlantic Quarterly* 99, no. 4 (Fall 2000): 819–40. See also Tomiko Yoda and Harry Harootunian, eds., *Japan after*

Japan: Social and Cultural Life from the Recessionary 1990s to the Present (Durham, NC: Duke University Press, 2006).

24. For an overview of the shifting location of war memory within postwar Japan, see, for example, Yoshida Yutaka, *Nihonjin no sensō-kan: Sengo shi no naka no henyō* [Japanese perspectives on the war: Their transformation within the postwar history] (Tokyo: Iwanami Shoten, 1995); Ishida Takeshi, *Kioku to bōkyaku no seijigaku: Dōka seisaku, sensō sekinin, shūgōteki kioku* [Political science of memory and forgetting: Assimilation policy, war responsibility, collective memory] (Tokyo: Akashi Shoten, 2000); Franziska Seraphim, *War Memory and Social Politics in Japan, 1945–2005* (Cambridge, MA: Harvard University Asia Center, 2006).

25. The historians' debate in the 1990s is yet another debate concerning modern subjectivity, which dates back not only to the immediate postwar era but further back to the prewar era. See Harry Harootunian, *Overcome by Modernity: History, Culture, and Community in Interwar Japan* (Princeton, NJ: Princeton University Press. 2000); and J. Victor Koschmann, *Revolution and Subjectivity in Postwar Japan* (Chicago: University of Chicago Press, 1996). On postwar Japanese social movements surrounding war memories, see Seraphim, *War Memory and Social Politics in Japan*.

26. Katō Norihiro, "Haisengo ron" [On postwar defeat], *Gunzō* 50, no. 1 (January 1995): 252–94; Takahashi Tetsuya, "Ojoku no kioku o megutte" [On the memories of disgrace], *Gunzō* 50, no. 3 (March 1995): 176–82. Katō and Takahashi developed their arguments in respective book forms: *Haisengo ron* [On postdefeat] (Tokyo: Kōdansha, 1997) and *Sengo sekinin ron* [On postwar responsibility] (Tokyo: Kōdansha, 1999).

27. For a concise overview of the debate in English, see Tessa Morris-Suzuki, "Unquiet Graves: Katō Norihiro and the Politics of Mourning," *Japanese Studies* 18, no. 1 (1998): 21–30.

28. Takahashi, *Sengo sekinin ron*, 163.

29. Takahashi, *Sengo sekinin ron*, 255.

30. Karatani Kōjin, et al., "Kyōdō tōgi: Sekinin to shutai o megutte" [Discussion: On responsibilities and the subject], *Hihyō kūkan* 2, no. 13 (April 1997): 6–40.

31. Nishikawa Nagao, "1995 nen 8 gatsu no gen'ei, aruiwa 'kokumin' to iu kaibutsu ni tsuite" [On the illusion of August 1995, or the monster called the "nation"], *Shisō* 856 (October 1995): 1–3, 3.

32. Yumiko Iida, "Between the Technique of Living an Endless Routine and the Madness of Absolute Degree Zero: Japanese Identity and the Crisis of Modernity in the 1990s," *positions: east asia cultures critique* 8, no. 2 (2000): 458.

33. Eric L. Santner, *Stranded Objects: Mourning, Memory, and Film in Postwar Germany* (Ithaca, NY: Cornell University Press, 1990). See also A. Dirk Moses, *German Intellectuals and the Nazi Past* (New York: Cambridge University Press, 2007), and "Stigma and Sacrifice in Postwar Germany," *History and Memory* 19, no. 2 (2007): 139–80, for an overview of the German intellectual debate on the stigmatized Germany identity.

34. On patriotic education in China, see Yinan He, "Remembering and Forgetting the War: Elite Mythmaking, Mass Reaction, and Sino-Japanese Relations, 1950–2006," *History and Memory* 19, no. 2 (2007): 43–74, and *The Search for Reconciliation: Sino-Japanese and German-Polish Relations since World War II* (New York: Cambridge University Press, 2009).

35. For a detailed historical study of Japanese repatriation from its empire, see Lori Watt, *When Empire Comes Home: Repatriation and Reintegration in Postwar Japan* (Cambridge, MA: Harvard University Asia Center, 2009). For the postwar recollection of their experiences, see Tamanoi, *Memory Maps*, chapter 3, and "Between Colonial Racism and Global Capitalism: Japanese Repatriates from Northeast China since 1946," *American Ethnologist* 30, no. 4 (2003): 527–39.

36. The Japanese image of the capital of Manchukuo was that of "paradise," as it was often described in the Manchuria travel industry in the 1930s. See Kō, " 'Rakudo' o hashiru kankō basu."

37. *Hikiageshas'* nostalgia is thus quite different from what Renato Rosaldo critiques as "imperialist nostalgia." See Renato Rosaldo, "Imperialist Nostalgia," *Representations* 26 (Spring 1989): 107–22.

38. Takeuchi Yoshimi, "Manshūkoku kenkyū no igi" [The meaning of studying Manchukuo], in *Takeuchi Yoshimi zenshū* [The complete works of Takeuchi Yoshimi], vol. 4 (Tokyo: Chikuma Shobō, 1980), 416.

39. The sentiments shared by many *hikiagesha* in their inability to mourn are social, different from what Alexander and Margarete Mitscherlich observed in their study of postwar Germany, where they sought psychological reasons for the inability to mourn the loss of Hitler among West Germans. The Mitscherlichs argue that "without a working-through of guilt, however belated, there could be no work of mourning" (50). They observed that the invisibility of other victims prevented Germans from mourning (25). In contrast, *hikiageshas'* inability to mourn their loss is precisely due to the visibility of Other victims, in their case, the Chinese. See Alexander and Margarete Mitscherlich, *The Inability to Mourn: Principles of Collective Behavior* (New York: Grove Press, 1975).

40. This is a phrase that my grandmother used to tell me and I encountered repeatedly among other Japanese repatriates from Manchuria.

41. The name of the association for repatriates from Changchun is not *Shinkyō* Association, as Changchun was called in Japanese during the Manchukuo period, but *Chōshun* Association, which is the Japanese pronunciation of the Chinese character for Changchun. On Manchuria-related Japanese associations, see Sakabe, *"Manshū" keiken no shakaigaku* and " 'Manshū' keiken no rekishi shakaigaku teki kōsatsu."

42. Louise Young, *Japan's Total Empire: Manchuria and the Culture of Wartime Imperialism* (Berkeley: University of California Press, 1998).

43. On the making of Japan's Manchuria in English, see, for example, Barbara J. Brooks, *Japan's Imperial Diplomacy: Consuls, Treaty Ports, and War in China, 1895–1938* (Honolulu: University of Hawai'i Press, 2000); Prasenjit Duara, *Sovereignty and Authenticity: Manchukuo and the East Asian Modern* (Lanham, MD: Rowman and Littlefield, 2003); Mark Driscoll, *Absolute Erotic, Absolute Grotesque: The Living, Dead, and Undead in Japan's Imperialism, 1895–1945* (Durham, NC: Duke University Press, 2010); Yoshihisa Tak Matsusaka, *The Making of Japanese Manchuria, 1904–1932* (Cambridge, MA: Harvard University Asia Center, 2001); Janis Mimura, *Planning for Empire: Reform Bureaucrats and the Japanese Wartime State* (Ithaca, NY: Cornell University Press, 2011); Rana Mitter, *The Manchurian Myth: Nationalism, Resistance, and Collaboration in Modern China* (Berkeley: University of California Press, 2000); Emer O'Dwyer, *Significant Soil: Settler Colonialism and Japan's Urban Empire in Manchuria* (Cambridge, MA: Harvard

University Asia Center, 2015); Mariko Asano Tamanoi, ed., *Crossed Histories: Manchuria in the Age of Empire* (Honolulu: University of Hawai'i Press, 2005); Daqing Yang, *Technology of Empire: Telecommunications and Japanese Expansion, 1883–1945* (Cambridge, MA: Harvard University Press, 2011); and Young, *Japan's Total Empire*.

44. Young, *Japan's Total Empire*, 247. Through his study of the urban planning and architecture of "Shinkyō" (Changchun), the former capital of Manchukuo, Koshizawa Akira shows in detail how the city was built as an ideal modern city. He demonstrates how the urban planning of Shinkyō was beyond the standard of Japanese cities at that time, and it took more than twenty years for Japan to achieve the same level of infrastructure in terms of running water, the sewer system, gas and electricity, telephone lines, and transportation. See Koshizawa, *Manshūkoku no shuto keikaku*.

45. Young, *Japan's Total Empire*, 12–13. Her observation echoes Ann Stoler's study, which shows how the colonies became "laboratories of modernity" in which the discourse of race was developed and experimented on in an attempt to stabilize European bourgeois identity alongside the emergence of the nation-state system. In so doing, Stoler persuasively illustrates how what is usually considered to be at the margins of modernity actually constitutes the core of modern projects. See Ann Stoler, *Race and the Education of Desire: Foucault's History of Sexuality and the Colonial Order of Things* (Durham, NC: Duke University Press, 1995).

46. Igarashi, *Bodies of Memory*.

47. Igarashi, *Bodies of Memory*, chapter 1.

48. Carol Gluck, "The 'End' of the Postwar: Japan at the Turn of the Millennium," *Public Culture* 10, no. 1 (1997): 1–23, 5. It should be noted that the inversion of victimhood after empire is not limited to Japan. As Caroline Elkins shows, after the British Imperial Army violently subdued the Mau Mau uprising in Kenya, which resulted in its independence, it was the British who recognized themselves as the victims while the newly independent Kenyan society suppressed its victimhood. See Caroline Elkins, *Imperial Reckoning: The Untold Story of Britain's Gulag in Kenya* (New York: Henry Holt, 2005).

49. Gluck, "The 'End' of the Postwar," 4. On Japan's "long postwar," see also Carol Gluck, "The Past in the Present," in *Postwar Japan as History*, ed. Andrew Gordon, 64–95 (Berkeley: University of California Press, 1993); and Harootunian, "Japan's Long Postwar."

50. As Carol Gluck puts it, "After the war, *sengo* had displaced Shōwa in historical consciousness." See Gluck, "The Past in the Present," 92.

51. Keizai Kikaku-chō [Economic Planning Agency], *Keizai hakusho* [Economic white paper], July 19, 1956.

52. Gluck, "The Past in the Present," 93.

53. One of the most telling examples of how the public memory of Japanese imperialism is displaced by that of war and Japanese suffering is found in the recently opened Shōwa Museum in central Tokyo. For an analysis of this museum, see Kerry Smith, "The Shōwa Hall: Memorializing Japan's War at Home," *The Public Historian* 24, no. 4 (2002): 35–64.

54. Fujiwara Tei, *Nagareru hoshi wa ikite iru* [Shooting stars are alive] (Tokyo: Hibiya shuppan, 1949).

55. The zero hour of 1945 separated prewar and postwar Japan as well as marking the start of "New China," as if the new political entity began on a clean slate within the

mainstream Japanese discourse. With this understanding of the new beginning, Japan as the failed colonizer disappeared from view. Articles on China even in progressive intellectual magazines in Japan such as *Chūō kōron* and *Kaizō* portrayed China as the New China under Mao in a celebratory and hopeful tone, emphasizing the discontinuity between China under Japanese control and China as a neighbor of postwar Japan. The same was true in Japanese social-scientific literature on Japan's immediate postwar era, as if the disappearance of the empire brought the natural disappearance of the consequences of the empire-building project.

56. Yoneyama, *Hiroshima Traces*; and Ran Zwigenberg, *Hiroshima: The Origins of Global Memory Culture* (Cambridge, UK: Cambridge University Press, 2014).

57. Gluck, "The 'End' of the Postwar," 5.

58. Gomikawa Junpei, *Ningen no jōken* [The human condition], vols. 1–6 (Tokyo: Bungei shunjū, 1979).

59. Kawamura Minato, *Manshū hōkai: "Daitōa bungaku" to sakkatachi* [The fall of Manchuria: "Great East Asian Prosperity literature" and its authors] (Tokyo: Bungei shunjū, 1997).

60. Gluck, "The 'End' of the Postwar," 8.

61. Kawamura, *Manshū hōkai*, 315–18.

62. Honda Katsuichi, *Chūgoku no tabi* [Journey through China] (Tokyo: Asahi shinbunsha, 1972).

63. Honda, *Chūgoku no tabi*, 8–9.

64. On *Chūgoku zanryū koji*, see Ide Magoroku, *Owarinaki tabi: "Chūgoku zanryū koji" no rekishi to genzai* [Endless journey: The history and the present of "Chūgoku zanryū koji"] (Tokyo: Iwanami shoten, 2004). Mariko Asano Tamanoi's study offers the Chinese side of the story. See Tamanoi, *Memory Maps*, chapter 4, and "Between Colonial Racism and Global Capitalism."

65. During their first visit in March 1981, thirty out of forty-seven orphans identified their Japanese relatives. Since then, more than thirty visits have been organized.

66. Gluck, "The Past in the Present," 85.

67. Yamazaki Toyoko, *Daichi no ko* [The child of the fatherland], vols. 1–3 (Tokyo: Bungei shunjū, 1991). Yamazaki is widely acclaimed for her historical and social epic novels, which are based on her extensive research. In preparation for writing *The Child of the Fatherland*, for example, Yamazaki spent several months in China conducting fieldwork, which she recounts in her *"Daichi no ko" to watashi* [The child of the fatherland and I] (Tokyo: Bungei shunjū, 1996).

68. While this chapter examines the touristic sites of encounters, chapters 4 and 5 will explore corporate sites of encounters by looking specifically at how increased Japanese direct investment in Dalian changed the topography of after empire for both Chinese and Japanese. On anthropological approaches to encounters, see Lieba Faier and Lisa Rofel, "Ethnographies of Encounter," *Annual Review of Anthropology* 43 (2014): 363–77.

69. Nakanishi Rei, *Akai tsuki* [The red moon], 2 vols. (Tokyo: Shinchōsha, 2001).

70. Motomiya Hiroshi, *Kuni ga moeru* [The country is burning], 9 vols. (Tokyo: Shūeisha, 2003–6).

71. This weekly comic magazine with its glossy cover of young women in bikinis or suggestive seminude clothing includes twenty to thirty comic installments every week.

Each story continues the following week, thus luring its readers to the magazine. Despite its semipornographic cover, and many scenes of violence and sex in its pages, the contents of the included comics range from historical graphic novels such as Motomiya's and social commentaries to stories about school, family, work, sports, and, most of all, sex, violence, and love stories. According to the data compiled by the Japan Magazine Publishers Association, *Young Jump* was the seventh most circulated magazine in 2004, with more than a million copies sold weekly. The majority of its readers are unmarried male college students and businessmen in their twenties and thirties. See Nihon zasshi kyōkai, ed., *Magajin dēta 2004* [Magazine data 2004] (Tokyo: Nihon zasshi kyōkai, 2005).

72. In the next chapter, we shall see how the Dalian municipal government presents Dalian as the land of opportunity to the Japanese business community and how Japanese businessmen, who are depressed by the decades-long recession in their country, discover the city as such.

73. Motomiya Hiroshi, "Kuni ga moeru" [The country is burning], *Young Jump*, October 7, 2004, 105–23.

74. *Tokyo nichinichi shinbun*, a Japanese daily newspaper, originally reported the event on November 30, December 4, 6, and 13, 1937, with a tone of live reporting on a sport match. This article and subsequent texts became the center of a high-profile legal battle by the subjects' surviving family members over libel. The two officers who allegedly participated in this match were executed in 1948 following the Nanjing Military Tribunal. In 1971, the publication of *Chūgoku no tabi* [Journey through China] (Tokyo: Asahi shinbunsha, 1971) by journalist Honda Katsuichi shook Japanese society, which had started to feel the shift from postwar recovery to postwar prosperity. In his book, Honda reported on the terrors of the Nanjing Massacre, including the infamous episode of *hyakunin giri*. The surviving family members sued Mainichi Shinbun, Honda Katsuichi, and Asahi Shinbun, which published Honda's book. On August 23, 2005, the Tokyo District Court ruled against their claim. Both the appeals court and the Supreme Court dismissed an appeal in 2006. The trial was emotionally charged, and the courtroom was always packed with left-leaning supporters of Honda Katsuichi and right-leaning supporters of the family members, with several court security guards intently monitoring the public for violence or verbal intrusion that could easily break out anytime during the court proceedings. For an analysis of debates on this issue in postwar Japan in English, see Bob Tadashi Wakabayashi, "The Nanking 100-Man Killing Contest Debate: War Guilt amid Fabricated Illusions, 1971–75," *Journal of Japanese Studies* 26, no. 2 (2000): 307–40.

75. Iris Chang, *The Rape of Nanking: The Forgotten Holocaust of World War II* (New York: Penguin Books, 1997).

76. Motomiya, "Kuni ga moeru", 118–19.

77. http://www.geocities.jp/nankin1937jp/page044.html.

78. As Marilyn Ivy points out, "It is around the place of photographs of mutilations (and the mutilations of photography) that the greatest agitation emerges." Marilyn Ivy, "Revenge and Recapitation in Recessionary Japan," *The South Atlantic Quarterly* 99, no. 4 (2000): 819–40, 821.

79. Motomiya Hiroshi, *Kuni ga moeru* [The country is burning], vols. 1–9, vol. 9 (Tokyo: Shūeisha, 2006), 152–55.

80. Hirsch, "The Generation of Postmemory," 106. See also her book, *The Generation of Postmemory*, and "Surviving Images: Holocaust Photographs and the Work of Postmemory."

81. Hirsch, "The Generation of Postmemory," 111.

82. Hirsch, "The Generation of Postmemory," 106.

83. Hirsch argues that postmemory "strives to reactivate and reembody" severed pasts. See "The Generation of Postmemory," 111.

84. "Chikyū no arukikata" henshūshitsu, *Chikyū no arukikata: Dairen to Chūgoku tōhoku chihō, 1999–2000* [Walking around the globe: Dalian and Northeast China, 1999–2000] (Tokyo: Diamond big sha, 1999), 168.

85. In his essay on the uncanny, Freud illuminates how the "uncanny" contains both familiarity and unfamiliarity. In discussing the convergence of the linguistic usage of *das Heimliche* (homely) and *das Unheimliche,* Freud points to how this term contains opposite meanings: "among its different shades of meaning the word '*heimlich*' exhibits one which is identical with its opposite, '*unheimlich*.' What is *heimlich* thus comes to be *unheimlich*" (224). He further explains, "This uncanny is in reality nothing new or alien, but something which is familiar and old-established in the mind and which has become alienated from it only through the process of repression" (241). He suggests that what is uncanny is the trace of the premodern.

My ethnographic observation in Changchun points to a different interpretation of the uncanny suggested by Mladen Dolar. Using Lacan, Dolar argues that what appears as uncanny is not the repressed premodern but the counterpart of modernity, the very product of modernity (7). The uncanny is the appearance of the lost part of modernity, the lack in modernity. From this perspective, it is not the lack or loss that produces anxiety but the lack of lack—the revelation of what is supposed to be unseen—that produces anxiety. Dolar writes, "What is uncanny is again the recuperation of the loss: the lost part destroys reality instead of completing it" (15). The presence of the uncanny is unsettling, because it is supposed to be unseen. When it becomes visible, it creates anxiety and fear. See Sigmund Freud, "The 'Uncanny,'" in *The Standard Edition of the Complete Psychological Works of Sigmund Freud*, vol. 17, ed. James Strachey, 217–56 (London: Hogarth Press, 1955), especially 224 and 241; and Mladen Dolar, "'I Shall Be with You on Your Wedding-Night': Lacan and the Uncanny," *October* 58 (Fall 1991): 5–23, especially 7 and 15.

86. For a concise overview of the history textbook controversy in the 1980s in English, see Arif Dirlik, "'Past Experience, If Not Forgotten, Is a Guide to the Future'; or, What Is in a Text? The Politics of History in Chinese-Japanese Relations," in *Japan in the World*, ed. Masao Miyoshi and H. D. Harootunian, 49–78 (Durham, NC: Duke University Press, 1993); and Laura Hein and Mark Selden, eds., *Censoring History: Citizenship and Memory in Japan, Germany, and the United States* (Armonk, NY: M. E. Sharpe, 2000).

87. Kuroyagi framed the historical issue between China and Japan within what Cathy Caruth refers to as referential practice—history as a "real" event that needs most of all to be visible in the place where it happened. Caruth's insight into the relationship between history and trauma is useful in understanding this Japanese visitor's profound disappointment. Writing in response to the claims of incommensurability of singular historical experiences, Caruth attempts to liberate the understanding of "history." Her detailed and imaginative analysis of texts reveals how intercultural sharing of trauma becomes pos-

sible when "history" is liberated from "simple models of experience and reference," which leave no room for possibility of history without the "immediate understanding" of this experience (11). Her study suggests that attempts at "seeing real history" at the site of where colonial violence took place, as this young Japanese man hoped to do, may do little to facilitate reconciliation (chapter 2). See Cathy Caruth, *Unclaimed Experience: Trauma, Narrative, and History* (Baltimore, MD: Johns Hopkins University Press, 1996).

88. Peter Sichrovsky, *Born Guilty: Children of Nazi Families*, trans. Jean Steinberg (New York: Basic Books, 1988), 171.

89. I borrow this title from Peter Sichrovsky's work on children of Nazi families in Germany in *Born Guilty*. Sichrovsky shows how many children of former Nazis, despite their wide-ranging relations to their parents' past, end up seeing themselves as overlooked victims of the history. They feel the weight of history, the guilt that they feel they have inherited from their parents but that they nevertheless feel their parents fail to acknowledge.

90. Caruth, *Unclaimed Experience*, 24.

91. The inverted gaze that many Japanese visitors to Changchun experience echoes the role of the gaze of the Other that Jacques Lacan elucidates: "In the scopic field, the gaze is outside, I am looked at, that is to say, I am a picture. This is the function that is found at the heart of the institution of the subject in the visible. What determines me, at the most profound level, in the visible, is the gaze that is outside. It is through the gaze that I enter light and it is from the gaze that I receive its effects." See Jacques Lacan, *The Four Fundamental Concepts of Psychoanalysis: The Seminar of Jacques Lacan, Book XI*, ed. Jacques-Alain Miller, trans. Alan Sheridan (New York: W. W. Norton, 1973), 106.

92. As Caruth puts it, the act of seeing atrocity photographs "erases . . . the reality of an event" due to "the inevitable self-referential reversal of the act of understanding." See Caruth, *Unclaimed Experience*, 29. Her analysis of the 1959 French film *Hiroshima mon amour* by Alain Resnais points to the scene in which a French actress visiting Hiroshima recognizes the catastrophe in Hiroshima as a referent to the end of the war (for her as a French national), framed within the narrative of French national history. While facing the Hiroshima cityscape, what she "sees" is not Hiroshima but her hometown in France.

93. Caruth, *Unclaimed Experience*, 29.

94. Karen Strassler's ethnographic study of Indonesian national imaginaries illustrates a similar structure of refraction that is mediated through photography taken by ethnic-minority Chinese Indonesian photographers. See Karen Strassler, *Refracted Visions: Popular Photography and National Modernity in Java* (Durham, NC: Duke University Press, 2010). While the experiences of Japanese tourists in Changchun echo the structure of refraction that is mediated by the Other, it is not the refraction itself that reveals the topography of guilt to them. Rather, it is the underlying moral economy that is framed within the refraction that conjures up this topography, as we will see further in chapter 4.

95. See Elazar Barkan, *The Guilt of the Nations: Restitution and Negotiating Historical Injustices* (New York: W. W. Norton, 2000), for an overview of how national guilt drives politics in various cultural contexts. Ian Buruma, in his *Wages of Guilt: Memories of War in Germany and Japan* (New York: Farrar, Straus, Giroux, 1994), compares Japanese and German attempts to come to terms with their respective fascist pasts through the lens of guilt.

96. On postwar responsibility (*sengo sekinin*), see Ōnuma Yasuaki, *Tōkyō saiban, sensō sekinin, sengo sekinin* [Tokyo Tribunal, war responsibility, postwar responsibility] (Tokyo: Tōshindō, 2007); Takahashi Tetsuya, *Sengo sekinin ron* [On postwar responsibility] (Tokyo: Kōdansha, 1999); and Utsumi Aiko, Ōnuma Yasuaki, Tanaka Hiroshi, and Katō Yōko, *Sengo sekinin: Ajia no manazashi ni kotaete* [Postwar responsibility: In response to the gaze of Asia] (Tokyo: Iwanami shoten, 2014).

97. On corruption in China, see, for example, Xiaobo Lü, *Cadres and Corruption: The Organizational Involution of the Chinese Communist Party* (Stanford, CA: Stanford University Press, 2000).

98. For a concise overview of the debate surrounding this debate in Germany, see Gavriel D. Rosenfeld, "'The Architects' Debate': Architectural Discourse and the Memory of Nazism in the Federal Republic of Germany, 1977–1997," *History and Memory* 9, no. 1/2 (Fall 1997): 189–225.

99. In chapter 5, we will see how the anxieties that the local Chinese project onto the Japanese inability to reckon with its imperial past play out in the Chinese postgenerations' attempts to come to terms with the losses inflicted through not only colonial modernity but also socialist and postsocialist modernities.

CHAPTER FOUR

1. The appeal of Western-style housing among the new middle class is not unique to Dalian. For example, observing a similar proliferation of new housing developments that evoke images of the West through architectural styles and naming practices in the city of Kunming in southern China, Li Zhang illustrates a tension between the desire for all things Western by the real estate market and middle-class consumers and a sense of nationalism expressed by the local government and intellectuals. In contrast, in Dalian what is notable is the lack of such a tension. See Li Zhang, *In Search of Paradise: Middle-Class Living in a Chinese Metropolis* (Ithaca, NY: Cornell University Press, 2010), chapter 3. On the recent proliferation of Western-style housing in other Chinese cities, see also Fulong Wu, "Transplanting Cityscapes: The Use of Imagined Globalization in Housing Commodification in Beijing," *Area* 36, no. 3 (2004): 227–34; and Davis Fraser, "Inventing Oasis: Luxury Housing Advertisements in Reconfiguring Domestic Space in Shanghai," in *The Consumer Revolution in Urban China*, ed. Deborah Davis, 25–53 (Berkeley: University of California Press, 2000).

2. For postcoloniality in Taiwan, see Leo Ching, "'Give Me Japan and Nothing Else!' Postcoloniality, Identity, and the Traces of Colonialism," *The South Atlantic Quarterly* 99, no. 4 (2000): 763–88, and *Becoming "Japanese": Colonial Taiwan and the Politics of Identity Formation* (Berkeley: University of California Press, 2000).

3. Gu Mingyi, Fang Jun, Ma Lifen, Wang Shengli, Zhang Qingshan, and Lü Linxiu, eds., *Dalian jin bainianshi* [A hundred-year modern history of Dalian], vols. 1–2 of *Diguo zhuyi qinlue Dalian shi congshu* [Collective works on the history of the imperialist invasion of Dalian], ed. Ma Lifen, et al. (Shenyang, China: Liaoning renmin chubanshe, 1999). Numerous other official publications about the city's history followed, including Ma Lifen, et al., eds., *Diguo zhuyi qinlue Dalian shi congshu* [Collected works on the history of the imperialist invasion of Dalian], 6 vols. (Shenyang, China: Liaoning renmin

chubanshe, 1999); and Wang Huiquan, ed. *Dalian bainian jianben* [Simplified edition of Dalian hundred years] (Dalian, China: Dalian Chubanshe, 1999).

4. Gu Mingyi, et al., eds., *Dalian jin bainianshi*, 3.

5. Gu Mingyi, et al., eds., *Dalian jin bainianshi*, 7.

6. On the history of Japanese settler colonialism in Dalian, see Emer O'Dwyer, *Significant Soil: Settler Colonialism and Japan's Urban Empire in Manchuria* (Cambridge, MA: Harvard University Asia Center, 2015).

7. Wang Huiquan, ed., *Dalian wushi nian* [Dalian fifty years] (Dalian, China: Dalian chubanshe, 1995); Dalian shi shizhi bangongshi [Dalian City Gazetteer Office], ed., *Kaishi quanmian jianshe shehui zhuyi shiqi de Dalian, 1957.1–1966.4* [Dalian during the early period of total construction of socialism, 1957.1–1966.4], Zhonggong Dalian dangshi ziliao congshu [Collective works on the Dalian Chinese Communist Party history], vol. 11 (Dalian, China: Dalian chubanshe, 1998); Gao Bo, *Dalianshi shehui he jingji fazhan gailan* [The overview of the social and economic development of Dalian] (Beijing: Zhongguo shangye chubanshe, 2002). In English, see Christian A. Hess, "From Colonial Jewel to Socialist Metropolis: Dalian 1895–1955" (PhD dissertation, University of California, San Diego, 2006), and "From Colonial Port to Socialist Metropolis: Imperialist Legacies and the Making of 'New Dalian,'" *Urban History* 38, no. 3 (December 2011): 373–90, for an historical overview of the city's transformation from Dalini to Dairen to Dalian.

8. Gao, *Dalianshi shehui he jingji fazhan gailan*, 30.

9. On the development of the private trade relations and the so-called LT Agreement between the two countries without diplomatic relations in English, see Kurt Wermer Redtke and Chengzhi Liao, *China's Relations with Japan, 1945–83: The Role of Liao Chengzhi* (Manchester: Manchester University Press, 1990).

10. Gu Mingyi, et al., eds., *Dalian jin bainianshi.*

11. Through her observation of silk-factory workers in Hanzhou, Lisa Rofel locates the project of modernity in reform-era China within a framework of long-deferred postcolonial desires. What the case of Dalian shows is the aggressive incorporation of colonial experiences into the course of the city's pursuit of modernity. Within this framework, the processes of pursuing modernity were not deferred by imperial aggressions, as Rofel observes elsewhere in China, but rather these foreign aggressions are understood to have set the first stage in the process toward today's Dalian. See Lisa Rofel, *Other Modernities: Gendered Yearnings in China after Socialism* (Berkeley: University of California Press, 1999).

12. Lisa M. Hoffman, *Patriotic Professionalism in Urban China: Fostering Talent* (Philadelphia: Temple University Press, 2010), 39.

13. By historicizing corporeal embodiment in China, Judith Farquhar shows how reform-era Chinese bodies have come to embody the high Maoist past. What makes the case in Dalian unique is that the narrative of corporeal embodiment instead emphasizes that Dalianites' bodies are repositories of its colonial past. See Judith Farquhar, *Appetites: Food and Sex in Post-Socialist China* (Durham, NC: Duke University Press, 2002).

14. On *suzhi*, see Ann Anagnost, "The Corporeal Politics of Quality (*Suzhi*)," *Public Culture* 16, no. 2 (2004): 189–208; Vanessa Fong, "Morality, Cosmopolitanism, or Academic Attainment? Discourses on "Quality" and Urban Chinese-Only-Children's Claims to Ideal Personhood," *City and Society* 19, no. 1 (2007): 86–113; Hoffman, *Patriotic Professionalism*

in Urban China; Carolyn L. Hsu, *Creating Market Socialism: How Ordinary People Are Shaping Class and Status in China* (Durham, NC: Duke University Press, 2007); Andrew Kipnis, "*Suzhi*: A Keyword Approach," *The China Quarterly* 186 (2006): 295–313; Lisa Rofel, *Desiring China: Experiments in Neoliberalism, Sexuality, and Public Culture* (Durham, NC: Duke University Press, 2007); Li Zhang, *Strangers in the City: Reconfigurations of Space, Power, and Social Networks within China's Floating Population* (Stanford, CA: Stanford University Press, 2001); and Tiantian Zheng, *Red Lights: The Lives of Sex Workers in Postsocialist China* (Minneapolis: University of Minnesota Press, 2009).

15. Whereas the usage of *suzhi* in Dalian highlights historicity embodied in workers' bodies, Ann Anagnost finds a lack of historicity within this discourse generally observed nationwide in China. *Suzhi* in her analysis is not perceived as something that builds on one's inheritance, as in the case of Dalianites. She shows how the proliferation of the discourse of *suzhi* has naturalized the newly formed structural power relations that divide the society into exploited migrant workers and the new middle class. Bodies of the new middle class are considered to embody *suzhi*, while bodies of migrant workers embody its lack, symbolizing the backwardness and the absence of civilization (*wenming*) that Chinese society believes must be overcome in order to be competitive in the global market. *Suzhi* thus represents a new set of values that have accumulated in bodies. As Anagnost succinctly puts it, the discourse of *suzhi* "yields surplus value not just in the economic realm but also in the realm of political representation. It works ideologically as a regime of representation through which subjects recognize their positions within the larger social order and thereby sets up the conditions for socioeconomic striving" (193). Her analysis emphasizes how *suzhi* is understood as a supplement, an added value to the body: "*Suzhi* is not something that naturally inheres in the body but is rather something that must be built into the body—a supplement that must be added to its 'bare life'" (193). The economic logic of capital accumulation takes another form in the realm of corporeal presence. The discourse of *suzhi* reenacts and legitimizes neoliberal economic logic, which she portrays as "the negation of history" (206). See Anagnost, "The Corporeal Politics of Quality (*Suzhi*)."

16. On the formation of a new generation of workers in Dalian, see Lisa M. Hoffman, *Patriotic Professionalism in Urban China*; "Guiding College Graduates to Work: Social Constructions of Labor Markets in Dalian," in *China Urban: Ethnographies of Contemporary Culture*, ed. Nancy N. Chen, Constance D. Clark, Suzanne Z. Gottschang, and Lyn Jeffery, 43–66 (Durham, NC: Duke University Press, 2001); "Urban Transformation and Professionalization: Translocality and Rationalities of Enterprise in Post-Mao China," in *Translocal China: Linkages, Identities, and the Reimagining of Space*, ed. Tim Oakes and Louisa Schein, 109–37 (London: Routledge, 2006); and "Autonomous Choices and Patriotic Professionalism: On Governmentality in Late-Socialist China," *Economy and Society* 35, no. 4 (November 2006): 550–70. See also Vanessa L. Fong, *Paradise Redefined: Transnational Chinese Students and the Quest for Flexible Citizenship in the Developed World* (Stanford, CA: Stanford University Press, 2011); and "Morality, Cosmopolitanism, or Academic Attainment?"

17. Nicholas B. Dirks, "History as a Sign of Modern," *Public Culture* 2, no. 2 (Spring 1990): 25–32.

18. While the discourse of *suzhi* justifies the class division between urban and rural,

the boundary between the two is blurring as Chinese society's engagement with the market economy deepens. The expansion of city limits and the rural-to-urban migration have opened up opportunities for rural desiring subjects to unsettle, co-opt, and challenge this divide. See, for example, Jonathan Bach, "'They Come in Peasants and Leave Citizens': Urban Villages and the Making of Shenzhen, China," *Cultural Anthropology* 25, no. 3 (2010): 425–58; Yan Hairong, *New Masters, New Servants: Migration, Development, and Women Workers in China* (Durham, NC: Duke University Press, 2008); Pun Ngai, *Made in China: Women Factory Workers in a Global Workplace* (Durham, NC: Duke University Press, 2005); Dorothy J. Solinger, *Contesting Citizenship in Urban China: Peasant Migrants, the State, and the Logic of the Market* (Berkeley: University of California Press, 1999); Winnie Won Yin Wong, *Van Gogh on Demand: China and the Readymade* (Chicago: University of Chicago Press, 2013); and Zhang, *Strangers in the City.*

19. On the centrality of desire and the desiring subject in post-Mao China, see Rofel, *Desiring China*, and Farquhar, *Appetites*.

20. This tax structure as well as the role of the Zone within the Chinese economy went through a major change in 2008. On March 16, 2007, the tenth National People's Congress adopted a new corporate-income-tax law, which imposes a flat 25 percent corporate tax rate across the board effective on January 1, 2008. Accordingly, preferential tax rates for foreign corporations located in special economic zones were abolished.

21. On the role of foreign direct investment in China's transition to a market-oriented economy, see Mary Elizabeth Gallagher, *Contagious Capitalism: Globalization and the Politics of Labor in China* (Princeton, NJ: Princeton University Press, 2005).

22. Michel Foucault, "Of Other Spaces," trans. Jay Miskowiec, *Diacritics* 16, no. 1 (Spring 1986): 22–27.

23. In his exploration of "other spaces," Foucault juxtaposes *heterotopia*, a term he adopted from medical science that refers to a displacement of organs in other spaces, with *utopia*, an illusionary space of perfection. In Foucault's description, heterotopias are articulations of utopias—illusory spaces of perfection—that often take the form of external countersites, where "the real sites . . . are simultaneously represented, contested, and inverted." The role of a heterotopia is either "to create a space of illusion that exposes every real space" or to create a space of compensation that enacts utopian illusion. His examples include brothels, which exemplify the former, and certain colonies, which exemplify the latter. See Foucault, "Of Other Spaces," 24.

24. Louise Young, *Japan's Total Empire: Manchuria and the Culture of Wartime Imperialism* (Berkeley: University of California Press, 1998).

25. In her analysis of resource extraction in Indonesia, Anna Lowenhaupt Tsing describes a similar process of socially constructing an image of a "frontier" devoid of local inhabitants through the discourse of development. See Anna Lowenhaupt Tsing, *Friction: An Ethnography of Global Connection* (Princeton, NJ: Princeton University Press, 2005). On the construction of special economic zones as urban spaces that draw on the modernist notion of tabula rasa planning, see Jonathan Bach, "Modernity and the Urban Imagination in Economic Zones," *Theory, Culture, and Society* 28, no. 5 (2011): 98–122.

26. For middle-class modernity as one of the central organizing principles of Japan's "long postwar," see Carol Gluck, "The 'End' of the Postwar: Japan at the Turn of the Millennium," *Public Culture* 10, no. 1 (1997): 1–23.

27. See Gendai yōgo henshūbu, ed., *Gendai yōgo no kiso chishiki 2007* [Basic knowledge of contemporary terms] (Tokyo: Jiyū Kokuminsha, 2006).

28. See, for example, Mizushima Hiroaki, *Netto kafe nanmin to hinkon Nippon* [Internet cafe refugees and poverty Japan] (Tokyo: Nihon terebi, 2007); NHK Special "wākingu puā" shuzai-han, ed., *Wākingu puā: Nihon o mushibamu yamai* [Working poor: A disease that undermines Japan] (Tokyo: Populasha, 2007); Tachibanaki Toshiaki, *Kakusa shakai: Nani ga mondai nano ka* [Society with disparity: What are the issues?] (Tokyo: Iwanami shoten, 2006); and Yuasa Makoto, *Han-hinkon: "Suberidai shakai" kara no dakkyaku* [Antipoverty: Escape from a slide society] (Tokyo: Iwanami shoten, 2008).

29. In contrast to the special economic zones in southern China, most notably the one in Shenzhen, which has attracted small- to medium-size companies, the majority of the corporations in the Dalian Economic and Technological Zone are brand-name global corporations. Dalian's factory-floor line workers in the Zone tend to be more educated and skilled than their southern counterparts, and they often expressed a strong sense of being part of the emerging middle class, a different tenor from what Pun Ngai observed in her ethnographic account of the day-to-day lives of sweatshop workers in Shenzhen. Furthermore, as Lisa Rofel observed in Hanzhou and Beijing, "class" in post-Mao China is less about socioeconomic standing than about one's ability to be a desiring subject. From a different register, Carolyn L. Hsu shows how the concept of *suzhi* has come to replace class as a measure of one's status in post-Mao China. See Pun Ngai, *Made in China: Women Factory Workers in a Global Workplace* (Durham, NC: Duke University Press, 2005); Rofel, *Desiring China*; and Hsu, *Creating Market Socialism*.

30. The opening scene of Yiyun Li's short story "Extra" vividly illustrates how Japanese corporations' televised commercials influenced and penetrated Chinese society on the cusp of socioeconomic transition. The story starts with a conversation between Granny Lin, who was just laid off from a garment factory, and her neighbor Auntie Wang: "There is always a road when you get into the mountain," Auntie Wang says to her upon being informed of Granny Lin's situation. The second line of a Toyota commercial slips out of Granny's mouth before she realizes it: "And there is a Toyota wherever there is a road." See Yiyun Li, *A Thousand Years of Good Prayers* (London: Fourth Estate, 2006), 3.

31. On the early development of Toshiba Dalian and the difficulties the Japanese management team faced in transplanting the Japanese corporate management style to China, see Arakawa Naoki, *Chūgoku de seizōgyō wa fukkatsu suru: Tōshiba dairensha no chōsen* [Revival of the manufacturing industry: Challenges of Toshiba Dalian] (Tokyo: Mita shuppankai, 1998).

32. Adam Smith, *An Inquiry into the Nature and Causes of the Wealth of Nations*, ed. Edwin Cannan (Chicago: University of Chicago Press, 1976 [1776]).

33. Adam Smith, *Wealth of Nations*, book I, chapter 1, 8–9.

34. For Smith on moral economy, see Adam Smith, *Wealth of Nations*, and *The Theory of Moral Sentiments*, ed. D. D. Raphael and A. L. Macfie (Indianapolis: Liberty Fund, 1982 [1759]). For Smith on morality, see Jerry Evensky, "Retrospectives: Ethics and the Invisible Hand," *Journal of Economic Perspectives* 7, no. 2 (1993): 197–205.

35. See "Joint Communiqué of the Government of Japan and the Government of the People's Republic of China," signed on September 29, 1972. The preamble states that "the Japanese side is keenly conscious of the responsibility for the serious damage that

Japan caused in the past to the Chinese people through war, and deeply reproaches itself." Following this statement, article five reads, "The Government of the People's Republic of China declares that in the interest of the friendship between the Chinese and the Japanese peoples, it renounces its demand for war reparation from Japan."

36. On the anthropological concept of the gift, which always incurs debt, see Marcel Mauss, *The Gift: Forms and Functions of Exchange in Archaic Societies* (New York: Routledge, 1970 [1924]).

37. In his critical reading of Mauss, Jacques Derrida reflects on how what is given in gift relations is not the thing that is presented but time for future repayment of the debt incurred through receiving a gift. See Jacques Derrida, *Given Time: I. Counterfeit Money*, trans. Peggy Kamuf (Chicago: University of Chicago Press, 1992).

38. "Koizumi shushō ra no ODA uchikiri hatsugen, Chūgoku shushō ga fukai kan" [Chinese Premier expressed discomfort at Japanese Prime Minister Koizumi's intention to discontinue the ODA], *Yomiuri shinbun*, December 3, 2004. See also Cao Haidong and Huang Xiaowei, "Riben Dui Hua Yuanzhu San Shi Nian" [Thirty years of Japan's aid to China], *Nanfang Zhoumo* [Southern Weekly], February 20, 2008, http://www.infzm.com/content/7707.

39. "Nazo no Nihonjin Dairen e: Nihonjin no me" [A mystery Japanese goes to Dalian: A Japanese view], *Bipure: Business and Play*, December 2002, 29.

40. "Nazo no Nihonjin Dairen e," *Bipure: Business and Play*, January 2003, 33.

41. For the centrality of the sex industry within the gendered corporate culture during the bubble-economy-era Japan, see Anne Allison, *Nightwork: Sexuality, Pleasure, and Corporate Masculinity in a Tokyo Hostess Club* (Chicago: University of Chicago Press, 1994).

42. For the key role the sex industry plays in China's new economy, see Tiantian Zheng, *Red Lights: The Lives of Sex Workers in Postsocialist China* (Minneapolis: University of Minnesota Press, 2009). On the role of the sex industry and sexuality among China's new rich, see John Osburg, *Anxious Wealth: Money and Morality among China's New Rich* (Stanford, CA: Stanford University Press, 2013).

43. Li Jiarui, "Dalian xinniang zai Riben xingfu zhenxiang" [The reality of happiness of Dalian brides in Japan], *Xinshangbao* [New Business News] (Dalian, China), March 30, 2003, 23.

44. *Oshin*, a widely popular and record-breaking morning drama series, was broadcast daily in 1983–84 by NHK (Japan Broadcasting Corporation, public broadcaster). It later became hugely popular worldwide, especially in developing countries. It portrays the rags-to-riches life story of a virtuous, conscientious, and persistent woman.

45. Based on her participant observation of lives of Dalian hostesses in karaoke bars catering to Chinese, Tiantian Zheng's engaging ethnography captures the dangers, vulnerability, and humiliation that these young women face daily. She also observes how hostesses have an easier time dealing with Japanese men, whom they describe as less chauvinistic than Chinese businessmen. See Zheng, *Red Lights*.

46. In her ethnography of karaoke clubs in Dalian, Tiantian Zheng shows how conspicuous consumption has become a site for Chinese men to recover masculinity. See Zheng, *Red Lights*.

47. Desiring to go abroad, of course, is not limited to Japan, nor is this pervasive yearning unique to Dalian. For example, Vanessa L. Fong shows how desiring to going

abroad—anywhere beyond China—has become a major life pursuit among the new generation of Dalianites. Julie Y. Chu provides a cultural analysis of Fuzhounese aspiration for overseas emigration to show how mobility has become a key cultural currency. See Fong, *Paradise Redefined*; and Julie Y. Chu, *Cosmologies of Credit: Transnational Mobility and the Politics of Destination in China* (Durham, NC: Duke University Press, 2010).

48. This feeding off of individual and national redemptive desires in Dalian echoes what Lisa Rofel observes in the emergence of the desiring subject and China's attempt to reposition itself within the new post–Cold War global order through the mediation of national public culture. See Rofel, *Desiring China*.

49. The construction of narratives—both individual and collective—has become a key mechanism for ordinary Chinese to make sense of the major social transformation in the post-Mao era; it is not unique to Dalian. As Carolyn L. Hsu succinctly puts it in her analysis of how ordinary people in Harbin are handling this transition, "The ordinary people in the city, in dialogue with the state and market forces, were collectively shaping the economic institutions of market socialism as well as moral discourse to support it." See Hsu, *Creating Market Socialism*, 4.

50. Data from Dalian shi Duiwai Maoyi Jingji Hezuo ju [Dalian Foreign Trade and Economic Cooperation Bureau].

51. In 1990, 83 percent of actual foreign investment in Dalian came from Japan. In 2002, the number dropped to 44 percent even though the investment amount increased from 150 million US dollars to 700 million US dollars. Data from Dalian shi Duiwai Maoyi Jingji Hezuo ju [Dalian Foreign Trade and Economic Cooperation Bureau].

52. Data from Dalian shi Duiwai Maoyi Jingji Hezuo ju [Dalian Foreign Trade and Economic Cooperation Bureau].

53. Data from *Dalian tongji nianjin* [Dalian statistical yearbook] and the Dalian municipal government homepage. Cited in Nihon bōeki shinkō kikō (JETRO) dairen jimusho, "Dairenshi gaikyō" [The overview of Dalian], September 2006, 12.

54. Kokusai Kōryū Kikin [Japan Foundation], "Nihongo nōryoku shiken kekka no gaiyō 2005" [The overview of the Japanese proficiency exam 2005].

55. For a social history of prewar Dalian as Japanese frontier, see Yanagisawa Asobu, *Nihonjin no shokuminchi keiken: Dairen Nihonjin shōkōgyōsha no rekishi* [Japanese colonial experience: The history of Japanese commercial and industrial entrepreneurs in Dalian] (Tokyo: Aoki shoten, 1999).

56. An English-language book published in New York in 1922 by the South Manchuria Railway Company, for example, promotes Manchuria as the "land of opportunities," as the book title unambiguously trumpets. South Manchuria Railway, *Manchuria, Land of Opportunities* (New York: South Manchuria Railway, 1922).

CHAPTER FIVE

1. "Xin shenghuo, jiu huiyi: guiguo nuxing fangtan" [New life, old memories: Interviews with women who returned from abroad], *Oggi: Jinri fengcai* 17 (March 2003): 120–23.

2. Theodor W. Adorno, "What Does Coming to Terms with the Past Mean?" in *Bit-*

burg in Moral and Political Perspective, ed. Geoffrey H. Hartman, 114–29 (Bloomington: Indiana University Press, 1986 [1959]).

3. He wrote, "'Coming to terms with the past' does not imply a serious working through of the past, the breaking of its spell through an act of clear consciousness. It suggests, rather, wishing to turn the page and, if possible, wiping it from memory." See Adorno, "What Does Coming to Terms with the Past Mean?" 115.

4. As he put it, "National Socialism lives on, and to this day we don't know whether it is only the ghost of what was so monstrous that it didn't even die off with its own death, or whether it never died in the first place. . . . I consider the continued existence of National Socialism *within* democracy potentially more threatening than the continued existence of fascist tendencies *against* democracy." See Adorno, "What Does Coming to Terms with the Past Mean?" 115.

5. Eva Hoffman, *After Such Knowledge: Memory, History and the Legacy of the Holocaust* (New York: Public Affairs, 2004).

6. This is a departure from Eva Hoffman's position—hence *despite* such knowledge—that no reconciliation is possible between Germans and Jews. As she puts it, "The gulf—moral, political, affective—between the victim and the perpetrator is almost absolute." See Hoffman, *After Such Knowledge*, 111.

7. Wang Huiquan, ed., *Dalian wushi nian* [Dalian fifty years] (Dalian, China: Dalian chubanshe, 1995), 198.

8. For the history of Onoda Cement, see Nihon Keiei Kenkyūjo [Japanese Management Research Institute], ed., *Onoda Semento hyakunen shi* [Centennial history of Onoda Cement] (Tokyo: Onoda Semento, 1981); Sunaga Noritake, "Manshū no yōgyō" [Ceramic industry in Manchuria], *Rikkyō keizaigaku kenkyū* [Rikkyo journal of economics] 59, no. 3 (2006): 63–99; and Soon-Won Park, *Colonial Industrialization and Labor in Korea: The Onoda Cement Factory* (Cambridge, MA: Harvard University Asia Center, 1999).

9. *Jeong v. Onoda Cement Co. Ltd.*, 2000 US Dist LEXIS 7985.

10. For the global context in which this case has evolved, see Lisa Yoneyama, "Traveling Memories, Contagious Justice: Americanization of Japanese War Crimes at the End of the Post-Cold War," *Journal of Asian American Studies* 6, no. 1 (2003): 57–93. For labor relations at Onoda Cement plants in Japanese-occupied Korea, see Park, *Colonial Industrialization and Labor in Korea*. Park mentions briefly the presence of forced-labor practices: "In late 1941, as the labor shortage intensified with the outbreak of the Pacific War, the Association for Korean Labor Affairs (Chōsen rōmu kyōkai) was established and made solely responsible for labor mobilization. Within the colonial government, the Labor Affairs Section was also hurriedly established. . . . one million Korean men and women were mobilized by force from 1939 to 1945" (44–45). Yet the body of her work painstakingly documents nuanced and complex social relations, which refuse to be reduced into "a simple, binary exploitation-resistance view of colonial Korea" (33). Perhaps, and precisely because of her approach, the defendant (Taiheiyo/Onoda Cement) quoted her book in their argument against Jeong's claims.

11. On January 15, 2003, Superior Court Judge Boland argued that the case could proceed because section 354.6 was constitutional, since its "enactment was an appropriate exercise of the state's sovereign powers." He justified the validity of section 354.6 "because

(1) no federal treaty or other law preempts it, (2) the enactment poses at most merely an incidental or indirect effect on foreign countries, (3) the statute does not violate constitutional due process, and (4) the claims it allows do not present non-justiciable political questions." On March 30, 2004, however, Judge Boland reversed his opinion to reflect the US Supreme Court decision on June 23, 2003. The Supreme Court ruled 5–4 that the California's Holocaust Victims Insurance Relief Act of 1999 was unconstitutional because it interfered with the federal government's foreign policy. Upon reviewing the Supreme Court case, Judge Boland overturned his own opinion in January 2003 and argued that the San Francisco Peace Treaty in 1951 preempts section 354.6 and thus California's law "conflicts with the foreign policy expressed in the 1951 Treaty." See *Taiheiyo Cement Corp. v Superior Court*, 105 Cal App 4th 398, 129 Cal Rptr 2d 451 (2003) Cal App LEXIS 57; *American Ins. Assn. v Garamendi*, 539 US 396 (2003); and *Taiheiyo Cement Corp. v Superior Court*, 117 Cal App 4th 380, 12 Cal Rptr 3d 32 (2004), 398.

12. Nihon Keiei Kenkyūjo, ed., *Onoda Semento hyakunen shi.*

13. On labor history in Manchuria, see Matsumura Takao, Xie Xueshi, and Eda Kenji, eds., *Mantetsu rōdōshi no kenkyū* [The labor history of the South Manchuria Railway Company] (Tokyo: Nihon keizai hyōronsha, 2002). The Chinese-language version of the same title is Xie Xueshi and Matsumura Takao, eds., *Mantie yu Zhongguo laogong* [The South Manchuria Railway Company and Chinese laborers] (Beijing: Shehui kexue wenxian chubanshe, 2003). For an overview of how Japanese corporations took part in the Japanese occupation of China from 1937 to 1945, see Shibata Yoshimasa, *Chūgoku senryōchi nikkei kigyō no katsudō* [Activities of Japanese corporations in occupied China] (Tokyo: Nihon keizai hyōronsha, 2008).

14. For a comprehensive overview of the mobilization of Chinese forced laborers, see Nishinarita Yutaka, *Chūgokujin kyōsei renkō* [Chinese forced labor] (Tokyo: Tokyo daigaku shuppankai, 2002). For a compilation of primary sources and analyses of them, see Tanaka Hiroshi, Arimitsu Ken, and Nakayama Taketoshi, eds., *Mikaiketsu no sengo hoshō: Towareru Nihon no kako to mirai* [Unresolved postwar compensation: Problematizing Japan's past and future] (Tokyo: Sōshisha, 2012); Tanaka Hiroshi, "Chūgokujin kyōsei renkō no rekishi to genzai" [The Chinese forced labor in history and today], in *Ringoku kara no kokuhatsu: Kyōsei renkō no kigyō sekinin 2* [Accusation from the neighbors: Corporate responsibility for forced labor 2], ed. Yamada Shōji and Tanaka Hiroshi (Tokyo: Sōshisha, 1996); Tanaka Hiroshi and Matsuzawa Tetsunari, eds., *Chūgokujin kyōsei renkō shiryō: "Gaimuhō hōkokusho" zen 5 bunsatsu hoka* [Source material on the Chinese forced labor: The reports of the Ministry of Foreign Affairs of Japan] (Tokyo: Gendai shokan, 1995); Tanaka Hiroshi, Utsumi Aiko, and Nīimi Takashi, eds., *Shiryō Chūgokujin kyōsei renkō no kiroku* [Source material: Records of the Chinese forced labor] (Tokyo: Akashi shoten, 1990); and Tanaka Hiroshi, Utsumi Aiko, and Ishitobi Jin, eds., *Shiryō Chūgokujin kyōsei renkō* [Source material: The Chinese forced labor] (Tokyo: Akashi shoten, 1987). For oral histories of the victims compiled in China, see He Tianyi, ed., *Erzhan lu Ri Zhongguo laogong koushushi* [Oral history of Japanese-captured Chinese forced laborers during the Second World War], 5 vols. (Jinan, China: Qilu shushe, 2005). In English, see Paul H. Kratoska, *Asian Labor in the Wartime Japanese Empire: Unknown Histories* (Armonk, NY: M. E. Sharpe, 2005).

15. Inose Kenzō, *Tsūkon no sanga: Ashio dōzan Chūgokujin kyōsei renkō no kiroku* [Poignant landscape: The record of the Ashio copper mine Chinese forced labor], revised and enlarged ed. (Utsunomiya, Japan: Zuisōsha, 1994 [1973]), 38–39.

16. Gaimushō Kanrikyoku [The Ministry of Foreign Affairs Management Bureau], *Kajin rōmusha shūrō jijō hōkoku (yōshi)* [The employment situation of Chinese laborers (summary)], March 1946. Reproduced in Tanaka Hiroshi and Matsuzawa Tetsunari, eds., *Chūgokujin kyōsei renkō shiryō* [Source material on the Chinese forced labor] (Tokyo: Gendai shokan, 1995), 6.

17. For an overview of the institutional and organizational structures of the "rabbit chase operation," see Tanaka, Utsumi, and Ishitobi, eds., *Shiryō Chūgokujin kyōsei renkō*, 590–611.

18. Wang Huiquan, ed., *Dalian wushi nian* [Dalian fifty years] (Dalian, China: Dalian chubanshe, 1995), 198.

19. Carol Gluck, "Operations of Memory: 'Comfort Women' and the World," in *Ruptured Histories: War and Memory in Post-Cold War Asia*, ed. Sheila Miyoshi Jager and Rana Mitter, 47–77 (Cambridge, MA: Harvard University Asia Center, 2007), 57.

20. "Scarred Landscape" here has a resonance to Ann Stoler's concept of "imperial debris," which was developed originally through a workshop titled "Scarred Landscape and Imperial Debris" at The New School in 2006. The collection of papers from this workshop was subsequently published as a volume edited by her: *Imperial Debris: On Ruins and Ruination* (Durham, NC: Duke University Press, 2013).

21. Bi Zhiwei and Liu Yi, "Wang Xuan jinri lai lian diaocha quzheng: Souji Riben xijunzhan zuie zhengju, wei wugu shouhaizhe shenzheng zhengyi" [Wang Xuan to arrive in Dalian for an evidence gathering trip: Investigating the evidence of the crimes of the Japanese biological warfare in order to extend justice to innocent victims], *Dalian ribao* [Dalian Daily] (Dalian, China), April 23, 2003, 1.

22. On August 27, 2002, the Tokyo Regional Court (Heisei 9 [wa] No. 16684, and Heisei 11 [wa] No. 27579) ruled against the plaintiffs, although Judge Iwata Kōji acknowledged the historical fact of germ warfare by the Japanese Army and that such an act was against the Hague Treaty. The appeals court at the Tokyo High Court (Heisei 14 [ne] No. 4815) upheld the lower court decision on July 19, 2005, and rejected the Chinese plaintiffs' request for compensation and official apology from the Japanese government. Judge Ōta Sachio argued that due to the doctrine of sovereign immunity under the Meiji Constitution (the so-called *kokka mutōseki no hōri*), the Imperial Japanese state was not liable for damages resulting from actions related to its exercise of state power (*kenryoku sayō*). The judge further argued that due to the Joint Communiqué of Japan and the People's Republic of China in 1972 (in which the Chinese government renounced reparation claims against Japan), the plaintiffs did not have the right to claim. On May 9, 2007, the Supreme Court dismissed the final appeal.

23. CCTV started "*gandong Zhongguo*" in 2002, and it has become an influential annual media event since then.

24. Fuchang Company's original company name in Japanese was Fukushō kōshi (Fukushō Company) when it was established in 1909 with Aioi Yoshitarō from the South Manchuria Railway Company as the president. Because of Aioi falling ill and the slump

in business due to the depression since 1920, the company faced a need for a fundamental rationalization of business operations. In 1926, with the South Manchuria Railway Company as the largest stockholder, Fukushō kakō kabushiki gaisha (Fukushō Chinese Labor Corporation) was born as a subsidiary of the South Manchuria Railway Company. See Yanagisawa Asobu, "Dairen futō" [Dalian port], in *Mantetsu rōdōshi no kenkyū* [The Labor history of the South Manchuria Railway Company], ed. Matsumura Takao, Xie Xueshi, and Eda Kenji (Tokyo: Nihon Keizai Hyōronsha, 2002), 249–84, esp. 256–58. Fuchang Company was one of the organizations in charge of recruiting and abducting Chinese for mobilization of labor forces. See Gaimushō Kanrikyoku [The Ministry of Foreign Affairs Management Bureau], *Kajin rōmusha shūrō jijō hōkoku (yōshi)* [The employment situation of Chinese laborers (summary)], reproduced in Tanaka and Matsuzawa, eds., *Chūgokujin kyōsei renkō shiryō*, 6.

25. On Manchuria tourism in 1930s and 1940s, see Kō En, "'Rakudo' o hashiru kankō basu: 1930 nendai no 'Manshū' toshi to teikoku no doramaturugī" [A tour bus in 'paradise': 'Manchurian' cities in the 1930s and the dramaturgy of the empire], in *Iwanami kōza kindai nihon no bunka shi 6: Kakudai suru modanitī*, ed. Yoshimi Shunya, et al., 215–53 (Tokyo: Iwanami shoten, 2002); and Kenneth J. Ruoff, *Imperial Japan at Its Zenith: The Wartime Celebration of the Empire's 2,600th Anniversary* (Ithaca, NY: Cornell University Press, 2010).

26. "Shōwa jūyonendo mansen shūgaku ryokōki (bunka yonen)" [Diary from the school trip to Manchuria and Korea in Showa 14 (senior in the Humanities)], August 28, 1939, Nara Women's University Archive (Kōshi kankei shiryō), no. 96, electronic document, http://www.nara-wu.ac.jp/nensi/96.htm, accessed May 20, 2007.

27. Fukushō Kakō Kabushiki Gaisha [Fukushō Chinese Labor Corporation], "Hekizansō" (brochure), 1929.

28. Fukushō Kakō Kabushiki Gaisha, "Hekizansō," 3.

29. Fukushō Kakō Kabushiki Gaisha, "Hekizansō," 3.

30. Fukushō Kakō Kabushiki Gaisha, "Hekizansō," 16.

31. Yanagisawa, "Dairen futō" [Dalian port].

32. Liu Yi, "Jinzhou you qinhua rijun xijun shiyanchang: Wang Xuan lai lian xunchu yiduan xian wei ren zhi de lishi" [In Jinzhou exists the Japanese Army germ experimentation site: Wang Xuan's visit to Dalian discovers little known history], *Dalian ribao* [Dalian Daily] (Dalian, China), April 26, 2003, 1.

33. On chemical-germ warfare by the Imperial Japanese Army, see Jing-Bao Nie, Nanyan Guo, Mark Selden, and Arthur Kleinman, eds., *Japan's Wartime Medical Atrocities: Comparative Inquiries in Science, History, and Ethics* (New York: Routledge, 2010); Yoshimi Yoshiaki, *Dokugasusen to nihongun* [Poison gas warfare and the Japanese Army] (Tokyo: Iwanami shoten, 2004); Awaya Kentarō and Yoshimi Yoshiaki, eds., *Dokugasu sen kankei shiryō* [Source materials on poison gas warfare] (Tokyo: Fuji shuppan, 1989); Bu Ping, ed., *Huaxue zhan* [Chemical warfare], Riben qinhua xin zuizheng xilie congshu, ed. Bu Ping and Xin Peilin (Haerbin, China: Heilongjiang renmin chubanshe, 1997).

34. On the Pingdingshan Massacre, see Honda Katsuichi, *Chūgoku no tabi* [Journey through China] (Tokyo: Asahi shinbunsha, 1972); and Inoue Hisashi and Kawakami Shirō, eds., *Heichōzan jiken shiryōshū* [Source materials on Pingdingshan Massacre] (Tokyo: Kashiwa shobō, 2012).

35. This is similar to Andreas Huyssen's depiction of historical museums as a "burial chamber of the past." See his *Twilight Memories: Marking Time in a Culture of Amnesia* (New York: Routledge, 1995), 15.

36. Hou Xiaoyun, "Gexing Wang Xuan de 'nüren weier'" [Wang Xuan's "feminine" personality], *Bandao Chenbao* [Peninsula Morning News] (Dalian, China), April 26, 2003, 4.

37. For an ethnographic study of China's new rich, see John Osburg, *Anxious Wealth: Money and Morality among China's New Rich* (Stanford, California: Stanford University Press, 2013).

38. Hou, "Gexing Wang Xuan de 'nüren weier.'"

39. Yu Linan and Liu Jia, "'Lujun bingyuan' shi wei wangong de xijun shiyanchang: Wang Xuan Dalian xunzheng gongzuo you xinjinzhan" ['Army Hospital' was the unfinished germ experimentation site: A new development in Wang Xuan's evidence-gathering visit in Dalian], *Xinshangbao* [New Business News] (Dalian, China), April 26, 2003, 6.

40. For example, Janis Mimura examines the role of the reform bureaucrats in the construction and management of Manchukuo. See Janis Mimura, *Planning for Empire: Reform Bureaucrats and the Japanese Wartime State* (Ithaca, NY: Cornell University Press, 2011).

41. Such discrepancy and the linkage between the two usages of *renzhen* exemplify what Rey Chow calls "entanglements," which "keep things apart" while "hold[ing] things together." See Rey Chow, *Entanglements, or Transmedial Thinking about Capture* (Durham, NC: Duke University Press, 2012), 12.

42. Hannah Arendt's observation of the trial of Nazi high official Adolf Eichmann captures this tension between instrumental and substantive reason, which creates a gap between conscientious individuals and collective outcomes. Arendt's analysis finds a middling, diligent bureaucrat who is aware above all of being conscientious when it comes to his duty, thus producing pride in his work that contributes to a brutal collective outcome. See Hannah Arendt, *Eichmann in Jerusalem: A Report on the Banality of Evil* (New York: Viking Press, 1963).

Japanese historian Yoshimi Yoshiaki examines a similar tension decades later and chronicles how ordinary Japanese became both the victims and active participants of Japanese fascism. See *Kusa no ne no fasizumu: Nihon minshū no sensō taiken* [Grassroots Fascism: The War Experience of the Japanese People] (Tokyo: University of Tokyo Press, 1987), which is translated into English under the same title: Yoshiaki Yoshimi, *Grassroots Fascism: The War Experience of the Japanese People*, trans. Ethan Mark (New York: Columbia University Press, 2015).

43. As I discussed briefly in the introductory section, Theodor Adorno, in his observation of postwar West Germany in the 1950s, argued that the slogan of coming to terms with the past only led to the effacement of memory unless it also addressed the objective social reality that disavows autonomous individuals. A response to this effect of the "force of the collective" within modern society is what he sought in the task of coming to terms with the past. See Adorno, "What Does Coming to Terms with the Past Mean?"

44. For an insightful analysis of public debates surrounding apology, see Norma Field, "War and Apology: Japan, Asia, the Fiftieth, and After," *positions: east asia cultures critique* 5, no. 1 (1997): 1–49; and Alexis Dudden, *Troubled Apologies among Japan, Korea, and the United States* (New York: Columbia University Press, 2008).

45. In spite of the rich literature on the history of the Japanese invasion of China, the topic of collaboration remains an underexplored area of study, despite the fact that such inquiries are essential for understanding the nature of colonial modernity and its afterlife. A few recent works in English fill this glaring gap. See Timothy Brook, *Collaboration: Japanese Agents and Local Elites in Wartime China* (Cambridge, MA: Harvard University Press, 2005); Poshek Fu, *Passivity, Resistance, and Collaboration: Intellectual Choices in Occupied Shanghai, 1937–1945* (Stanford, CA: Stanford University Press, 1993); and Rana Mitter, *The Manchurian Myth: Nationalism, Resistance, and Collaboration in Modern China* (Berkeley: University of California Press, 2000).

CHAPTER SIX

1. On July 22, 1989, construction workers unearthed the remains of more than a hundred human individuals at the construction site for the new National Institute of Health building in Shinjuku. Since the site was once that of the Japanese Army Medical College and only steps away from the former laboratory of Ishii Shirō, who taught bacteriology at the college and was in charge of the Unit 731 human biological experimentation site in Northeast China, speculation emerged that the remains belonged to victims of human experiments by the Japanese Army. Suspicion intensified when the Japanese government ordered the Shinjuku Ward office to cremate and bury the remains without delay. A group of citizens organized a movement to preserve the remains for further examination and filed a lawsuit on September 2, 1993 (Heisei 5 [gyō u] No. 244), which Tanaka and other lawyers represented. The case eventually went to the Supreme Court (Heisei 8 [gyō tsu] No. 67), which ruled against the plaintiffs on December 19, 2000.

2. "Negative inheritance" (*fu no isan*) is a vernacular Japanese term often used to refer to unaccounted-for pasts stemming from Japanese imperialism. In Chinese, such remainders are often referred to as "Second World War remainder issues" (*erzhan yiliu wenti*) or "postwar remainder issues" (*zhanhou yiliu wenti*).

3. Cathy Caruth, *Unclaimed Experience: Trauma, Narrative, and History* (Baltimore, MD: Johns Hopkins University Press, 1996), 24.

4. Using the lens of gender analysis, Hyunah Yang problematizes this slippage. She shows how the voices of former Korean comfort women were constructed within the sexualized national framework. See Hyunah Yang, "Re-Membering the Korean Military Comfort Women: Nationalism, Sexuality, and Silence," in *Dangerous Women: Gender and Korean Nationalism*, ed. Elaine H. Kim and Chugmoo Choi, 123–39 (New York: Routledge, 2008).

5. In their analysis of the appropriation of the Other's suffering, Arthur and Joan Kleinman critically examine how trauma stories become the symbolic capital to mobilize physical resources and to establish the figure of the victim. Likewise, Jean and John Comaroff observe that the recent global proliferation of legal redress for past violence has turned sufferings and pain into "political currency." The economy of debt depicted in my ethnography demonstrates the circulation of this symbolic currency at the micro- and macroaxes of national inheritance. See Arthur Kleinman and Joan Kleinman, "The Appeal of Experience; The Dismay of Images: Cultural Appropriations of Suffering in Our

Times," in *Social Suffering*, ed. Arthur Kleinman, Veena Das, and Margaret Lock, 1–23 (Berkeley: University of California Press, 1997); and Jean Comaroff and John L. Comaroff, *Theory from the South: Or, How Euro-America Is Evolving toward Africa* (Boulder: Paradigm, 2012), 147.

6. China was not the only victim nation that prioritized formal economy over moral economy in pursuit of wealth accumulation. Similar to the 1972 Joint Communiqué between PRC and Japan, the South Korean government renounced its right to claim reparation from Japan in exchange for future economic cooperation arrangements in the 1965 treaty between South Korea and Japan ("Treaty on Basic Relations between Japan and the Republic of Korea" and the accompanying "Agreement between Japan and the Republic of Korea Concerning the Settlement of Problems in Regard to Property and Claims and Economic Cooperation").

7. Ann Stoler underscores the dimension of action in her use of a verb rather than a noun in presenting processes of ruination and imperial debris: "Our focus is less on the noun *ruin* than on 'ruination' as an active, ongoing process that allocates imperial debris differentially and *ruin* as a violent verb that unites apparently disparate moments, places, and objects." Ann Laura Stoler, "Introduction: 'The Rot Remains': From Ruins to Ruination," in *Imperial Debris: On Ruins and Ruination*, ed. Ann Laura Stoler, 1–35 (Durham, NC: Duke University Press, 2013), 7.

8. As I have explained, my exploration of the concept of inheritance in relation to betrayal is inspired by Jacques Derrida's search for the specters of Marx at the moment of the demise of socialism in Europe. See Jacques Derrida, *Specters of Marx: The State of the Debt, the Work of Mourning, and the New International*, trans. Gayatri Chakravorty Spivak, corrected ed. (New York: Routledge, 1994).

9. Theodor W. Adorno, "What Does Coming to Terms with the Past Mean?" in *Bitburg in Moral and Political Perspective*, ed. Geoffrey H. Hartman, 114–29 (Bloomington: Indiana University Press, 1986).

10. On China's recent global expansion, see Elizabeth C. Economy and Michael Levi, *By All Means Necessary: How China's Resource Quest Is Changing the World* (New York: Oxford University Press, 2014); Howard W. French, *China's Second Continent: How a Million Migrants Are Building a New Empire in Africa* (New York: Knopf, 2014); Ching Kwan Lee, "Raw Encounters: Chinese Managers, African Workers, and the Politics of Casualization in Africa's Chinese Enclaves," *The China Quarterly* 199 (2009): 647–66; Barry Sautman and Hairong Yan, "African Perspectives on China-Africa Links," *The China Quarterly* 199 (2009): 728–59; David Shambaugh, *China Goes Global: The Partial Power* (New York: Oxford University Press, 2013); and Odd Arne Westad, *Restless Empire: China and the World Since 1750* (New York: Basic Books, 2012).

11. Reported on July 16, 2014, on *Yomiuri Shimbun* online: http://www.yomiuri.co.jp/economy/20140715-OYT1T50208.html, accessed on July 17, 2014.

12. The case was originally filed in the Tokyo District Court on January 25, 2007 (Heisei 19 [wa] No. 1441), and the court denied the plaintiffs' claims on May 24, 2010. On September 21, 2012, the Tokyo High Court rejected the plaintiffs' claims (Heisei 22 [ne] No. 4283). The Supreme Court of Japan dismissed the appeal on October 28, 2014.

The case is one of several lawsuits filed by Chinese civilian victims, who seek compensation through the Japanese legal system for deaths and injuries—estimated at more than 2,000 cases throughout China—caused by deadly remainders of Japanese imperialism in China after Japan's defeat in 1945.

13. Tokyo High Court decision (Heisei 22 [ne] No. 4283), 4–51.

14. Tokyo High Court decision (Heisei 22 [ne] No. 4283), 51–55.

15. Tokyo High Court decision (Heisei 22 [ne] No. 4283), 55–81.

16. Tokyo High Court decision (Heisei 22 [ne] No. 4283), 58 and 68.

17. Tokyo High Court decision (Heisei 22 [ne] No. 4283), 58.

18. Tokyo High Court decision (Heisei 22 [ne] No. 4283), 72.

19. Tokyo High Court decision (Heisei 22 [ne] No. 4283), 62–67.

20. The lawyers representing the Qiqihar victims go into detail pointing out the Japanese state's inaction but have no words for the role of the Chinese counterpart. The court document that the plaintiffs' lawyers submitted only points out, instead, that in June 1987 at the Conference on Disarmament in Geneva, the Chinese government argued that those countries that had abandoned chemical weapons had responsibility for disposing them. While China did not name Japan, this prompted the two countries to initiate discussion on this topic. The lawyers' documents further note that in August 1990, the Chinese government officially requested the Japanese government to resolve the issue. This resulted in the first Sino-Japanese Specialist Meeting in September 1993. During the second meeting in September 1994, the Chinese delegation framed the issue as an *economic* issue: "The way in which the issue is addressed is not timely enough, and we request that the Japanese government accelerate the pace. This issue is affecting the economic construction since the issue is sensitive as we anticipate further damage if the issue is left unaddressed, which can damage the national sentiment. We thus wish the Japanese side to understand the urgency of the matter."

21. Parallel to what Eric Santner reveals in his analysis of the inability to mourn in postwar Germany, the pronoun *we* bears the scars of history for the Japanese. See Eric L. Santner, *Stranded Objects: Mourning, Memory, and Film in Postwar Germany* (Ithaca, NY: Cornell University Press, 1990).

22. I would like to thank the anonymous reviewer from the Weatherhead Series for pointing out this aspect of the term *renzhen* and for directing me to explore tensions contained within asymmetrical truth claims among victims and perpetrators.

23. In her exploration of victimhood through the twin conceptual lenses of mimesis and sacrifice, Rey Chow points to the duplicity contained within the sacred. Her observation that sanctified victimhood could lead to sacrifice (a form of abandonment) echoes the duplicity expressed in the abandonment and the evasion of accountability resulting from the adherence to victimhood in a pure sanctified form. See Rey Chow, *Entanglements, or Transmedial Thinking about Capture* (Durham, NC: Duke University Press, 2012), especially chapter 4, "Sacrifice, Mimesis, and the Theorizing of Victimhood," 81–105.

24. On March 18, 2014, the Beijing No. 1 Intermediate People's Court officially accepted the lawsuit submitted on February 26, 2014, by a group of forty wartime forced-labor victims and their bereaved family members, who seek compensation and apologies from Mitsubishi Material Corporation and Nippon Coke and Engineering Company (formerly Mitsui Mining).

This development in China follows a similar but even more dramatic shift that took place within the South Korean judiciary. Ever since the landmark decision by the South Korean Constitutional Court in 2011 to declare unconstitutional the South Korean government's prohibition on individual compensation claims by its citizens against Japan, some Korean plaintiffs who lost in the forced-labor cases in Japan have filed and won cases in the South Korean courts in quick succession, and more cases are yet to come. A different gate of law is now open to South Korean victims in their home country, allowing them to stand before the law within their jurisdiction. This new development in South Korea has spurred renewed interest among Chinese victims, lawyers, and activists to seek legal redress within Chinese jurisdiction. For the South Korean landmark case at the Constitutional Court, see "Challenge against Act of Omission Involving Article 3 of the 'Agreement on the Settlement of Problem Concerning Property and Claims and the Economic Cooperation between the Republic of Korea and Japan'" (23-2[A] KCCR 366, *2006Hun-Ma788*, August 30, 2011). See also another landmark decision by the Supreme Court of Korea on May 24, 2012 (*2009Da22549*), which echoed the 2011 South Korean Constitutional Court decision in recognizing the individual rights to claim compensation from Japan.

25. These cases were submitted to Hebei High Court on December 27, 2000 (forced-labor case), Zhejiang High Court on May 12, 2003 (biological-warfare case), Shanghai High Court on September 5, 2003 (forced-labor case), Shandong High Court on September 16, 2010 (forced-labor case), and Chongqing High Court on September 10, 2012 (air-raid case). In one of these cases involving a major Japanese corporation, after the court refused to accept the case, the lead Chinese lawyer for the plaintiffs was pressured by a high-ranking local government official, who expressed strong concerns that such a lawsuit might jeopardize ongoing negotiations with this corporation to invest in the region. Many plaintiffs in the compensation lawsuits shared with me how until very recently they had received various forms of threats from the Chinese authorities, so much so that they felt the need to change their phone numbers frequently. Such incidents point to how formal economy was often prioritized over moral economy.

26. On the legal structure of abandonment and duplicity after empire in East Asia, see Yukiko Koga, "Between the Law: The Unmaking of Empire and Law's Imperial Amnesia," *Law and Social Inquiry* 41, issue 2 (Spring 2016): 402–34.

BIBLIOGRAPHY

Abbas, Ackbar. *Hong Kong: Culture and the Politics of Disappearance*. Minneapolis: University of Minnesota Press, 1997.

Adorno, Theodor W. "What Does Coming to Terms with the Past Mean?" In *Bitburg in Moral and Political Perspective*, edited by Geoffrey H. Hartman, 114–29. Bloomington: Indiana University Press, 1986.

Allison, Anne. *Nightwork: Sexuality, Pleasure, and Corporate Masculinity in a Tokyo Hostess Club*. Chicago: University of Chicago Press, 1994.

———. *Precarious Japan*. Durham, NC: Duke University Press, 2013.

Anagnost, Ann. "The Corporeal Politics of Quality (*Suzhi*)." *Public Culture* 16, no. 2 (2004): 189–208.

———. *National Past-Times: Narrative, Representation, and Power in Modern China*. Durham, NC: Duke University Press, 1997.

Aoki Fukiko. *731*. Tokyo: Shinchōsha, 2005.

Arakawa Naoki. *Chūgoku de seizōgyō wa fukkatsu suru: Tōshiba dairensha no chōsen* [Revival of the manufacturing industry: Challenges of Toshiba Dalian]. Tokyo: Mita shuppankai, 1998.

Arendt, Hannah. *Eichmann in Jerusalem: A Report on the Banality of Evil*. New York: Viking Press, 1963.

Asano Toyomi. *Sengo Nihon no baishō mondai to Higashi Ajia chiiki saihen: Seikyūken to rekishi ninshiki mondai no kigen* [Japanese postwar reparation and reconfiguration of East Asia region: Right to claim reparation and the origin of historical consciousness problem]. Tokyo: Jigakusha shuppan, 2013.

Awaya Kentarō and Yoshimi Yoshiaki, eds. *Dokugasu sen kankei shiryō* [Source materials on poison gas warfare]. Tokyo: Fuji shuppan, 1989.

Bach, Jonathan. "Modernity and the Urban Imagination in Economic Zones." *Theory, Culture, and Society* 28, no. 5 (2011): 98–122.

———. "'The Taste Remains': Consumption, (N)ostalgia, and the Production of East Germany." *Public Culture* 14, no. 3 (Fall 2002): 545–56.

———. "'They Come in Peasants and Leave Citizens': Urban Villages and the Making of Shenzhen, China." *Cultural Anthropology* 25, no. 3 (2010): 425–58.

Barkan, Elazar. *The Guilt of the Nations: Restitution and Negotiating Historical Injustices*. New York: W. W. Norton, 2000.

Barlow, Tani E. "~~Colonialism~~'s Career in Postwar China Studies." *positions: east asia cultures critique* 1, no. 1 (1993): 224–67.

———. "Debates over Colonial Modernity in East Asian and Another Alternative." *Cultural Studies* 26, no. 5 (2012): 617–44.

———, ed. *Formations of Colonial Modernity in East Asia*. Durham, NC: Duke University Press, 1997.

———. "Introduction: On 'Colonial Modernity.'" In *Formations of Colonial Modernity in East Asia*, edited by Barlow, 1–20. Durham, NC: Duke University Press, 1997.

Bi Zhiwei and Liu Yi. "Wang Xuan jinri lai lian diaocha quzheng: Souji Riben xijunzhan zuie zhengju, wei wugu shouhaizhe shenzheng zhengyi" [Wang Xuan to arrive in Dalian for an evidence gathering trip: Investigating the evidence of the crimes of the Japanese biological warfare in order to extend justice to innocent victims]. *Dalian ribao* [Dalian Daily] (Dalian, China), April 23, 2003, 1.

Bissell, William Cunningham. "Engaging Colonial Nostalgia." *Cultural Anthropology* 20, no. 2 (2005): 215–48.

Bix, Herbert P. "Japanese Imperialism and the Manchurian Economy, 1900–31." *The China Quarterly* 51 (July–September 1972): 425–43.

Boym, Svetlana. *The Future of Nostalgia*. New York: Basic Books, 2001.

Breen, John, ed. *Yasukuni, the War Dead and the Struggle for Japan's Past*. New York: Columbia University Press, 2008.

Brook, Timothy. *Collaboration: Japanese Agents and Local Elites in Wartime China*. Cambridge, MA: Harvard University Press, 2005.

Brooks, Barbara J. *Japan's Imperial Diplomacy: Consuls, Treaty Ports, and War in China, 1895–1938*. Honolulu: University of Hawai'i Press, 2000.

Buck, David D. "Railway City and National Capital: Two Faces of the Modern in Changchun." In *Remaking the Chinese City: Modernity and National Identity, 1900–1950*, edited by Joseph W. Esherick, 65–89. Honolulu: University of Hawai'i Press, 2000.

Bu Ping, ed. *Huaxue zhan* [Chemical warfare]. Riben qinhua xin zuizheng xilie congshu [Series on the new evidence on the Japanese invasion of China], edited by Bu Ping and Xin Peilin. Haerbin, China: Heilongjiang renmin chubanshe, 1997.

Buruma, Ian. *Wages of Guilt: Memories of War in Germany and Japan*. New York: Farrar, Straus, Giroux, 1994.

Campos, Michelle U. *Ottoman Brothers: Muslims, Christians, and Jews in Early Twentieth-Century Palestine*. Stanford, CA: Stanford University Press, 2010.

Cao Haidong and Huang Xiaowei. "Riben dui Hua yuanzhu san shi nian" [Thirty years of Japan's aid to China]. *Nanfang zhoumo* [Southern weekly], February 20, 2008. http://www.infzm.com/content/7707.

Carter, James H. *Creating a Chinese Harbin: Nationalism in an International City, 1916–1932*. Ithaca, NY: Cornell University Press, 2002.

Caruth, Cathy. *Unclaimed Experience: Trauma, Narrative, and History*. Baltimore, MD: Johns Hopkins University Press, 1996.

Chang, Iris. *The Rape of Nanking: The Forgotten Holocaust of World War II*. New York: Penguin Books, 1997.

Chari, Sharad, and Katherine Verdery. "Thinking between the Posts: Postcolonialism, Postsocialism, and Ethnography after the Cold War." *Comparative Studies in Society and History* 51, no. 1 (2009): 6–34.

Chen, Nancy N., Constance D. Clark, Suzanne Z. Gottschang, and Lyn Jeffery, eds. *China Urban: Ethnographies of Contemporary Culture*. Durham, NC: Duke University Press, 2001.

Chen, Kuan-Hsing. *Asia as Method: Toward Deimperialization*. Durham, NC: Duke University Press, 2010.

Chiasson, Blaine R. *Administering the Colonizer: Manchuria's Russians under Chinese Rule, 1918–29*. Vancouver: UBC Press, 2010.

Chikyū no arukikata: Dairen to Chūgoku tōhoku Chihō, 1999–2000 [How to walk around the globe: Dalian and Northeast China]. Tokyo: Diamond biggu sha, 1999.

Ching, Leo. *Becoming "Japanese": Colonial Taiwan and the Politics of Identity Formation*. Berkeley: University of California Press, 2000.

———. "'Give Me Japan and Nothing Else!': Postcoloniality, Identity, and the Traces of Colonialism." *The South Atlantic Quarterly* 99, no. 4 (2000): 763–88.

Cho, Mun Young. *The Specter of the People: Urban Poverty in Northeast China*. Ithaca, NY: Cornell University Press, 2013.

Choi, Chungmoo. "The Discourse of Decolonization and Popular Memory: South Korea." *positions: east asia cultures critique* 1, no. 1 (1993): 77–102.

Chou, Shun-hsin. "Railway Development and Economic Growth in Manchuria." *The China Quarterly* 45 (January–March 1972): 57–84.

Chow, Rey. *Entanglements, or Transmedial Thinking about Capture*. Durham, NC: Duke University Press, 2012.

Chu, Julie Y. *Cosmologies of Credit: Transnational Mobility and the Politics of Destination in China*. Durham, NC: Duke University Press, 2010.

Clausen, Søren, and Stig Thøgersen. *The Making of a Chinese City: History and Historiography in Harbin*. Armonk, NY: M. E. Sharpe, 1995.

Coble, Parks M. "China's 'New Remembering' of the Anti-Japanese War of Resistance, 1937–1945." *The China Quarterly* 190 (2007): 394–410.

Cole, Jennifer. "The Work of Memory in Madagascar." *American Ethnologist* 25, no. 4 (1998): 610–33.

Collins, John. "Ruins, Redemption, and Brazil's Imperial Exception." In *Imperial Debris: On Ruins and Ruination*, edited by Ann Laura Stoler, 162–93. Durham, NC: Duke University Press, 2013.

Comaroff, Jean, and John Comaroff. *Of Revelation and Revolution, Vol. 1: Christianity, Colonialism, and Consciousness in South Africa*. Chicago: University of Chicago Press, 1991.

———. *Theory from the South: Or, How Euro-America Is Evolving toward Africa*. Boulder: Paradigm, 2012.

Cooper, Frederick. *Citizenship between Empire and Nation: Remaking France and French Africa, 1945–1960*. Princeton, NJ: Princeton University Press, 2014.

Coronil, Fernando. "After Empire: Reflections on Imperialism from the Americas." In *Imperial Formations*, edited by Ann Laura Stoler, Carole McGranahan, and Peter C. Perdue, 241–71. Santa Fe, NM: School for Advanced Research Press, 2007.

———. "Editor's Column: The End of Postcolonial Theory? A Roundtable with Sunil Agnani, Fernando Coronil, Gaurav Desai, Mamadou Diouf, Simon Gikandi, Susie Tharu, and Jennifer Wenzel." *Publications of the Modern Language Association* 122, no. 3 (2007): 633–51.

Dalian kaifaqu zhaoshang zhongxin [Dalian Foreign Investment Service Center]. "Dairen kaihatsuku toushi annai 2004 nen, Riwenban" [Dalian development zone investment guide 2004, Japanese version].

Dalian shi duiwai maoyi jingji hezuo ju [Dalian Foreign Trade and Economic Cooperation Bureau]. "Dairenshi toushi gaido" [Dalian investment guide]. n.d.

Dalian shi shizhi bangongshi [Dalian City Gazetteer Office], ed. *Kaishi quanmian jianshe shehui zhuyi shiqi de Dalian, 1957.1–1966.4* [Dalian during the early period of total construction of socialism, 1957.1–1966.4]. Zhonggong Dalian dangshi ziliao congshu [Collective works on the Dalian Chinese Communist Party history], edited by Dalian shi shizhi bangongshi, vol. 11. Dalian, China: Dalian chubanshe, 1998.

Das, Veena. *Life and Words: Violence and the Descent into the Ordinary*. Foreword by Stanley Cavell. Berkeley: University of California Press, 2007.

Davies, David J. "Old Zhiqing Photos: Nostalgia and the 'Spirit' of the Cultural Revolution." *The China Review* 5, no. 2 (Fall 2005): 97–123.

Denton, Kirk A. "Horror and Atrocity: Memory of Japanese Imperialism in Chinese Museums." In *Re-envisioning the Chinese Revolution: The Politics and Poetics of Collective Memories in Reform China*, edited by Ching Kwan Lee and Guobin Yang, 245–86. Stanford, CA: Stanford University Press, 2007.

Derrida, Jacques. *Given Time: I. Counterfeit Money*. Translated by Peggy Kamuf. Chicago: University of Chicago Press, 1991.

———. *Specters of Marx: The State of the Debt, the Work of Mourning, and the New International*. Translated by Peggy Kamuf. New York: Routledge, 1994.

Dirks, Nicholas B. *Castes of Mind: Colonialism and the Making of Modern India*. Princeton, NJ: Princeton University Press, 2001.

———. "History as a Sign of Modern." *Public Culture* 2, no. 2 (Spring 1990): 25–32.

Dirlik, Arif. "'Past Experience, If Not Forgotten, Is a Guide to the Future'; or, What Is in a Text? The Politics of History in Chinese-Japanese Relations." In *Japan in the World*, edited by Masao Miyoshi and H. D. Harootunian, 49–78. Durham, NC: Duke University Press, 1993.

———. "The Postcolonial Aura: Third World Criticism in the Age of Global Capitalism." *Critical Inquiry* 20 (Winter 1994): 328–56.

Dolar, Mladen. "'I Shall Be with You on Your Wedding-Night': Lacan and the Uncanny." *October* 58 (Fall 1991): 5–23.

Dower, John W. *Embracing Defeat: Japan in the Wake of World War II*. New York: W. W. Norton, 2000.

———. *Ways of Forgetting, Ways of Remembering: Japan in the Modern World*. New York: New Press, 2012.

Draper, Nicholas. *The Price of Emancipation: Slave-Ownership, Compensation and British Society at the End of Slavery*. New York: Cambridge University Press, 2013.

Driscoll, Mark. *Absolute Erotic, Absolute Grotesque: The Living, Dead, and Undead in Japan's Imperialism, 1895–1945*. Durham, NC: Duke University Press, 2010.

Drucker, Peter F. "The End of Japan, Inc.? An Economic Monolith Fractures." *Foreign Affairs* 72, no. 2 (Spring 1993): 10–15.

Duan Guangda and Ji Fenghui. *Lishi huimou: Ershi shiji de Haerbin* [Glancing back at history: Twentieth-century Harbin]. 3 vols. Vol. 1. Harbin, China: Haerbin chubanshe, 1998.

Duara, Prasenjit. "Introduction: The Decolonization of Asia and African in the Twentieth Century." In *Decolonization: Perspectives from Now and Then*, edited by Prasenjit Duara, 1–18. New York: Routledge, 2004.

———. *Rescuing History from the Nation: Questioning Narratives of Modern China*. Chicago: University of Chicago Press, 1995.

———. *Sovereignty and Authenticity: Manchukuo and the East Asian Modern*. Lanham, MD: Rowman and Littlefield, 2003.

Dudden, Alexis. *Troubled Apologies among Japan, Korea, and the United States*. New York: Columbia University Press, 2008.

Duus, Peter, Ramon H. Myers, and Mark R. Peattie, eds. *The Japanese Informal Empire in China, 1895–1937*. Princeton, NJ: Princeton University Press, 1989.

Economy, Elizabeth C., and Michael Levi. *By All Means Necessary: How China's Resource Quest Is Changing the World*. New York: Oxford University Press, 2014.

Edelman, Marc. "E. P. Thompson and Moral Economies." In *A Companion to Moral Anthropology*, edited by Didier Fassin, 49–66. Oxford: Wiley-Blackwell, 2012.

Elkins, Caroline. *Imperial Reckoning: The Untold Story of Britain's Gulag in Kenya*. New York: Henry Holt, 2005.

Elkins, Caroline, and Susan Pedersen, eds. *Settler Colonialism in the Twentieth Century: Projects, Practices, Legacies*. New York: Routledge, 2005.

Elliott, Mark C. "Chuantong Zhongguo shi yi ge diguo ma?" [Was the traditional China an empire?]. *Dushu* (Beijing), January 2014, 29–40.

———. *The Manchu Way: The Eight Banners and Ethnic Identity in Late Imperial China*. Stanford, CA: Stanford University Press, 2001.

Esherick, Joseph W., ed. *Remaking the Chinese City: Modernity and National Identity, 1900–1950*. Honolulu: University of Hawai'i Press, 2000.

Evensky, Jerry. "Retrospectives: Ethics and the Invisible Hand." *Journal of Economic Perspectives* 7, no. 2 (1993): 197–205.

Faier, Lieba, and Lisa Rofel. "Ethnographies of Encounter." *Annual Review of Anthropology* 43 (2014): 363–77.

Farquhar, Judith. *Appetites: Food and Sex in Post-Socialist China*. Durham, NC: Duke University Press, 2002.

Fassin, Didier "Compassion and Repression: The Moral Economy of Immigration Policies in France." *Cultural Anthropology* 20, no. 3 (2005): 362–87

Fassin, Didier, and Richard Rechtman. "Compassion and Repression: The Moral Economy of Immigration Policies in France." *Cultural Anthropology* 20, no. 3 (2005): 362–87.

———. *The Empire of Trauma: An Inquiry into the Condition of Victimhood*. Translated by Rachel Gomme. Princeton, NJ: Princeton University Press, 2009.

Field, Norma. "War and Apology: Japan, Asia, the Fiftieth, and After." *positions: east asia cultures critique* 5, no. 1 (1997): 1–49.

Fogel, Joshua A., ed. *The Nanjing Massacre in History and Historiography*. Berkeley: University of California Press, 2000.

Fong, Vanessa L. "Morality, Cosmopolitanism, or Academic Attainment? Discourses on 'Quality' and Urban Chinese-Only-Children's Claims to Ideal Personhood." *City and Society* 19, no. 1 (2007): 86–113.

———. *Only Hope: Coming of Age under China's One-Child Policy*. Stanford, CA: Stanford University Press, 2004.

———. *Paradise Redefined: Transnational Chinese Students and the Quest for Flexible Citizenship in the Developed World*. Stanford, CA: Stanford University Press, 2011.

Foucault, Michel. "Of Other Spaces." Translated by Jay Miskowiec. *Diacritics* 16, no. 1 (Spring 1986): 22–27.

Fraser, Davis. "Inventing Oasis: Luxury Housing Advertisements in Reconfiguring Domestic Space in Shanghai." In *The Consumer Revolution in Urban China*, edited by Deborah Davis, 25–53. Berkeley: University of California Press, 2000.

French, Howard W. *China's Second Continent: How a Million Migrants Are Building a New Empire in Africa*. New York: Knopf, 2014.

Freud, Sigmund. "The 'Uncanny.'" In *The Standard Edition of the Complete Psychological Works of Sigmund Freud*, vol. 17, edited by James Strachey, 217–56. London: Hogarth Press, 1955.

Friedmann, John. *China's Urban Transition*. Minneapolis: University of Minnesota Press, 2005.

Fu, Poshek. *Passivity, Resistance, and Collaboration: Intellectual Choices in Occupied Shanghai, 1937–1945*. Stanford, CA: Stanford University Press, 1993.

Fujimori Terunobu and Wan Tan, eds. *Zenchōsa higashi Ajia kindai no toshi to kenchikū, 1840–1945* [A comprehensive study of East Asian architecture and urban planning, 1840–1945]. Tokyo: Chikuma shobō, 1996.

Fujitani, Takashi, Geoffrey M. White, and Lisa Yoneyama, eds. *Perilous Memories: The Asia-Pacific War(s)*. Durham, NC: Duke University Press, 2001.

Fujiwara Tei. *Nagareru hoshi wa ikite iru* [Shooting stars are alive]. Tokyo: Hibiya shuppan, 1949.

Fukushō kakō kabushiki gaisha [Fukushō Chinese Labor Corporation]. "Hekizansō" (brochure). 1929.

Gaimushō kanrikyoku [Ministry of Foreign Affairs Management Bureau]. *Kajin rōmusha shūrō jijō hōkoku (yōshi)* [The employment situation of Chinese laborers (summary)]. March 1946. Reproduced in *Chūgokujin kyōsei renkō shiryō* [Source material on the Chinese forced labor], edited by Tanaka Hiroshi and Matsuzawa Tetsunari. Tokyo: Gendai shokan, 1995.

Gallagher, Kevin, and Roberto Porzecanski. *The Dragon in the Room: China and the Future of Latin American Industrialization*. Stanford, CA: Stanford University Press, 2010.

Gallagher, Mary Elizabeth. *Contagious Capitalism: Globalization and the Politics of Labor in China*. Princeton, NJ: Princeton University Press, 2005.

Gamsa, Mark. "Harbin in Comparative Perspective." *Urban History* 37, no. 1 (2010): 136–49.

Gao Bo. *Dalianshi shehui he jingji fazhan gailan* [The overview of the social and economic development of Dalian]. Beijing: Zhongguo shangye chubanshe, 2002.

Gao Ling, Xiao Shuyuan, and Shi Fang. *Lishi huimou: Ershi shiji de Haerbin* [Glancing back at history: Twentieth-century Harbin]. 3 vols. Vol. 2. Harbin, China: Haerbin chubanshe, 1998.

Gao, Xiaoyan. *Nihongun no iki dokugas heiki: Chūgokujin higaisha wa uttaeru* [The chemical weapons abandoned by the Japanese Imperial Army: Appeals of Chinese victims]. Translated by Yamabe Yukiko and Miyazaki Kyōshirō. Tokyo: Akashi shoten, 1996.

Gendai yōgo henshūbu [Editorial department of contemporary terms], ed. *Gendai yōgo no kiso chishiki 2007* [Basic knowledge of contemporary terms 2007]. Tokyo: Jiyū kokuminsha, 2006.

Gluck, Carol. "The 'End' of the Postwar: Japan at the Turn of the Millennium." *Public Culture* 10, no. 1 (1997): 1–23.

———. "Operations of Memory: 'Comfort Women' and the World." In *Ruptured Histories: War, Memory, and the Post-Cold War in Asia*, edited by Sheila Miyoshi Jager and Rana Mitter, 47–77. Cambridge, MA: Harvard University Asia Center, 2007.

———. "The Past in the Present." In *Postwar Japan as History*, edited by Andrew Gordon, 64–95. Berkeley: University of California Press, 1993.

Gomikawa Junpei. *Ningen no jōken* [The human condition]. 6 vols. Tokyo: Bungei shunjū, 1979.

Gotō Mitsuo. "Nihonkoku kenpō seiteishi ni okeru 'Nihon kokumin' to 'gaikokujin'" ["Japanese people" and "foreigner" in the drafting of Japanese Constitution]. *Hikaku hōgaku* [Comparative law review] 45, no. 3 (2012): 1–28.

———. "Nihonkoku kenpō 10-jō: Kokusekihō to kyūshokuminchi shusshinsha" [Japanese Constitution Article 10: Japanese nationality law and former colonial subjects]. *Waseda shakai kagaku sōgō kenkyū* [Waseda studies in social sciences] 13, no. 3 (2013): 19–39.

Gottschang, Thomas R., and Diana Lary. *Swallows and Settlers: The Great Migration from North China to Manchuria*. Ann Arbor: University of Michigan Press, 2000.

Gries, Peter Hays. "China's 'New Thinking' on Japan." *The China Quarterly* 184 (2005): 831–50.

Gu Mingyi, Fang Jun, Ma Lifen, Wang Shengli, Zhang Qingshan, and Lü Linxiu, eds. *Dalian jin bainianshi* [A hundred-year modern history of Dalian]. Vols. 1–2 of *Diguo zhuyi qinlue Dalian shi congshu* [Collective works on the history of the imperialist invasion of Dalian], edited by Ma Lifen, et al. Shenyang, China: Liaoning renmin chubanshe, 1999.

Gu Wanchun and Li Rongxian. *Changchun chengshi bianqian* [The transformation of Changchun urban space]. Changchun, China: Changchun chubanshe, 1998.

Guo, Qinghua. "Changchun: Unfinished Capital Planning of Manzhouguo, 1932–42." *Urban History* 31, no. 1 (May 2004): 100–117.

———. "Shenyang: The Manchurian Ideal Capital City and Imperial Palace, 1625–43." *Urban History* 27, no. 3 (2000): 344–59.

Haerbinshi jianzhu weiyuanhui. *Sheng Suofeiya Jiaotang* [St. Sophia Cathedral]. Harbin, China: Haerbinshi jianzhu weiyuanhui, 1997.

Hairong, Yan. *New Masters, New Servants: Migration, Development, and Women Workers in China*. Durham, NC: Duke University Press, 2008.

Han, Clara. *Life in Debt: Times of Care and Violence in Neoliberal Chile*. Berkeley: University of California Press, 2012.

Harootunian, Harry. "Japan's Long Postwar: The Trick of Memory and the Ruse of History." *The South Atlantic Quarterly* 99, no. 4 (Fall 2000): 715–40.

———. *Overcome by Modernity: History, Culture, and Community in Interwar Japan*. Princeton, NJ: Princeton University Press, 2000.

Harris, Sheldon H. *Factories of Death: Japanese Biological Warfare, 1932–1945, and the American Cover-Up*. New York: Routledge, 1994.

Hashiya Hiroshi. "Sōru no kenchiku: Shokuminchika to kindaika" [Architecture in Seoul: Colonization and modernization]. In *Kindai Nihon to higashi Ajia: Kokusai kōryū saikō* [Modern Japan and East Asia: Reconsidering international exchange], edited by Yūzō Katō, 209–34. Tokyo: Chikuma shobō, 1995.

He Tianyi, ed. *Erzhan lu Ri Zhongguo laogong koushushi* [Oral history of Japanese-captured Chinese forced laborers during the Second World War]. 5 vols. Jinan, China: Qilu shushe, 2005.

He, Yinan. "Remembering and Forgetting the War: Elite Mythmaking, Mass Reaction, and Sino-Japanese Relations, 1950–2006." *History and Memory* 19, no. 2 (Fall 2007): 43–74.

———. *The Search for Reconciliation: Sino-Japanese and German-Polish Relations since World War II*. New York: Cambridge University Press, 2009.

Hein, Laura, and Mark Selden, eds. *Censoring History: Citizenship and Memory in Japan, Germany, and the United States*. Armonk, NY: M. E. Sharpe, 2000.

Hess, Christian A. "From Colonial Jewel to Socialist Metropolis: Dalian 1895–1955." PhD dissertation, University of California, San Diego, 2006.

———. "From Colonial Port to Socialist Metropolis: Imperialist Legacies and the Making of 'New Dalian.'" *Urban History* 38, no. 3 (December 2011): 373–90.

Hevia, James L. "Remembering the Century of Humiliation: The Yuanming Gardens and Dagu Forts Museums." In *Ruptured Histories: War, Memory, and the Post-Cold War in Asia*, edited by Sheila Miyoshi Jager and Rana Mitter, 192–208. Cambridge, MA: Harvard University Press, 2007.

Hirsch, Marianne. "The Generation of Postmemory." *Poetics Today* 29, no. 1 (2008): 103–28.

———. *The Generation of Postmemory: Writing and Visual Culture after the Holocaust*. New York: Columbia University Press, 2012.

———. "Surviving Images: Holocaust Photographs and the Work of Postmemory." *The Yale Journal of Criticism* 14, no. 1 (2001): 5–37.

Hoffman, Eva. *After Such Knowledge: Memory, History, and the Legacy of the Holocaust*. New York: Public Affairs, 2004.

Hoffman, Lisa M. "Autonomous Choices and Patriotic Professionalism: On Governmentality in Late-Socialist China." *Economy and Society* 35, no. 4 (November 2006): 550–70.

———. "Guiding College Graduates to Work: Social Constructions of Labor Markets in Dalian." In *China Urban: Ethnographies of Contemporary Culture*, edited by Nancy N. Chen, Constance D. Clark, Suzanne Z. Gottschang, and Lyn Jeffery, 43–66. Durham, NC: Duke University Press, 2001.

———. *Patriotic Professionalism in Urban China: Fostering Talent*. Philadelphia: Temple University Press, 2010.

———. "Urban Transformation and Professionalization: Translocality and Rationalities of Enterprise in Post-Mao China." In *Translocal China: Linkages, Identities, and the Reimagining of Space*, edited by Tim Oakes and Louisa Schein, 109–37. New York: Routledge, 2006.

Honda Katsuichi. *Chūgoku no tabi* [Journey through China]. Tokyo: Asahi shinbunsha, 1972.

Horkheimer, Max, and Theodor W. Adorno. *Dialectic of Enlightenment*. Translated by John Cumming. New York: Continuum, 1987.

Hou Xiaoyun. "Gexing Wang Xuan de 'nüren weier'" [Wang Xuan's "feminine" personality]. *Bandao chenbao* [Peninsula Morning News] (Dalian, China), April 26, 2003, 4.

Hsu, Carolyn L. *Creating Market Socialism: How Ordinary People Are Shaping Class and Status in China*. Durham, NC: Duke University Press, 2007.

Hubbert, Jennifer. "Revolution *Is* a Dinner Party: Cultural Revolution Restaurants in Contemporary China." *The China Review* 5, no. 2 (2005): 123–48.

Huo Liaoyuan and Cui Guoxi. *Cong lunxian dao jiefang: 1931 nian dao 1948 nian de Changchun* [From surrender to liberation: Changchun from 1931 to 1948]. Changchun wenshi ziliao, vol. 47. Changchun, China: "Changchun wenshi ziliao" bianjibu, 1995.

Huyssen, Andreas. *Twilight Memories: Marking Time in a Culture of Amnesia*. New York: Routledge, 1995.

Ide Magoroku. *Owarinaki tabi: "Chūgoku zanryū koji" no rekishi to genzai* [Endless journey: The history and the present of "Chūgoku zanryū koji"]. Tokyo: Iwanami shoten, 2004.

Igarashi, Yoshikuni. *Bodies of Memory: Narratives of War in Postwar Japanese Culture, 1945–1970*. Princeton, NJ: Princeton University Press, 2000.

Iida, Yumiko. "Between the Technique of Living an Endless Routine and the Madness of Absolute Degree Zero: Japanese Identity and the Crisis of Modernity in the 1990s." *positions: east asia cultures critique* 8, no. 2 (2000): 234–63.

Iijima Yōichi. *Ō no shintai toshi: Showa tennō no jidai to kenchiku* [The city as the emperor's body: The era of the Showa Emperor and its architecture]. Tokyo: Seidosha, 1996.

Inose Kenzō. *Tsūkon no sanga: Ashio dōzan Chūgokujin kyōsei renkō no kiroku* [Poignant landscape: The record of the Ashio copper mine Chinese forced labor]. Revised and enlarged edition. Utsunomiya, Japan: Zuisōsha, 1994 [1973].

Inoue Hisashi and Kawakami Shirō, eds. *Heichōzan jiken shiryōshū* [Source materials on Pingdingshan Massacre]. Tokyo: Kashiwa shobō, 2012.

Ishida Takeshi. *Kioku to bōkyaku no seijigaku: Dōka seisaku, sensō sekinin, shūgōteki kioku* [Political science of memory and forgetting: Assimilation policy, war responsibility, collective memory]. Tokyo: Akashi shoten, 2000.

Ivy, Marilyn. *Discourses of the Vanishing: Modernity, Phantasm, Japan*. Chicago: University of Chicago Press, 1995.

———. "Revenge and Recapitation in Recessionary Japan." *The South Atlantic Quarterly* 99, no. 4 (Fall 2000): 819–40.

Iwasaki Minoru and Takahashi Tetsuya. "Taidan: 'monogatari' no haikyo kara" [Discussion: From the ruins of "narratives"]. *Gendai shisō* 25, no. 8 (July 1997): 128–56.

Jacobs, Andrew. "China Is Wordless on Traumas of Communists' Rise." *New York Times*, October 2, 2009, A4.

Jager, Sheila Miyoshi, and Rana Mitter, eds. *Ruptured Histories: War, Memory, and the Post-Cold War in Asia*. Cambridge, MA: Harvard University Press, 2007.

Ji Fenghui. "Chengshi guangchang" [City square]. *Heilongjiang chenbao* (Harbin, China), May 8, 2002.

———. *Haerbin xungen* [The roots of Harbin]. Harbin, China: Haerbin chubanshe, 1996.

———. *Huashuo Haerbin* [Talk about Harbin]. Harbin, China: Heilongjiang renmin chubanshe, 2002.

———. "Zhuanjia wei wo shi bainian qingdian xianji" [Experts offer advice on our city's centenary celebration]. *Xinwanbao* (Harbin, China), December 14, 1994.

Kahn, Joseph. "Where's Mao? Chinese Revise History Books." *New York Times*, September 1, 2006, A1 and A6.

Kang Sang-jung. *Orientarizumu no kanata e: Kindai bunka hihan* [Beyond Orientalism: Critique of modern culture]. Tokyo: Iwanami shoten, 1996.

Karatani Kōjin, et al. "Kyōdō tōgi: Sekinin to shutai o megutte" [Discussion: On responsibilities and the subject]. *Hihyō kūkan* 2, no. 13 (April 1997): 6–40.

Karatoska, Paul H., ed. *Asian Labor in the Wartime Japanese Empire: Unknown Histories*. Armonk, NY: M. E. Sharpe, 2005.

Katō Norihiro. "Haisengo ron" [On postwar defeat]. *Gunzō* 50, no. 1 (January 1995): 252–94.

———. *Haisengo ron* [On postwar defeat]. Tokyo: Kōdansha, 1997.

Kawamura Minato. *Manshū hōkai: "daitōa bungaku" to sakkatachi* [The fall of Manchuria: "Great East Asian Prosperity literature" and its writers]. Tokyo: Bungei shunjū, 1997.

Keizai kikaku-chō [Economic Planning Agency]. *Keizai hakusho* [Economic white paper], July 19, 1956.

Kemen, Antoine. "Shenyang, Privatisation in the Vanguard of Chinese Socialism." In *Privatizing the State*, edited by Béatrice Hibou, 11–94. New York: Columbia University Press, 2004.

Kim, Elaine H., and Chungmoo Choi, eds. *Dangerous Women: Gender and Korean Nationalism*. New York: Routledge, 1998.

Kipnis, Andrew. "*Suzhi*: A Keyword Approach." *The China Quarterly* 186 (2006): 295–313.

Kishida Hideto. "Manshū kenkoku jisshūnen to sono kenchiku" [The tenth anniversary of Manchukuo and its architecture]. *Manshū kenchiku zasshi* 22, no. 11 (1942).

Kleinman, Arthur. *What Really Matters: Living a Moral Life amidst Uncertainty and Danger*. New York: Oxford University Press, 2006.

Kleinman, Arthur, Yunxiang Yan, Jing Jun, Sing Lee, Everett Zhang, Pan Tianshu, Wu Fei, and Jinhua Guo. *Deep China: The Moral Life of the Person: What Anthropology and Psychiatry Tell Us about China Today*. Berkeley: University of California Press, 2011.

Kō En. "Kioku sangyō to shite no tsūrizumu: Sengo ni okeru nihonjin no 'manshū' kankō" [Tourism as a memory industry: Japanese tourism of "Manchuria" in the postwar]. *Gendai shisō* 29, no. 4 (2001): 219–29.

———. "'Rakudo' o hashiru kankō basu: 1930 nendai no 'Manshū' toshi to teikoku no doramaturugī" [A tour bus in "paradise": "Manchurian" cities in the 1930s and the dramaturgy of the empire]. In *Iwanami kōza kindai nihon no bunka shi 6: Kakudai suru modanitī* [Iwanami studies on the cultural history of modern Japan 6: Expanding modernity], edited by Yoshimi Shunya, et al., 215–53. Tokyo: Iwanami shoten, 2002.

Koga, Yukiko. "Accounting for Silence: Inheritance, Debt, and the Moral Economy of Legal Redress in China and Japan." *American Ethnologist* 40, no. 3 (2013): 494–507.

———. "Between the Law: The Unmaking of Empire and Law's Imperial Amnesia." *Law and Social Inquiry* 41, issue 2 (Spring 2016): 402–34.

"Koizumi shushō ra no ODA uchikiri hatsugen, Chūgoku shushō ga fukai kan" [Chinese Premier expressed discomfort at Japanese Prime Minister Koizumi's intention to discontinue the ODA]. *Yomiuri shinbun* (Tokyo), December 3, 2004.

Kokusai kōryū kikin [Japan Foundation]. "Nihongo nōryoku shiken kekka no gaiyō 2005" [The overview of the Japanese proficiency exam 2005].

Koschmann, J. Victor. *Revolution and Subjectivity in Postwar Japan*. Chicago: University of Chicago Press, 1996.

Koshizawa Akira. *Manshūkoku no shuto keikaku: Tokyo no genzai to mirai o tou* [The urban planning of the Manchurian capital: Questioning the present and the future of Tokyo]. Tokyo: Nihon keizai hyōronsha, 1988.

Kratoska, Paul H. *Asian Labor in the Wartime Japanese Empire: Unknown Histories*. Armonk, NY: M. E. Sharpe, 2005.

Kushner, Barak. *Men to Devils, Devils to Men: Japanese War Crimes and Chinese Justice*. Cambridge, MA: Harvard University Press, 2015.

Kwon, Nayoung Aimee. *Intimate Empire: Collaboration and Colonial Modernity in Korea and Japan*. Durham, NC: Duke University Press, 2015.

Lacan, Jacques. *The Four Fundamental Concepts of Psychoanalysis: The Seminar of Jacques Lacan, Book XI*. Edited by Jacques-Alain Miller. Translated by Alan Sheridan. New York: W. W. Norton, 1973.

Lahusen, Thomas. "A Place Called Harbin: Reflections on a Centennial." *The China Quarterly* 154 (June 1998): 400–410.

Landsberg, Alison. *Prosthetic Memory: The Transformation of American Remembrance in the Age of Mass Culture*. New York: Columbia University Press, 2004.

Lee, Ching Kwan. *Against the Law: Labor Protests in China's Rustbelt and Sunbelt*. Berkeley: University of California Press, 2007.

———. "Raw Encounters: Chinese Managers, African Workers, and the Politics of Casualization in Africa's Chinese Enclaves." *The China Quarterly* 199 (2009): 647–66.

———. "The 'Revenge of History': Collective Memories and Labor Protests in Northeastern China." *Ethnography* 1, no. 2 (2000): 217–37.

Lee, Chong-Sik. *Revolutionary Struggle in Manchuria: Chinese Communism and Soviet Interest, 1922–1945*. Berkeley: University of California Press, 1983.

Li Debin. *Lishi huimou: Ershi shiji de Haerbin* [Glancing back at history: Twentieth-century Harbin]. 3 vols. Vol. 3. Harbin, China: Haerbin chubanshe, 1998.

Li, Jie. *Shanghai Homes: Palimpsests of Private Life*. New York: Columbia University Press, 2014.

Li Shuxiao, ed. *Haerbin jiuying* [Old photos of Harbin]. Beijing: Renmin meishu chubanshe, 2000.

Li, Yiyun. *A Thousand Years of Good Prayers*. London: Fourth Estate, 2006.

Li Zhensheng. *Red-Color News Soldier*. Introduction by Jonathan Spence. London: Phaidon Press, 2003.

Liu Jingsong and Zheng Min. "'Suofeiya' bu hui wangji: Haerbin Suofeiya Jiaotang Guangchang zonghe zhengzhi zhuiji" [Unforgettable "Sophia": A follow-up report on the comprehensive renewal of Harbin St. Sophia Cathedral Square]. *Shenghuobao* (Harbin, China), September 7, 1997, 1 and 15.

Liu Yi. "Jinzhou you qinhua rijun xijun shiyanchang: Wang Xuan lai lian xunchu yiduan xian wei ren zhi de lishi" [In Jinzhou exists the Japanese Army germ experimentation site: Wang Xuan's visit to Dalian discovers little-known history]. *Dalian ribao* [Dalian Daily] (Dalian, China), April 26, 2003, 1.

Logan, John, ed. *The New Chinese City: Globalization and Market Reform*. Cambridge, MA: Blackwell, 2001.

Lu Xiangdong. "Hashi zhaokai Haerbin chengshi jiyuan lunzhenghui" [Harbin city organizes Harbin city origin conference]. *Shenghuobao* (Harbin, China), December 14, 1994.

Lü, Xiaobo. *Cadres and Corruption: The Organizational Involution of the Chinese Communist Party*. Stanford, CA: Stanford University Press, 2000.

Ma Lifen, et al., eds. *Diguo zhuyi qinlue Dalian shi congshu* [Collected works on the history of the imperialist invasion of Dalian]. 6 vols. Shenyang, China: Liaoning renmin chubanshe, 1999.

Maki Yōjirō. "Chūgoku ga kushami o suruto . . . : Shudōken o ubawareta nihon keizai" [When China sneezes . . . : Japanese economy without hegemony]. *Ekonomisuto* [Economist] 82, no. 38, extra edition (July 11, 2004): 46–49.

Matsumura Takao, Xie Xueshi, and Eda Kenji, eds. *Mantetsu rōdōshi no kenkyū* [The labor history of the South Manchuria Railway Company]. Tokyo: Nihon keizai hyōronsha, 2002.

Matsusaka, Yoshihisa Tak. *The Making of Japanese Manchuria, 1904–1932*. Cambridge, MA: Harvard University Asia Center, 2001.

Mauss, Marcel. *The Gift: The Form and Reason for Exchange in Archaic Societies*. Translated by W. D. Halls. Foreword by Mary Douglas. New York: W. W. Norton, 1990 [1924].

Miller, Ian Jared. *The Nature of the Beasts: Empire and Exhibition at the Tokyo Imperial Zoo*. Berkeley: University of California Press, 2013.

Mimura, Janis. *Planning for Empire: Reform Bureaucrats and the Japanese Wartime State*. Ithaca, NY: Cornell University Press, 2011.

Mitscherlich, Alexander and Margarete. *The Inability to Mourn: Principles of Collective Behavior*. New York: Grove Press, 1975.

Mitter, Rana. "Behind the Scenes at the Museum: Nationalism, History and Memory in the Beijing War of Resistance Museum, 1987–1997." *The China Quarterly* 161 (2000): 279–93.

———. "China's 'Good War': Voices, Locations, and Generations in the Interpretation of the War of Resistance to Japan." In *Ruptured Histories: War, Memory, and the*

Post-Cold War in Asia, edited by Sheila Miyoshi Jager and Rana Mitter, 172–91. Cambridge, MA: Harvard University Asia Center, 2007.

———. *The Manchurian Myth: Nationalism, Resistance, and Collaboration in Modern China*. Berkeley: University of California Press, 2000.

Mizushima Asaho, ed. *Mirai sōzō to shite no "sengo hoshō": "Kako no seisan" o koete* ["Postwar compensation" as the creation of the future: Beyond "settling accounts"]. Genjin Booklet no. 39. Tokyo: Gendai jinbunsha, 2003.

Mizushima Hiroaki. *Netto kafe nanmin to hinkon Nippon* [Internet cafe refugees and poverty Japan]. Tokyo: Nihon terebi, 2007.

Morimoto Seiichi. *Akuma no hōshoku: Dai 731 butai no senritsu no zenbō!* [Devil's gluttony: The chilling reality of Unit 731!]. Tokyo: Kadokawa shoten, 1983.

Morris, Rosalind C. *In the Place of Origins: Modernity and Its Mediums in Northern Thailand*. Durham, NC: Duke University Press, 2000.

Morris-Suzuki, Tessa. *Borderline Japan: Foreigners and Frontier Controls in the Postwar Era*. New York: Cambridge University Press, 2010.

———. "Unquiet Graves: Katō Norihiro and the Politics of Mourning." *Japanese Studies* 18, no. 1 (1998): 21–30.

Moses, A. Dirk. *German Intellectuals and the Nazi Past*. New York: Cambridge University Press, 2007.

———. "Stigma and Sacrifice in Postwar Germany." *History and Memory* 19, no. 2 (2007): 139–80.

Motomiya Hiroshi. *Kuni ga moeru* [The country is burning]. 9 vols. Tokyo: Shūeisha, 2003–6.

———. "Kuni ga moeru" [The country is burning]. *Young Jump*, October 7, 2004, 105–23.

Myers, Ramon H. "Japanese Imperialism in Manchuria: The South Manchuria Railway Company, 1906–1933." In *The Japanese Informal Empire in China, 1895–1937*, edited by Peter Duus, Ramon H. Myers, and Mark R. Peattie, 101–32. Princeton, NJ: Princeton University Press, 1989.

Nakanishi Rei. *Akai tsuki* [The red moon]. 2 vols. Tokyo: Shinchōsha, 2001.

Nelson, Christopher. *Dancing with the Dead: Memory, Performance, and Everyday Life in Postwar Okinawa*. Durham, NC: Duke University Press, 2008.

Ngai, Pun. *Made in China: Women Factory Workers in a Global Workplace*. Durham, NC: Duke University Press, 2005.

NHK Special "wākingu puā" shuzai-han [Research team on "working poor"], ed. *Wākingu puā: Nihon o mushibamu yamai* [Working poor: A disease that undermines Japan]. Tokyo: Populasha, 2007.

Nie, Jing-Bao, Nanyan Guo, Mark Selden, and Arthur Kleinman, eds. *Japan's Wartime Medical Atrocities: Comparative Inquiries in Science, History, and Ethics*. New York: Routledge, 2010.

Nihon bōeki shinkō kikō (JETRO) dairen jimusho [Japan External Trade Organization Dalian Office]. "Dairenshi gaikyō" [The overview of Dalian]. September 2006.

Nihon keiei kenkyūjo [Japanese Management Research Institute], ed. *Onoda Semento hyakunen shi* [Centennial history of Onoda Cement]. Tokyo: Onoda Semento, 1981.

Nihon zasshi kyōkai [Japan Magazine Association], ed. *Magajin dēta 2004* [Magazine data 2004]. Tokyo: Nihon zasshi kyōkai, 2005.

Nishikawa Nagao. "1995 nen 8 gatsu no gen'ei, aruiwa 'kokumin' to iu kaibutsu ni tsuite" [On the illusion of August 1995, or the monster called the "national subject"]. *Shisō* 856 (October 1995): 1–3.

Nishinarita Yutaka. *Chūgokujin kyōsei renkō* [Chinese forced labor]. Tokyo: Tokyo daigaku shuppankai, 2002.

Nishizawa Yasuhiko. *"Manshū" toshi monogatari: Harubin, Dairen, Shinyō, Chōshun* [The tales of "Manchurian" cities: Harbin, Dalian, Shengyang, Changchun]. Tokyo: Kawaide shobō shinsha, 1996.

Nixon, Rob. *Slow Violence and the Environmentalism of the Poor*. Cambridge, MA: Harvard University Press, 2011.

O'Dwyer, Emer. *Significant Soil: Settler Colonialism and Japan's Urban Empire in Manchuria*. Cambridge, MA: Harvard University Asia Center, 2015.

Ōnuma Yasuaki. *Tan'itsu minzoku shakai no shinwa o koete: Zainichi Kankoku Chōsenjin to shutsunyūkoku kanri taisei* [Beyond the myth of a single ethnic society: Koreans in Japan and the emigration and immigration administration]. Tokyo: Tōshindō, 1986.

———. *Tōkyō saiban, sensō sekinin, sengo sekinin* [Tokyo Tribunal, war responsibility, postwar responsibility]. Tokyo: Tōshindō, 2007.

———. *Zainichi Kankoku Chōsenjin no kokuseki to jinken* [Nationality and human rights of Koreans in Japan]. Tokyo: Tōshindō, 2004.

Orr, James Joseph. *The Victim as Hero: Ideologies of Peace and National Identity in Postwar Japan*. Honolulu: University of Hawai'i Press, 2001.

Osburg, John. *Anxious Wealth: Money and Morality among China's New Rich*. Stanford, CA: Stanford University Press, 2013.

Park, Soon-Won. *Colonial Industrialization and Labor in Korea: The Onoda Cement Factory*. Cambridge, MA: Harvard University Asia Center, 1999.

Povinelli, Elizabeth A. *Economies of Abandonment: Social Belonging and Endurance in Late Liberalism*. Durham NC: Duke University Press, 2011.

Qu Wei and Li Xuxiao, eds. *Youtairen zai Haerbin* [The Jews in Harbin]. Beijing: Shehui kexue xenxian chubanshe, 2003.

Redtke, Kurt Wermer, and Chengzhi Liao. *China's Relations with Japan, 1945–83: The Role of Liao Chengzhi*. Manchester: Manchester University Press, 1990.

Renmin jiaoyu chubanshe lishi shi [People's education press history department], ed. *Jiu nian yiwu jiaoyu san nianzhi chuji zhongxue jiaokeshu: Zhongguo lishi* [Elementary level junior high textbook for the nine-year compulsory education: Chinese history]. Beijing: Renmin jiaoyu chubanshe, 2002.

Rofel, Lisa. *Desiring China: Experiments in Neoliberalism, Sexuality, and Public Culture*. Durham, NC: Duke University Press, 2007.

———. *Other Modernities: Gendered Yearnings in China after Socialism*. Berkeley: University of California Press, 1999.

Rosaldo, Renato. "Imperialist Nostalgia." *Representations* 26 (Spring 1989): 107–22.

Rosenfeld, Gavriel D. "'The Architects' Debate': Architectural Discourse and the Memory of Nazism in the Federal Republic of Germany, 1977–1997." *History and Memory* 9, no. 1/2 (Fall 1997): 189–225.

Rothberg, Michael. "Introduction: Between Memory and Memory: From Lieux de mémoire to Noeuds de mémoire." *Yale French Studies* 118/119, *Noeuds de mémoire: Multidirectional Memory in Postwar French and Francophone Culture* (2010): 3–12.

———. *Multidirectional Memory: Remembering the Holocaust in the Age of Decolonization*. Stanford, CA: Stanford University Press, 2009.

Rothberg, Michael, and Yasemin Yildiz. "Memory Citizenship: Migrant Archives of Holocaust Remembrance in Contemporary Germany." *Parallax* 17, no. 4 (2011): 32–48.

Ruoff, Kenneth J. *Imperial Japan at Its Zenith: The Wartime Celebration of the Empire's 2,600th Anniversary*. Ithaca, NY: Cornell University Press, 2010.

Sakabe Shōko. *"Manshū" keiken no shakaigaku: Shokuminchi no kioku no katachi* [Sociology of "Manchuria" experiences: Forms of memory of the colony]. Tokyo: Sekai shisōsha, 2008.

———. "'Manshū' keiken no rekishi shakaigaku teki kōsatsu: 'Manshū' dōsōkai no jirei o tōshite" [A sociohistorical analysis of "Manchuria" experience: A case of "Manchuria" reunion associations]. *Kyoto shakaigaku nenpō* 7 (1999): 101–20.

Sakai, Naoki. *Translation and Subjectivity*. Minneapolis: University of Minnesota Press, 1997.

Santner, Eric L. *Stranded Objects: Mourning, Memory, and Film in Postwar Germany*. Ithaca, NY: Cornell University Press, 1990.

Satō Takeo. "Shina tairiku ni okeru gaikoku kenchiku to sono seiji hyōgen" [Foreign architecture in China and its political expression]. *Kenchiku zasshi* 691 (1942).

Sautman, Barry, and Hairong Yan. "African Perspectives on China-Africa Links." *The China Quarterly* 199 (2009): 728–59.

Scott, David. *Omens of Adversity: Tragedy, Time, Memory, Justice*. Durham, NC: Duke University Press, 2014.

Scott, James C. *The Moral Economy of the Peasant: Rebellion and Subsistence in Southeast Asia*. New Haven, CT: Yale University Press, 1976.

Seraphim, Franziska. *War Memory and Social Politics in Japan, 1945–2005*. Cambridge, MA: Harvard University Asia Center, 2006.

Shambaugh, David. *China Goes Global: The Partial Power*. New York: Oxford University Press, 2013.

Shen Yan. *Changchun weiman yizhi daguan* [An overview of the architectural remainders of fake Manchukuo in Changchun]. Changchun, China: Jilin sheying chubanshe, 2002.

Shibata Yoshimasa. *Chūgoku senryōchi nikkei kigyō no katsudō* [Activities of Japanese corporations in occupied China]. Tokyo: Nihon keizai hyōronsha, 2008.

Shin, Gi-Wook, and Michael Robinson, eds. *Colonial Modernity in Korea*. Cambridge, MA: Harvard University Press, 1999.

"Shōwa jūyonendo mansen shūgaku ryokōki (bunka yonen)" [Diary from the school trip to Manchuria and Korea in Showa 14 (senior in the humanities)], August 28, 1939. Nara Women's University Archive (kōshi kankei shiryō), no. 96. Electronic document, http://www.nara-wu.ac.jp/nensi/96.htm, accessed May 20, 2007.

Sichrovsky, Peter. *Born Guilty: Children of Nazi Families*. Translated by Jean Steinberg. New York: Basic Books, 1988.

Smith, Adam. *An Inquiry into the Nature and Causes of the Wealth of Nations*. Edited by Edwin Cannan. Chicago: University of Chicago Press, 1976 [1776].

———. *The Theory of Moral Sentiments*. Edited by D. D. Raphael and A. L. Macfie, *The Glasgow Edition of the Works and Correspondence of Adam Smith*. Indianapolis: Liberty Fund, 1982 [1759].

Smith, Kerry. "The Shōwa Hall: Memorializing Japan's War at Home." *The Public Historian* 24, no. 4 (2002): 35–64.

Soh, C. Sarah. *The Comfort Women: Sexual Violence and Postcolonial Memory in Korea and Japan*. Chicago: University of Chicago Press, 2008.

Solinger, Dorothy J. *Contesting Citizenship in Urban China: Peasant Migrants, the State, and the Logic of the Market*. Berkeley: University of California Press, 1999.

Song Hongyan. *Donghang xiao Bali* [Paris of the East]. Harbin, China: Heilongjiang kexue jishu chubanshe, 2001.

South Manchuria Railway. *Manchuria, Land of Opportunities*. New York: South Manchuria Railway, 1922.

Spiegelman, Art. *Maus I: A Survivor's Tale: My Father Bleeds History*. New York: Pantheon, 1986.

Stewart, Susan. *On Longing: Narratives of the Miniature, the Gigantic, the Souvenir, the Collection*. Durham, NC: Duke University Press, 1993.

Stoler, Ann Laura. *Carnal Knowledge and Imperial Power*. Berkeley: University of California Press, 2002.

———, ed. *Imperial Debris: On Ruins and Ruination*. Durham, NC: Duke University Press, 2013.

———. "Imperial Debris: Reflections on Ruins and Ruination." *Cultural Anthropology* 23, no. 2 (2008): 191–219.

———. *Race and the Education of Desire: Foucault's History of Sexuality and the Colonial Order of Things*. Durham, NC: Duke University Press, 1995.

Stoler, Ann Laura, and Frederick Cooper. "Between Metropole and Colony: Rethinking a Research Agenda." In *Tensions of Empire: Colonial Cultures in a Bourgeois World*, edited by Frederick Cooper and Ann Laura Stoler, 1–54. Berkeley: University of California Press, 1997.

Strassler, Karen. *Refracted Visions: Popular Photography and National Modernity in Java*. Durham, NC: Duke University Press, 2010.

Sunaga Noritake. "Manshū no yōgyō" [Ceramic industry in Manchuria]. *Rikkyō keizaigaku kenkyū* [Rikkyo Journal of Economics] 59, no. 3 (2006): 63–99.

Swislocki, Mark. *Culinary Nostalgia: Regional Food Culture and the Urban Experience in Shanghai*. Stanford, CA: Stanford University Press, 2009.

Tachibanaki Toshiaki. *Kakusa shakai: Nani ga mondai nano ka?* [Society with disparity: What are the issues?]. Tokyo: Iwanami shoten, 2006.

Takahashi Tetsuya. "Ojoku no kioku o megutte" [On the memories of disgrace]. *Gunzō* 50, no. 3 (March 1995): 176–82.

———. *Sengo sekinin ron* [On postwar responsibility]. Tokyo: Kōdansha, 1999.

Takenaka, Akiko. *Yasukuni Shrine: History, Memory and Japan's Unending Postwar.* Honolulu: University of Hawai'i Press, 2015.

Takeuchi Yoshimi. "Manshūkoku kenkyu no igi" [The meaning of studying Manchukuo]. In *Takeuchi Yoshimi zenshū* [The complete works of Takeuchi Yoshimi], vol. 4. Tokyo: Chikuma shobō, 1980.

Tamanoi, Mariko Asano. "Between Colonial Racism and Global Capitalism: Japanese Repatriates from Northeast China since 1946." *American Ethnologist* 30, no. 4 (2003): 527–39.

———, ed. *Crossed Histories: Manchuria in the Age of Empire.* Honolulu: University of Hawai'i Press, 2005.

———. *Memory Maps: The State and Manchuria in Postwar Japan.* Honolulu: University of Hawai'i Press, 2009.

Tanaka Hiroshi. "Chūgokujin kyōsei renkō no rekishi to genzai" [The Chinese forced labor in history and today]. In *Ringoku kara no kokuhatsu: Kyōsei renkō no kigyō sekinin 2* [Accusation from the neighbors: Corporate responsibility for forced labor 2], edited by Yamada Shōji and Tanaka Hiroshi. Tokyo: Sōshisha, 1996.

Tanaka Hiroshi, Utsumi Aiko, and Ishitobi Jin, eds. *Shiryō Chūgokujin kyōsei renkō* [Source material: The Chinese forced labor]. Tokyo: Akashi shoten, 1987.

Tanaka Hiroshi, Utsumi Aiko, and Nīimi Takashi, eds. *Shiryō Chūgokujin kyōsei renkō no kiroku* [Source material: Records of the Chinese forced labor]. Tokyo: Akashi shoten, 1990.

Tanaka Hiroshi, Arimitsu Ken, and Nakayama Taketoshi, eds. *Mikaiketsu no sengo hoshō: Towareru Nihon no kako to mirai* [Unresolved postwar compensation: Problematizing Japan's past and future]. Tokyo: Sōshisha, 2012.

Tanaka Hiroshi and Matsuzawa Tetsunari, eds. *Chūgokujin kyōsei renkō shiryō: "Gaimuhō hōkokusho" zen 5 bunsatsu hoka* [Source material on the Chinese forced labor: The reports of the Ministry of Foreign Affairs of Japan]. Tokyo: Gendai shokan, 1995.

Tang Jige, et al. *Changchun erbai nian* [Two-hundred-year history of Changchun]. Changchun, China: Changchunshi Zhengxie, 2000.

Taussig, Michael. *Shamanism, Colonialism, and the Wild Man: A Study in Terror and Healing.* Chicago: University of Chicago Press, 1987.

Thompson, E. P. "The Moral Economy of the English Crowd in the Eighteenth Century." *Past and Present* 50 (February 1971): 76–136.

Tsing, Anna Lowenhaupt. *Friction: An Ethnography of Global Connection.* Princeton, NJ: Princeton University Press, 2005.

Uchida, Jun. *Brokers of Empire: Japanese Settler Colonialism in Korea, 1876–1945.* Cambridge, MA: Harvard University Press, 2011.

Utsumi Aiko, Ōnuma Yasuaki, Tanaka Hiroshi, and Katō Yōko. *Sengo sekinin: Ajia no manazashi ni kotaete* [Postwar responsibility: In response to the gaze of Asia]. Tokyo: Iwanami shoten, 2014.

Verdery, Katherine. *The Political Lives of Dead Bodies: Reburial and Postsocialist Change.* New York: Columbia University Press, 1999.

Vidler, Anthony. *The Architectural Uncanny: Essays in the Modern Unhomely.* Cambridge, MA: MIT Press, 1992.

Wakabayashi, Bob Tadashi. "The Nanking 100-Man Killing Contest Debate: War Guilt amid Fabricated Illusions, 1971–75." *Journal of Japanese Studies* 26, no. 2 (2000): 307–40.

Waldron, Arthur. "China's New Remembering of World War II: The Case of Zhang Zizhong." *Modern Asian Studies* 30, no. 4 (1996): 869–99.

Wang Dexin. "Haerbin de chengshi qiyuan yu chengshi jiyuan (1)" [The origin of the city and the historical beginning of the city of Harbin (1)]. *Xinwanbao* (Harbin, China), April 10, 1992.

———. "Haerbin de chengshi qiyuan yu chengshi jiyuan (2)" [The origin of the city and the historical beginning of the city of Harbin (2)]. *Xinwanbao* (Harbin, China), April 13, 1992.

Wang Huiquan, ed. *Dalian bainian jianben* [Simplified edition of Dalian hundred years]. Dalian, China: Dalian chubanshe, 1999.

———, ed. *Dalian wushi nian* [Dalian fifty years]. Dalian, China: Dalian chubanshe, 1995.

Wang Yuechuan. *Hou zhiminzhuyi yu xinlishizhuyi wenlun* [Literary theory of postcolonialism and New Historicism]. Jinan, China: Shandong jiaoyu chubanshe, 1999.

Wang Yulang. "Du 'Haerbin chengshi jiyuan de qisuan shijian'" [Reading "the historical origin of Harbin"]. *Xinwanbao* (Harbin, China), April 3, 1992.

———. "Zaidu 'Haerbin chengshi jiyuan de qisuan shijian'" [Rereading "the historical origin of Harbin"]. *Xinwanbao* (Harbin, China), April 6, 1992.

Wang, Zheng. *Never Forget National Humiliation: Historical Memory in Chinese Politics and Foreign Relations*. New York: Columbia University Press, 2012.

Watson, Rubie S. "Memory, History, and Opposition under State Socialism: An Introduction." In *Memory, History and Opposition under State Socialism*, edited by Rubie S. Watson, 1–20. Santa Fe, NM: School of American Research Press, 1994.

Watt, Lori. *When Empire Comes Home: Repatriation and Reintegration in Postwar Japan*. Cambridge, MA: Harvard University Asia Center, 2009.

Westad, Odd Arne. *Restless Empire: China and the World since 1750*. New York: Basic Books, 2012.

Weston, Timothy B. "'Learn from Daqing': More Dark Clouds for Workers in State-Owned Enterprises." *Journal of Contemporary China* 11, no. 33 (2002): 721–34.

Wilder, Gary. *The French Imperial Nation-State: Negritude and Colonial Humanism between the Two World Wars*. Chicago: University of Chicago Press, 2005.

Wolff, David. *To the Harbin Station: The Liberal Alternative in Russian Manchuria, 1898–1914*. Stanford, CA: Stanford University Press, 1999.

Wong, Winnie Won Yin. *Van Gogh on Demand: China and the Readymade*. Chicago: University of Chicago Press, 2013.

Wu, Fulong. "Transplanting Cityscapes: The Use of Imagined Globalization in Housing Commodification in Beijing." *Area* 36, no. 3 (2004): 227–34.

Xie Xueshi and Matsumura Takao, eds. *Mantie yu Zhongguo laogong* [The South Manchuria Railway Company and Chinese laborers]. Beijing: Shehui kexue wenxian chubanshe, 2003.

Xinhua meiri dianxunshe [Xinhua daily telecommunications company], ed. *Jizhu Changchun* [Remembering Changchun]. Beijing: Xinhua chubanshe, 2000.

"Xin shenghuo, jiu huiyi: Guiguo nuxing fangtan" [New life, old memories: Interviews with women who returned from abroad]. *Oggi: Jinri fengcai* 17 (March 2003): 120–23.

Xue Yanwen and Zhang Xueshan, eds. *Zhiqing lao zhaopian* [Old zhiqing photos]. Tianjin, China: Baihua wenyi chubanshe, 1998.

Yamazaki Toyoko. *Daichi no ko* [The child of the fatherland]. Vols. 1–4. Tokyo: Bungei shunjū, 1994.

———. *Daichi no ko to watashi* [The child of the fatherland and I]. Tokyo: Bungei shunjū, 1999.

Yanagisawa Asobu. "Dairen futō" [Dalian port]. In *Mantetsu rōdōshi no kenkyū* [The labor history of the South Manchuria Railway Company], edited by Matsumura Takao, Xie Xueshi, and Eda Kenji, 249–84. Tokyo: Nihon keizai hyōronsha, 2002.

———. *Nihonjin no shokuminchi keiken: Dairen nihonjin shōkōgyōsha no rekishi* [Japanese colonial experience: The history of Japanese commercial and industrial entrepreneurs in Dalian]. Tokyo: Aoki shoten, 1999.

Yang, Daqing. *Technology of Empire: Telecommunications and Japanese Expansion, 1883–1945*. Cambridge, MA: Harvard University Press, 2011.

Yang, Guobin. "China's *Zhiqing* Generation: Nostalgia, Identity, and Cultural Resistance in the 1990s." *Modern China* 29, no. 3 (July 2003): 267–96.

———. "Days of Old Are Not Puffs of Smoke: Three Hypotheses on Collective Memories of the Cultural Revolution." *The China Review* 5, no. 2 (Fall 2005): 13–41.

Yang, Mayfair Mei-Hui. *Gifts, Favors and Banquets: The Art of Social Relationships in China*. Ithaca, NY: Cornell University Press, 1994.

———. "Spatial Struggles: Postcolonial Complex, State Disenchantment, and Popular Reappropriation of Space in Rural Southeast China." *Journal of Asian Studies* 63, no. 3 (August 2004): 719–55.

Yoda, Tomiko, and Harry Harootunian, eds. *Japan after Japan: Social and Cultural Life from the Recessionary 1990s to the Present*. Durham, NC: Duke University Press, 2006.

Yoneyama, Lisa. *Hiroshima Traces: Time, Space, and the Dialectics of Memory*. Berkeley: University of California Press, 1999.

———. "Traveling Memories, Contagious Justice: Americanization of Japanese War Crimes at the End of the Post-Cold War." *Journal of Asian American Studies* 6, no. 1 (2003): 57–93.

Yoshida, Takashi. *The Making of the "Rape of Nanking": History and Memory in Japan, China, and the United States*. New York: Oxford University Press, 2006.

Yoshida Yutaka. *Nihonjin no sensō-kan: Sengo shi no naka no henyō* [Japanese perspectives on the war: Their transformation within the postwar history]. Tokyo: Iwanami shoten, 1995.

Yoshimi Yoshiaki. *Comfort Women: Sexual Slavery in the Japanese Military during World War II*. Translated by Suzanne O'Brien. New York: Columbia University Press, 2000.

———. *Dokugasusen to nihongun* [Poison gas warfare and the Japanese Army]. Tokyo: Iwanami shoten, 2004.

———. *Grassroots Fascism: The War Experience of the Japanese People*. Translated by Ethan Mark. New York: Columbia University Press, 2015.

———. *Kusa no ne no fasizumu: Nihon minshū no sensō taiken* [Grassroots Fascism: The War Experience of the Japanese People]. Tokyo: University of Tokyo Press, 1987.

Young, Louise. *Japan's Total Empire: Manchuria and the Culture of Wartime Imperialism*. Berkeley: University of California Press, 1998.

Yu Linan and Liu Jia. "'Lujun bingyuan' shi wei wangong de xijun shiyanchang: Wang Xuan Dalian xunzheng gongzuo you xinjinzhan" ["Army Hospital" was the unfinished germ experimentation site: A new development in Wang Xuan's evidence gathering visit in Dalian]. *Xinshangbao* [New Business News] (Dalian, China), April 26, 2003, 6.

Yu Wenxiu. "Sheng cheng xuezhe yantao Haerbin jianchengri" [Experts discuss Harbin's birthday]. *Heilongjiang chenbao* (Harbin, China), December 14, 1994.

Yuan Xiaoguang. "Haerbin, natian shi ni de shengri" [Harbin, when is your birthday]. *Shenghuobao* (Harbin, China), March 17, 1996.

Yuasa Makoto. *Han-hinkon: "Suberidai shakai" kara no dakkyaku* [Antipoverty: Escape from a slide society]. Tokyo: Iwanami shoten, 2008.

Yue, Ming-Bao. "Nostalgia for the Future: Cultural Revolution Memory in Two Transnational Chinese Narratives." *The China Review* 5, no. 2 (Fall 2005): 43–63.

Zarrow, Peter. *After Empire: The Conceptual Transformation of the Chinese State, 1885–1924*. Stanford, CA: Stanford University Press, 2012.

Zeng Yizhi. *Cheng yu ren: Haerbin gushi* [The city and the people: Stories of Harbin]. Haerbin, China: Heilongjiang renmin chubanshe, 2003.

Zhang Fushan. *Lishi huimou: Haerbin shihua* [Glancing back at history: A narrative history of Harbin]. Harbin, China: Haerbin chubanshe, 1998.

Zhang, Li. *In Search of Paradise: Middle-Class Living in a Chinese Metropolis*. Ithaca, NY: Cornell University Press, 2010.

———. *Strangers in the City: Reconfigurations of Space, Power, and Social Network within China's Floating Population*. Stanford, CA: Stanford University Press, 2001.

Zheng Min, Wen Ting, and Liu Jingsong. "Ta fang Sheng Suofeiya Dajiaotang" [Investigation of St. Sophia Cathedral]. *Shenghuobao* (Harbin, China), January 5, 1997.

Zheng, Tiantian. *Red Lights: The Lives of Sex Workers in Postsocialist China*. Minneapolis: University of Minnesota Press, 2009.

"Zhong Ri guanxi shi de xin pianzhan" [A new chapter to the history of China and Japan]. *Renmin ribao* [People's Daily] (Beijing), September 30, 1972, shelun [editorial], 2.

"Zhou Enlai zongli de zhujiu ci zai huanying Tianzhong shouxiang yanhui shang" [Premier Zhou Enlai's speech at the banquet to welcome Prime Minister Tanaka]. *Renmin ribao* [People's Daily] (Beijing), September 26, 1972, 3.

Žižek, Slavoj. "Eastern Europe's Republics of Gilead." *New Left Review* 1, no. 183 (1990): 50–56.

Zwigenberg, Ran. *Hiroshima: The Origins of Global Memory Culture*. Cambridge: Cambridge University Press, 2014.

INDEX

Chinese and Japanese terms are indicated with [C] and [J] respectively. Page numbers in italic refer to captions. While the nature of ethnography defies the idea of summation, page numbers in bold indicate sections that give the gist of key concepts.